Birth of a
Nation'hood

Birth of a Nation'hood

Gaze, Script, and Spectacle in the
O.J. Simpson Case

*Edited by Toni Morrison and
Claudia Brodsky Lacour*

Introduction by Toni Morrison

Pantheon Books
NEW YORK

Library of Congress Cataloging-in-Publication Data

Birth of a nation'hood : gaze, script, and spectacle in the O.J.
    Simpson case / edited by Toni Morrison and Claudia Brodsky Lacour.
        p.   cm.
    Includes bibliographical references.
    ISBN 0-679-75893-3
        1. Simpson, O. J., 1947- —Trials, litigation, etc.   2. Trials
(Murder)—California—Los Angeles.   3. Discrimination in criminal
justice administration—United States.   I. Morrison, Toni.
II. Lacour, Claudia Brodsky, 1955-
KF224.S485B57   1997
345.73'02523'0979494—dc20
[347.30525230979494]

Random House Web Address: http://www.randomhouse.com/

BOOK DESIGN BY LAURA HAMMOND HOUGH
Printed in the United States of America
FIRST EDITION
9   8   7   6   5   4   3   2   1

Contents

The Official Story: vii
Dead Man Golfing
Introduction by Toni Morrison

The Greatest Story Ever Sold: 3
Marketing and the O.J. Simpson Trial
George Lipsitz

The O.J. Simpson Trial: 31
Who Was Improperly "Playing the Race Card"?
A. Leon Higginbotham, Jr.,
Aderson Bellegarde François, and Linda Y. Yueh

Dismissed or Banished?   57
A Testament to the Reasonableness of the Simpson Jury
Nikol G. Alexander and Drucilla Cornell

Color-blind Dreams and Racial Nightmares: 97
Reconfiguring Racism in the Post–Civil Rights Era
Kimberlé Williams Crenshaw

Bigger and O.J. 169
Ishmael Reed

"Hertz, Don't It?" 197
*Becoming Colorless and Staying Black in the Crossover
of O.J. Simpson*
Leola Johnson and David Roediger

If the Genes Fit, How Do You Acquit? 241
O.J. and Science
Andrew Ross

American Kabuki 273
Patricia J. Williams

The Unbearable Darkness of Being: 293
"Fresh" Thoughts on Race, Sex, and the Simpsons
Ann duCille

Eye, the Jury 339
Armond White

The "Interest" of the Simpson Trial: 367
*Spectacle, National History, and the Notion of
Disinterested Judgment*
Claudia Brodsky Lacour

About the Contributors 414

The Official Story:
Dead Man Golfing
Introduction by Toni Morrison

W e have been deceived. We thought he loved us. Now we know that everything we saw was false. Each purposeful gesture, the welcoming smile, the instant understanding of how we felt and what we needed. Even before we knew what was in our best interests, he seemed to anticipate and execute it right on cue. He gentled us toward our finer instincts; toward the medicine that would cure us; toward the rest we needed. He imitated our language in structure and content. And all with the most charming good nature—joy even. So obvious was his fidelity we had no doubt he would lay down his life for us. It seemed inherent, in his nature, so to speak. It was what he was born for.

It was not so. Not only did he not love us, he loathed and despised us. All the time he was planning to kill us. And if he is let go, he will do it again; kill more of us. Why? Because he is an animal. Cunning, manipulative, subtle, but savage nevertheless. How could we have been so deceived? How could we have let our vigilance become so clouded? Was it the coast—dulcet, permissive, delusional? The weather—a long narcotic calm, enervating heat? The long journey to get to where we were? Or was it perhaps our need to be deceived? Desperate to be that effortlessly and deeply loved, had we fashioned and secured our own blindfolds?

Sitting in the courthouse at the trial watching Justice sway her scales; listening to sworn depositions; seeing the witnesses relive their horror, the survivors of the *San Dominick* could have pondered along those lines over the trial of the Senegalese man who, with a dagger and ferocious single-mindedness, took by murder control of a vessel in order to reverse his fortune, and who, in so doing, disrupted for a little while the routine business of the trade that bought and sold him. That trial took place in 1799 at the close of the eighteenth century, but an end-of-century population of watchers anywhere in the United States (or the world) has had similar thoughts concerning the case of Orenthal J. Simpson. Both are tales centering on the shock of deception; the sudden transformation of the unbelievable into belief.

Like the readers of Herman Melville's "Benito Cereno," contemporary "readers" of the Simpson case have been encouraged to move from a previous assessment of Mr. Simpson as an affable athlete/spokesperson to a judgment of him as a wild dog. He is clearly, according to mainstream wisdom, the latter. And the wild dog portrait layered over him contains a further incompatibility: cool, cunning, even intelligent malfeasance or raging, mindless, brutal insanity. The language developing around him portrays a thoughtful, meditating murderer capable of slick and icy-cold deliberations *and/or* a mindless, sponta-neous killer—a kind of lucky buffoon. That each cluster of adjectives cancels out the other is of no moment since contra-diction, incoherence and emotional disorder "fit" when the sub-ject is black. A single, unarmed black man on the ground surrounded by twelve rioting police can be seen as a major threat to the police. A beaten up, sexually assaulted black girl wakes up in a hospital and is "convicted" of raping and defiling herself. To ask why? how? is to put a rhetorical question—not a serious one worthy of serious response. Difficult explanations are folded into the general miasma of black incoherence.

In the Simpson case the prosecution put forward a motive (jealous rage) to explain Mr. Simpson's alleged feral behavior, but with the accumulation of hard evidence they did not have to prove its credibility. They needed a coherent case, not a coherent defendant. "Senseless" is the term most often applied to crime (and criminals) anyway.

In Melville's narrative, the clutch of the plot is the control the author exercises over the reader. An American captain boards a ship in disrepair with gifts of food and good intentions. What he sees is what he is socialized to see: docile if disorderly blacks; a frail, un-manly [read "un-American"] captain attended by a devoted Senegalese. The American captain spends the day on board the *San Dominick*, happily observing, inquiring, chatting and arranging relief for the distressed ship's population. Any mild uneasiness he feels is quickly obliterated by his supreme confidence in his assessment of the order of things. He is unmindful of nefarious plots, hints of danger, until he is about to return to his own ship. At that point the Senegalese and all of the captives behave in such a manner that, at last, the American realizes that he has been the dupe of the black men, who are in fact in rebellion, and that not service but the murder of white people has been in operation all the while. The long deferment of this realization is understandable partly because of his trusting nature but mostly because of his certainty that blacks were incapable of so planned, so intricate an undertaking. Melville, releasing and withholding, massaging and sabotaging, rationalizing and raising doubt, hiding and exposing, tells the story of an innocent white captain while simultaneously critiquing the racist foundations of that innocence.

Initially we are led to believe we are watching the behavior of a natural servant: adept, reassuring. Finally we learn ("in a flash" along with the American if we are not paying attention, earlier if we are) that all the while we were watching a traitor whose rage to kill is suppressed or set free at will. The Senegalese, "in whose rude face ... like a shepherd's dog ... sorrow and affection were equally blended," morphs from faithful dog to "snakishly writhing" murderer. Melville describes the American's epiphany: "Now with scales dropped from his eyes he saw the negroes, not in misrule, not in tumult, ... but with mask torn away, flourishing hatchets and knives, in ferocious piratical revolt. Like delirious black dervishes...." In the morphing process the transition from one thing to another thing is not quicker than the eye, but, because of its speed and facility, the radical change appears inevitable. The new features appear to be already embedded in the original. The abrupt switch of the Senegalese from one kind of animal to another is easy: first because the modifying terms are limited to the non- or barely human, but most important because the reversal is played out with and on a black man. Illogic, contradiction, deception are understood to be fundamental characteristics of blacks and in judging them there need be no ground or reason for a contrary or more complicated view. For centuries the debate in human versus animal discourse has rested on blacks, thus relegating to them the essence of contradiction. Even when permitted conceptually to enter the kingdom of *Homo sapiens,* blacks have historically been viewed as either submissive children, violent ones, or both at once. Very few African Americans of a certain generation can forget how the infamous eleventh edition of the *Encyclopaedia Britannica* put it: "the mental condition of the negro is very similar to that of a child, normally good-natured and cheerful, but subject to sudden fits of emotion ... capable of performing acts of singular atrocity ... but often exhibiting in the capacity of servant a dog-like fidelity." When the scholarly vocabulary of race is itself primitive the belief-language of popular culture is equally retarded. What might be illogical for a white is easily possible for a black who has never been required to make, assumed to make, or described as making "sense." Therefore when race is at play the leap from one judgment (faithful dog) to its complete opposite (treacherous snake) is a trained reflex. From this reductive viewpoint blacks are seen to live outside "reason" in a world of phenomena in which motive or its absence is sheltered from debate. Or, as a William Faulkner character put it, "a nigger is not a person so much as a form of behavior."

The gap between these two opposing and mutually cancelling perceptions forms an unbreachable chasm, and the need to know which label is correct ought to stimulate a search for reasonable explanations of such shape-shifting behavior. Insights into motivation, however, do not arrive when the lens is misty with racist assumptions. When the "delirious" irrational behavior of the blacks (How dare they try to go free? How evil. How stupid. Did they really think they could get away with it?) is given a human context we are able to discover another narrative. The other story

Melville is (not) telling, yet is provoking us to discover for ourselves, is a complicated, powerful racial narrative in which the
denial of racism is an ignorance of the most dangerous kind.

Readers of *True Crime* stories are accustomed to tales that
require the perfect marriage of Jekyll and Hyde, of perfidy accompanied by superhuman gifts, of outrageous luck in the grip of a
psychotic episode. They are fictions styled for popular taste and
the satisfaction of discovering once again that, however clever,
the villain is known even if not brought to justice. Yet it is
precisely the absence of a rational analysis of behavior that
leads one to the thought(less) process the American captain in
"Benito Cereno" entertained. And it is the absence of a rational
analysis of behavior that is so disturbing in the O.J. Simpson
case. Given the propensity to ascribe irrationality to black behavior; given the planned versus unplanned, the subtle mind versus
mindlessness that the alleged motive and the murderous actions
had to embrace; given the difficulties the "time line" presented
in believability; given the claims of race as a blinding force for
the defendant and the jury, it would be interesting and possibly
revealing to try to imagine an un-raced figure executing the murders. Not a race-transcending "crossover" into the white world;
not a beloved, faithful hero capable of betraying whites and
"falling" back into blackness, but a figure functioning within the
bounds of credibility, but beyond the hysteria of race-inflected
rationales.

I have wasted piles of paper trying to complete a believable
narrative of such a figure. Using all of the admissible evidence,
the time line put forward by the prosecution, the dotty explanations of things never found (weapon, blood-steeped clothes,
etc.), the movements the killer is assumed to have made, I tried
to construct a plot any reader would accept. I shaped it as fiction
because fiction has its own internal laws of character logic where

action and chance and psychology must work together to illuminate character. In other words, its standards of believability are higher than those in life. Even (especially) in the world of magic, of science fiction, of fantasy, a certain level of coherence must be achieved. I tried it with a cunning, pre-meditating killer. I tried it as an explosive, spontaneous slaughter. I gave the character an intricate interior life; then a simpler one. I made him a drug user; a drug hater; a devoted father; an indifferent father; a violent husband; a patient husband . . . All my efforts collapsed into nonsense. Without the support of black irrationality, without the license provided by the convictions of the *Encyclopaedia Britannica,* the fictional case not only could not be made, it was silly.

The gargantuanism of the trial—its invention of wild dogs and angels, stick figures and clowns, its out-lawry—aroused immediate suspicion. Examining the weight the case has come to have, one is struck by how quickly guilt was the popular verdict. It may have been this early gigantism that made Mr. Simpson's guilt increasingly remote to some African Americans. Not because they knew or loved him (not even because he is black); nor because they suspected foul play. Early on it began to look like white mischief—the kind that surfaces when the opportunity to gaze voluptuously at a black body presents itself. The narrative of the entertainment media and their "breaking story" confederates was so powerfully insistent on guilt, so uninterested in any other scenario, it began to look like a media pogrom, a lynching with its iconography intact: a chase, a cuffing, a mob, name calling, a white female victim, and most of all the heat, the panting, the flared nostrils of a pack already eager to convict. For many, black and white, the passion they felt in the wake of the media onslaught was real, hinging as it did on violence and treachery. Mr. Simpson became the repository of fear. Every woman who

had felt or witnessed the insensate brutality of men, who had tenderly touched her body where bruises, swellings and breaks
limned the violence she had suffered, saw in him the lover she had
(or should have) fled. Men who had let their guard down and
actually loved this charming black man, men who relished the
comfort they felt in his company, or remembered the beauty of
his runs—forever, it seemed—across fields long and wide must
have felt they had loved the wrong kind of man. The media's
instant and obvious preference for a guilty man created an early if
not immediate public rage at having been deceived, of having profoundly flawed judgment. Mr. Simpson was accused of multiple
murder. But he was guilty of personal treason.

A woman opens her door, steps out and has her head
chopped off. A man performs a neighborly gesture and is cut to
pieces. The media response to this obscenity was excessive,
manipulative and generally obfuscatory. But the blood it smelled
belonged not to the victims but to the prey—a potent sensation
aroused by the site and sight of a fallen, treacherous, violent
black body, and sustained by the historical association of such a
body with violence as dread entertainment.

Within the fecund, self-perpetuating meta-narrative that
has followed, not only has the gravitas of the crimes *in themselves*
been lost and forsaken in favor of excitement and frivolity and
profit, not only has the resolution of the trial been declared
inoperative, the race-based nature of the narrative is reduced to
a footnote, an aside, a secondary debate about whether race mattered in the case and if so, how deplorable. There seems to be a
universal sorrow that these proceedings were distorted, sullied
by race, that its intervention was false, even shrewd; that it
should have been (and but for the isolate Mr. Fuhrman and an
"uneducated" [read black] jury, could have been) race-free—
confined wholly to non-race-inflected evidence, a disinterested

legal process in which even to mention race as a major factor rips away the blindfold that Justice wears and forces her to make decisions based on visual bias. Such massive denial of the social (even the material) world, a denial which found its best and worst expression in the "race card" phrase, still has the capacity to astonish.

Although some of the media made an effort at restraint, flecks of saliva regularly soiled its reportage. The predictable pounce on every scrap, every leak, every mucus thread of lie or gossip associated with these proceedings revolted and mesmerized. And while media avarice and shamelessness were remarked upon and condemned by the avaricious and the shameless, and while the aggression of the journalists, photographers, commentators and hucksters was routinely deplored by the aggressors themselves, the reporters (collectors and distributors of the narrative) seemed somehow as helpless as fawns in the industry headlights with as much choice as bullets in the barrel of corporate media guns. If there were journalists eager to get other stories before the public, their disappointment at seeing their efforts repeatedly collapse must have been deeply painful. The marketing of every iota of the case had its own relentless power and there was no competition between dollars and disinterested analysis. Between dollars and a rival story. Dollars won.

Yet something more was going on; something more than a hot property of mayhem loaded with the thrill that a mixture of fame, sex, death, money and race produces. That something more was the construction of a national narrative, an official story. One of the most alarming aspects of the Simpson case is the shotgun wedding of the commodified, marketplace story and the official story.

A national narrative is born in and from chaos. Its purpose is to restore or imitate order and to minimize confusion about what is at stake and who will pay the price of dissension. Once, long ago, these stories developed slowly. They became over time national epics, written, sung, performed and archived in the culture as memory, ideology and art.

In some modern nations the construction of a national narrative is given over to a government agency and their uniformed enforcers. Government-owned or -controlled press and electronic media carry whatever message is deemed necessary to the health or status quo of the body politic: that the dead are disappeared; that the bloody crisis is the fault of the oppressed; that the problems are alien; that justice is accessible to the deserving and all is well.

In other nations the manufacture of a public truth is harder—cautioned and delayed by a free press, an openly dissident citizenry, a reversible electorate. Normally, in a democratic climate, managed opinion proceeds at a moderate pace. Recently, however, democratic discourses are suborned by sudden, accelerated, sustained blasts of media messages—visual and in print—that rapidly enforce the narrative and truncate alternative opinion. The raison d'être of this narrative may vary, but its job is straightforward: the production of belief. In order to succeed it must monopolize the process of legitimacy. It need not "win" hands down; it need not persuade all parties. It needs only to control the presumptions and postulates of the discussion. For the very struggle for monopoly assures the name and reach of the debate. Spectacle is the best means by which an official story is formed and is a superior mechanism for guaranteeing its longevity. Spectacle offers signs, symbols and images that are more pervasive and persuasive than print and which can smoothly parody thought. The symbolic language that emanates from unforeseen events supplies media with the raw material from which a narrative emerges—already scripted, fully spectacularized and riveting in its gazeability. The fortuitousness of the event which contributes to the construction of a public verity can mislead us into thinking that the power of persuasion lies in the events themselves, when in fact it is the already understood and agreed-upon interpretation of the events that is sold and distributed as public truth. Underneath the commodified story (of violence, sex, race, etc.) is a cultural one. While it is the commercial value of the story as product that gave the Simpson case its gigantism, it is the force of the cultural narrative that gives it its staying power. The spectacle is the narrative; the narrative is spectacularized and both monopolize appearance and social reality. Interested only in developing itself, the spectacle is immune to correction. Even and especially when panels are assembled to critique the process, the dialogue is confined to the terms the spectacle has set.

It was clear from the beginning that the real (as opposed to legal) possibility of Mr. Simpson's innocence was a story that had no legs and would not walk, let alone sell. Such a story would be a very sad (but not uncommon) one of a double murder by assailants unknown. A best-seller story requires the familiar ingredients of "a good read": fame, death, money, sex, villains and, of course, pace. (How often we heard commentators grumble about the boring days, the absence of "drama"; how often they cut away from explications of hard evidence because it was "droning," untheatrical; how often witnesses were judged as good based not on what they had to say, but on their "performance"—on how much the camera loved them.) In a culture dominated by images, Mr. Simpson is ideal—already an entertainer with a surfeit of the talents successful entertainers have. Also, he is black. When race culpability or pathology is added to this market brew, profits soar and the narrative coalesces quickly, takes on another form and moves from commodity to lore. In short, to an official story.

In the case of Mr. Simpson the theme of racial culpability rapidly became obvious.

First came the assertion/denial of race. A kind of double-speak in which race is both flagged and erased. There was a quick made-for-television movie, shown before the trial. It featured a brutal, repellant, already-convicted-in-the-film's-eye version of Mr. Simpson. The plot ended just before the main character does the deed the viewer is programmed to accept as reality. The darkened photograph on the cover of a national magazine—a decision to distort inconceivable with another alleged killer Timothy McVeigh—was an early harbinger of how this narrative was going to be scripted. Racial irrationality in all of its manifestations was soon imposed on all language, all visuals that referenced the story.

The official story obliterates any narrative that is counter to it. Nowhere is there a narrative of the literal innocence of Mr. Simpson. There are hints, equivocations, protective covers, but such a story is unimaginable. And unprofitable. "Reasonable doubts" of his guilt in court have become pervasive doubts of his innocence in the media. Just as the real lives of the Senegalese and his fellows are largely unimagined, imagining the consequences of a provably innocent Mr. Simpson is lethal. What if the punditocracy is wrong? What if the average person has been ambushed on the "information highway"? By now, the interests are so vested the official story is already in gear to protect itself. The rehabilitation of Detective Fuhrman will soon come. No book or interview time will be orchestrated for any but those convinced of or flirting with Mr. Simpson's guilt.

The verdict, unenforcable by the spectacle, ran counter to its agenda and had to be instantly voided. The story of racial incompetence, which was the theme all along, was reinforced by the attack on the jury as incapable of making an intelligent decision, as being (unlike other juries) grossly uneducated. The presumption of innocence demanded of them is being called "ethnic bias," a sort of lunatic, vaguely illegal "sympathy" rather than a prerequisite courts are bound to demand. Jury nullification becomes the topic of the day. The messengers of this view of the jury (journalists, commentators, even lawyers) see themselves as the American captain in Melville's story saw himself: objective (or maybe too trusting in their dealings with blacks), non-racist truth-seekers, innocent transcribers of a language they may truly believe is unraced.

Racial deviance was further detected in the polls. If these polls are correct twenty-five percent of the white population—more whites than the *total* number of African Americans in the nation—resist the official story and believe Mr. Simpson to be innocent. But, like the non-black jurors, they are erased, swallowed in the maw of the official narrative; blackened by default. Their resistance to the official story does not count. Nowhere was the jury described as "mixed." In any case, both groups are dismissed: the blacks who believe Mr. Simpson innocent are exhibiting ethnic closure; the whites who agree are suffering from liberal paralysis.

Part of the resistance to a blanket condemnation of Mr. Simpson may be a wariness of a tale that emerged fully formed, one that needed so much volume, space, and required amazing sleight of hand and tongue in cheek. A story that kept telling us that we were asking for it like a new breakfast cereal we simply had to have. Force feeding us until we thought the taste was our own invention, our own hunger.

Excised from the official story is Mr. Simpson's life among and within his black family. The official story has limited his biography to an insolent, womanizing golf life. Although it is promoted as a life of sexual prowess, drugs, alcohol, infidelity and violence—characteristics associated with black male misbe-havior—it is lived in an all-white world. A separate world with walls so high even the running champion could not scale them. We are repeatedly told he "never did anything for his commu-nity," meaning he was not a vocal, high-profile activist, although why Hertz (or Nike, Hanes, Pepsi, Midas or any company) would choose a black activist as its spokesperson is not made clear. In addition, the children he had with his second wife have been scripted as white children with no relationship with or rela-tion to their sisters and brother, aunts and grandmother, cousins or any of the Simpsons who are African Americans. His children by his first wife have provoked no media interest (lucky for them). This surgical excision functions under the guise of the enforced racelessness of the case—a guise that works if whites are the only ones who are unraced, neutral. Consider the "whitening" of his "black" children; the clear assumption that they are "safe" with the white side of their family. (Racelessness was a hope, a goal, Mr. Simpson, like many many others, believed had come to fruition in his own life and was possible in all our lives. But dec-larations that racism is irrelevant, over or confined to the past are premature fantasies.)

The effectiveness of the official story can be seen in several quarters. Many African Americans found themselves intimidated in the workplace, unwilling to voice even minor aspects of a counter-narrative lest they be accused of . . . what? showing race preference? It was easier to say nothing or agree.

Women were especially intimidated—because to question the story amounted to approving of or dismissing domestic violence.

Some people were persuaded of Mr. Simpson's guilt by hunches; some by their own examinations of the examinations, but most had no choice in the wake of the official story. Even the huge problems associated with and discrediting the DNA-verified blood samples have been eliminated from common parlance. There is blood, after all. In the popular mind's eye there is a scene like something out of *The Shining.* The house at Rockingham awash in blood. Great splashes in the foyer, up the stairs, cascading down the edge of a porcelain sink. Smears and globs of it everywhere: car, bedroom, socks. The 1.4 cc; the .07 of a drop; the flecks smaller than a child's littlest fingernail grow in the imagination, flood and saturate exponentially to "all that blood. What about all that blood?" Or whatever the amount, it is conclusively identified. The wide scientific controversy about the inclusionary properties of DNA, about the absolute, unequivocal necessity for flawless handling in order to get anything but worthless results, are read as the intellectual nit-picking of eggheads and therefore dismissed.

It is important to note that police methods can alter perception in the construction of a public truth. And one of the chief arguments in the Simpson case was whether police corruption was absurd or isolate. The story avoided as best it could whether corruption was endemic. It suggested that "massive" collusion would be necessary to pull off such a thing as tampering with evidence—and, since we are in the race-denying mode, what would be the motive? For middle and upper classes the police are the praetorian guard. They are the men in blue who riot for them, in place of them, who are implacable in their pursuit of the disorderly, the unhoused and the criminal, and who sometimes have to violate law to enforce it. For whites to consider police corruption as systemic rather than occasional is to place themselves in the untenable position of being shielded *by,* rather than protected from, chaos. The desire for protection from blacks at all costs encourages recklessness and the weapon of choice may be an arrow tipped with poison at both ends.

Acknowledging the predatory nature of a psychotic cadre within the police force would necessitate the suppression of the ultimate social nightmare: one in which pockets of gestapo turn their "commitment to law and order" on to *them;* break into *their* houses without warrants; manipulate evidence against *them,* handcuff *them.* To open up that debate (as Alan Dershowitz tried to do) proved too toxic for the body politic and was expunged from the official story. It would take the whole department to effect such a conspiracy, wouldn't it? "Conspiracy" is a term routinely used to end further analysis—a junk word applicable to boneheads hooked on JFK lore and alien landings. Laughable. Many African Americans agree. Evidence placement and tampering doesn't need the conspiracy of a whole department. Such actions need only what they have: averted eyes and trained "testilying." The ordinary everyday experience of African Americans with the police is acknowledged, but since blacks and criminality are understood to go hand in hand, the outrage that should be the consequence of lawless police is muted. The New York Dirty Thirty (the 30th Precinct in Harlem that had preyed on the population for years) and the Philadelphia police (now testifying to years and years of planting evidence and brutality) are both scandals among many more that broke in the last three years, one during the year Mr. Simpson's attorneys put forth police misconduct as a factor in the collection of evidence.

Another issue the official story both exposed and blanketed is the matter of domestic abuse, by which is meant the physical harm males do to females—the reverse being rare, warranted, a joke or all three. There are patently excessive responses to these claims. A six-year-old boy was suspended for kissing a girl classmate on the cheek (prompting the question of whether expulsion would have been the consequence if she had kissed him). And there are undoubtedly some fabrications, abuse being the easiest and most effective claim in divorce settlements. But the more recent understandings of the law and the unassailable argument of men and women who are trying to get the general population and the courts to take this issue seriously lead toward one conclusion: a female must not be physically accosted by a male under any circumstances—excepting a demonstrable threat to his or somebody's life. That means whatever the reasons, there are no excuses. If she slaps him, he is not to retaliate in like manner. If she curses him, humiliates him or degrades him, he must not hit her. If she betrays him with another sexual partner, he must not hit her. If she abuses his children or burns his supper; wrecks his car or chops off his penis; whether she is shooting up, messing up or cleaning up, he must not hit her. Why? Because he is stronger. The power relationship is unequal. (Except when she is armed.)

As for sexual assault, the thinking is similar. Rape is a criminal act whatever the circumstances. A woman riding the subway nude may be guilty of indecency, but she may not be raped. If she invites or even sells sex at 10:00 and refuses it at 10:45, the partner who disregards her refusal and forces sex is guilty of rape. If she is drunk, asleep, mentally defective, paralyzed or dead, she must not be raped. Why? Because sexual congress must be by consent. And males are stronger.

Trying to ensure that view has been difficult partly because the masculinist side of the debate (She was "asking" for it) still pervades, but also because in the negotiation of power, the physical strength and the allegedly uncontrollable sexual hunger of males are seen as unequalizing factors. The unpopular counter-argument that concerns female responsibility in these matters of power is a subversive, almost treasonable one. Men must be retrained and socialized into non-aggressive, respectful behavior. But women, whose historically repressive social education has

been ruthless and whose self-esteem has been systematically plun-
dered, are understood to have no responsibility. As long as the
wildly irresponsible claim of "It doesn't matter what she does" is
the answer to the helpless, hopeless idiocy of "She made me do
it," the complicity in power/abuse relationships will be unad-
dressed. It *does* matter what she does. And she can't *make* you. But
the dialogue that lies between those two positions is being buried
under the detritus of the Simpson case. His "not really" blackness damns him because not only has he admitted and been convicted of spousal abuse, sexual brutality is part of the package
when anyone "falls" back (or is returned) into the metaphorical
ghetto. The people opposed to Mr. Simpson's speaking engage-
ments say that his censure is necessary because he is a batterer. I
should think that would confirm his place in the domestic abuse
dialogue, assuming that, rather than monologue, is the agenda.

Within this official story are issues that can remake and
unmake America: violence, class, race, capitalism, the control
and distribution of information, equitable justice, constitutional
guarantees, privacy, patriarchal power, to name a few. But the
grammar of the meta-narrative has been forcibly limited to the
question, Did he? The answer is available to some, certainly to
Mr. Simpson, but any other answer is a hunch—educated or
uninformed, but still a hunch. So the substitute question is, Do
you think he did it? As a stripped-down, litmus test question it
gets an answer: Yes, I do. No, I don't. But the question is not
stripped down; it is loaded with additional meaning. It has
become a ploy disguised as a disinterested query that really asks,
Are "they" guilty or innocent? "They" meaning we blacks, those
blacks, we men, those men. Are "they" getting away with murder?

As troubling as the development of a national story is,
equally troubling are the subsequent efforts to secure it, render it

unimpeachable—all the way from silencing the defendant to slandering any attempt to contest the official story.

The sustained determination to shut Mr. Simpson up, we are told, is the result of profound moral outrage, and his need for funds is felt to be an insult. (He is liable for child support and damages, but is permitted only to distribute money, not earn any.) He tries to market a self-justifying video; interviews on TV shows (except the black one) are cancelled. Mr. Simpson just "calls in" from distant unspecified places to comment on what the meta-narrative is deploying. To the spectacle he is a disembodied voice, a phantom, a social cadaver and a minor irritant in the official gaze, which cracks occasionally to expose him golfing. A "dead" man arrogantly alive. This silencing is very interesting. If what Mr. Simpson has to say is so worthless, so self-serving, why not let him join the other worthless narrators loading the airwaves? If he is lying, what is there to fear but another televised distortion among a flood of them? The official story has apparently won the confidence of almost everybody. The censorship is not seen for what it is: a blatant attempt to control the narrative by dismissing or trivializing all counter-narratives—narratives that neither support the market story, which is still earning money, nor intervene in the agenda of the official story. The feelings and comments of anti-Simpson forces are solicited daily. In the civil case no phalanx of reporters seek friends or family of Mr. Simpson to note or report their response to the case. Only the plaintiffs get to speak and contribute to the shape of this narrative. There is no investigation of any alternative story, and if there is to be one, the burden of producing it is not on the district attorney or on investigative reporting, but on Mr. Simpson himself. So it is passing odd that he has the onus to reveal a story he is forbidden to tell.

Eeny, meeny miney moe
Catch a nigger by the toe
If he hollers
Let him go.

Let him go? If he hollers—if he speaks? Let him go? Then, by all means, he must not speak a word.

There will be no multi-million-dollar contracts signed for a neutral investigative book describing, advancing or even hinting strongly at any other narrative—a narrative more complicated than the one that echoes the spectacle's rapture and mainstream's desire. Any such story will be thrown into the refuse heap of vested interests, of ethnic bias or discredited liberal reasoning. It is socially correct to doubt his innocence but it is literally safer to declare him guilty. Instead of "nigger lover," "murderer!" is shouted to his associates and well-wishers. Instead of burning crosses stuck in yards, death threats are e-mailed or dropped in mailboxes. To avoid snubbing, disdain and threats the protective cover is "I think he did it, but had I been on the jury I would have acquitted him." It is an odd opinion reminiscent of the "I think he did it, but I think he'll walk" statement heard so often at the beginning of the case, a statement uneasily close to "I think he did it, but I hope he walks." What could that possibly mean? If convinced of his guilt, why connect it with freedom? Does it mean Mr. Simpson is or should be above conviction, jail-time, execution? Or is it the fusion of the race-inflected official story and a longing for a living black man repeating forever a narrative of black insufficiency?

It is curious how satisfying the idea of Mr. Simpson as a dead man golfing has become. The pity belongs to the dead; but according to headlines, cover stories and book titles the status of American tragedy belongs to Mr. Simpson. Is that another denial of race or a signal of its presence? If he is guilty, isn't "tragedy" a bit grand? And why "American," one wonders?

I began this essay with "Benito Cereno," an American tale in which, because the racist point of view of the narrator is hidden, the watcher is forced to discover racism as the paramount theme, the axis upon which all the action turns. Like Melville's "long benighted" captain, most white Americans are still in denial—that is, public denial. And to suggest how these denials inform and are informed by culture I would like to end with another American narrative.

The film *Birth of a Nation*, based on the novel *The Klansman*, gathered up and solidified post–Civil War America's assumptions of and desires for white supremacy. The Simpson spectacle has become an enunciation of post–Civil Rights discourse on black deviance. Both of these sagas have race at their nexus. Not in spite of but because of the overdetermined claims: that race was "inserted" in the trial, or that the trial "became" about race, or that it degenerated into a racial referendum, it is clear that the Simpson official narrative, like *Birth of a Nation*, is ruled by race. Like *Birth of a Nation*, the case has generated a newer, more sophisticated national narrative of racial supremacy. But it is still the old sham white supremacy forever wedded to and dependent upon faux black inferiority.

They are out to break him, said one of Mr. Simpson's lawyers after the trial. And, of this date, it is hard to see how they can fail. The appetite for a live head on a stick is ravenous. So, perhaps, we will see what the American captain in Melville's fiction saw and wanted to see: the head of the Negro "fixed on a pole in the Plaza." But that was not all there was to see. Melville pushes the image beyond the desires of the American captain to insinuate into the reader's mind a far more complex issue. He does not use the Senegalese's proper name toward the end; instead Melville applies the generic label "the black," as if to stress the point implied: unlike a white, the black individual is forced to stand in for the entire race.

The official story has thrown Mr. Simpson into that representative role. He is not an individual who underwent and was acquitted from a murder trial. He has become the whole race needing correction, incarceration, censoring, silencing; the race that needs its civil rights disassembled; the race that is sign and symbol of domestic violence; the race that has made trial by jury a luxury rather than a right and placed affirmative action legislation in even greater jeopardy. This is the consequence and function of official stories: to impose the will of a dominant culture. It is *Birth of a Nation* writ large—menacingly and pointedly for the 'hood.

Birth of a Nation'hood

The Greatest Story Ever Sold:
Marketing and the
O.J. Simpson Trial
George Lipsitz

"When you have this kind of public awareness and preconditioning, the long-term cash-in has got to be enormous."
—Jack Myers, President, Myers Communications[1]

"The public hates itself for its fascination with O.J. Simpson."
—David Bartlett, President, Radio-Television News Directors Association[2]

Prosecutors in Los Angeles announce the filing of first-degree murder charges against a handsome and athletic African-American man. They claim that he used deadly force in assaulting a white woman and her male companion on a quiet street in an affluent section on the west side of Los Angeles. The defendant is represented by prominent defense attorney Johnnie Cochran, who claims that serious and deliberate misconduct on the part of law enforcement officers has tainted the evidence against his client. After a much publicized trial, the jury reaches a verdict.

The jury finds the defendant guilty and sends him to prison, where he remains to this day. The man is not, however, O.J. Simpson. He is Elmer "Geronimo" Pratt, a former deputy defense minister of the Black Panther Party, who has been incarcerated for nearly twenty-five years for his alleged involvement in the 1968 killing of Caroline Olsen and the wounding of Kenneth Olsen near a Santa Monica tennis court. Before coming to Los Angeles to enter UCLA on the GI Bill, Pratt served two tours of duty in Vietnam, where he was a decorated paratrooper. After receiving an honorable discharge from the service, he entered college and became active in radical political organizations, including the Los Angeles chapter of the Black Panther Party. After assassins (egged on by the Federal Bureau of Investigation's COINTELPRO project) shot and killed local Panther leaders Alprentice "Bunchy" Carter and Jon Huggins, Pratt became a key leader of the group.

At Pratt's trial in 1972, prosecutors claimed that a car resembling his was seen near the site of the crime, that the murder weapon had been found in Jon Huggins's house, and that Kenneth Olsen, who survived the attack, had positively identified Pratt as the culprit. In addition, an expelled member of the Black Panther Party, Julio Carl Butler, gave testimony damaging to the defendant. For his part, Pratt denied any knowledge of the attack on the Olsens, claiming that he had been hundreds of miles away in Oakland, California, when the crime was committed. Prosecutors and police officials did not tell the jury that Kenneth Olsen had identified at least three other suspects before responding to police prodding to name Pratt as the man who killed Caroline Olsen. They did not disclose that the barrel was missing from the alleged murder weapon, making it impossible to conduct tests that could connect it definitively to the crime. They did not produce wiretap evidence that might have corroborated Pratt's story that he was in Oakland at the time of the attack.

In their 1988 book, *Agents of Repression*, Ward Churchill and Jim Vander Wall revealed that agents from the Los Angeles office of the Federal Bureau of Investigation targeted Pratt for special surveillance and prosecution as early as 1969 because of his political activities. Internal reports from the Los Angeles office of the bureau described Pratt as "a key Black extremist," and informed supervisors in Washington, D.C., that "constant consideration is given to the possibility of utilization of counter-intelligence measures with efforts being directed toward neutralizing Pratt as an effective BPP (Black Panther Party) functionary."[3] Los Angeles Police Department officers arrested Pratt several times on an assortment of charges, all of which were dropped or resulted in acquittals before they attempted to connect him to the killing of Caroline Olsen.[4] Pratt was in jail awaiting trial in 1971 when he learned that his wife, Sandra Lane Pratt, had been murdered. She was eight months pregnant when she was shot five times at close range and killed. Although her body was found stuffed inside a sleeping bag alongside an L.A. freeway, the police department conducted no serious investigation into her death. Law enforcement officials also denied permission to Geronimo Pratt to view his wife's body or to attend her funeral.[5]

Churchill and Vander Wall point out that key prosecution witness Julio Carl Butler had been a deputy sheriff before joining the Black Panther Party, that he has been identified as an FBI infiltrator of the Black Panthers by Louis Tackwood, who himself worked as an undercover agent in Black nationalist groups, and that even though Butler pleaded guilty to four major felonies, he received only a probationary sentence and has subsequently been allowed to complete law school and enter the California bar association.[6] Former FBI Agent M. Wesley Swearingen also claimed in a 1995 book that Carl Butler was an informant for the Los Angeles Police Department and for the FBI. Swearingen noted that the bureau closed its file on Butler before the trial so that they could say he was "not an FBI informant," and he alleged that the government indeed possessed wiretap logs proving that Pratt was in the San Francisco Bay Area before and after the shooting of Caroline Olsen. When Swearingen tried to check the bureau's wiretap records, he was told that the logs from November 15 to December 20, 1968, were "missing."[7] A member of the jury that convicted Pratt in 1972 now says that she believes that they would never have reached a verdict of guilty had they known about the wiretap evidence or about the allegations that Butler had been an informant.[8]

Geronimo Pratt's story is at least as dramatic and as interesting as O.J. Simpson's. It is a story of murder and misconduct, of lost liberty and a ruined reputation. Yet it is not a story that will sell. Pratt may well be an innocent man imprisoned for a crime that he did not commit, a prisoner framed for his political activities. But he does not have the necessary qualifications to be a famous black criminal defendant like the man we might refer to as Johnnie Cochran's other client—O.J. Simpson. His story has no details about interracial sex, no intimations of drug use, no spectacular spousal abuse. Although he managed to secure the services of Johnnie Cochran, he had no "dream team" of lawyers working for $650 per hour, no ability to pay forensic consultants the $50,000 per week that they received from Simpson.[9] Most important, Geronimo Pratt's story will not sell because it goes against the grain of the story-telling apparatuses of commercial culture that place entertainment and consumer purchases at the center of the social world. Pratt's story is about politics, racism, and history; consequently, he remains unknown to most of the public, cannot get a rehearing of his case based on newly discovered evidence, and he sits in a prison cell. Simpson's story is about sex and celebrities, about professional sports, Hollywood films, and television commercials; consequently, his story is universally known. Simpson may be guilty, but he is a free man today. Pratt may be innocent, but he remains incarcerated and virtually unknown.

In publicizing the O.J. Simpson case, media conglomerates publicized themselves and the world in which they work. The "salability" of this story stemmed from its smooth fit with the long history of sales that preceded it—sales of individual celebrity images, cross-marketing campaigns aimed at connecting fame to commercial endorsements, and the general dramatization of wealth and material goods that forms the subtext of so many television commercials, Hollywood films, and even news broadcasts. The O.J. Simpson case was about an entertainment figure, but it also was entertainment. The reach and scope of media interest in the trial bears a close relation to the financial benefits that media outlets derived from selling the kind of story that fit neatly into their preexisting categories. The Simpson story made huge amounts of money for cable and broadcast television networks, for tabloid newspapers and magazines, and for the merchandisers whose videotapes and books have only just begun to reach the market. But beyond its utility as a means for capital accumulation, the Simpson trial also enables us to ask and answer questions about the power of publicity, the meaning of money, and the interpenetration of public and private concerns in our culture. Why did this story take on the proportions that it did? What were its uses and effects? What can we say about a society that spends so much of its time and resources on a story like this one?

Cultural theorist Arthur Kroker claims that nothing happens in our society unless it happens on television. Of course we know that this is not quite correct, that one of the problems with television programs is that they do so little to reflect the realities that people confront every day. Kroker's overstatement is perhaps a deliberate provocation designed to get our attention, to emphasize the central role played by commercial culture in framing public events and private concerns. But even if Kroker's formulation is flawed, the obverse of it is certainly true: If something happens over and over again on television, then it certainly "happens" to all of us. Television played the key role in the Simpson case in many ways. The trial was telecast live, and its details were aired endlessly on news and entertainment programs. The case opened up whole new television markets with gavel-to-gavel coverage on cable and broadcast outlets. It helped spur the development of new programs and the creation of new celebrities through specialized discussions on cable channels. It provided a constant frame of reference for late-night comedians, talk shows, and news features, and even served as the source of a new line of Halloween masks featuring the case's central "characters."

Simpson's status as an already-famous celebrity gave his case a particularly significant meaning to television programming not just because he has appeared often in the medium as an athlete, broadcaster, film star, and spokesperson famous for his commercial endorsements but rather his prominence in diverse areas of entertainment gave him the kind of visibility that television loves to recycle and repackage. His segueing from athletics to entertainment to news simply augmented that capacity, or rather, to be more precise, brought the news where news directors, advertisers, and public relations firms deeply desire it to be—squarely within the realm of entertainment. Commercial television in the United States has long rested on intertextual engagement with other media—television presents motion pictures, sporting events, and concerts; it mixes celebrities from different realms of endeavor on talk and game shows; it engages in relentless cross-programming, plugging purchases of other kinds of entertainment by placing television at the nexus of publishing, broadcasting, filmmaking, music recording, and shopping. Television stars make films that enable them to appear on talk shows to prepare audiences for their best-selling books, which give them name recognition valuable for product endorsements, etc. As Daniel Czitrom noted years ago, nearly everything on television is an advertisement for some form of entertainment or product available in another medium; the "infomercial" or program-length commercial that dominates late-night programming on cable is simply a refinement of what the medium does more crudely elsewhere.

The Simpson trial became a story that was easy to sell, in part, because it seemed to replicate so perfectly the world of commercial television and its generic conventions. The athlete/actor/celebrity defendant charged with murder could have come out of *Murder, She Wrote* or *Columbo* while the details about his residence and vehicles might fit easily into segments of *Dallas, Dynasty,* or *Life Styles of the Rich and Famous.* For experienced television viewers, courtroom confrontations enacted half-remembered episodes of *L.A. Law, Perry Mason,* and *Quincy,* while the history of unheeded claims of spousal abuse evoked the concerns and conflicts often aired in the movie-of-the-week. The search for justice by grieving relatives and the short, glamorous lives of the victims sparked associations with daily soap operas or weekly serial dramas. Indeed, one source of public dissatisfaction with the trial, with its participants and its outcome, seems to stem from the failure of the trial to fit the frame that television established for it, to come to a "happy ending" in the form of an unambiguous verdict of guilty—which certainly would have been the case had this been simply a television melodrama. But instead of following the clearly defined character roles and unambiguous narrative closures offered by television programs, the trial and its participants instead reflected the ambiguities, uncertainties, and contradictions of everyday life and its complex social relations, giving the entire enterprise the look of being out of control in comparison to the other stories that television tells and sells.

From start to finish, the O.J. Simpson story demonstrated an eerie engagement with, and an unusual affinity for, the money-making mechanisms within commercial culture. If it was something less than the trial of the century in terms of legal significance, it was certainly the "sale" of the century in terms of its ability to bring together the various apparatuses of advertising, publicity, spectator sports, motion pictures, television, and marketing into a unified totality generating money-making opportunities at every turn. A major Los Angeles radio station gave defense witness Brian "Kato" Kaelin his own talk show because of the trial. One outside "expert" frequently employed by television networks during the trial, attorney Gerry Spence parlayed his guest commentaries on the Simpson case on a variety of programs into his own televised talk show on CNBC. The William Morris Agency won a hotly contested battle to serve as theatrical and public relations representative for lead prosecutor Marcia Clark.[10] Edward Billet Productions purportedly offered Judge Lance Ito $1 million to star in a new version of the television program *The People's Court*.[11] Industry experts confided to *Advertising Age* reporters that "Simpson-related marketing could produce as much as $1 billion in media and merchandising sales." During the trial, Simpson had his lawyers take out patent protection for his full name as well as for his nicknames "O.J." and "The Juice," and had them file more than fifty lawsuits against merchandisers marketing items bearing his name. In addition, Simpson negotiated deals for a video, a book, pay-per-view interviews, and other projects that might eventually net as much as $18 million.[12]

During the trial, jurors were dismissed for allegedly keeping notes designed to aid them in writing books about their experiences. One dismissed juror published a book that came out before the trial ended. After the verdict, some jurors asked television producers and magazine editors for as much as $100,000 for interviews; one agreed to pose nude for *Playboy*.[13] Prosecutor Christopher Darden and chief defense lawyer Robert Shapiro produced highly publicized and broadly marketed books that appeared some six months after the trial. In his book, Darden accused a member of Simpson's defense team of drafting a book on a laptop computer even while the trial was taking place. Journalist Brent Staples speculated in the *New York Times* that Shapiro hired Alan Dershowitz as part of the defense team not for his potential contributions to the actual case but mainly to prevent Dershowitz from serving as a television analyst and making comments that might embarrass Shapiro.[14] Proof of Mark Fuhrman's perjury did not emerge through vigorous cross-examination but rather from remarks he made to an aspiring screenwriter in the hope that he could have his real and imagined deeds as a member of the Los Angeles Police Department immortalized and publicized in a Hollywood film.[15]

The story of O.J. Simpson on trial sold well. CNN (the Cable News Network) presented 631 hours of direct televised coverage of the Simpson trial, attracting an average of 2.2 million viewers at any given time. This content increased the channel's ratings and revenues by close to fifty percent.[16] On the day of the verdict, an unusually large number of daytime viewers—representing forty-two percent of the nation's television homes and more than ninety percent of the sets actually in use—were tuned to channels covering the case. For the entire week leading up to the verdict, Simpson programming gave CNN fourteen of the fifteen most-watched basic cable programs. Court TV, available in only about twenty-four million homes, nonetheless accounted for three of the most-watched shows on cable during the fall 1995 ratings period.[17] Industry officials attributed much of cable television's collective twenty-five percent jump in ratings between 1994 and 1995 to the Simpson case.[18] Tabloid television shows featuring the Simpson story registered dramatic gains as well. During the week when the verdict was announced, *Entertainment Tonight* secured an audience that was thirty-nine percent larger than the previous week's. *Inside Edition* increased its viewership by twenty-four percent over the same time period the previous year, while *American Journal* attracted double its average audience for that season.[19]

Mass circulation magazines devoted fifty-four cover stories to the Simpson case during the last half of 1994, and ninety cover stories to it during 1995—almost three times the attention they gave to their second favorite cover story personality, television talk-show host Oprah Winfrey.[20] More than one million Internet users visited CNN's O.J. Simpson Web site in the first six hours after the trial verdict, an average of 3,800 per minute.[21] A live interview with O.J. Simpson in January 1996 enabled Black Entertainment Television (BET) to reach three million households and secure the highest ratings in the channel's sixteen-year history, easily surpassing the previous high of 1.2 million households, much less its average viewership of 300,000 homes in prime time. The network did not pay Simpson for this interview as he initially requested, but they did allow him to purchase time before and after the program to advertise his mail-order video available for purchase at $29.95 apiece.[22]

Stories about the O.J. Simpson trial enjoyed a powerful presence in the market, in part because they could draw on the main themes that organize television discourse in the United States: the primacy of products as the center of social life, the stimulation and management of appetites, and alarm about the family in jeopardy. A story linking any two of these categories will always make the news (i.e., a news event that resembles a popular motion picture—"a real-life *Home Alone* right here in your town," the existence of a new product that can affect your appetite for another product—"Will a new exercise machine help you quit smoking?" "Are you eating fat-free foods and still gaining weight? Find out why at eleven."). A story that links all three is even better—i.e., "Could your child be receiving sexually explicit images on the Internet?" One reason why the O.J. Simpson trial became so prominent in the media is because it contained all these elements necessary for televisual representation: it was a story about products, appetites, and the family in jeopardy.

O.J. Simpson's identity immediately raises associations with products. Over the years, he has done commercials as a spokesperson for Hertz Rent A Car, Chevrolet, Wilson Sporting Goods, and Royal Crown Cola. He has been visible as a commodity himself, as a football player, as an announcer for ABC television's *Monday Night Football* games, as an actor in motion pictures, including the *Naked Gun* series, as a motivational speaker at corporate events, and as a personality on exercise videos. In addition, he has become wealthy from these endeavors and lives a visibly affluent life. Each part of his career has served as a form of advertising for the other parts: his fame as a football player gave him an edge as an actor; his visibility as both an actor and athlete made him more desirable for commercial endorsements. His sources of fame are mutually reinforcing, and this history makes him quite desirable as the object of news or feature stories on television. Audiences will recognize him; their attention will translate into future commodity purchases. O.J. replicates the kinds of cross-marketing fundamental to television's relationship to other media.

These days, fame itself can be the most important part of a product. For example, low-wage women workers in Indonesia who sew Air Jordan athletic shoes for Nike receive wages of about $1.35 per hour. The shoes they make cost Nike about $5 a pair in materials and labor—but sell for anywhere from $45 to $80 in the United States. Michael Jordan receives $20 million per year to endorse these shoes, more than the total wages of all of Nike's workers in all six of their workplaces combined. Thus, Jordan's fame is worth more to Nike than the workers' labor; his reputation and visibility are themselves commodities more valuable than his own work as a basketball player (for which he receives about one-fifth the amount he gets for endorsements).[23] When fame is connected with a product, both become enhanced in value and both are more likely to appear on television.

Media coverage of the Simpson trial drew upon and reinforced the connection between Simpson and commodities. Coincidentally, the key pieces of material evidence in the trial were almost all commodities: the white Bronco and the Rolls Royce, the mysterious knife and the expensive Italian shoes, the unusual pair of designer leather gloves, some missing luggage, a golf bag, and even O.J.'s socks. Like testimony about the swimming pool, guest house, or video equipment on Simpson's property, the prominence of these items allowed journalists to report the news and talk about shopping at the same time. "News" reports on the trial paid close attention to Robert Shapiro's ties and Marcia Clark's hairstyles. Perhaps that preoccupation with appearances helps explain a recurrent preoccupation in Christopher Darden's book on the trial—what reviewer Adam Hochschild describes as Darden's "suitomania"—a compulsion to comment on other attorney's "expensive suits," Simpson's "thousand-dollar suit," and Johnnie Cochran's "off-white linen suit."[24]

The priority given to products in televisual discourse makes the issue of appetites crucially important. Commercials promote desire by projecting images of plenitude and fulfillment through commodity accumulation, but they also raise anxieties about desires that get out of control. Some commercials profess to monitor consumption by describing the dangers of reckless or foolish indulgences, for which they sell remedies ranging from indigestion medicine to diet pills to rehabilitation from drug, alcohol, or gambling addictions. In a similar way, television programs often work the same way, to inflame our desires but make us fear excess at the same time. In the Simpson case, the same things that made O.J. a symbol of fulfilled desires also made him a focal point for rumination about uncurbed appetites, cocaine use, indiscriminate sex, and unrestrained violence. John Fiske points out the ways in which tabloid newspaper accounts particularly emphasized these connections with stories like "Sex Secrets That Drove O.J. Crazy" and "Shocking Truth About Nicole's 911 Call, O.J. Caught Her Making Love While Kids Slept in the Next Room."[25] The talents that brought him wealth may have led him to use drugs. The good looks that made him a movie star may have enabled him to engage in obsessive extramarital sexual escapades. The physical strength that made him a successful athlete may have enabled him to murder two people brutally.

Finally, there is the issue of the family in jeopardy. This is a major theme of television drama, comedy, and news as well as a central preoccupation of commercials. As literary scholars Nancy Armstrong and Roddy Reid remind us, it is an old theme, one that dates back to the mid-nineteenth century, when domestic fiction first became a profitable market item. They argue that the theme emerged less because families actually experienced new threats from the world at large but instead because the best way to constitute the middle-class family as a consumption unit organized around the acquisition of household products was to create fearful images of the outside world and then "sell" the family as a defense against them.[26] To this day, the family is described in the media largely in terms of affection, intimacy, and its role as "a haven in a heartless world," with little open acknowledgment of its central role as a site for consumption, as an economic unit that transfers wealth and property across generations, and as an entity coveted by marketers who divide each family into separate market segments.

Like previous forms of commercial culture aimed at families, television endeavors to describe the family as always in jeopardy—but also to jeopardize it more fully by making commercial culture the arbiter of proper family behavior. The authority of the products and the people on television always appears more impressive than the authority of one's own family. Television organizes the family into separate market segments watching different programs (Monday night football, late-afternoon talk shows, Saturday morning cartoons) at different times of the day. In order to fulfill its project completely, the television industry ideally would like to detach everyone from their connections to roles other than shopping, thus enabling television to sell them things around the clock. But to market products effectively, they must be represented as non-commodities, as essentially vehicles for creating and preserving affection, intimacy, and interpersonal relations. This contradiction creates an unstable, volatile, and ultimately unresolvable anxiety that is always susceptible to media manipulation.

The Simpson trial revolved around narratives of family closure and rupture. One tabloid ran a picture of O.J., Nicole, and their first child with the caption: "How this dream family portrait turned into a murderous nightmare."[27] Was Nicole

Brown's marriage to a wealthy and handsome celebrity the fulfillment of the dreams of an Orange County suburban girl, or was it a cruel deception that trapped her in a tempestuous relationship with a jealous, violent, and philandering husband? Did O.J. love Nicole and their children as evidenced by his presence at the recital the day that Nicole was murdered, or was his attention merely a device to control others while allowing himself unbridled liberty? Both sides used family solidarity as an emblem of what was at stake for their side; the Goldman family's public weeping and timely press conferences served the prosecution in the same way that the tight family circle of sisters and O.J.'s mother presented "proof" of Simpson's virtue in the eyes of the defense. Hints of a sexual relationship between Nicole Brown Simpson and Ron Goldman or between Nicole and Kato Kaelin had to be quashed by the prosecution, while O.J.'s romantic and sexual entanglements with other women had to be narrativized as irrelevant to his devotion to Nicole. From an entertainment perspective, the issue was not so much character or motivation for murder but rather exposure of the close relationship between foundational narratives of family fidelity and the lived experiences that revealed them as fictions. As in the daytime soap opera or nighttime serial drama, family ties become invoked all the more passionately in the abstract as they disintegrate in actual practice. Affirmation of the family as the center of the social world is required, but that affirmation can exist easily alongside practices that contradict it.

The primacy of property, appetites, and the family in jeopardy in television discourse made the Simpson trial unusually susceptible to media exposure. In any art form, it is easy to go with the conventions and core grammar of the form and difficult to go against it. The Simpson trial was a story that could be told easily on television because television had long been involved in preparing the audience for stories like this one. Just as the Western films of John Ford seemed immediately credible to audiences accustomed to previous representations of the region in the paintings of Remington and Russell, on the covers of Western novels, and through performances of the Wild West Show, the O.J. Simpson trial could be immediately comprehended as "true" by viewers accustomed to television and its conventions.[28] In this context, there is no danger of overexposure; even disgust at the media attention devoted to the Simpson trial can be easily incorporated into the narrative—simply another aspect of the Simpson case that can be marketed on its own as a topic for discussion on talk shows or as the subject of magazine articles.

It is difficult not to feel contempt for the processes that employ powerful and sophisticated communications media for the kinds of voyeurism, idle speculation, and trivialities that dominated coverage of the Simpson trial. Its pervasive presence certainly raises serious questions about the society in which we live. Yet the stories that the media sells would not work if they did not serve some purpose, if they did not engage the attention and interest of audiences. We might do well to defer our judgment about whether we like or dislike the world that the Simpson trial reveals to us until we understand how and why the story worked, what wounds it salved, and what desires it actually expressed. In an essay about the popular culture of the 1930s, C.L.R. James offered some ideas that might help us understand the fascination with O.J. Simpson today. James argued that people who perceive themselves as restricted and constrained by their life circumstances turn to popular culture for compensatory stories about "free individuals who go out into the world and settle their problems by free activity and individualistic methods."[29] Movie stars and celebrities "live grandly and boldly," enjoying the freedom that others desire for themselves. Fictional and real lawbreakers offer special opportunities for investment and engagement because their stories titillate millions of people with the fantasy of active living. According to James, stories filled with bloodshed, violence, and the freedom from restraint that they symbolize allow audiences to release "the bitterness, hate, fear, and sadism which simmer just below the surface."[30] For James, the source of popular anger lay in the Great Depression, in the lost hopes, blasted aspirations, cultural disillusionments, and economic hard times engendered by economic collapse in the 1930s. It is certainly possible that economic restructuring and cultural change tied to deindustrialization, globalization, and the stagnation of real wages has had a similar effect on our own time.

James felt that fascination with popular heroes in the 1930s provided "an outlet for cheated, defrauded personality in vicarious living through a few striking personalities."[31] With no freedom to make meaningful choices about work or politics, people turn to popular culture, where at least some choices seem possible. At the same time, people resent the freedoms they project onto their heroes, mixing adoration of famous individuals with "murderous rejection" of them. The intolerable impotence and rage of everyday life ultimately leads us to desire the downfall of the idols we have created. This is a perversion, James contends, but one inherent "in a society in which the actual deepest desires of the masses cannot find expression."[32]

Yet for James, what mattered most about the stories that sell was less their immediate uses and effects on audiences but rather their ideological role in preventing other stories from emerging, stories about history, power, and social relations. This was true in the Simpson case, especially in respect to race. The very affinities for products, appetites, and the family in jeopardy that drove the Simpson saga as a media event also made it nearly impossible for public discourse to go beyond the frames and boundaries imposed by television's rhetorical and ideological conventions.

Even *Time* magazine agreed with arts curator Thelma Golden that "if Nicole had been black, this case would have been on a cover of *Jet* magazine and not much more."[33] In a society dominated by property, appetites, and family-in-jeopardy stories, race should disappear, but in a racialized society, concepts like property, appetites, and the family in jeopardy have racial implications. Throughout much of the 1980s and 1990s, television has linked accumulation and protection of property, descriptions of uncontrolled appetites, and threats to the family to racialized and racist imagery.[34] Media images and political discourse over the past two decades have hinged upon stories that connect crime, drugs, and family disintegration to nonwhite communities, while presenting whites as besieged.[35] On television, Black people who do not belong on *The Cosby Show* belong on *Cops.* Once these images have been circulated and recirculated, they are extremely difficult to displace. As historian Nathan Irvin Huggins remarked years ago about the enduring and poisonous power of the minstrel show "darkie," Black people have found it very difficult to "step out of character" either on or off stage because white people are often so attached to the images that they have created about Blacks. Elements in the trial that conformed to the story already in place about racial identity could be comprehended easily by the audience. Elements that contradicted it made the story harder to sell. Thus, the story of a guilty O.J. could easily fit this scenario, especially after national newsmagazines printed Simpson's mug shot and artificially darkened his picture on their covers in order to accentuate the threat that he embodied (and, as John Fiske points out, to promote "impulse" buys by whites for those very magazines).[36] The story of an innocent, O.J., or at least of a technically not-guilty O.J. because the largely black jury believed that the prosecution's case did not meet the legal standards of proof beyond a reasonable doubt, was a story that went against the grain of the narrative already in place.

Yet racial categories accounted for much of the emotional charge carried by the Simpson trial and verdict. How could it have been otherwise in a case involving a Black defendant and two white victims? Race provided the trial with its most significant subtext, and the racial identities of the judge, attorneys, witnesses, and, most of all, jurors, played a major role in determining what stories could be told and sold. Efforts to commodify racial identity proved easy. *Tonight Show* host Jay Leno and New York senator Alphonse D'Amato attracted different degrees of criticism when Leno presented a recurrent skit featuring the "Dancing Itos" (bearded Japanese men in judges' robes performing a French cancan) and D'Amato impersonated Ito speaking in a Japanese accent (which Ito does not have) during an appearance on the Don Imus radio show. But even though they transgressed the boundaries of taste and tolerance, D'Amato and Leno correctly assumed that racial identity could "play" in the media as a joke, as an anxious expression of the intrusion of otherness in a media discourse that assumes audiences are white. But more complicated stories about race, and racism, could not so easily fit the commodified form of television discourse.

Detective Mark Fuhrman's testimony—and perjury—provides a case in point. Before he took the stand, print journalists reported that Fuhrman had applied for disability benefits on the grounds that his service in the Los Angeles Police Department

had left him with a violent hatred toward Blacks and other
"minority" groups. Prosecutors denied these stories and provided
the press with a completely different "spin"—that Fuhrman was
a distinguished and disciplined professional. When F. Lee Bailey's
initial cross-examination failed to crack Fuhrman's cover story,
press reports gushed about how effective a witness Fuhrman had
been, how handsome he was, and how credible his testimony
seemed to be. They overlooked Fuhrman's preposterous assertion
that the police did not consider Simpson to be a suspect and consequently did not need a search warrant when Fuhrman climbed
over a fence to inspect the grounds of Simpson's estate. These
same accounts ridiculed Bailey for asserting that Fuhrman might
harbor racist antipathies toward Blacks. Fuhrman's "composure"
and media-friendly appearance (handsome, white, and male) led
the press to imbue his story with credibility. When definitive evidence emerged that Fuhrman had committed perjury, that he not
only had used the word "nigger" in conversation but also was a
racist ideologue who boasted privately about using his position as
a police officer to brutalize suspects and enact his own racist
beliefs, the response was very strange. Rather than expressing
anger that a police officer had compromised an important murder case by lying in court and by boasting about breaking the law,
media outlets and callers to talk shows largely adopted the prosecution's line of argument, treating Fuhrman like an unsuccessful
character whose part had to be written out of the show. They
admitted that Fuhrman was "a racist," but contended that his
racism was personal and had nothing to do with the widespread
practices of the Los Angeles Police Department (witness Chief
Gates) or the prosecutor's office.

No one was expected to take responsibility for Fuhrman's
racism, even the detective himself, who was allowed to plead "no
contest" and avoid jail for his misconduct, getting off with a

$200 fine and three years of probation with no conditions except that he obey the law from now on—a condition that most of us experience as a matter of course. By treating racism as individual rather than institutional, Fuhrman's "racism" could in no way be allowed to taint the police department that hired and promoted him, and that continued to place him in positions where he could abuse his authority. It could not be permitted to reflect badly on the prosecutors who relied on his testimony despite what they knew about him, who ridiculed claims that Fuhrman was a racist; but when these claims were shown to be true, those involved absolved themselves of any blame and took no steps to prosecute the detective for perjury. However, when Johnnie Cochran used Fuhrman's racism to undermine the credibility of his testimony, the Goldman family, prosecutors, and an overwhelming number of media commentators reacted with indignation and outrage. People who could find no racism in Mark Fuhrman now felt quite comfortable in condemning Cochran for "playing the race card." If Fuhrman's racism was a personal attribute that could not be used to undermine the credibility of any other white person or any social institution run by whites, Cochran, the jury, and all of Black America could easily be indicted as "reverse racists" for the Simpson verdict. As Lewis Gordon points out, "What the aftermath of the O.J. Simpson case has shown about contemporary racial ideology in the U.S. is that it is considered bad taste, a violation of protocol, for blacks to identify racism where racism exists."[37]

Los Angeles district attorney Gil Garcetti set the stage for most of the reaction to the verdict when he accused the majority Black jury of being "emotive" rather than intellectual in their deliberations.[38] Facing a potentially difficult reelection campaign because his office had also failed to secure convictions in the highly publicized Menendez case the previous year, Garcetti had ample political incentive to shift the blame for this acquittal away from the prosecutors and police and on to the jury. But his choice of blaming the intellectual failings of the jury was no accident; it built upon long-standing slurs of black people, to be sure, but also on the 1994 public relations campaign by right-wing foundations like the John M. Olin Foundation on behalf of *The Bell Curve.* This book drew upon the most regressive and white supremacist traditions of eugenics to spin a story about the innate mental inferiority of Black people. Although thoroughly discredited as science by every reputable critic, neoconservatives continued to circulate and praise the book because it enabled them to evade responsibility for their own actions in destroying the social welfare safety net and abandoning enforcement of civil rights laws over the past two decades, blaming the disasters that their policies have brought to communities of color on the alleged "biological" inferiority of minorities themselves. Garcetti's comments also played into the public relations campaign waged by Congressional Republicans during and after the 1994 electoral campaign through the "Contract with America," which tried to reframe civil rights by presenting white people as the victims of "reverse discrimination" rather than as the perpetrators of discrimination against people of color.

Popular reaction to the Simpson case followed the line of least resistance in the realm of media logic. Consequently, *The Bell Curve* and the "Contract with America" provided a framework for denouncing the verdict, the jury, and Johnnie Cochran while absolving Fuhrman, the prosecutors, and the LAPD. Just as Dan Quayle attributed the 1992 Los Angeles riots to the "poverty of values" in the inner city (which he blamed on the television program *Murphy Brown* letting its lead character have a baby without getting married), political leaders and media commentators "blamed" the Simpson verdict on the propensity of Black people to "blame" their problems on racism. Peniel Joseph attributes this dynamic to what he calls the "equal opportunity racism" of the present day, which "seeks to exculpate white America's unrepentant racism by claiming that blacks are just as 'racist'; and in some cases (such as the Simpson case) can be worse than whites."[39] One reason why this line of argument sometimes works effectively rests upon the logic of the media, on the fact that *The Bell Curve,* the "Contract with America," and Quayle's attacks on *Murphy Brown* so easily recapitulate commercial media's concerns about property, appetites, and the family in jeopardy. White racist acts like Fuhrman's, or those of Charles Stuart (who killed his pregnant wife in Boston in 1992 to get insurance money, and then blamed the attack on a Black man) or Susan Smith (who drowned her two young sons in South Carolina in 1994 and blamed the crime on a Black man) never register as nodes in a network of white racist blame-fixing, but instead get dismissed as the acts of individuals who themselves get dismissed as aberrations. On the other hand, broad systematic practices like discrimination in housing, employment, and education are too remote and impersonal for media treatment—until a white individual claims to be a victim of "reverse" discrimination. The real racism that millions of people face very day is thus either too localized or too generalized to secure media attention; but stories like the Simpson trial, which use race as a way of dramatizing already known stories about products, appetites, and the family in jeopardy, attain unlimited coverage.

The core preoccupations of commercial media determine the stories that sell, and these, in turn, become the stories we tell. But this framework means that some important stories cannot be told. During the O.J. Simpson case, particular angles escaped media scrutiny entirely because they could not fit the format that places products, appetites, and the family in jeopardy at the center of the social world. For example, in the midst of all the attention given to O.J. Simpson's possessions, escapades, and costs of his own defense, where was the detailed scrutiny of how California's Proposition 13 (the tax-limitation ballot initiative of 1978 that has funneled millions of dollars to multinational corporations, small businesses, and homeowners at the expense of general tax revenues) constrained the prosecution? How can local prosecutors ever win a case against wealthy individuals with unlimited resources for their defense when budget constraints so badly limit the resources and personnel available to the representatives of the public? In addition, what was the role of Simpson's celebrity status in the police decision to do so little about the nine cases of spousal abuse at the Simpson home to which they had been summoned? Former LAPD officer Mike Rothmiller has charged that the Organized Crime Intelligence Division of the department uses informants, wiretaps, cameras, and personal surveillance to monitor "all kinds of celebrities." Rothmiller claims that the department gathers embarrassing evidence about the personal lives of celebrities so that it will have leverage with important people and can secure their cooperation for initiatives that the department desires. Is it possible that the police had to fabricate the story that Simpson was not a suspect when they climbed the wall of his estate not only to protect the evidence they seized on that occasion but because admitting that he was a suspect would make them reveal sources of information that might call public attention to the secretive duties of the OCID?

Proposition 13 and the activities of the OCID could not be related to the Simpson story as told by the media because they break the frame that limits social life to a series of personal problems and acts of consumption. They require attention to broad structural processes and acknowledgment of deeply unequal conditions and opportunities in our society. They cannot coast on their similarity to previous media messages; they do not reference the primacy of products, anxiety about appetites, or fears about the family as they have come to us in mediated texts over the years. But if the stories that sell monopolize the stories we tell, we will have no way to understand, analyze, or alter the very serious structural problems our society faces. As a character in Leslie Marmon Silko's novel *Ceremony* explains, "as long as people believed the lies, they would never be able to see what had been done to them or what they were doing to each other."[40] Stories can be a means of expanding our horizons and augmenting our understanding, but they can also be a means for imprisoning us just as surely and just as securely as we can be imprisoned by stone walls and iron bars. Just ask Geronimo Pratt.

Notes

1.   Joe Mandrese and Jeff Jensen, " 'Trial of a Century,' Break of a Lifetime," *Advertising Age*, October 9, 1995, p. 1.

2.   Christopher Stern, "Cameras in Courts Take a Hit," *Broadcasting & Cable*, October 9, 1995, p. 10.

3.   Ward Churchill and Jim Vander Wall, *Agents of Repression: The FBI's Secret Wars Against the Black Panther Party and the American Indian Movement* (Boston: South End Press, 1988), pp. 79, 85.

4.   *Ibid.*, p. 79.

5.   *Ibid.*, pp. 87–88, 409.

6.   *Ibid.*, pp. 90, 91, 406.

7.   M. Wesley Swearingen, *FBI Secrets: An Agent's Exposé* (Boston: South End Press, 1995), pp. 84–86.

8.   Mumia Abu-Jamal, "Parole Denied for Geronimo Pratt—Again," *New Pittsburgh Courier*, April 17, 1996, p. A-7.

9.   Anonymous, "Taxing: The O.J. Simpson Trial," *The Economist,* June 17, 1995, p. 31.

10. Rich Brown, "The Juice Powers Some Players," *Broadcasting & Cable,* October 9, 1995, p. 10.

11. Mandrese and Jensen, " 'Trial of a Century,' Break of a Lifetime," p. 41.

12. *Ibid.,* p. 1; Michael Wilke, "O.J. verdict: 'Hero' days are over," *Advertising Age,* October 2, 1995, p. 8.

13. Cynthia Littleton, "Verdict Propels Tabloid Ratings," *Broadcasting & Cable,* October 9, 1995, p. 7.

14. Brent Staples, "Millions for Defense," *New York Times Book Review,* April 28, 1996, p. 15; Adam Hochschild, "Closing Argument," *New York Times Book Review,* April 28, 1996, p. 15.

15. Hochschild, "Closing Argument," p. 15.

16. Steve McClellan, "All Eyes on O.J.," *Broadcasting & Cable,* October 9, 1995, p. 6; Mandrese and Jensen, " 'Trial of a Century,' Break of a Lifetime," p. 1.

17. Joe Mandrese and Thomas Tyler, "Simpson Shakes New TV Season," *Advertising Age,* October 16, 1995, p. 48.

18. *Ibid.;* Jim McConville, "Down Is Up for Cable Networks," *Broadcasting & Cable,* October 30, 1995, p. 51.

19. Littleton, "Verdict Propels Tabloid Ratings," p. 7.

20. Julie Johnson, "O.J. Scores Again on '95 Covers," *Advertising Age,* January 1, 1996, p. 4.

21. Mark Berniker, "CNN Web Site Flooded with O.J. Interest," *Broadcasting & Cable,* October 9, 1995, p. 71.

22. J.M., "O.J. Simpson Interview Scores Big for BET," *Broadcasting & Cable,* January 29, 1996, p. 7.

23. Richard Barnet and John Cavenagh, *Global Dreams, Imperial Corporations and the New World Order* (New York: Simon and Schuster, 1994), pp. 325–29.

24. Hochschild, "Closing Argument," p. 14.

25. John Fiske, *Media Matters: Everyday Culture and Political Change* (Minneapolis: University of Minnesota Press, 1994), p. xix.

26. Nancy Armstrong, *Desire in Domestic Fiction* (New York: Oxford, 1985); Roddy Reid, *Families in Jeopardy* (Stanford: Stanford University Press, 1994).

27. Fiske, *Media Matters,* p. xix.

28. William Howze, "John Ford's Celluloid Canvas," *Southwest Media Review* 3 (1985).

29.   C.L.R. James, *American Civilization* (New York and London: Blackwell, 1994), p. 127.

30.   *Ibid.*

31.   James, *American Civilization*, p. 158.

32.   *Ibid.*, p. 148.

33.   *Time*, October 9, 1995, p. 39.

34.   Jimmie Reeves and Rich Campbell, *Cracked Coverage* (Durham, N.C.: Duke University Press, 1994); Herman Gray, *Watching Race: Television and the Struggle for 'Blackness'* (Minneapolis: University of Minnesota Press, 1995).

35.   Gray, *Watching Race*, p. 23.

36.   Fiske, *Media Matters*, p. xvi.

37.   Lewis R. Gordon, "A Lynching Well Lost," *The Black Scholar* v. 25, n. 4 (1995), p. 37.

38.   Peniel E. Joseph, " 'Black' Reconstructed: White Supremacy in Post Civil Rights America," *The Black Scholar* v. 25, n. 4 (1995), p. 53.

39.   *Ibid.*, p. 52.

40.   Leslie Marmon Silko, *Ceremony* (New York: New American Library, 1977), p. 199.

The O.J. Simpson Trial: Who Was Improperly "Playing the Race Card"?

A. Leon Higginbotham, Jr.,
Aderson Bellegarde François,
and Linda Y. Yueh

A Duality of Standards: Did the Defense Improperly "Play the Race Card" or Rationally Conduct a Fair Defense Strategy?

The case of *The People v. Orenthal James Simpson* has come to be seen by many as a metaphor for the seemingly intractable problems of race in America. Yet, for all of the incalculable hours of media attention and endless public comment by both observers and trial participants, many of the "lessons" drawn from the trial by commentators and a large segment of the public were deceptive. The most blatantly deceptive of these lessons is what now has become the conventional wisdom that in using detective Mark Fuhrman's racism as a test of his credibility, the Simpson defense team had *improperly and unjustifiably* "played the race card." That conclusion is false. Rather than establishing that the defense strategy was improper or unethical, when carefully analyzed, many of the critiques of the defense team's strategies reveal far more the latent and explicit biases of the commentators and the duality of standards the public still uses to judge African-American criminal defendants and African-American lawyers.

The purpose of this article is to analyze the concept of "playing the race card," and whether the perceptions of *who* improperly "plays the race card"[1] are reflective of larger societal racial attitudes. Therefore, was the core of the condemnation that the defense team improperly "played the race card" predicated more on some unarticulated and, perhaps, unrecognized racial biases of the critics than on any real deficiencies or inappropriateness of the defense strategy? All persons are products of the culture of our society and may have feelings, attitudes, and hostilities of which they are not fully aware. One of the intriguing questions regarding some of the critics of Johnnie Cochran and of the defense strategies is: Would they be more tolerant of the same type of aggressive conduct by a white lawyer on behalf of a white defendant? In short, to ask the question that Professor Cornel West raises: "Does race matter?"[2] Essential to this analysis is the answer to the question of why so many commentators were perturbed by the fact that the defense revealed on the evidentiary record before the jury that a significant witness, whose credibility was crucial, had often used the word "nigger," and frequently spoke disparagingly about African Americans.

The Simpson Case as a Symbol
of America's Racial Anxiety

In America, the "race card" is usually played as part of a zero-sum game in which any gain by African Americans—real or imagined—is considered to be a loss by whites. The Simpson case was no different. In the aftermath of the not-guilty verdict, with all of the self-righteous teeth-gnashing by many whites and the self-congratulatory chest-thumping by many African Americans, one would have thought that whites had suffered a grievous defeat and African Americans had won a great victory. Not so. Not even close. In this country, when race is at issue—and race was absolutely at issue in the Simpson trial and in the public reaction to the verdict—things are never really what they appear to be. When defense attorney Johnnie Cochran pointed out that police officers Fuhrman and Vannatter were the "twin devils of deception" when they hid and lied about their racist views behind façades of perfect respectability, he could have been talking about the issue of race; for in American society, race is often a great deceiver, an untrustworthy messenger, a misleading conjurer, an even more incredible witness than Mark Fuhrman testifying under oath that he had *not* used the word "nigger" in the past ten years.

It follows then that even though many African Americans were intent on celebrating the verdict, the mass of African Americans in fact won nothing or very little. Mr. Simpson's acquittal did not and will not redress the discriminatory treatment many African Americans continue to face in the criminal justice system. Moreover, whatever symbolic satisfaction some African Americans may have enjoyed from seeing "one of our own" finally "beat the system" should have disappeared with the realization that Mr. Simpson, as evidenced by the life he led before the trial in his heyday of professional football and later media stardom, did not, for a single moment, consider himself to be "one of our own." He never spent any considerable effort as an advocate for the eradication of the systemic racism that engulfs most African Americans.

On the other hand, many whites, notwithstanding their very public "wither the nation" rhetoric after the Simpson verdict was announced, actually themselves engaged in a favorite American pastime: playing the race card, or, more accurately, playing the race game. And they played it with such sincere intensity, such deep concentration, and such card-shark skill as to make Johnnie Cochran's superb performance during the trial seem like the fumblings of a wholly incompetent attorney who did not understand the legal concepts of relevance and the other legal precedents for the admissibility of evidence in a criminal trial.

Thus, in the aftermath of the not-guilty verdict, the public was asked to believe that the acquittal of Mr. Simpson was a symptom, if not an outright cause, of racial division in this country. Robert Shapiro, one of Mr. Simpson's attorneys, no less, was perhaps the first to introduce this theme when he declared in a nationally televised interview with Barbara Walters on the news program 20/20 on October 3, 1995. "Not only did we play the race card, we dealt it from the bottom of the deck." In a separate interview on October 6, 1995, with the commentator Larry King, Mr. Shapiro continued: ". . . we played the race card, that's what happened. We have divided the blacks and the whites in an unnecessary way." Christopher Darden, one of the prosecuting attorneys, picked up Mr. Shapiro's theme. When asked during an interview with Barbara Walters on the news program 20/20 on October 6, 1995, whether Mr. Cochran had played the race card from the bottom of the deck as Mr. Shapiro claimed, Mr. Darden replied: "He played the race card from the bottom of the deck, from inside his shirtsleeve, he played it as well as anybody I've seen it played." Later, in his book, *In Contempt*, published a few months after the trial, Mr. Darden, like Mr. Shapiro during the Larry King interview, seemed to ascribe the very cause of racial division to the trial itself. He wrote: "As the case became more and more about race, I watched helplessly as it ripped the scabs off America's [racial] wounds."[3]

A chorus of commentators soon joined in the Shapiro-Darden song about how the defense had, as Mr. Shapiro claimed, "played the race card from the bottom of the deck," and how the verdict had, as Mr. Darden put it, "picked the scabs off America's [racial] wounds." Clarence Page, the political columnist, declared, "Mr. Cochran played more than the race card. He played the whole deck."[4] Representative Bob Dornan of California complained: "I think it was a racist decision."[5]

Perhaps the most deceptive statement of all was uttered with a purported neutrality when Andy Rooney, the famed *60 Minutes* correspondent, declared that "[t]he [Simpson] acquittal was the worst thing that's happened to race relations in 40 years."[6] Worse than what? one wanted to ask Mr. Rooney: Worse than the bombing of the 16th Street Baptist Church in Birmingham, and the killing of four schoolchildren in 1963? Worse than the slaying of Medgar Evers in 1963, of James Chaney, Andrew Goodman, and Michael Schwerner in 1964, of Jimmie Lee Jackson, Reverend James Reeb, and Viola Gregg Liuzzo in 1965, or of dozens of other civil rights martyrs in the 1960s? Worse even than the assassination of Martin Luther King?

Mr. Rooney was not the only Jeremiah shouting about the end of racial progress. Marshall Wittmann, a senior fellow at the conservative think tank The Heritage Foundation, mused:

"[W]hat we're seeing now is thirty years of moving from a color-blind society to a balkanized society."[7] Even newspaper editorials joined in. The *Los Angeles Times* called the verdict "a sad commentary on American racial divisions."[8] The *Seattle Times* wondered: "What kind of society can flourish when members of a community—whether defined as Los Angeles or the United States—believe that Justice is based on skin color?"[9] *USA Today* concluded, "[t]he verdict in the O.J. Simpson trial has left White Americans bitter, cynical about the criminal justice system, and overwhelmingly convinced that race relations will worsen as a result."[10]

The immediate lesson that the public was supposed to learn from all of this hand-wringing is that race-consciousness, whether invidious or benign, is always impermissible, and that whenever race is used, whether such use is rational or irrational, the result will be as unfair as the not-guilty verdict that supposedly allowed Mr. Simpson to get away with murder. For example, William Bennett, the former secretary of education during the Reagan administration, reflected during an October 8, 1995, interview on the Sunday news program *This Week With David Brinkley:* "To get beyond racism, we need to get beyond the use of preference by race. . . . We have had thirty years of affirmative action. We have been thinking of race, we have been counting by race, we have been admitting and awarding by race, and now we are shocked to find a jury judges by race. I think we should go back to what [Martin Luther] King was talking about." Dinesh D'Souza, author of the conservative polemic *The End of Racism,* took a similar and quite common view during a debate on the October 8, 1995, CNN news program *The Color of Justice.* He maintained: "What the verdict shows is we live in a racially intoxicated society. . . . So, I think a positive thing to come out of the verdict is for whites and for all Americans to ask themselves, do we want race to be embedded in our laws, our policy, our voting, our education, our hiring, our promotion of government contracts; or should we begin to de-racialize our society?" George Will, one of the respected "elders" of current conservative dogma, concluded in a *Washington Post* column: "Another chilling residue of this [verdict] should be the realization that nothing—no institution, no pattern of civility—is spared the ravages of racial thinking. For more than a generation now, public policies such as affirmative action, the racial spoils system and the cult of 'diversity' have been teaching the nation that groupthink is virtuous.... Given all this, it is not surprising that the jurors had no pangs of conscience about regarding Simpson as a member of a group—and not seeing his victims at all. People who think 'race-conscious remedies' for this or that can be benign are partly to blame."[11] The deeper moral that these commentators were asking the public to take from the trial is that the use of race—being the root of all social evils—had to be eradicated from American society; from affirmative action to college admissions, from congressional redistricting to government contracts. The supposed logic of their comments is that once race-consciousness is wiped out completely from our collective psyche and from all government programs, we will yet be able to achieve the glorious dream of a color-blind society.

In short, the trial and acquittal of Mr. Simpson became something infinitely greater than the trial and acquittal of one man for the murder of two people. It became the symbol of racial division, the proof of the evils of race-consciousness, the marker for racial injustice, the premonitory sign of the dying of the dream of a color-blind society. It did not seem to matter very much that the Simpson defense team was within its legal, ethical, and professional duty to raise the racial issue. Nor did it seem to matter very much that the lessons the public was asked to draw from the trial were ahistorical to say the least.

Testing Credibility and Bias
by the Rules of Evidence

For decades, the jurisprudence of the federal and California courts have recognized that a court or jury may properly determine that a witness's testimony is not credible if that witness either lies on the stand with regard to a material issue, or displays a specific bias toward a particular defendant or a general prejudice toward the defendant's gender, religion, ethnicity, or—yes—even race.

The standard set of instructions to the jury that federal judges have used for more than three decades[12] recommends that jurors always be told that "as jurors, [they] are the sole and exclusive judges of the credibility of each of the witnesses called to testify . . . and that [they] may decide to believe all of that witness' testimony, only a portion of it, or none of it." The instructions continue that "if a person is shown to have knowingly testified falsely concerning any important or material matter, [jurors] obviously have a right to distrust the testimony of such an individual concerning other matters."[13]

Moreover, the U.S. Supreme Court has stressed the need to test a witness's credibility against that witness's bias "by means of cross-examination directed toward revealing possible biases, prejudices, or ulterior motives of the witness as they may relate directly to issues or personalities in the case at hand." Federal appellate courts, following the lead of the Supreme Court, have also held as much. As one such court has put it: "the law recognizes 'the force of a hostile emotion, as influencing the probability of truth-telling . . . ; and a partiality of mind is therefore always relevant as discrediting the witness and affecting the weight of his testimony.' . . . Prejudice toward a group of which defendant is a part may be a source of partiality against the defendant."[14]

Similar to the rulings of the federal courts, Section 780 of the California Evidence Code specifically permits the court or jury, in determining the credibility of a witness, to consider, among other things, "the existence or nonexistence of a bias, interest, or other motive"; and "a statement made by [the witness] that is inconsistent with any part of his testimony at hearing." Pursuant to that rule, as recently as March 1996, the Court of Appeals of California reaffirmed their long-standing doctrine that "where . . . a witness is knowingly false in one part of his testimony, the jury may distrust other portions of his testimony as well."[15]

The foregoing cases, statutes, and jury instructions represent a formal modern enactment of the ancient maxim *falsus in uno, falsus in omnibus*—originally construed as "he who speaks falsely on one point will speak falsely upon all"—and serve as means to enforce the Supreme Court's admonishment that "the exposure of a witness's motivation in testifying is a proper and important function of the constitutionally protected right of cross-examination." This plethora of unequivocal state and federal jurisprudential precedents sanctioned the defense team's efforts to inquire about the racial bias of detective Mark Fuhrman.

Was Mark Fuhrman Biased?

The Simpson trial presented the case of an African-American man accused of killing his white ex-wife and her white male friend. Mark Fuhrman, the prosecution's main police witness, whom Mr. Cochran referred to as a "lying genocidal racist," once admitted that "when he sees a nigger driving with a white woman, he pulls them over" for no reason other than the fact that the man is African American and the woman is white. So strong was Mr. Fuhrman's bias toward African Americans that he wished "nothing more than to see all niggers gathered together and killed." So deep were Mr. Fuhrman's prejudices that he allowed himself to be taped using the word "nigger" at least forty-two times. Yet, when questioned on the stand about whether he harbored a bias toward African Americans, Mr. Fuhrman denied that he did so. Indeed, Mr. Fuhrman went on to emphatically deny having used the word "nigger" at all in the past ten years.

The jury, therefore, had at least four reasons to consider Mr. Fuhrman a less than credible witness against Mr. Simpson. First, the fact that Mr. Fuhrman lied about using the word "nigger" (*falsus in uno*) meant that he could have been lying about other aspects of his testimony (*falsus in omnibus*). Second, the jury had cause to disbelieve Mr. Fuhrman's testimony because Mr. Fuhrman perjured himself on the witness stand when he testified that he had not used the word "nigger" in the past ten years, when in fact he had been taped saying it at least forty-two times. Third, the jury could have reasonably determined that Mr. Fuhrman was biased against Mr. Simpson for having been married to a white woman because Mr. Fuhrman held and acted upon a strong bias against interracial couples made up of African-American men and white women. Fourth, the jury could have reasonably found that Mr. Fuhrman's investigation and testimony against Mr. Simpson was tainted because it was Mr. Fuhrman's fervent wish to have "all niggers gathered together and killed." Thus, the Simpson defense team had a legal and professional obligation to introduce to the jury this very substantial and damning evidence of Mr. Fuhrman's lack of credibility.

This may seem to be an obvious point. However, during and after the trial, it appeared as if most Americans considered it morally wrong, socially irresponsible, and generally "unfair" for Mr. Cochran and his co-counsel to have "interjected" race into the trial.

Why was it unfair?

If Different Biases Had Been Involved, Would the Commentators Have Been as Critical of a Defense Counsel's Strategy to Raise the Issue of Race, or Gender, or Religion?

Any critical evaluation of the fairness of the commentary on the O.J. Simpson case should start with the assessment that there were several factors present during the trial that affected the public reaction to the verdict and that may have led commentators to claim that the defense improperly "played the race card": the race of the defendant, his fame and wealth, the race and gender of the victims, the race of the main police witnesses, the particular racial bias held by these witnesses, the race of lead counsel for the defense, and even the race of the judge. Since the interplay of these factors undoubtedly contributed to the incorrect perception that the defense had improperly played the race card, it then follows that changing one or more of these factors might also conceivably alter the perception that the defense improperly interjected race into the trial.

For example, if the main police witnesses had been African Americans with a history of hatred of and hostility toward whites, and if O.J. Simpson had been white, would the commentators have been as critical of any defense counsel who

raised "the bias issue" as to the black police officers' prior conduct? Or, if Mr. Simpson's wife had been black, would these
same commentators have been just as vehement in condemning
the verdict as an outrage?

There are several other scenarios that could be hypothe-
sized in order to raise the issue as to what the response would be
if the gender or race or religion of the defendant had been different, or if the religion or race or gender of the victim had been
different. Underlying all these scenarios described below is the
basic question of whether, assuming that the violence and the
commission of the crime were precisely the same, the intensity
of the criticism would have been the same, less, or more, if the
variables as to race, gender, or religion were different than those
involved in the O.J. Simpson case.

If the defendant had been Catholic, and the prosecution's
main police witness had a history of calling Catholics "devil sinners" and then lying about it on the witness stand, arresting,
without justification, Catholics for traffic violations on their
way home from church, and wishing that "all devil sinners
should be gathered together and killed," would the critics claim
that it was unfair for the defense to introduce evidence that
the prosecution witness was a lying, anti-Catholic bigot? Probably not.

If the defendant had been Jewish, and the prosecution's
main police witness had a history of calling Jewish individuals
"kikes" and then lying about it on the witness stand, automati-
cally stopping any motorist wearing a yarmulke, and wishing
that "all kikes should be gathered together and killed," would the
critics claim that it was unfair for the defense to introduce evidence that the witness was a lying, anti-Semitic neo-Nazi? Probably not.

If the defendant had been a woman, and the prosecution's main police witness had a history of calling women "bitches" and then lying about it on the witness stand, sexually harassing women at work, and wishing that "all bitches should be gathered together and killed," would the critics claim that it was unfair for the defense to introduce evidence that the witness was a lying, misogynistic harasser? Probably not.

If the defendant had been gay, and the prosecution's main police witness had a history of calling gays "faggots" and then lying about it on the witness stand, arresting any men seen holding hands, and wishing that "all faggots should be gathered together and killed," would the critics claim that it was unfair to introduce evidence that the witness was a lying, genocidal homophobe? Probably not.

Would it be unfair for the defense to argue that any witness—particularly a law enforcement officer charged with protecting all citizens—who harbors and acts upon sexist, anti-Catholic, anti-Semitic, or homophobic tendencies should be disbelieved when the defendant against whom the witness is testifying represents the very object of the witness's hate? Probably not.

Under any of the above scenarios, would the defense be accused of unfairly playing the gender card, or the religion card, or the ethnicity card, or the sexual-orientation card? Probably not.

Would the defense's trial strategy be considered a symptom or a cause of the division of America along gender, religious, ethnic, or sexual-orientation lines? Probably not.

Would the trial be used as an argument against policies designed to enhance the role of women in the workplace on the ground that they unfairly divide men and women; or against granting tax-exempt status to Catholic churches on the ground that it unfairly divides Catholics from non-Catholics; or against the United States' considerable foreign aid to Israel on the ground that it unfairly divides Jews and Gentiles; or against prosecuting gay-bias crimes on the ground that it unfairly divides heterosexuals from homosexuals? Probably not.

Some of these hypotheticals may sound farfetched, and some of the connections made between these hypothetical trials and particular public policies may seem absurd, but this is largely how the public reacted to the Simpson trial and verdict. For example, if a seemingly guilty Jewish defendant is acquitted because the defense showed that the prosecution's main police witness was a lying neo-Nazi, no one would seriously argue that the unjust verdict was a symptom of ethnic division and that the government should therefore stop favoring Israel with foreign aid. Instead, most people would agree that the testimony of an avowed neo-Nazi should carry very little weight against a Jewish defendant. Most people would also recognize that even if the Jewish defendant was indeed guilty, the issue of his unjust acquittal would have nothing to do whatsoever with foreign aid to Israel.

Yet, in the Simpson case, most commentators insisted on finding it unfair for the defense to have pointed out to the jury that Mr. Fuhrman was a confirmed racist and that his testimony against Mr. Simpson could reasonably have been deemed incredible by the jury. Moreover, these same commentators did not think it intellectually incoherent to link the acquittal of Mr. Simpson—unjust or otherwise—with issues as historically complex and as politically charged as the use of race in affirmative action or college admissions. Instead, the not-guilty verdict was used as the most recent and most vivid premonitory sign of the threat of race-consciousness to the dream of a color-blind society.

The Tensions between the Rhetoric of Seeking a Color-blind Society and the Reality of Living in a Race-conscious Nation

One of the ironies in the responses to the Simpson case was that the public seems to expect the dream of the color-blind society to become real, even though public policies in terms of race seem destined to never make it so. For example, in the area of the criminal justice system, justice is clearly not yet color-blind. Blacks represent only 12 percent of the general population but comprise 48 percent of the prison population. One in three black men ages 20–29 are under the supervision of the criminal justice system. There are more black men in prisons than there are in college. Nationwide, the fastest growing segment of the prison population are black women. In the last five years alone, the number of black women in prison, in jail, or on parole has increased by 78 percent.

In 1992, a longitudinal study commissioned by the Federal Judicial Center reported that "there has always been a tendency for the sentences of whites to be lower than the sentences of nonwhites, a difference that, unfortunately, has become larger over time. In 1984, the average sentence for blacks was 28 percent higher than that for whites. *By 1990, the average sentence for blacks was 49 percent higher than that for whites.*"[16]

By 1994, sentencing disparities had worsened, and a study of the Federal Judicial Center noted that "among offenders who engaged in conduct warranting a mandatory minimum, white offenders were less likely than blacks or Hispanics to receive the mandatory minimum term. In addition, since the mandatory minimums have been enacted, the gap between the average sentences of blacks and those of other groups has grown wider." For example, the 1994 study considered the racial disparity in sentencing for crack and powder cocaine. The authors stated: "Statutes having a disparate impact on blacks include those that make offenses involving five or more grams of crack cocaine (a weekend's supply to a serious abuser) subject to the same mandatory minimum term of five years in prison as offenses involving 100 times that amount of powder cocaine. Because blacks are more likely to be prosecuted for crack offenses and whites for powder cocaine offenses, the long sentence lengths for smaller amounts of crack lead to longer sentences for blacks."[17]

In 1995, three members of the U.S. Sentencing Commission testified before the U.S. Senate Judiciary Committee about these disparities. Commissioner Wayne A. Budd, a former U.S. Attorney for the District of Massachusetts, conceded that "in spite of the fact that the majority of crack users are White, more than 90 percent of all crack cocaine offenders sentenced in federal court were Black; six percent were Hispanic, and four percent were White."[18]

O.J. Simpson's acquittal in October 1995 has had and will have no impact in decreasing the number of blacks who are going into our criminal justice system at an alarming rate. Probably not one African American in prison will receive any benefit by reason of Simpson's not-guilty verdict. Yet, his single acquittal has been used as a justification to decrease the already limited options in our society for minorities, particularly blacks and Latinos. By using the O.J. Simpson case as a scapegoat, many of these critics are refusing to recognize the fundamental disparities in our society and our often minuscule progress, as revealed in the following data on gaps in income and unemployment between African Americans and whites.

The Income Gap

In 1969, the median family income for blacks was $22,000. In 1993, it declined to $21,550.[19] Or, in other words, the black family median income was 61 percent of what whites earned in 1969, and in 1993, *declined* to 55 percent of that of white families.

The per capita income of blacks in 1993 was $9,860, which was approximately 59 percent of white per capita income.

EARNINGS BY FULL-TIME WORKERS   Black men earned a median income of $24,680 in 1979, but by 1993 they experienced a *drop* in median income to $23,020. In addition, the income gap between black men and white men *reduced only slightly* from 1979 to 1993, from black men earning 73 percent of white men's income to 74 percent.

For black women, their earnings in 1993 ($19,820) were comparable to the earnings of white women in 1979. Overall, earnings for both black and white women increased from 1979 to 1993; however, the income gap between black and white women *worsened* from 92 percent to 90 percent.

The income gap between blacks and whites has narrowed only slightly from 1979 to 1993. A black individual in 1993 earned *fifty-nine cents* on the dollar earned by a white individual. The income gap has been reduced slightly for black men, while the earnings gap has worsened for black women, who earned in 1993 what white women earned almost two decades ago in 1974.

The median family income for blacks has decreased while it has increased for whites. In fact, the real median income for black families has not improved in the last twenty-four years. Blacks, whether individually or as a family, earn only about half of that of whites.

The Unemployment Gap

In both 1980 and 1993, the unemployment rate for blacks was more than twice that of whites: approximately 14 percent versus 6 percent in both periods. In 1994, blacks comprised 12.7 percent of the U.S. population, but 21 percent of the unemployed.

In the area of jobs, a black individual is *twice as likely* as a white individual to be unemployed. The unemployment rate for black teenagers and young adults is estimated to be an astounding 40 to 60 percent.[20]

The Poverty Gap

In 1993, the poverty rate for black families was 31 percent (2.5 million) as compared with 9 percent (5.4 million) for white families. Black families were *three and a half times* more likely to be poor than white families. In addition, the poverty gap has remained *unchanged* over the past twenty-four years.

For individuals, the poverty rate for blacks (33%) is almost *threefold* that of whites (12%), and this gap has also been unchanged for the past twenty-four years.

The poverty rate for black individuals has increased in the last twenty-four years. Black individuals are twice as likely as white individuals to be poor and a greater proportion of black families are in poverty today than in 1969.

These statistics reveal a startling gap between what proponents of a color-blind society believe is possible for America and the racist reality that many African Americans and people of color face every day of their lives. This myth that race-consciousness is an evil that must be overcome, rather than a remedy for racism, is espoused even by the U.S. Supreme Court, which gives it the imprimatur of the law. In the recent congressional redistricting case of *Shaw v. Reno,* the Supreme Court stated that "racial [consciousness], even for remedial purposes ... threatens to carry us further from the goal of a political system in which race no longer matters, a goal ... to which the Nation continues to aspire."[21] Unfortunately, as enticing and simple as this proposition may seem, race-consciousness is unlikely to be what is keeping this country from achieving a system in which "race no longer matters." The uncomfortable reality is that neither our society nor our criminal justice system is color-blind. The solution must be that rather than deny that race matters, the courts and the legislature must embrace measures, such as majority-minority districts in voting, that take race into account for benign purposes. Race-consciousness by itself is not an evil but rather a reality that must be recognized even as America hopes to be and continues to strive to be a nation in which the color of one's skin is of no consequence. It is only when race-consciousness is attacked in order to maintain the status quo of white dominance that Americans are moved "further from the goal of a political system in which race no longer matters."

Conclusion

Perhaps it is both inevitable and understandable that the Simpson case would be used as a metaphor for the seemingly intractable problem of race in America. In the larger scheme, the case did not really involve any major public policy issues. However, the public paid so much attention to the trial that by the time the verdict was finally announced, there seemed to be a need to infuse the case with a measure of deeper social importance in order to justify all of the time and money spent on it. Unfortunately, the lessons that most Americans took from the trial were wrong.

Is the case actually a metaphor for race in this country? Are there any relevant lessons to be learned from it?

Mr. Simpson is most certainly guilty of having abused his ex-wife, Nicole Brown Simpson, and he may or may not be guilty of having killed her and her friend, Ronald Goldman. Most people would agree that Mr. Simpson was never adequately punished for abusing his ex-wife, and many believe that he was unjustly acquitted of murdering her and her friend. Those who hold this view made it more than amply clear that they consider Mr. Simpson's acquittal to be a moral outrage. To the extent that their belief in Mr. Simpson's guilt is sincere, their sense of outrage must be respected even by those who would believe equally sincerely in Mr. Simpson's innocence. As such, the unseemly celebration of the verdict by some African Americans is a blunt reminder that even those who themselves have suffered injustice can sometimes forget how deep is the cut when justice is—or appears to have been—denied. Celebrating the acquittal of Mr. Simpson—and this can never be said too often or too clearly—was not the finest hour for those African Americans who made the terrible mistake of confusing for a hero a man who regularly beat his wife.

Still, in the days following the verdict, one sometimes wished that the loud volume of voices denouncing or defending the verdict was lowered—if only a little bit and if only for a little while—out of respect for the grieving and the dead. After all, the idea of a just victory held by those who believed Mr. Simpson innocent, and the sense of moral outrage felt by those who thought him guilty, can never be equal in substance or in depth to the pain shared by the victims' families, who never again will get to see, hear, touch, or hold the loved ones they lost in that double murder. And perhaps, in some way, the cacophony of vocal reaction to the verdict only made heavier the burden of grief these families carried and no doubt carry still; as if the public recrimination over the verdict only served to rake over and over again the dirt from the freshly covered graves of the victims, revealing in the churned-up mud corpses only half buried and souls only half put to rest.

Perhaps it is only in that way that the trial and the verdict may—carefully, very carefully—be used as a metaphor for race in America. The victims' graves were not the only ones that were disturbed by the public recrimination over the verdict. In the process, we also stirred up the shallow grave where is stored the vestiges of centuries of slavery, segregation, racial oppression, biases, and prejudices, also revealing in that ancient muddy racial pit corpses only half buried and souls only half put to rest. The trial was merely the shovel we used to dig up that grave.

The Simpson trial *did not create* the racial tensions that American society experiences and desperately attempts to conceal. To pretend to be shocked at the differences in racial attitudes in the reactions to the verdict is, therefore, more than a little disingenuous. The "racial divide" in public opinion over the verdict is not a phenomenon newly created by the Simpson trial; it has existed all along, and it took the tragic double murder of two innocent people to expose the hypocrisy of our collective consciousness. It is this same self-deception that Americans engage in when politicians and even the courts declare that race-conscious remedies in public policies are evils that keep us from reaching the promised land of a color-blind society. It is this same deception that leads well-meaning individuals to question the continued relevance of affirmative action programs, the need for benign measures to correct past injustices in the arena of voting, and even the importance of diversity in education. This deception is not new, for it serves an ancient American need to maintain the status quo of white dominance.

But are there deeper lessons to be learned from the Simpson trial? We learned from the trial that the racism in the average police department is no better or worse than the racism in society at large; the Rodney King incident hopefully taught us that already. We learned that African Americans and whites view the criminal justice system differently; most African Americans have been aware of that fact for a long time and probably so have a great number of whites. We learned that the wealthy and the famous can usually afford to buy a little more "justice" than the rest of us; most Americans, of whatever race, already knew that too. However, there may yet be a final lesson to be learned if we can see the trial for what it was: a case where a seemingly guilty man went free because the main witness against him was a racist. That realization may then teach us not to believe that racial prejudice belongs to the days that are behind us, that our divisive history is buried in deep graves, and that we are somehow cleansed of personal biases or that our eyes can no longer see racial difference. If we continue to deceive ourselves, then the pain and the morbid fascination that Americans endured through the Simpson trial were a waste of time.

Americans must attempt to see that race is the great deceiver and that our only chance to reach the glorious noon of true equality when colorblindness is the reality is in our ability to accommodate the differences in racial experiences. Johnnie Cochran's last statement to the jury was not an appeal to racial division (as it is commonly perceived to be) but an exhortation for the jurors to rise above the issue of race. He reminded the jury "[t]hat this has been a search for truth. That no matter how bad it looks, if truth is out there on the scaffold, and wrong is in here on the throne, remember that the scaffold always sways the future and beyond the dim unknown standeth the same God for all people keeping watch above his own." Perhaps we, as a society, can also learn to be better than what we are by stripping away our self-deceptions with respect to race. In our attempts to accommodate our racial differences, we might also remember one thing that we have in common: "the same God for all people keeping watch above his own." If the Simpson trial embodies no deeper meaning, it will have been worthwhile if it can ask us, as the jurors were asked, to attempt to be—and strive to be—better than what we are now as Americans.

Postscript

On October 2, 1996 (after this article had been set into galleys), Mark Fuhrman pleaded no contest to a count of perjury.[22] The felony complaint charged Fuhrman with having "willfully . . . state[d] as true a *material* matter which he knew to be false, to wit: that he had not addressed any Black person as a 'nigger' or spoken about Black people as 'niggers' in the past ten years."[23]

Although Fuhrman states that he "deeply regrets the effect his testimony has had on the general public, the Los Angeles Police Department and its employees, and his family," it is significant that he does not apologize to African Americans for his denigration of them and the discriminatory treatment he had imposed on them in the past.[24] There is not one line in his no-contest plea that indicates a scintilla of remorse for his diatribes against African Americans over the years. With Fuhrman showing no remorse as to his racism over the years or in the Simpson case, he was put on probation for three years and fined $200.

One great irony is that although the media gave endless coverage throughout the trial to the claim that the Simpson defense team "played the race card," their coverage was minuscule as to Fuhrman's plea of no contest to his blatant perjury. Fuhrman's

testimony was sufficiently nefarious to constitute perjury on a
"material matter," for which he was indicted, for which he pled no
contest, and for which he was sentenced. But, based on the relative lack of media attention, it seems as if the critics of the Simpson defense team are more tolerant of perjury involving racist
statements by a white police officer than they are of the legal
tenets of rational advocacy, relevant cross-examination, and the
challenging of the credibility of key witnesses when utilized by
defense attorneys on behalf of a black defendant.

Notes

1. The concept "playing the race card" was perhaps first used by Presi-
    dent Nixon and the Republicans as part of the "Southern strategy" to
    capture the white votes of the South through a call to establish white
    supremacy. In particular, it often refers to Nixon's bargain with Sena-
    tor Strom Thurmond and other Southern conservatives, whereby
    Thurmond would deliver the South if Nixon would ease up on federal
    efforts at school desegregation in return. For books that discuss
    Nixon's Southern strategy, see Kevin P. Phillips, *The Emerging Republican
    Majority* (New York: Arlington House, 1969); John Murphy and Harold
    S. Gulliver, *The Southern Strategy* (New York: Charles Scribner's Sons,
    1971); Stephen E. Ambrose, *Nixon: The Triumph of a Politician, 1962–1972*
    (New York: Simon and Schuster, 1989); Earle Black and Merle Black,
    Politics and Society in the South (Cambridge, MA: Harvard University Press,
    1987); and Joseph A. Aistrop, *The Southern Strategy Revisited—Republican
    Top-Down Advancement in the South* (Kentucky: University of Kentucky
    Press, 1996).
2. Cornel West, *Race Matters* (Boston: Beacon Press, 1993).
3. Christopher A. Darden, *In Contempt* (New York: Regan Books/
    HarperCollins, 1996), p. 11.
4. Clarence Page, "An Entire Deck of Race Cards," *The Baltimore Sun*,
    October 5, 1995, p. 25A.
5. CNN, *Inside Politics*, October 4, 1995.

6. CBS, *60 Minutes*, October 8, 1995.

7. *Time*, October 9, 1995, p. 36.

8. "A City Divided," *Los Angeles Times*, October 4, 1995, p. 38.

9. *Seattle Times*, October 4, 1995.

10. "A Nation More Divided," *USA Today*, October 9, 1995, p. 5A.

11. "Jury Fell Short of Even Lowest Expectations," *Chicago Sun-Times*, October 5, 1995, p. 41.

12. Devitt et al., 1 *Federal Jury Practice and Instructions Civil and Criminal* § 1501, p. 465 (4th ed. 1992).

13. Ibid.

14. *U.S. v. Kartman*, 417 F.2d 893, 897 (1969).

15. *Vallbona v. Springer*, 43 Cal. App. 4th 1525 (1996).

16. Federal Judicial Center, *The General Effect of Mandatory Minimum Prison Terms*, p. 20 (1992) (emphasis added).

17. Federal Judicial Center, *The Consequences of Mandatory Minimum Prison Terms: A Summary of Recent Findings*, p. 23 (1994).

18. U.S. Sentencing Commission, News Release, p. 1 (August 10, 1995).

19. The statistical data from this section are taken from the reports by the Bureau of the Census; Claudette E. Bennett, *The Black Population in the United States: March 1994 and 1993*, U.S. Bureau of the Census, Current Population Reports, P20-480; and *1990 Census of Population: Characteristics of the Black Population*, U.S. Department of Commerce, Economics and Statistics Administration, Bureau of the Census, October 1994. All figures are in real dollars, adjusted for inflation, with 1993 as the base year.

20. The Labor Department stated that the unemployment rate among black teenagers was 43.8 percent in May 1996. However, the National Urban League estimates the figure to be 60.5 percent, factoring in hidden unemployment ingredients such as discouraged and involuntary part-time workers. National Urban League, *State of Black America* (1994).

21. *Shaw v. Reno*, 509 U.S. 630, 657 (1993).

22. The cross-examination of Mark Fuhrman on March 15, 1996, had been as follows:

    Q. "I will rephrase it. I want you to assume that perhaps at sometime since 1985 or 6, you addressed a member of the African American race as a nigger. Is it possible that you have forgotten that act on your part?"

    A. "No, it is not possible."

Q. "Are you therefore saying that you have not used that word in the past ten years, Detective Fuhrman?"

A. "Yes, that is what I'm saying."

Q. "And you say under oath that you have not addressed any black person as a nigger or spoken about black people as niggers in the past ten years, Detective Fuhrman."

A. "That's what I'm saying, sir."

Q. "So that anyone who comes to this court and quotes you as using that word in dealing with African Americans would be a liar, would they not, Detective Fuhrman?"

A. "Yes, they would."

Q. "All of them, correct."

A. "All of them."

See Official Transcript, which gives a "Personal History in lieu of Probation Report." *The People of the State of California v. Mark Fuhrman*, No. BA109273, Superior Court of the State of California for the County of Los Angeles (October 2, 1996), pp. 4–5. (Quoting from *People v. Simpson*, Vol. 107, p. 18899).

23.   See Felony Complaint in *The People of the State of California v. Mark Fuhrman*, No. BA109273, Municipal Court of Los Angeles County, Los Angeles Judicial District (October 2, 1996), p. 2 (emphasis added). *See* Guilty Plea/Probation Order in *The People of the State of California v. Mark Fuhrman*, No. BA109273, Superior Court of the State of California for the County of Los Angeles (October 2, 1996), pp. 25–26.

24.   See Official Transcript, which gives a "Personal History in lieu of Probation Report." *The People of the State of California v. Mark Fuhrman*, pp. 5–6.

Dismissed or Banished?
A Testament to the
Reasonableness of the
Simpson Jury
Nikol G. Alexander and
Drucilla Cornell

Introduction

The O.J. Simpson trial kept millions of Americans glued to their TV sets. Watching the trial day in and day out gave many the sense that they could have a solidly based opinion about whether or not O.J. committed the crime. After all, they watched the trial unfold in minute detail. They as well as the jury saw the presentation of the evidence. Committed viewers watched the direct and cross-examination of all the witnesses. Then there were the endless talk shows about the trial. In bars, restaurants, and supermarkets around the country, people debated about whether or not O.J. murdered Nicole Simpson. The question almost always asked in the endless debates was factual: Did he do it? The one fact that everyone knew was that a horrible murder of two people took place and that someone did it. The trial was frequently portrayed in the media as a search for truth, a search that, given the widespread access to television coverage, could be taken up by the nation as a whole and not just by the jury.

This portrayal, however, misunderstands the abstract requirements of political morality embedded in the constitutional principles that guide our criminal justice system. Under our Constitution a criminal trial is not a no-holds-barred search for truth, in which no murderer can escape the righteous punishment he or she deserves. The jurors are mandated by the requirements of our Constitution to maintain a presumption of the innocence of the accused until he or she is proven guilty.[1] This presumption has been interpreted over the centuries to be basic to the political ideal of freedom from state persecution elaborated in the Bill of Rights. And it is not surprising that this presumption has been interpreted as fundamental to individual freedom, given the history of how the United States was constituted as an independent government. Many of the colonists were fleeing religious and political persecution and had personally experienced the injustice of imprisonment without legal recourse. The institution of the jury system is justified as a further check against the danger of an authoritarian executive power. The ideal of a jury of one's peers institutionalized the relationship between the checks on the government and the ideal that the people as a citizenry should be involved in protecting each other from an unjust criminal system. The jurors then would not have been fulfilling their civic duty if they had simply sought to answer the question: Did he do it? They were mandated instead to ask (and answer) a different question: Did the prosecution prove the guilt of the accused beyond a reasonable doubt? When we assess the verdict we have to remember the requirements of our Constitution that are imposed upon all juries, including the one in the Simpson trial.

In this essay we challenge the popular consensus amongst white Americans that the O.J. jury knowingly let a guilty man go free because the majority of the jurors were black and blacks will simply not usually convict other blacks. We assert to the contrary that the jury earnestly strove to meet its civic duty. First, we turn to the reflections of some of the jurors on the glaring weaknesses in the prosecution's case. Given the magnitude of the reforms proposed in light of the Simpson verdict, we believe that the analysis of the prosecution's case by the actual jurors should be given more serious attention than it has previously received. To this end, we review some of the jurors' more critical observations regarding evidentiary production and witness credibility in the case. After illustrating how the jurors' careful consideration on the legal issues presented to them contradicts the common rhetoric about their lack of sophistication and racial bias, we address other arguments levied against the jurors, including those by some members of the feminist community. Finally, we expose the racial fantasies behind the characterizations of the jurors as both unreasonable and irrational. We argue that the implications of such characterizations when given as acceptable reasons for legal reform legitimate the banishment of African Americans from the body politic.

Reasonable Women

In *Madam Foreman*,[2] a book written with Tom Byrnes, foreman Armanda Cooley and two of her colleagues on the jury, Carrie

Bess and Marsha Rubin-Jackson, explain the reasons for their judgment that the prosecution did not—and perhaps could not (given the incompetence of the LAPD)—prove their case against O.J. beyond a reasonable doubt. As the book reveals, the three jurors of *Madam Foreman* were government employees (a fact that would undoubtedly surprise more than a few people) and were conscientiously involved in the execution of their duties. Regrettably, this book has been given little public attention, even though it provides one of the few lengthy and systematic discussions by actual jurors of the reasons for their verdict. Unlike so many of the other books discussing the trial, it did not make the *New York Times* best-seller list. Indeed, it is difficult to find in bookstores. Yet the jurors' own reasons need to be heard before they can be judged. Thus, we begin by giving these women the hearing they ought to receive if their verdict is to be judged fairly. We turn now to their reasons for their verdict.

The jurors' first concern was the mishandling of the blood evidence. The second, inevitably connected to the first, was the complete lack of credibility of key witnesses for the LAPD, witnesses who were absolutely crucial for the prosecution's case because of the role they played in gathering and maintaining the evidence. The third was the seeming impossibility of Simpson doing all he allegedly did at the crime scene, including committing the murders, in the time frame presented by the prosecution.

Let us turn first to the jurors' analysis of the mishandling of the blood evidence. (Since there was error after error made in the gathering and the maintaining of the blood evidence, we cannot discuss each and every contradiction that the jurors noticed and commented upon in their deliberations; hence, we focus on a few significant discrepancies in the blood evidence that most troubled the jury.) From the outset, there was the question of how much blood was drawn from O.J. in the first place. Knowing exactly how much blood was drawn was crucially important for determining whether any blood was missing and if so, how much was missing from the vial. The notion that blood could be missing raised questions in the jurors' minds that needed to be addressed. As Marsha Rubin-Jackson said, "That was one of my turnaround points because there was always talk around how there was blood missing, there was blood missing, there was blood missing... Then you're getting the first blood, what, a week later, two weeks later on the fence?"[3]

Given that the blood vial was not checked-in properly and was instead kept in Detective Philip Vannatter's possession for hours, it was necessary to establish how much blood was taken initially to dispel doubt that some blood at the crime scene had been planted. As Carrie Bess explained:

> It was the same story over and over again when it came to how evidence was collected and stored. I had a hard time with Mr. Peratis. His first testimony as a witness was okay. But when he had to go back again and indicate he's not sure about how much blood he drew I had a problem because he's been a nurse for what, twenty, thirty years? He draws blood all the time. I figured if you're doing this on a consistent basis, I have a problem when you state you didn't know how much you draw. Because his testimony in the first place was, "Yes, I did draw 8 cc's. It could have been 7.9 or 8.1 because this is something I do all the time. It would have been either under 1 cc or over 1." But then, all of a sudden, the new testimony is he doesn't know, the syringe was turned a different way and it was a 10 cc syringe instead of an 8 cc syringe. I had a real problem with that.[4]

Then there were serious problems for these three women jurors with the blood samples on the gate and in Simpson's Bronco. The first serious implausibility had to do with unanswered questions as to why the police did not notice the blood on the fence when they first examined the crime scene. Cooley describes her own reaction:

> I also thought, personally, that blood was planted on the fence simply because when they first made the collections it wasn't there. And I feel that if it was there whoever did the collecting would have seen it. I cannot understand how, if you're out and you are looking especially for blood drops, you can say, "Oops, I found these on the back of the fence." I would assume that someone would do that. If they didn't then that tells me someone did not do a very good job. Then two weeks later you come back and look, and if there is still blood there and you can see it with the naked eye, why wasn't it seen in the beginning? This is not a new fence. This is not another link of the fence. So, personally, I felt that the blood was planted.[5]

The suspicion that the blood was planted was intensified by the fact that there was EDTA in the blood samples gathered from the rear gate at the crime scene and not in the samples gathered two weeks earlier from the terra-cotta walkway. EDTA (ethylenediamine tetra-acetic acid) is a chelating and sequestering agent that is used as the medium for the placement of the blood in DNA testing. EDTA may also appear naturally at certain levels in the human body. But the same person at a given time will either have EDTA in the blood or not. EDTA is produced as part of the body's mechanism to counterbalance chemical reactions produced by substances that do not mix well when they are combined. Above a certain level, EDTA can put a person at risk of excessive bleeding, because it is an anticoagulant.

Since it would be medically impossible for some blood samples from the same crime scene and the same person to have EDTA in them and not others, a suspicion had to be raised in the jurors' minds as to how this impossibility had occurred in these blood samples, especially since EDTA is also used in DNA testing. The jurors also wanted to know exactly how high the level of EDTA was in the sample in which it appeared to judge whether it was consistent with a person's ability to tolerate that level without excessive bleeding. Due to faulty machinery the exact level of EDTA in the sample was difficult to ascertain.

Obviously, the prosecution wanted to convince the jury that the EDTA had been naturally produced in O.J.'s blood and was not the result of prior chemical processing before it was purportedly collected. But simply to assert that EDTA can be naturally produced could not solve the jury's problem since their concern was that, even if that was the case, the EDTA should have been in all of the samples. The answer that EDTA degenerates along with other contents of the blood also did not and could not assuage the suspicion raised by the discrepancy in the sample because the sample on the gate was found two weeks after the crime; therefore, the contents of that sample should have been more degenerated.

The jurors also criticized the police for letting the samples from the walkway degenerate to the point that they could not be tested by the most reliable DNA test. The drops on the walkway were degraded because they were left for hours inside the LAPD crime scene truck on a stifling hot day. The truck's refrigeration unit continually broke down and therefore could not be used to store the blood. However, even though the less precise test was used, the women accepted that the tests were reliable enough to provide sufficient markers to show a high probability that it was O.J.'s DNA in the blood. (A marker is a crucial gene in the DNA molecule. The more markers in the sample, the more precise the exclusion process of other human beings can be.) The defense stressed the lack of significant degradation of the blood samples on the fence as itself raising suspicion since they were gathered on July 3rd, more than two weeks after the crime. It is also the case that the more precise DNA test could only be used on these samples. Therefore, the DNA in the samples from the gate could be subjected to more comparison tests than the DNA in the other samples. Thus, any suspicion about the legitimacy of the sample would also call into question the most precise DNA reading offered in the case.

Critics of the jury have argued that the police would not have had any incentive to plant blood on the gate because the less reliable test still demonstrated a good probability that O.J. was present at the crime scene. But, let us compare what the two tests can show. Tests run on three drops of blood from other sections of the crime scene showed that 1 person out of 240,000 had DNA with the markers found in the sample. The fourth blood drop, also from other sections of the crime scene, showed that 1 out of 5,200 could have had the markers found in that particular sample. The fifth blood drop, found on the gate, was the only one that could be subjected to the RFLP test. It was the drop subjected to that test that showed that only 1 out of 57 billion people could have those markers. The difference between the two tests is obviously extremely significant in proving the prosecution's case. The police could not know beforehand how the degeneration of the blood samples would undermine the effectiveness of the DNA testing. It is not hard to imagine the panic that set in once it was understood just how badly the blood sample in the truck had been allowed to degenerate. It is not difficult to imagine that that panic alone could have motivated at least one or some of the police in charge of the crime scene to try to make up for the consequences of their irresponsible handling of the blood samples in the truck. But, it was not for the jury to speculate about why the police might have done what they did. The inconsistencies presented by the evidence were enough to raise a suspicion in the minds of the jurors, a suspicion that went unanswered by the prosecution. Cooley explains why she questioned the legitimacy of the blood sample on the gate:

> Okay, maybe it was O.J.'s blood at Bundy. It was O.J.'s blood on the gate. All I could say after hearing all that was, well, maybe it was but you let this blood degrade. You should have been there doing your job. Now you want to tell us that EDTA was on the blood at the gate. It should have deteriorated along with the other sample, especially two weeks later. EDTA is something that's found in all of us but there is such a narrow margin. Because if it was that high, our blood wouldn't clot. So why didn't that deteriorate too?[6]

Recall that the level of the EDTA was relevant to whether or not it had been naturally produced and whether it was also at a level that could be tolerated without causing excessive bleeding. The expert witnesses who testified as to how much EDTA was in the blood sample also raised questions about how accurately the blood was analyzed. Bess explained her concern:

> They were looking to see how much EDTA was in there and in order to see it you have to have all these ions in there for it to be present.... And Herbert MacDonell

stated that the ions were there, all of them. But the guy who tested the EDTA said it wasn't fair and all the signs showed the same wave length. When he was asked about it, about all the wave lengths being the same, he said that was just noise in the machine. That the machine was noisy. So the question we had was, How can you call this set "noise" and tell us we should ignore it, even though it had all the same frequencies as the one that represented the presence of the ions? So I think he picked the parts that he wanted. And so that was questionable.[7]

All three jurors commented on how seriously they took the need to educate themselves about the DNA evidence. They were absolutely clear in their own minds as to how critical the DNA evidence was to the case as a whole. Were they able to assess the legal significance of the DNA evidence, even though they were not experts? Cooley insisted that they made the necessary effort to do so. She describes her own experience:

> On the whole I did not find DNA too complicated to grasp because Barry Scheck took time to explain it and we really observed and listened to what those people were telling us. Now, granted we may not be experts in the field because we never studied DNA. I understood that there's degrading of DNA. I understood the amount of blood it took to really come up with a good reading. I understood when they talked about the autorads and those aliels [alleles]. Day in and day out they talked about them.[8]

The implausibility of the time cited for first discovering the blood on the console of the Bronco also raised the possibility that the blood was planted as well. As Cooley explains, "I had problems understanding how they found the blood smears on the console of the Bronco. Why were they seen after they had torn the inside of this car completely up? They should have been detected immediately. And all of a sudden, you know a week or so later you are just detecting that. I felt it looked planted."[9]

The more serious problem for Cooley was the inevitability of contamination, given how the blood sample was collected:

> My biggest problem was that there were .07 cc's of blood in the Bronco. Total. But you go back days, weeks later and get some more. Now, we don't know what could have happened between that time. Here's the vehicle down at the O.P.J. Anyone could have gone down there and got anything. We don't know what you got going. We don't know anything about the swatches, which were wet in certain places. You have to take all these things into consideration. Why were these swatches wet? If you say you put all these swatches in a drying area, we're looking at contamination for sure.[10]

The jurors also raised questions as to why, when Simpson purportedly had such a bad cut on his hand, there was no blood on the glove found at Rockingham. They made it clear that it was an overall pattern in the handling and gathering of the evidence that began to raise doubts in their minds as to the coherence of the state's case—at least in its presentation of the blood samples.

In addition to their concerns about the evidence, the three jurors also found the police witnesses completely lacking in credibility. They all agreed that Vannatter's mishandling of the blood samples remained incomprehensible to them. The stated reasons for his actions simply did not make any sense. Detective Mark Fuhrman was caught in an outright lie. During his direct examination he denied ever using the "n" word. Once the jurors heard the tapes it was clear that he had indeed used the "n" word. The tapes were the reason that Bess discredited Fuhrman. "Up until they brought the tapes out, I thought O.J. was gone. Because I really had not discredited Fuhrman, I really hadn't. I just figured here's a sharp cop. This guy was really on it and he was just lucky enough to find every damn thing when it came to the evidence. I'm just figuring that he is one of those lucky cops . . . that he must have been a hell of a detective, and then I come to find out he was a, you know . . ."[11]

Rubin-Jackson, on the other hand, was convinced even before she heard the tapes that Fuhrman was lying about his racist attitudes, yet she did not allow that to discredit his entire testimony. It was only when she had heard the tapes that she concluded that he had utterly discredited himself.

> His getting up there saying he had never said nigger and I'm thinking, Oh, come on now, I know you're lying about that. It didn't discredit his whole testimony to me. But after they had validated the tapes and the court had confirmed they were his tapes, there was no need for them to bring him back.[12]

The discrediting of Fuhrman effectively undermined the prosecution's case. His comments and attitudes about racist language, specifically, and racism, generally, were relevant because they were solicited on cross-examination to establish a motive for planting evidence. Furthermore, the tapes documenting his racist views and use of epithets not only provided a possible motive for tampering with the evidence, they more generally called Fuhrman's credibility into question. There was also the criticism that the prosecution should have recognized how Fuhrman's lack of credibility as a witness had damaged their case, and that they should have handled their obvious problem with him differently. Bess, for example, declares:

> I am surprised that the prosecuting attorneys let it go so far knowing that they had a problem with Fuhrman as opposed to bringing it out to us. I think it would have been a much different situation because we had an opportunity to throw out all or any part of Fuhrman's testimony. And Fuhrman was the trial. Fuhrman found the hat...Fuhrman found the glove. Fuhrman found the blood. Fuhrman did everything. When you throw it out, what case did you have? You've got reasonable doubt right there before you even get to the criminalist. Why didn't the prosecuting attorneys know that they had built their case on what Fuhrman had said along with Vannatter? Why didn't they protect themselves by clarifying that Fuhrman situation as opposed to him taking the fifth and just leaving them holding the bag?[13]

As the jurors suggest, the prosecution could have preempted this issue by raising any potentially damaging information regarding Fuhrman on direct examination, but they chose not to avail themselves of this time-honored lawyering tactic. In the end, the three women stressed that they discredited Fuhrman because he was a liar, not because he was a racist.

Finally, the time frame offered by the prosecution in which O.J. purportedly killed Simpson and Goldman, and then took actions to cover his tracks, also troubled the three jurors. As Rubin-Jackson explained:

My doubt was over the time. I didn't think one man could have done all that damage in that length of time and get back to the house without help . . . And they kept saying that he did it alone. That he did this all by himself. I kept saying I just don't see how that could happen. Maybe that was my biggest thing. The time frame bothered me. I just had too many questions. Driving up there with the shovel. So what did he do? Take the shovel and go back to the house and dig a hole and bury the clothes? He didn't have that much time by himself and they never presented to me that he had any help. Then, on the other hand, what happened to those dark clothes he was wearing at the recital? I was really stuck for a while.[14]

The women took up their jobs with utmost seriousness. They all spoke eloquently about their struggle to be true to the legal standard they were asked to apply. They sought to give Simpson a fair hearing and to refuse a "rush to judgment," which is exactly what they thought the police had done. Indeed, the jurors did not condemn the police for a racist conspiracy. Instead, these jurors attributed police incompetence to "the rush to judgment," which led the police to make initial errors that they later tried to cover up, which eventually undermined the prosecution's case against O.J. The jurors only found out after the trial the extent to which O.J. had already been tried by the media. To quote Cooley:

I think the media decided this case early on. I also think the fact that a lot of people out there judged Mr. Simpson guilty from the jump street is a violation of the law. The law states you are innocent until proven guilty. They needed to see someone punished from jump street. They had these preconceived ideas and it[']s not fair. The court never asked us if we personally thought the man was guilty of murder or not. The court provided us a law we had to go by and that's it.[15]

Indeed, as Rubin-Jackson stated, "I have not declared him innocent at all."[16]

Given their commitment to the conscientious execution of their duties, the women were shocked by the public response to their verdict. The jurors vehemently denied being influenced by some of the much-publicized flaws in the prosecution's case. For example, these women did not believe that the June 15 demonstration in which O.J. purportedly could not get the gloves on his hands actually showed that they did not fit. Rubin-Jackson expressed her skepticism about the demonstration:

> Sure you know they fit. They were, I shouldn't even say expensive, I should say a good leather glove. And a good leather glove isn't gonna stretch that much. Like a leather shoe. It dries and then it[']s tight. You put it on and it stretches. He was putting the glove on like this, she says splaying her fingers. And I must have had an expression on my face because as he stood there, it was like he was talking to me and he went, "They don't fit. They would have fit anybody."[17]

They were particularly insulted by the accusation that they played "the race card" in their deliberations. For them, this accusation is itself a form of racism—as much as the media presentations of the black jurors having no capacity for reason. They vehemently, and to our minds rightly, protested the unfairness of being blamed for social ills when they simply did the job that was required of them as jurors. As Cooley argues:

> We're taking the burden from NOW (National Organization for Women) organization. When I signed up for jury duty, I didn't see the state of California vs. NOW, the state of California vs. Racism, the state of California versus all these things. All I saw was the state of California versus Orenthal James Simpson. Out of this we got political wars. We got wars with the judicial system. We're hearing that we set this world back on its toes from square one. The hell if we have. These things have always been here. They have always been camouflaged. Don't blame us.[18]

But blamed they have been. Two counteracting stories to the one we have presented in which the jurors are judged as reasonable citizens whose verdict was also reasonable have been widely circulated. We turn to those stories now.

"Colored" Perspectives

The jurors on the Simpson jury have been accused of having a "colored" perspective on their unquestioning acceptance of evidence of police violations of the Fourth Amendment, such as the warrantless search of Simpson's house. Yet, even commentators who challenge the verdict as an emotional response in the face of purportedly overwhelming evidence do not deny that there was evidence of serious violations of the Fourth Amendment. These infractions (including, one assumes, its openly racist justification of Mark Fuhrman's testimony) were portrayed by an editorial in *The New Republic* (exemplary in its expression of the general public's widely held views of the jurors) as "small lies and inconsistencies on the part of the police,"[19] which would not have led anyone whose perspective was not "colored" to reach the verdict of not guilty. In the same editorial, the inability to see straight was also attributed to class, the so-called dumbing down of the jury, who were supposedly picked "for their ignorance and credulity and hermetic isolation from civil society. The Simpson jury," we are told, "looked not very much like America."[20] More specifically, in the editorialist's view, their "ignorance" explains their incapacity to objectively judge the evidence, their "credulity" led to their emotional reaction to the LAPD, and, in the final analysis, their "tribal identifications" with O.J. drove them to put the facts aside and let a guilty man go free. In light of this perspective, one has to wonder if the writers of the editorial knew anything, for example, about the employment status of the jurors.

There has been widespread misrepresentation in the media about what kind of people were on the jury, misrepresentations that do not relate to the actual experiences or socioeconomic backgrounds of these three African-American women. Armanda Cooley is a fifty-one-year-old woman who is an administrative assistant (III) for the county of Los Angeles. She is responsible for monitoring outside collection agency contracts. Her job is to ensure that the contracts are correctly governed by the rules and regulations established by the state and the county. (In 1990, Armanda Cooley won the Employee of the Year Commendation.) Marsha Rubin-Jackson works as a mail carrier for the U.S. Postal Service. Carrie Bess is a clerk for the U.S. Postal Service. She has worked for the post office for twenty-three years. Although she does not yet have a college degree (one of her main goals as a young woman was to graduate from college), she has regularly taken classes at Los Angeles Trade Technical College. It is a peculiar view of government employees to describe them as isolated from civil society. The government is the nation's biggest employer; hence, the suggestion that this jury did not "look much like America"—at least according to socioeconomic profiles—is a curious one indeed.

Regarding the degree to which the jurors were viewed as acting rationally, it was in the sense that they had the goal of protesting police abuse and used the means of jury nullification to achieve it. Even if the jurors were understood to be rational, they were still accused of using the means of nullification to guarantee the "primacy of tribal identifications"[21] rather than fulfilling the requirements of citizenship. Yet there was *not one* juror on the O.J. jury who gave as a reason for his or her own vote on the jury the political use of nullification. A number of jurors, including the three women in *Madam Foreman*, have spoken directly to the issue of nullification. As we have already discussed, the jurors in *Madam Foreman* were appalled to learn that they stood accused of nullification, or any other form of "playing the race card."

Rubin-Jackson responded to the accusation that the jury's verdict was deliberate nullification as follows:

> I don't understand how people could say that I let someone go because he was . . . If I hadn't been on the trial and O.J. had been my relative and it was proven to me that he killed two people, he'd be in prison. I don't care who he is or what color he is. People don't know me. They've passed judgment on me. You tell the world I created this big division. This division was there before I was even part of the jury. I have never been part of any type of division. It angers me.

It really angers me for people to say that because I was a black woman, I let this black man go. If they had proven to me that this black man had killed two people, that black man would be in prison. Simple as that.[22]

When juror six, Mr. Cryer, was asked directly about nullification, whether or not he was "moved" by Johnnie Cochran's appeal in his closing statement to "send a message," he replied: "Well, move—I mean no, it didn't move me. I kind of, like probably had a little chuckle about it, like, 'OK, Johnnie, I get your point.' "[23] When asked to describe the deliberations, he responded, "They were very organized, very concise. Everyone was very respectful with each other and very orderly."[24] Mr. Cryer clearly stated that he made his judgment based on the legal standard of reasonable doubt and not on speculation or belief about O.J.'s guilt or innocence. Identification with O.J. as a black man did not, according to Cryer, play a role in his own judgment.

> STONE PHILLIPS: Did it cross your mind that maybe he did it?
> CRYER: Sure. Sure, it did.
> PHILLIPS: Does it still cross your mind?
> CRYER: No, not anymore. Not anymore.
> PHILLIPS: It's not just a case of reasonable doubt. You believe he didn't commit the crime?
> CRYER: I'd say it's probably more a case of reasonable doubt than . . . than I know he did commit the crime.[25]

Cryer also explicitly denied that the African-American jurors put pressure on the white and Hispanic jurors who initially voted guilty:

PHILLIPS: The two jurors that voted to convict, what do they . . . what do they have to say? You . . . can you recall what . . . what the discussion center[ed] on?

CRYER: Now, Stone, the only thing I can tell you about that, first of all, is that those individuals were never identified. Until this day I still don't know.

PHILLIPS: So those people didn't come forward and say I think he is guilty in the course of deliberations, even though they had voted that way.

CRYER: No.

PHILLIPS: So, there really wasn't any discussion about . . .

CRYER: No, what I am saying is, there was discussion, but the discussion was always in a broad sense. It was never that, "Oh, I think this piece of evidence points to—I know he was not guilty, or this piece of evidence points to" . . . it was broad deliberation in the fact that we all sat down and decided to share our opinions about the evidence and the testimony.[26]

Mr. Cryer describes the jury's process as an exchange of reasons, with each juror being open to hearing the assessments of others on the jury. He does not describe the attuning of ends and already established opinions in which a compromise was reached, which favored the majority of blacks on the jury and in which the white and the Hispanic jurors submitted to their racial identification with O.J. The black jurors describe the process as reasoning together, as respectfully taking up each other's judgments as reasons. According to Cooley, there was no discussion of the issue of race in the deliberations.

Not only have the jurors said repeatedly that they did not play the "race card," Rubin-Jackson points out that if she were

to have played the so-called race card, she would have played it
with different results for O.J.:

> What do people want? I asked myself. Forty acres and a
> mule, sweetheart. Everybody needs to know that the racial
> cards that were played in the actual courtroom were not
> played or by any means used in the deliberation room. It
> wasn't racist going in. It wasn't a racist case. If that were
> the case we could have been angry at O.J. for being with a
> white woman. It could be either way. We didn't even see
> racism in this. But think about it. Being black women, we
> could have been angry as heck at O.J. for going with a
> white woman. But that wasn't the case.[27]

The Undeserved Feminist Critique

Jonetta Rose Barras exemplifies the feminist critique that the
women jurors completely lost sight of the significance of
spousal abuse. "Gone from the minds of the majority female
jury," she writes, "were issues of spousal abuse; gone were the
scenes of an obsessive and possessive husband who became
enraged at the sight of his ex-wife in another man's arms."[28] Barras is simply inaccurate in her statements as to what was "gone"
from the minds of the jury.[29] Again, let us turn to how the
women jurors in *Madam Foreman* analyzed the evidence that was
presented to them of O.J.'s abuse of Nicole. For Cooley, "One
of the most confusing aspects of the trial in hindsight was why
the prosecution didn't introduce additional evidence about O.J.
abusing Nicole."[30] The prosecution did not effectively present a
pattern of abuse, according to these women jurors. The prosecu-

tion presented isolated incidents in 1985, 1989, and 1993. The jurors did not doubt that O.J. had on those occasions abused Nicole. For the three women jurors in *Madam Foreman*, abuse certainly could provide a motive for murder, but they would have wanted to see a more consistent pattern in order to find O.J.'s abuse a motive for murder in this case. To quote Cooley:

> If it had been something a little more consistent—because we went from '89 to '93—I would have looked at it differently. But based on what we saw in the evidence, I could not lay a heavy consideration as far as that being a motive. I feel that if a person is capable of extreme rage then these types of things happen more often than once every four or five years.[31]

This is one of the many examples of blaming the jury for not giving sufficient weight to evidence they did not have. The general public knew there was such a consistent pattern of abuse, but the jury did not.

Even so, there is no rational basis to assume that the jurors were insensitive to issues of violence against women. Bess, for instance, strongly disagrees with the position voiced by some white feminists that African-American women generally shrug off abuse as the way of the world. She explains that, although "it was stated that maybe black women do not look at spousal abuse as seriously as white women . . . I say women are women and abuse is abuse. I divorced my husband after three years because he came home and jumped on me and I left. I never went back."[32] In Bess's case we have a woman who refused to put up with an abusive husband. The irony is that to refuse to listen to her is to disregard her experience of abuse and her resistance to it.

"The Rush to Judgment"?

But what about the speed at which the decision was reached? Doesn't that alone show that serious deliberation didn't take place? Doesn't it show that the jury simply expressed their identification as blacks by their vote?

Cooley attempted to be as systematic as possible in her organization of the jury's deliberations. The jurors initially took a secret ballot. In that vote two jurors voted for the verdict of innocent. Only one of these jurors identified herself. After the vote a number of jurors began to raise questions about the prosecution's evidence. Cooley felt the discussion was becoming disorganized so she intervened to summarize the central issues that everyone agreed had to be addressed. She remembers,

> And that's when I intervened and said, "Wait a minute, we've got all these issues that we need to discuss, which was Allan Parks information, information about the glove, information about the EDTA and information about the puncture wounds and the wounds on Mr. Goldman.
>
> "Wait a minute," I said. "We'll get to all this information, but let's just take one thing at a time." And that's what we did. I asked Carrie to pass out the evidence books.[33]

There was unanimous agreement from the beginning of the deliberations that the fact that there was EDTA in the blood samples on the gate at Bundy raised serious questions as to whether or not the blood on the gate had been planted. Thus the validity of using the RFLP-tested blood to carry the prosecution's case would have been severely undermined by a showing that it had been planted. Indeed, the failure of the prosecution to adequately explain the presence of EDTA in these samples was one of the most decisive factors in the jury's verdict. Cooley in particular wanted to emphasize that Fuhrman was not as influential in their verdict as he was portrayed to be in the press.

> One thing I would like to get straight was that Fuhrman was not the main reason we came to our decision. And I am glad he did not come into our conversation until toward the end of our deliberation. I think a lot of hostility would have set in early on based on the fact that he denied that he ever used the "n" word, that type of thing. Remember we never got to hear all of the tapes, we just heard certain segments. But Fuhrman did not come up until the end. And when he came up juror #1290 said, "Well, we know he's a liar. So we don't even have to deal with that." Certain other comments came up about him, but other than that, he never even came up as part of our reasoning.[34]

Once the deliberations got under way it became clear that even the jurors who had initially voted guilty shared the same concerns about the evidentiary production in the prosecution's case. Of course, the jurors were aware that the prosecution, which carried the burden of persuasion throughout the trial, might have been able to effectively answer their questions about the evidence. But their conclusion was the prosecution did not meet its burden and therefore did not dispel the doubt that was raised by the evidence.

Cooley summarizes why the jury was able to reach their verdict as quickly as they did:

> There has been a lot of criticism about how long—or short—the deliberation was. I say where is it written how

long the deliberations should be? Number one, we were in lockup for eight or nine months. You had nobody you could talk to about the case. Nobody to judge any type of feelings, to answer some of the questions that are on your mind. After the day ended—after you had dinner, after you watched a movie—when you're in that room by yourself at night, you're deliberating with yourself. You're going over what happened in the courtroom. What you felt about it. What questions you have. When they come up the next time, you'll be able to fill in those voids at the next day's session. So it did not take another nine months in that room to deliberate the case because everybody was going through the same thing. But none of us knew that until we walked into the deliberation room. When we all united, it was just like a cloak had been lifted. We walked into that room and discovered that everybody was in tune with the same thing.[35]

In the end all the jurors who have been interviewed agree that they reached the verdict they did because the prosecution did not prove its case against O.J. Simpson.

Banished to the Realm of the Phenomenal[36]

We are not claiming that race did not play a role in the trial. In our wholly racialized society it is impossible for race not to play a role in the murder trial of a black man accused of murdering his white ex-wife. Race is so deeply embedded in our unconscious identifications that it is inextricable from any sense of who we are. The jurors, in fact, specifically commented on how race played a role in the trial. They noted that because the majority of them were black, they were spoken down to by the lawyers and by many of the expert witnesses. They spoke about how the prosecution used Chris Darden because the DAs felt they needed a black to address an almost entirely black jury. Indeed, they criticized Darden for making serious mistakes in the presentation of the prosecution's case because he felt that black women could not understand the abstract concept of DNA evidence. Darden has since justified his use of the glove demonstration so as to confirm the women's suspicions of his view of their intelligence. He believed they needed a picture (i.e., the glove fits) in order to be convinced that O.J. was guilty. But not only did the women not need a "picture," they saw right through Darden, regretting that he had been influenced by racist views of African-American women. They noted that, even if O.J. Simpson was black, he had left the black community to live in a white world.

They also spoke of a shared concern about the inability of an alternative juror to abide by his job as a citizen because of his hatred of white people. But all the jurors interviewed insisted that their verdict was not an emotional reaction to Fuhrman's racism. Nor was it based on a racial identification with O.J. Nor did they engage in a deliberate act of nullification "to send the LAPD a message." All three of the women jurors in *Madam Foreman* felt that the attacks on the jurors in the press were racist in that they portrayed the jury as not being intellectually capable of the analytic tasks demanded by jury duty. We agree with them that this is indeed a racist judgment.

The jury gave reasons for their verdict consistent with their roles as jurors. They have said over and over again that they struggled to assess the evidence in accordance with the legal standards they were instructed to use. To accord them the basic respect of taking up their reasons as reasons is the most minimal demand imposed upon us by even the most modest egalitarian ideal: that all of us are to be regarded as equal to the tasks of citizenship. Furthermore, the jurors should be accorded this basic respect because there is no reason not to do so. There is no evidence that they behaved irrationally, moreover. They met their civic duty and should be recognized for having done so.

This modest suggestion in the context of the furor that has followed the Simpson trial becomes a form of witnessing to the larger political significance of the attacks on the jury, which also have been broadened to include all African Americans. The implicit (sometimes explicit) charge is that African Americans do not have the necessary capacities "to be" up to the demands of citizenship. We highlight the words "to be" deliberately to indicate that some of the charges against the jury implicate at the very least an unconscious imagining of African Americans as a "lesser" form of being, barely human. It is against the background of a long history of banishing African Americans to the "realm of the phenomenal" that the defense of the reasonableness of the jury takes on the political significance it does as a form of witnessing to the continuing degradation of African Americans. When we claim that the jurors were reasonable, we mean that they analyzed the evidence of the case in accordance with the requirements of public morality imposed upon them by the Constitution. African Americans are judged as less than persons when they are judged as incapable of these capacities. They are denied equal citizenship in a most basic sense.

Full citizenship as we understand it entails treatment as an equal, not just equal treatment. A crucial aspect of what it means to be treated as an equal is that each of us is to be evaluated by the public institutions of the government, and its representatives, as free and equal persons capable of reasonableness and rationality. More specifically, all of us should be judged equal to the tasks of citizenship; that is, of having those capacities needed for the fulfillment of civic duty. This is a normative psychological judgment demanded by the ideal of constitutional democracy, not an empirical judgment of our actual abilities. As we have seen in the case of the O.J. jurors, African Americans still frequently do not have attributed to them either by the public institutions that make up the government or by white citizens with whom they ideally would share a public life the capacities of reasonableness and rationality.[37]

The disparaging comments made about the jury were degrading because they assumed that African Americans as a group were a lesser form of human being, incapable of either reason or rationality and, thus, of the tasks demanded by citizenship. Degradation in this specific sense is inseparable from what Toni Morrison has termed Africanism—a trope that has been put to wide and varied use by white people. It is "a disabling virus [that] has become in the Eurocentric tradition that American education favors, both a way of talking about and a way of policing matters of class, sexual license, and repression, formations and exercises of power, and meditations on ethics and accountability."[38]

This "disabling virus" has clearly infected the "meditations on ethics and accountability" that have followed in the wake of the O.J. verdict. The disabling virus that sadly infects our public discourse is inseparable from the process of metaphoric transference that demonizes color and gives us a form of life where we see black as a brand of inferiority. Linguistically, metaphoric transference can operate in several ways. Metaphor functions to describe relationships. *My daughter's skin is like "burnished gold"* . . . [39] By so doing it can enable us to see and think about our world differently. In the case of the daughter's skin, for instance, the metaphor evokes the brilliance of her flesh; it assumes no normative meaning. But when the process of metaphoric transference is buried under the habits of usage and the load of unconscious fears, representations of our reality become choked. We can't see different possibilities of representation and the new relationships that might grow out of them. *Black is like...* is an example of metaphoric transference. These loaded meanings collapse the relationship of similarity into an identity which we see as the truth of what it means to be "black." We then see this color as both a fact of a people and as a true description of them. We learn to see "black" as an identity only through this process. This is why many children, for example, under the age of four (unless they are raised in a household in which the word is used to designate a people and/or a judgment about them) will not identify persons as black. Through metaphoric transference, "black" comes to represent a whole set of characteristics that are then tucked into the word as its inherent meaning.

Let's take our example of "burnished gold" to help us make our point as clearly as possible. If the color of burnished gold came to be identified with a particular people, so that when we spoke of the "burnished golds," anyone who knew the language well would know the qualities that were being either appreciated or degraded just by the use of the expression; then the color would stand for a complex set of normative judgments about the people. In our culture and in our common usage, we have no "burnished gold" people that, with those words, spring to life with an identity. But this is the type of metaphorical transference that frequently recurs with regard to race. The meaning of the color black in the literature of our country is then encompassed in the trope of Africanism. Africanism in turn is inseparable from our country's symbolic history in which the tension between declared freedom and the enslavement of African Americans generated, and continues to generate, enormous anxieties that demand alleviation through justification for the existence of such a brutal institution. Justification implicates an unnoted metaphoric transference in which "black" becomes identified with a true mark of inferiority.

The "reasoning"—and we put reason in quotation marks to note its failure to live up to its claim to be reasonable—is circular. Blacks are inferior because they are black; they are colored with all the scary connotations of the word. This imagined identity of what it means to be black is then imposed as the unequal treatment that then purportedly makes its own case. Nor do we find this imagined identity projected onto the O.J. jurors alone. African Americans are regularly portrayed as mentally infirm, sexually uncontrolled, and hopelessly violent, and this projected identity continues to direct our public discourse on affirmative action, family welfare, and crime. Sadly, many of the attitudes expressed in the wake of the O.J. Simpson verdict illustrate the way in which racism can infect our public discourse and make us blind to its operation. Fantasies about what it means to be black allow government institutions, as well as white citizens, to rationalize behavior that is in fact based on unconscious fears expressed in projected identifications. One tragic result of this for our body politic is scapegoating. Ignoring all evidence to the contrary, for instance, many have convinced themselves that there is a growing mass of AFDC recipients—all gold-clad, Cadillac-driving women named Sapphire—bankrupting the government with exorbitant cash outlays and, to boot, eroding the moral character of the country. The justification of racism is inseparable, in other words, from an imagined African-American identity intertwined with the meaning of the word black.

Whiteness in turn comes to make sense only against its opposite blackness. Whiteness even as an adjective (one only needs to read the definitions in the Oxford dictionary to believe us) stands in for the noncolor: the neutral. White is paradoxically viewed as the noncolor color. This paradoxical view of whiteness influences the way in which we think about race. Race—especially in discussions involving African Americans—is usually taken to mean nonwhite people. We generally do not speak of white people as having a race.

Moreover, as we all know from the movies, white is also the color of "good guys": the color of reason rather than irrationality. But when we argue that capacities such as reasonableness and rationality have been whitewashed, we do not mean that they are white or male and therefore should be condemned. We mean exactly the opposite. We seek to expose the process by which these properties have been unconsciously whitened, by affirming throughout this essay that this view of these qualities is not true.

The frozen language of racial discourse makes it difficult for whites to understand the actions of African Americans other than in terms consistent with fantasies about the normative meanings of color. Thus, whites "de-code" the meaning of African-American actions through the grid established by the metaphysical condensation of metaphorical transference into an apparently unshakable reality. A classic example of how racialized discourse leads to the misrepresentation of a particular action is the reading given by some whites in both the press and the public of Mr. Cryer's raised fist to O.J. after the verdict was announced. This gesture, read in the strongest possible manner, proved to some whites that at least Mr. Cryer had engaged in jury nullification. Mr. Cryer explained his action differently:

> PHILLIPS: After the verdict was read, you raised a clenched fist.
> CRYER: Mm-hmm.

PHILLIPS: A signal to O.J.

CRYER: Not a signal. Actually, all it was, was a hey man, have a nice life and enjoy it. Go get your kids and go with that. That's all it was, not a signal or a sign or anything. It was just, "Hey man, have a good time. Enjoy it."[40]

Mr. Cryer tells us that he did not mean to indicate racial identification with O.J. by his raised fist. Yet his action has been understood in accordance with white perceptions of the meaning of the raised fist. The so-called race card that the jury purportedly "played" is a textbook example of an appeal to the trope of Africanism to give meaning to their verdict. But as we have argued throughout, there is no evidence that supports this attribution of motive to this jury. They have said loud and clear and over and over again that they reached their verdict because the prosecution did not prove its case beyond a reasonable doubt. Why can't we hear them? If we hear them, why can't we believe them? Why can't we accord them the basic respect that the reasons they gave are *reasons*, not signs of "tribal identifications"? The lens of stereotype and caricature that distorts political analysis of the serious problems our country faces now also makes unnoteworthy the racialized contempt African Americans confront. Indeed, one measure of African-American devaluation is the extent and severity of the suffering and assault that can transpire without comment. The women on the O.J. jury have testified to their pain at being portrayed in the press, in legal commentaries, and in calls for jury reform as stupid, racially biased, and insensitive to the problem of wife battering. The imposed shame they have had to endure has not received much, if any, public attention.

Racialized coloration disguises an irrational and unreasonable judgment about the capacities of African Americans and other minority citizens. The irrationality and unreasonableness of the judgment disappears into the fantasies of truth about the meanings of color. As citizens we need to struggle to de-couple the unconscious process by which we give meaning to color from the inherent judgments these processes disguise. Treatment as an equal does not require colorblindness. It does, however, demand this de-coupling—opening us up to a world in which "colors" no longer mark any one of us as inferior—as a justification for banishing any one of us to the realm of the phenomenal. The attribution of reasonableness to the jurors operates against the misrepresentation of African Americans "through the demonizing and reifying [of] the range of color on a palette."[41] We do not just demand this attribution as a political antidote to the fetishization of "blackness" that has fixed racist justifications in our political discourse, although this stirring up of the so-called ground for racism is clearly part of our goal. We do so because we believe it to be a fair and accurate assessment of the jury's verdict.

Is There a Constitutional Crisis?

Since we have argued that the jury's verdict was reasonable, we reject legal reforms that implicitly, let alone explicitly, are tailored to "improve" the criminal justice system by effectively taking African Americans out of it because of their purported inability to fulfill the task of jury duty. We are in a constitutional crisis, signified by the failure of many Americans and, more specifically, the institutions of the government (the police obviously included) to adhere to the fundamental premise of a democratic society that all of its citizens are to be regarded as equal. When Marcia Clark in her role as a public prosecutor, for example, states, "Liberals don't want to admit it, but a majority

black jury won't convict in a case like this. They won't bring justice,"[42] she effectively denies the equal standing of African
Americans as citizens.

Given our analysis of at least one aspect of the constitutional crisis, it cannot be cured by further undermining the protection of the Fourth Amendment and, more specifically, the
exclusionary rule, nor by jury reform that would replace our current jury system drawn from the populace at large with a jury of
legal professionals (i.e., lawyers and judges).

Nothing in our attribution of reasonableness to the jury
commits us to a position on the actual guilt or innocence of O.J.
Simpson. Indeed, we deliberately refuse to speculate on his guilt
or innocence, since that would be all we would be doing, speculating. Under our Constitution, a jury trial is not just a search for
the guilty party. A jury trial must be consistent with regard to
the notion that each one of us is an equal citizen and more particularly to our physical integrity and our safety from invasion of
places of retreat from public domains. We strongly endorse the
Fourth Amendment's protection of physical integrity and the
safety from invasion of places of retreat. Moreover, this kind of
protection from state coercion is so basic to what it means to be
valued as a citizen that it is fundamental to all the other rights
demanded by the recognition of our equal citizenship.[43] Again,
we need to stress that as a matter of day-to-day life, African
Americans have been persistently and unequally subjected to
state coercion and particularly police abuse in a manner that
white citizens have not. For us, then, any further undermining of
the Fourth Amendment can only heighten the constitutional crisis, since it represents such a significant blindness to the unequal
suffering of African Americans at the hands of the police, and
in general the coercive power of the state.

The assaults on the jury system and the reforms that have been suggested (for example, that we should adopt a system in which legal professionals rather than ordinary citizens perform deliberative functions) denies the equivalent evaluation of each one of us as up to the basic tasks of citizenship. They also do not rationally follow from an assessment of this jury's deliberations. The suggestion that more educated jurors would have been more objective or better able to decipher the complex evidence and argumentation presented at trial are, at best, unpersuasive. First, as demonstrated above, the jurors had a more than adequate grasp of the key legal concepts and evidentiary considerations used during the trial. What is really at issue is the inability of many critics to comprehend the difference between legal and factual guilt, and, given that the evidence presented at trial was not overwhelmingly on the side of the prosecution's case, the possibility that there could have been reasonable doubt. Second, such comments also wrongly assume that more educated or white jurors would have been more detached from "emotional" considerations of race. Formal education alone does not purge people of their unconscious fantasies. In fact, even lawyers have proven to be quite irrational in their thinking about the case. One law school professor is now teaching a course whose title— "The Jury System, From John Jay to O.J.: Did He Kill It, Too?"—has as its basic assumption that one largely black jury destroyed an otherwise perfectly functioning legal system. Educated citizens—lawyers not excluded—are simply not immune to racism.

We need to stress the point that the advocacy of jury reform because African-American people are not equal to the tasks of citizenship is not consistent with their equality and freedom.

More strongly put, the argument that African Americans are incapable of meeting the demands of jury duty legitimates their banishment from the normative political community established by our Constitution.

Thus, the overtly racist reactions to the O.J. verdict should be viewed as an opportunity to expose how pervasive fantasies about the inequality of African Americans are in our culture. It is the reaction to the verdict that should serve as a warning. These fantasies must not be allowed in our public culture and discourse of legal reform as if they were legitimate reasons to transform a fundamental political institution such as jury system.

However, we are not arguing that there are no reforms of our criminal justice system that could be made and justified in accordance with the ideal while still using the O.J. trial as an example of the need for reform. The O.J trial necessitates that we examine key aspects of our criminal justice system, from the role of money in building a defense to the advisability of having an entire trial televised. The jurors in *Madam Foreman* spoke persuasively about the "hell" of being sequestered. We certainly need to examine whether or not sequestration of the jury is too toilsome an imposition in spite of the purpose it is to serve. But these reforms, when they are made in our public political culture, must meet the ideal of public reason. The reaction to the O.J. verdict calls us all to vigilance against letting racist fantasies pass into the discourse of our public culture as if they were reasons for reform.

Notes

The authors would like to thank the following for their encouragement and insightful comments: Elizabeth Chambliss, Dasa Duhacek, Greg DeFreitas,

Ronald Dworkin, Laurie Gaughran, Rose M. Harris, Toni Morrison, Sara Murphy, Eloise Segal, and Gayle Tate. This essay is dedicated to Shirley Bourne.

1. We agree with Ronald Dworkin that many of the clauses in our Constitution—particularly those that protect individuals and minorities from government—demand a moral reading because they elaborate abstract principles of political morality. See Ronald Dworkin, "The Moral Reading and the Majoritarian Premise" in *Freedom's Law* (Cambridge: Harvard University Press, 1996), pp. 7–12.

2. *Madam Foreman: A Rush to Judgement?* (Los Angeles: Dove Books, 1995).

3. *Ibid.*, p. 23.

4. *Ibid.*, pp. 116–17.

5. *Ibid.*, p. 122.

6. *Ibid.*, p. 120.

7. *Ibid.*

8. *Ibid.*, p. 118.

9. *Ibid.*, p. 122.

10. *Ibid.*, p. 119.

11. *Ibid.*, p. 200.

12. *Ibid.*

13. *Ibid.*, p. 187.

14. *Ibid.*, p. 131.

15. *Ibid.*, p. 25.

16. *Ibid.*, p. 131.

17. *Ibid.*, p. 126.

18. *Ibid.*, pp. 140, 141.

19. See the editorial "Reasonable Doubt," *The New Republic*, October 23, 1995, p. 8.

20. If one looks at the facts of who goes to college in our society, the jury does "look like America"—if one includes African Americans in that vision. By the age of twenty-five, 25.6 percent of white men receive a college degree. Only 11 percent of African-American men receive a college degree. Only 11.8 percent of African-American women go to college, as compared to 19 percent of white women. The disproportionately lower socioeconomic status of African Americans and Hispanics frustrates their efforts to receive college educations. First, the majority of African Americans remain trapped in what some economists have called the secondary labor market, where job instability and low earnings make the

direct costs of tuition, books, etc., harder to bear. Second, family income needs to play a role in who can afford to forgo wages from full-time jobs for the number of years it takes to complete college. The containment in the secondary labor market gives a partial explanation of why fewer African Americans and Hispanics go to college themselves. See Gregory DeFreitas, *Inequality at Work* (New York: Oxford University Press, 1991); and Samuel Bowles and Herbert Gintis, *Schooling in Capitalist America* (New York: Basic Books, 1976). Studies have also shown the continuing role of de facto segregation in discriminating against both African Americans and Hispanics in the school system itself. (See Gary Orfeld, *Status of School Desegregation: The Next Generation* [Washington: U.S. Department of Education, 1992].) Despite these obstacles, many African Americans and Hispanics, like Carrie Bess, continue to work toward attaining degrees.

21.   See *Madam Foreman*, p. 8.

22.   *Ibid.*, p. 184.

23.   *Dateline NBC,* October 6, 1995.

24.   *Ibid.*

25.   *Ibid.*

26.   *Ibid.*

27.   *Ibid.*

28.   "My Race, My Gender," *The New Republic,* October 23, 1995.

29.   Some commentators' efforts at analyzing the case were frustrated by the way we continue to conceptualize the categories of race and gender. More specifically, although there has been an attempt to theorize about the intersection or interrelationship of these and other categories, in terms of the O.J. trial, many have chosen to view race and gender as mutually exclusive categories. Some like Jonetta Barras, who are committed to fighting domestic abuse, have wrongly assumed that "race," as a separate and distinct consideration (i.e., as something that can be distilled from class or gender issues) is more "important" for Black women—an idea that Black feminists have worked to discredit for some time. When feminists join in the voices condemning the jury's inability to reason or to sidestep the putative imperatives of racial bonding, they share in the propagation and legitimation of racist fantasies about African Americans. As feminists, we most particularly do not want to join the voices that implicitly or explicitly degrade the women on the jury by refusing to give them credibility. For an examination of the categories of race and gender as mutually constitutive,

see Rose M. Harris, "Signifying Race and Gender: Discursive Strategies in Feminist Theory and Black Politics," forthcoming dissertation, Rutgers University, 1997.

30. See *Madam Foreman*, p. 184

31. *Ibid.*

32. *Ibid.*

33. *Ibid.*, p. 126.

34. *Ibid.*, p. 159.

35. *Ibid.*, p. 161.

36. The phrase "banished to the realm of the phenomenal"—initially coined by one of the authors (Alexander)—implies the Kantian framework to which our argument appeals. (Slavery, for example, is the most brutal form of banishing African Americans to the realm of the phenomenal, human beings cruelly treated as beasts of burden, to be bought and sold.) Immanuel Kant elaborated and philosophically defended a radical divide that marked us in our human "being." As physical creatures we are part of the world of nature, rent by desires and wants. As beings capable of moral reasoning and, more specifically, of the self-conscious causality that is the rational will, we are also noumenal selves. Neither of the authors accepts in full the Kantian metaphysics that justify this radical divide in our human being. Indeed, one of the authors has ethically questioned the cost to ourselves of a strictly Kantian morality. See Drucilla Cornell, "The Ethical Message of Negative Dialectics," in *The Philosophy of the Limit* (New York: Routledge, 1992). With that caveat we accept the fundamental premise of Rawls's Kantian constructivism that at the heart of the moral appeal of a modern, politically liberal society is the underlying idea that each one of us is to be regarded as a free and equal person capable of both reasonableness and rationality.

37. See John Rawls, *Political Liberalism* (Cambridge: Harvard University Press, 1992, pp. 48–54), to distinguish the reasonable and the rational as categories in political philosophy.

38. See Toni Morrison, *Playing in the Dark* (New York: Vintage, 1993), p. 7.

39. The reference to "burnished gold" is from a recently discovered poem by the Greek poet Sappho (notes from translations on file with the authors).

40. *Dateline NBC*, October 6, 1995.

41. See Morrison, *Playing in the Dark*, p. 7.

42.   *New York Times,* October 6, 1995, p. A18.
43.   See Henry Shue, *Basic Rights* (Princeton: Princeton University Press, 1989) and Drucilla Cornell, *The Imaginary Domain* (New York: Routledge, 1995), ch. 1, for a more detailed argument for this position.

Color-blind Dreams and Racial Nightmares:

Reconfiguring Racism in the Post–Civil Rights Era

Kimberlé Williams Crenshaw

Introduction

Of the many startling dimensions of the O.J. Simpson saga, perhaps few are as remarkable as the manner in which Simpson has been transformed into a new symbol of a reconfigured vision of racism. From the day of the murders to the controversial acquittal, the domain of racism has been gradually but unmistakably re-envisioned. Racism, represented during the civil rights era through images such as white lynch mobs proudly displaying their "strange fruit," or defiant white defendants acquitted by all-white juries for various racial atrocities, has now been represented in snapshots depicting blacks sharing high-fives and dancing in the streets to celebrate the acquittal of one of "their own."

In this newly configured narrative of racism, the evil manifested in the actions of racist juries of the past is recalled not in
the racial contours of the criminal justice system, nor in the
tense and oppressive dynamics between the LAPD and the
African-American community in Los Angeles, but in the lawless
actions of the largely black jury and the outrageous celebrations
of hordes of African Americans. In its most extreme articulation, African-American celebration of Simpson's acquittal is
framed as a virtual endorsement of the murders of Nicole
Brown and Ronald Goldman. Thus, this "trial of the century"
has now come to represent a travesty of justice in which O.J.
Simpson, once the embodiment of racial transcendence, is transformed into an agent and beneficiary of an empty gesture of
racial payback.[1]

That Simpson, whose fleet-footedness on the football field
was replicated in his nimble transcendence of celebrity culture's
color line, would ultimately be captured by the specter of race
that he hoped to escape is one of the extraordinary ironies of this
case. Simpson's transition from color-blind dream to racial nightmare, however, is not merely fate's version of gallows humor. This
irony has much more earthly antecedents, conceived within the
very ideological framework that embraced Simpson as a symbol
of a color-blind ideal and later spat him out as the embodiment
of black criminality and irresponsibility.

The goal of this article is to uncover how the narrative
structure of Simpson's transformation—along with the polariz-
ing discourse on the verdict and a host of other reactions to the
Simpson tragedy—was initially framed within the narrow parameters of the dominant vision of race reform, a vision principally
organized around the concept of colorblindness.

Although the dominance of this vision was manifested in
myriad rhetorical gestures that presumed a race-neutral social

context, underlying these performative imperatives were white/ black power relations that differed only in degree from those that prevailed in pre–civil rights America, and a range of racist sentiments among large sectors of the white population that were never fully disciplined by the color-blind paradigm. In fact, the convergence of these opposing pressures were factors contributing to the disintegrating consensus around the paradigm even among the sector that constituted its principal supporters: the moderate and liberal elite.

The gaps between the color-blind ideology and the dynamics of racial power are nowhere more acute than in the areas of criminal justice, interracial sex, and especially, the intersection of the two. Thus, while pundits intoned from the beginning that this would not be a race case, the underlying dynamics that formed the material and discursive backdrop of the case guaranteed that race would not lay dormant for long.

Even the scripted declarations that this would not be a race case was itself a constitutive dimension of the racial dynamics of the case. Of course, pundits were correct that the case was not *exclusively* about race: it was in fact "about" any number of things. It was first and foremost about a double murder. It was also about gender, media, culture, and justice—one can read almost any contemporary issue through its lens. Yet the very terms of the initial denial regarding race reflected an investment in a color-blind ideology that seemed to command an approach to race that noticeably diverged from the manner in which other factors were framed.

The operation of this ideology was suggested by the emergence of the metaphor "playing the race card," frequently deployed to stigmatize attempts to question the role that racial power might play as the drama unfolded, while efforts to frame the case around domestic violence, for example, were rarely if ever dismissed with a parallel response of "playing the gender" card. Indeed, claims about the role of class, celebrity, or even gender were readily entertained, while similar claims about the role of race were routinely rejected.

In the earliest stages of the case, the wishful belief that race would not play a role was accompanied by a studied practice of denying the rather obvious racial dimensions of the case. Such factors included, for example, the setting of the crime in a city awash in racial tension and civil unrest over racism within the police department, the involvement of a well-known black celebrity in a sexually charged, interracial crime, and the deep patterns of racial and cultural segregation that contributed to sharply divergent views on the integrity of the criminal justice system and the likelihood that Simpson could get a fair trial.

Although these were all race-related conditions that decades of liberal reformism had failed to alter fundamentally, pundits virtually stumbled over themselves in honing to the color-blind imperatives of the dominant race ideology. No better symbol of colorblindness's simultaneous production and erasure of underlying dynamics of racial power could be found than in the very terms in which Simpson was initially portrayed. Mainstream commentators, perhaps in a preemptive response to possible concerns about whether Simpson could receive a fair trial, were quick to comment that Simpson was not thought of (by whites) as an African American, but as simply a "race-neutral" celebrity. Yet such "assurances" unwittingly revealed an underlying racial logic in which blackness remained as a suspect category that Simpson had been fortunate to escape. Implicitly, a defendant who *was* thought of as black might well have reason to worry.

Such commentary revealed as well the tortured etiquette of a color-blind performance. In such terms the acknowledgment of

Simpson's blackness was necessarily accompanied by a claim that this blackness was not noticed. This cross-your-heart promise not to notice the obvious constitutes a key dimension of the color-blind imperative that Neil Gotanda aptly labels "non-recognition." This technique of "noticing but not considering race" implicitly involves recognition of the racial category and a transformation or sublimation of that recognition so that the racial label is not "considered" ... in the employer's decision-making process. Of course, as Gotanda goes on to point out, non-recognition is a technical fiction. "(I)t is impossible to not think about a subject without having first thought about it at least a little." In reality, "an individual's assertion that he 'saw but did not consider race,' can be interpreted as a recognition of race and its attendant social implications, followed by suppression of that recognition. In other words, although non-recognition is literally impossible, colorblindness requires people to act as though it is."[2]

This tortured construction of colorblindness reflected the logic of liberal race reform and the particular ways in which it constructs racism and racial justice. Elites who undertook and shepherded the race reform project understood racism as a distortion of consciousness which was eventually correctable by a normative commitment to colorblindness. As Gary Peller argues, this dominant conception of racism "locate[d] racial oppression in the social structure of prejudice and stereotypes based on skin color, and ... [identified] progress with the transcendence of a racial consciousness about the world."[3] Although elites diverged on the question of whether remedial uses of race consciousness were legitimate, there was broad agreement that colorblindness was the eventual goal of racial justice.

On an ideological level, colorblindness eventually emerged as the dominant ideological framework within which the problem of racism and the imperative of racial justice would be understood. Yet at the structural level, the broad-scale institutional reforms that would have been necessary to eradicate patterns of white dominance and black subordination were only tentatively approached and eventually abandoned. The combination of the triumph of the discursive paradigm of colorblindness, and the failure of the structural reforms set the stage for the peculiar performative dynamics of the Simpson trial.

Colorblindness required a performance from its adherents in the Simpson case that proved increasingly difficult to sustain as the telltale signs of the aborted institutional reform project emerged. Indeed, as the case progressed, this color-blind performance began to take on the qualities of a D— melodrama in which the audience's ability to suspend its disbelief is undermined by the cumulative effect of artificial scenery, woodenly delivered lines, misplaced props, and gut-wrenching overacting. The plausibility of the color-blind narrative throughout the trial was compromised by the convergence of a number of factors: the inability of the district attorney to persuasively present racist police and potentially unconstitutional police practices as alternatively nonexistent or inconsequential, the refusal of the celebrated color-blind defendant to offer a color-blind defense, the unwillingness of the African-American community in Los Angeles to suspend their suspicions about the LAPD, and the ultimate refusal of millions of whites to suppress their beliefs about black paranoia, lawlessness, and bias.

The Color-blind Paradigm

This very public disintegration of the color-blind narrative raises, of course, questions about its normative dominance within the equality discourses of the race reform era. Colorblindness figured prominently within the liberal vision of race reform, a vision that framed the objectives of equality and the domains of racial power in narrow terms. Formal equality, constituted through the removal of formal racial barriers and animated by the normative objective of colorblindness, presented the objectives and practice of equality as one in which racial structures and racial identities have been "e-raced."[4] In color-blind ideology, the achievement of equality is measured by the formal removal of race categories across society. The goal of a color-blind world is one in which race is precluded as a source of identification or analysis; its antithesis is color consciousness of any sort. Pursuant to this understanding, the moral force of racial equality is mobilized within contemporary settings to stigmatize not only apartheid-era practices but also efforts to identify and challenge manifestations of institutionalized racial power. It is not necessary, therefore, to redistribute racial capital; color-blind discourse almost singularly achieves its mighty mission by simply suspending traditional signs of race and racism.

Of course, the mere *e*-racing of the dynamics of racial power cannot wholly disrupt these deep historical and cultural patterns. E-racing neither forestalls the redeployment of racist discourses nor buries the color line beyond discovery. As revealed in the proliferation of commentary that framed Simpson's acquittal in terms of black lawlessness and irresponsibility, traditional articulations of black otherness are easily recovered. Race, suspended in the buffer zone, remains ready to reappear as an interpretive frame to justify racial disparities in American life and to legitimize, when necessary, the marginalization and the circumvention of African Americans.

The discourse surrounding the Simpson case represents a popularized enactment of this vision of race and its concomi-

tant definition of racism. In this vision, racism is represented
as isolated, aberrational, and relegated to a distant past. The
frequent deployment of the metaphor of the "race card," for
example, presumes a social terrain devoid of race until it is (ille-
gitimately) introduced. Racism in this vision remains relevant
primarily as an historical concept, relevant only to mark the contrast between an enlightened present and a distant and unfortunate past. Within this racially enlightened era, not only are
whites expected to adopt a color-blind performance, but African
Americans are expected to approach the occasional discovery of
racist actors or actions with cool rationality rather than with
hysteria or paranoia.

The progression of the race discourse surrounding the O.J.
Simpson trial reflects this intricate pattern of race and reform in
the post–apartheid era. I have previously argued that race reform
projects organized around such a narrow understanding of the
scope of racial power would ultimately reproduce racial hierarchy
and legitimize material inequality through invoking, in cultural
terms, the same ideological justifications that had previously been
rejected as racist when presented in biological terms.[5]

The logic of white supremacy had been premised on the
inherent inferiority of blacks and the equally fallacious assumptions of the superiority of whites by whites. This ideological
assignment of differential value to blacks and whites was produced and supported by a wide variety of discourses, including
science, religion, and the humanities. Within traditional white
supremacist paradigms, blacks were imagined to be lascivious,
emotional, and childlike, while whites were regarded as industri-
ous, pious, rational, and mature. Liberal reform consisted of the

formal rejection of ideologies of black inferiority and the erasure of barriers that marked off various institutions and other social spaces as black and white respectively. In the post—apartheid world, blacks and whites were deemed formally equal, capable of competing for and within spaces previously segregated by law and culture.

Yet this reform project failed to produce a fundamental redistribution of racial power, nor did it eradicate white racism. While formal equality, along with some race-conscious remedial strategies, did produce a sizable (but vulnerable) black middle class, the mass transformation of the structural and institutional elements of the extant power structure was abandoned before it was ever fully conceived. Clearly one dimension of the retreat from the broader project of racial reform was grounded in a legitimate concern that pushing such a project forward might well unleash volatile and potentially uncontainable reactions from the broader white public. As Alan Freeman argued, "needs basic to the class structure" including maintenance of the myths of vested rights and equality of opportunity, constituted barriers to a more aggressive project of race-based redistribution.[6]

Moreover, despite the lofty goals of color-blind visionaries, racist sentiments were as often simply suppressed as they were eradicated. Thus while the triumph of the ideology of colorblindness has effectively rendered explicit racist discourse entirely unsuitable within mainstream political debate, a residual degree of racist sentiment among a substantial part of the white population remains amenable to appropriately coded racial appeals.

The disappointing returns from the liberal reformist agenda were prefigured by conceptual limitations within the contours of colorblindness itself. It stood to reason, for example, that if black subordination could no longer be justified by reference to stereotypes of black inferiority, then justifications for white dominance would similarly have to be rethought. Yet the rejection of ideologies of black exclusion and inferiority was not met with any rethinking of the nature and legitimacy of white dominance in American institutions. Racism was framed only in terms of the formal exclusion of nonwhites, not in terms of the privileging of whiteness.[7] Formal equality merely mandated the formal "erasure" of the institution's whiteness, primarily through the removal of explicit racial barriers.

Under this narrow conception of reform, limited deals were made that gave selected blacks some of the social capital of whiteness, but the cultural economy continued to disproportionately reward values, perspectives, and practices traditionally associated with white institutions. To be sure whiteness was transformed, but in the most limited of senses: white schools would be just "schools," white firms would be "equal opportunity employers," and white society would simply be "society." Equality would not require a fundamental dismantling of any formally white spaces, or the redistribution of white social capital. Race equality simply meant that blacks would have a shot—though not necessarily an equal shot—at getting some for themselves.

Perhaps the ingredient that made the whole story plausible, at least to many whites, was the inclusion of a small number of African Americans into the new and improved American fantasy. Although the opportunities presented by the promise of erasure were inaccessible to many African Americans, some would receive conditional passes to cross racial lines. Nowhere was this logic more carefully orchestrated than in celebrity culture, where its ultimate expression was the very public e-racing of the few blacks who had "crossed over" with the standard blessing of "we don't think of them as black."

The racial line, however, was still discernible even in the discourse of racial transcendence. The "other side of the tracks" from which the lucky few "crossed over" was still racially defined space. For O.J. Simpson, the trip originated from the most concentrated of racially defined spaces: *the projects*. Simpson clearly had traveled from a raced space, yet the promised land that he crossed over into was represented as a colorless terrain. Despite claims to the contrary, the terms of Simpson's migration never rendered his race entirely invisible. Rather, like old money—new money relations, the e-raced would be treated like those who were born into racial privilege, though everyone knew the difference between the truly privileged and the newly entitled. This was the color-blind deal, unless, of course, something were to happen where the race lines simply had to be redrawn.

This limited scope of racial equality endorsed by the liberal paradigm rejected broader and more progressive understandings of racial power. These broader visions understood racism not solely in terms of racially motivated discrimination, but instead as patterns of cultural and institutional power, exercised by dominant groups against others. Thus the problem of racism was not limited to the practice of discrimination or a mere departure from colorblindness: it was reflected in patterns of subordination that had become naturalized and entrenched within a post–apartheid society. Mere formal equality and its superficial erasures could not respond to this dimension of power.

This alternative understanding of racial power rejects the color-blind imperative as well as the premises underlying the standard articulations of intergrationism. Gary Peller observes that a contrasting vision of race and racial formation rejects integrationist premises that blacks and whites are the same. "[T]he idea of race as the organizing basis for group-consciousness asserts that blacks and white are different, in the sense of coming from different communities, neighborhoods, churches, families and histories." In this alternative conception of race, "differences between whites and blacks [are located] in social history." In constructing race as an historical and social phenomenon, Peller rejects the notion of race consciousness as an inherently suspect distortion of consciousness. Peller and other progressive critics of color-blind ideologies neither shy away from the reality of subjective difference nor do they reject the remedial deployment of race-conscious policies. The former is to be presumed in a world in which social and historical differences between races continue to manifest; the latter is necessary to push forward the broader project of structural and institutional reform in light of these differences.

Yet the rejection of color-blind ideology is not solely the province of race-conscious progressives. In part to offset potential contradictions between the formal discourse of racial equality on the one hand and the social and political realities of black marginalization and disempowerment on the other, race has gradually reemerged from both the center and the right as a discourse of legitimation. The continuing marginal condition of African Americans within the post–apartheid society has been a stubborn fact that can not be dismissed. Either the claims of equality's promise have been false and much more radical remedial strategies are warranted, or there is something wrong with blacks that formal equality simply cannot "fix."

In this context have emerged racial reality bites,[8] essentially a redeployment of rejected stereotypes under the new and improved frame of cultural or moral difference. Race consciousness has reemerged from the right in contemporary political discourses to explain racial inequalities in cultural and even moral terms. This re-racing of inequality implicitly challenges a key plank of the liberal paradigm that presumed the essential similarity between races, while assumptions and beliefs about racial difference had previously figured within color-blind paradigms as racial prejudice. In the new "frank" talk about a host of issues, blackness reemerges as a repository for a range of pathologies. Even biology has been reintroduced in public discourse as constituting an essential racial difference.[9] From AM radio's generic shock jocks to right-wing academics Dinesh D'Souza and Charles Murray, re-racing is the thrill of today's social discourse. Talking "honestly" about crime, unwed motherhood, and morality essentially means talking about race. The process of having e-raced blacks now provides the moral distance from the racings of the past so that one can rest comfortably in the belief that, although talking "honestly" now sounds suspiciously similar to the pre–civil rights justification for everything from sterilization to lynching, this race postreform discourse is different. Un-eracing is not old-style racing; it is merely putting certain commonsense observations and facts back into social discourse in the spirit of candor rather than prejudice.

Against this backdrop of the ideological paradigm of colorblindness, and its underlying dynamics of racial power, numerous dimensions of the discourse around the Simpson case can be better understood. Not only did this ideological framework shape the diverging black/white investments in Simpson, but color-blind assumptions also framed black perspectives as "biased" in contrast to a putative "objective," "Westside" analysis. The absolutely disastrous attempt by the prosecution to cover up obvious credibility problems and the bizarre perfor-

mance of Christopher Darden are similarly related to a contradiction between performative rhetorics and institutional realities
—only this tension is grounded in the rhetoric of bureaucratic
control of the police and prosecutorial commitment to rules of
constitutional protection. These complex dynamics enormously
complicate the meaning of the Simpson verdict, yet within the
racialized travesty narrative, they are reduced to a singular plane
of injustice.

O.J. Simpson: The Essential Symbol of the Color-blind Ideal

The Simpson case is a racial drama written within the contours
of the dominant color-blind paradigm. Simpson's high-profile e-
racing, and his subsequent re-racing in the wake of his arrest for
the murder of Nicole Brown Simpson and Ron Goldman, represents a popular embodiment of the dominant conception of
racial reform, including its contradictions and its ultimate
embodiment of historical patterns of racial power.

As an icon, O.J. Simpson has occupied a unique category as
the ultimate racial boundary crosser: he emerged from the black
underbrush and crossed over into race neutrality. Said one commentator: "Simpson had long reigned as one of America's best-
loved black celebrities. The football hero had crossed the color
line to become what marketing experts call race neutral."[10] One
may wonder, however, how it is possible to cross a racial line that
presumably divides black and white and simply become "neutral." Neutral functions here as a euphemism for white; indeed
both terms have been used somewhat interchangeably to describe
Simpson's popularity.[11] This unconscious equating of whiteness

with neutrality is even more pronounced in the description of, as one commentator put it, Simpson's "taste" in women.[12] "Simpson possessed a race-neutral style, which included dating white women . . ."[13]

Here, a specific racial preference is described as "race neutral," while a hypothetical preference for black women would presumably be race specific. The very terms of these descriptions reveal that Simpson's image was not grounded in a "race neutrality" as such, but in an apparent ability to neutralize his blackness by acquiring the accoutrements of whiteness.[14]

This popularized image of Simpson as an icon of racial neutrality reveals the manner in which whiteness, maintained as a dominant default sensibility, is legitimized as race neutral even as the border that Simpson crossed is readily acknowledged to set apart racial spaces. Apparently, one crosses from blackness into "neutrality" as one becomes acceptable to, familiar with, and embraced by whites.

The conditional status of Simpson's crossover position, however, was revealed in the almost reflexive recovering of his raced past in the many speculative (and premature) analyses of his fall into criminality. Invoking Simpson's past racial identity, one commentator offered:

> But for all of their talent and skill, they [Simpson's lawyers] cannot return the permanent smile upon a *race-neutral* face America used to know as O.J. It is a *different* face we see now, a face from another time, another place. An essential face that predates the toney address and the wife who stepped out of a Beach Boys song. [His white friends] exist on the far side of the divide now. They can offer him their best wishes. But they cannot help him. If

he is to save himself, O.J. Simpson may have to find himself. Regardless of the verdict, that journey—not the
hairs, the gloves, the hat, the blood, the DNA—may prove
to be the more revealing pieces of an evidence trail that
ultimately took a kid from the projects on Potrero Hill to
the mansions of Brentwood . . . and back again.[15]

This quasi-morality tale, while gesturing toward some deeper
meaning, ultimately reduces itself to a singsong wag that all of
Simpson's lawyers and all of his men couldn't make O.J. white
again.

Pundits throughout the nation produced similar analyses,
wondering in disillusioned tones whether the guy next door was
still the O.J. everybody thought they knew, or was he really the
essential "other" from across the tracks.

Was he the Hertz pitchman with the eternal smile who
company surveys revealed was "colorless" to the American
public? Or did he still carry much of the cruel persona of
the gang leader he had been, the kid who pulled robberies
and who once said, "It wasn't a weekend if there wasn't a
fight. I enjoyed it."[16]

Here, violence is located in opposition to Simpson's acquired colorlessness; his gang affiliation easily positioned the
"other" O.J. that "we don't know" as a black thug from the other
side of the tracks. Elsewhere, Simpson's wife beating was similarly framed as a marker of his essential otherness: "Simpson
beat his ex-wife at least once. Suddenly, it seemed, an old friend
has become a stranger."[17] In this classic othering of domestic
violence, men who beat their wives don't live next door, they

don't play golf, and they don't come into our living rooms. "We" simply don't know them.

Nowhere was Simpson's symbolic "return" to his essential blackness more graphically illustrated and debated than in the *Time* magazine cover that darkened his face.[18] Many African Americans saw in the illustration proof of their suspicions that race would certainly shape public discourse around the case. Even whites who steadfastly denied that race would have anything to do with the case were troubled by *Time*'s cover illustration. *Time* ultimately issued an explanation for the illustration in which it denied that the artistically inspired darkening of Simpson was racially motivated. Of course, *Time*'s disclaimer of conscious motivation was entirely plausible. However, its belief that this was responsive to concerns about the racial underpinnings of its artistic choice revealed how anemic the dominant understanding of racism really was.

Nonetheless, the criticism singularly directed against *Time* was another dimension of a massive inability to even recognize, much less interrogate, racial narratives proliferating elsewhere. Indeed, *Time*'s controversial cover only visually represented the story that was disseminated by *Newsweek* and repeated in several other venues. The frequent references to Othello, for example, and the ready connections drawn between the savage actions of which Simpson was accused and a troubled pre–race-neutral past all suggested that the killings marked the reemergence of a suppressed ghetto persona. Although *Time* simply offered a graphic depiction of the narrative that its competitors were hawking elsewhere, somehow the artistic illustration of this racial thinking went a little too far too fast.[19] Re-racing Simpson had to be a bit more gradual: it needed to be written and spoken before the story could be "artistically rendered."

Setting the Racial Drama: Divergent Racial Investments in O.J.

"One of My Best Friends Was Black"

Much of the early white response to the accusations against Simpson was mournful. Most articulated this tone as an expression of sadness that a hero had fallen. Yet the constant pairing of this attitude with the invocation of Simpson's "race neutral" appeal seemed to suggest that something more was lost in Simpson's fall. As Meri Nan-Ama Danquah surmised:

> White people liked O.J. They liked liking him, too. Liking him proved they were not racists. O.J. redeemed them.
>
> Whites never feel that O.J. hated them. For decades, pictures showed him wide-eyed and a little open-mouthed like a kid glancing up from a birthday cake. He was race-neutral, like Colin Powell or Nat King Cole.[20]

Simpson and perhaps a few other African Americans reinforce wishful beliefs that American society *has* reformed, in spite of the marginalization of masses of African Americans who live lives largely separate and remote from the majority of white Americans. Like the all-purpose refrain "some of my best friends are black," liking Simpson proved that however one reacted to other blacks, or however blacks were generally positioned in society, it had nothing to do with racism. Simpson confirmed not only that blacks could rise above their historically consigned status, but that whites would accept them when they managed to do so.

"Colored on TV!"

African-Americans' investment in Simpson was not nearly as celebratory as that of many whites.[21] The realities of racial disempowerment and social marginalities are not so easily cabined and tamed by the mere existence of an O.J. Simpson. The pervasive sense of the marginal status of black America, along with the reality that there is little remaining commitment to improving the economic and political status of African Americans, render it generally unlikely that Simpson's elite Brentwood lifestyle could convince most African Americans that social life was truly open and fluid. Little of Simpson's Brentwood existence could deflect the burning realities of contemporary black life. So why would Simpson be meaningful to African Americans at all? Indeed, as many whites somewhat self-servingly argued in the verdict's aftermath, Simpson had done little for the African-American community.[22]

Despite Simpson's distanced social existence, many African Americans did maintain some investment in him—not as a symbol of society's transcendence of racism but, rather, as a representation of one of the few "concessions" made by white America in the wake of black demands for societal change. One of the concessions that African Americans won from the massive mobilization during the sixties was the inclusion of minuscule numbers of African Americans into celebrity culture. In order for formal equality to be a meaningful social policy, the formal rejection of white supremacy would have to be conveyed through mass culture as well as through law.

Thus, some blacks gained a place in the self-representation of American culture far different from those prescribed for blacks—the maid, the criminal, and the downtrodden. Indeed, for many blacks who lived through the reform decades, one of the most significant ways that life is different now is that there are African Americans in celebrity culture. During the lifetime of even the youngest baby boomers, black figures in the media were so rare that all African-American activity would grind to a halt when a black appeared on TV. The call would go out, "black on TV" (actually, at the time, it was "colored on TV"), and people would literally run to the set to catch a glimpse of the momentary representation of black America on the public stage.

There seemed to be an implicit understanding that the fate of the individual colored person on TV somehow was tied to the interests of the group. There was some truth to that. The performance of the "colored on TV" was symbolically important not because their success meant that any African American could rise to the ranks of celebrity, but because many believed that African-American success on the public stage might combat the widespread beliefs in black inferiority. The performance was ameliorative in more personal ways as well. Celebrity blacks broke barriers that were frequently unimaginable to those raised in apartheid America. For some blacks, there was enormous pride in seeing folks who looked like them participating in the American fantasy. Yet, there was also concern that any poor performance would reflect negatively on the race.[23] Many observers held their breath or whispered silent prayers that the "colored on TV" would fare well.

Potentially more important in understanding black investment in celebrities, many of whom African Americans had little input in choosing, was that many believed that at the end of the day racism might intervene even in the lives of these chosen few. To be sure, Simpson clearly won a lottery in the sense that he among millions would be welcomed into the fantasy life of American celebrity culture. His life *was* different from that of most African Americans. Yet many African Americans believed as well that Simpson could not fully escape the reality of his black skin, a reality that was seen as a burden or a barrier no matter how fast or surefooted he might be. Thus,

Simpson's fall from grace was potentially meaningful because it suggested that even the few who won the celebrity lottery might still be divested of everything on the basis of the one thing they continued to share with the rest of African Americans—their race.

These diverging white and black perspectives on Simpson set in motion a collision that guaranteed that this case would on some level be about race, regardless of Simpson's guilt or innocence. To whites, the fact that Simpson had been embraced as the embodiment of a color-blind ideal preempted any possibility that race would or should play a role in the case. To many African Americans, Simpson's race-neutral persona did not immunize him against any and all forms of racism, especially when his color-blind image began to tarnish. Indeed, to some African Americans, the very fact that the Bentley-driving, golf-playing, white-womanizing Simpson was in such trouble raised the possibility that the features that made Simpson appear to be race neutral to more elite whites rendered him potentially vulnerable to the racist sentiments of others.

In fact, the race-neutral space in which Simpson was temporarily suspended was bound to collapse. When it did, the discourse about what this collapse meant and who was responsible for it gave rise to even more racial divergence surrounding the case. The case would reveal deep conflicts about the nature of American society and would uncover the widely divergent attitudes on such basic matters as the trustworthiness of police and the legitimacy of the criminal justice process. After the smoke cleared it would also be revealed that underlying the dominant paradigm of color-blind equality lay a trove of white racial power exercised against the black community through a disciplinary rhetoric of bias and uncivility.

The Trial, the Race Card, and Testilying

A central contradiction within contemporary reform ideology is manifested through the invocation of neutrality as the normative measure of fairness and equality, even as racial power is exercised and expressed. Throughout the Simpson trial, the "race card" metaphor effectively captured the formal dimensions of the color-blind performance and revealed it to be an effective means of camouflaging the dynamics of racial power. Under the metaphor of the "race card," raising the issue of racism was characterized as a disingenuous act that was especially dangerous and unethical in circumstances surrounding the trial. Raising the question of racism thus evoked an immediate response of disciplinary zeal.

Early in the pretrial period, *The New Yorker* published an essay by Jeffrey Toobin in which Detective Mark Fuhrman's troubling record of racism was revealed along the outlines of a possible defense strategy.[24] Although the evidence uncovered by Toobin revealed a scandalous disregard by the Los Angeles Police Department for the lives of blacks and Latinos with whom Fuhrman was likely to come into contact, many commentators were far more troubled by the fact that the pages of the highly respected *New Yorker* magazine would be used to peddle a damaging and unlikely story. Critics in and outside of the media criticized Toobin, giving tabloid publishers the opportunity to welcome Toobin and *The New Yorker* into the fold.[25]

Simultaneously, legal commentators and pundits expressed their requisite outrage by calling for professional sanctions against the defense team even before the evidence was ever presented.[26] Toobin himself labeled the defense "monstrous," and sought to justify the publication of the story as newsworthy on these grounds. At this point, it became evident how race was to be positioned in mainstream discourse around the Simpson case. No longer used solely to frame the rise and fall of Simpson, race was reconfigured as a defense ploy, a "card" unscrupulously played rather than a potentially substantive issue to be explored. The fierce tone of the criticism against the defense team suggested the underlying operation of another metaphor, that of crying fire in a crowded theater. Los Angeles, it was argued, was rife with racial tension following the Rodney King beating, the acquittal of the officers involved, the subsequent civil disturbance, and the Reginald Denney trial. To those Los Angelenos anxious to put those unfortunate events behind them, framing the defense around a racial conspiracy seemed the embodiment of irresponsibility.

The circumstances that rendered the "race play" so irresponsible, of course, simultaneously belied claims that the racist frame-up theory was simply incredulous. In the wake of the King beating, the blue-ribbon Christopher Commission had uncovered a troubling culture within the LAPD that condoned racist behavior and jeopardized the rights of the people of Los Angeles, particularly African Americans and Latinos. But the facts uncovered by the Christopher Commission's report proved to be far less compelling against the political realities of strong Westside support for the LAPD. Some of the Commissions' recommendations were implemented; however, resistance throughout the ranks is significant. Tensions between the LAPD and the African-American community continue to exist, yet beyond the formal implementation of community policing and the provision of sensitivity training, there is little political pressure to do more. Elite concerns about brutality and tensions between the department and the black community waned as the Rodney King fiasco receded into history. Concerns about hampering the police effectiveness in fighting crime once again took center stage.[27]

The framing of the Fuhrman controversy as the inexcusable reason for Simpson's acquittal provides apt illustration of the "race card" metaphor. It also suggests the operation of an intersecting discourse of police reform, a discourse which, like colorblindness, achieved a rhetorical dominance that is at odds with underlying realities. The widespread characterization of the Fuhrman issue as a simple race play first overlooked what should have been a police scandal. Moreover, the prosecution was fully aware of Fuhrman's credibility problems: at best, Fuhrman was simply a skillful liar, and at worst, Fuhrman was a rogue cop, clearly not the kind of witness upon whom to rest a high-profile case. Yet Marcia Clark presented Fuhrman in a manner that dripped of righteous indignation. Defending Fuhrman's credibility, Clark proclaimed, "In a very hideous and damaging way, they have attempted to speak of Mark Fuhrman with the most vicious of allegations concerning racism."[28]

Subsequent revelations that Fuhrman not only lied about his use of the word "nigger" but also bragged about engaging in gross police misconduct were simply cabined and excised from the case.

Clark's decision to prop up Fuhrman, along with other decisions that the prosecution made, revealed the extent to which police practices that breed mistrust within the African-American community are so woven into the fabric of criminal justice that pulling this thread might cause an entire case to unravel. It also illustrates yet another dichotomous relationship between a reform-based ideology and underlying realities, in this instance, between the ideology of tight bureaucratic and constitutional control of the police and actual police practices on the ground. In this sense, the courtroom performance of "appropriate police procedures" parallels with the performance of "colorblindness." Indeed, the constitutional and bureaucratic rules applicable to police procedures grew out of a reformist project that developed simultaneously with liberal race reform. Yet like colorblindness, these reforms are honored principally through a discursive performance that sharply diverges from the underlying realities.

Efforts to subject police procedures to constitutional norms grew out of a broader project of state modernization. Within the context of policing, the objectives of modernization involved reducing arbitrary police power and making policing less dependent on sheer violence. Courts issued constitutional rule designed to curb police brutality and unchecked investigatory powers. Constitutional rules mandated that police follow specific investigatory procedures, provide legal representation at defendants' requests, respect limitations on searches and seizures, and maintain strict limitations on the use of deadly force. Additional bureaucratization brought into play greater reliance on scientific evidence in criminal proceedings and a greater investment in rehabilitation over retribution. Like colorblindness, rhetorical adherence to the rules of constitutionally imposed restraints has been largely successful. Yet such rhetoric is belied by the everyday practices of "modernized" policing along with the prosecutorial reliance on the fruits of these practices. It seems to be taken for granted that on one hand, there are elaborate rules constraining police prerogatives, and that on the other, such rules often appear to be disregarded.

This contradiction between rhetoric and reality was rather amazingly revealed by the police investigation and their subsequent testimony in the Simpson case. Given the department's recognition from the very start that this would be a high-profile case, it stands to reason that the officers would investigate this one "by the book." But the pattern of shading the formal rules seems to have been so deeply ingrained that the investigators appeared to have forgotten what the book actually required. This is most obvious in the detectives' warrantless entry into Simpson's estate. Vannatter's later application for a search warrant—filed several hours after the police had occupied Simpson's property—was based on inaccuracies that were bound to come out in the subsequent trial. As the defense later uncovered, the police investigation was full of other irregularities—some of them of constitutional magnitude, others which seemed to compromise the most basic rules of investigatory integrity. If only to avoid embarrassment, it would seem that investigators minimally accustomed to following basic procedural rules would have proceeded much more carefully.

Although the officers' on-site investigation diverged from the constitutional and bureaucratic commands of police procedure, their courtroom testimony reflected a full awareness of the performative aspect of the relevant rules. Indeed, Vannatter's testimony regarding the warrantless search fell within the very narrow exceptions to a warrantless entry, provided his testimony was believed.

It is doubtful, of course, that anyone believed his story, just as it was doubtful that anyone believed Fuhrman's testimony regarding his use of a racial epithet. But the circumstances seemed to require that everyone (except, of course, the defense) act as though they did, or else key evidence in the case would have been thrown out. Thus, Clark's over-the-top defense of Fuhrman was joined by yet another implausible declaration of rule compliance and police credibility.

One might wonder, nonetheless, why Marcia Clark risked putting Fuhrman on the witness stand in the first place, thus placing the prosecution's case in unnecessary jeopardy. One might also wonder how any credit was ever given to the implausible claim made by Detectives Vannatter and Lange that their initial decision to leave a fresh crime scene and rush over to

Simpson's estate was prompted by their desire to inform Simpson of his ex-wife's death and subsequently to intervene in a possible assault in progress. Indeed, jurors have indicated that many
of their doubts rested with the prosecution's straight-faced
reliance on doubtful police testimony. Forewoman Armanda
Cooley expressed the doubts of many jurors who questioned
Vannatter's testimony: "Why would he even get up there with
that lie? Why didn't he just tell the truth? Don't tell me you're
going to go to the house because you think maybe the same
thing is happening over on Rockingham and you're concerned
about the Rockingham family. And then the first person you
send in the door is the daughter. If you're so concerned, you're
the police, why don't you walk through the door with your guns
drawn saying what the spiel is you give."[29] Defense team member
Alan Dershowitz had earlier prompted a storm of controversy
by suggesting that "testilying" was a common practice among
police.[30] Yet the relative ease with which the police told, the
prosecution presented, and the judge accepted so implausible a
story seems to affirm that "testilying" is so institutionalized and
so taken for granted that everyone involved in the criminal justice process must be willing to suspend their disbelief and act as
if these stories were plausible.

It is here that the failed project of color-blind race reform
converges with the limited scope of police constraint. One of the
reasons why testilying is a workable way to resolve the contradiction between the rhetoric and reality of modern policing is that
support for police reform was always tempered by the fear that
such constraints might compromise the effectiveness of police in
containing crime. In light of the limited ideological and material
scope of race reform, the concrete fear of crime continues to
reflect a racial dimension. The problem of testilying, by contrast,
raises few concerns among the elite and other populations who

are largely exempt from police procedures or have so rarely been subjected to them that they have little personal concern about the threat such practices represent.

Thus, the viability of testilying as a means of resolving what to many seem to be conflicting demands upon the police reflects particular relations of race and class power. Race figures prominently in this equation by investing police with a formal credibility that trumps the testimony of many African Americans and others who are most likely to be familiar with the realities of an unpoliced police force.

The formal commands of constitutional protection and fairness are thus honored through a superficial performance that frequently involves the police, the district attorney, and the judge. The likelihood that this courtroom script diverges substantially from what actually happens outside usually warrants little commentary. Yet in the context of the Simpson case, the business as usual attitude of the police and prosecutors no doubt contributed to the reasonable doubts of the jury. Indeed, two distinct features of this case proved to be fatal to the prosecution's fortunes: first, a jury that was unlikely to suspend its disbelief of implausible narratives, and second a defendant with enough financial resources to uncover the many divergences between the courtroom script and the actual investigation.

Within this context, the role that Assistant District Attorney Christopher Darden played deserves closer scrutiny.

Assistant District Attorney Christopher Darden's own portrayal in this debacle is particularly remarkable because it weaves together a chaotic mélange of his many attempts to reconcile his desire to win this case with his intimate knowledge of police irregularities and his foreboding sense that both Fuhrman and Vannatter were disasters waiting to happen.[31] This early knowledge is particularly remarkable in light of Darden's subsequent condemnation of the very jury that he knew would doubt the credibility of Fuhrman and Detective Philip Vannatter. Darden understood, perhaps more than his colleagues, why the jury might be wary of Fuhrman and also doubt the veracity of the other officers. Darden had previously investigated police misconduct and had struggled to prosecute LAPD officers who had committed the kind of police abuses Fuhrman was accused of. Moreover, Darden acknowledged the possibility that his colleagues might have used him as a tool to bolster the credibility of a controversial witness to preclude a potentially negative jury reaction. Recounting Clark's decision to assign both Fuhrman and Vannatter to him, Darden responded,

> Damn. We had talked about this, but to hear it was like getting kicked. Those two were the most controversial witnesses in the case, the two who could turn the case, lose it for us.[32]

Considering the possibility that the assignment was part of the prosecution's own racial strategy, Darden remembers wondering

> if my colleagues thought they could "sneak" Fuhrman and Vannatter through by giving them to the black guy. Did they think black jurors were so stupid that they would believe any witnesses I presented just because I was black too? It was ludicrous. Black jurors would do what any black person would do, what any person would do. They would evaluate the testimony and—if they didn't believe a witness—it wouldn't matter if Martin Luther King put him on the stand. The only thing that having me "sneak" these witnesses would accomplish is that the jury would

decide I was being used and I would lose any credibility I had in front of them.[33]

Notwithstanding this momentary lucidity, Darden ultimately rejected the possibility that his colleagues had used him in their own strategic race play.[34] As a consequence, Darden's clear recognition that jurors would not buy the Fuhrman whitewash was wholly jettisoned in Darden's postverdict condemnation of the jury. His candid assessment of the jury's likely reaction to his role was either forgotten or dismissed, perhaps as a consequence of his confidence in Clark's integrity.[35]

Convinced that Fuhrman was lying about his use of the epithet, Darden eventually declined to examine him, but was nonetheless satisfied when they managed to keep out damaging information about him.[36]

Darden's argument to Judge Lance Ito concerning the inadmissibility of Fuhrman's use of racial epithets hinted at his ultimate rejection of the jury as blinded and incompetent. In trying to "save" the case by suppressing evidence of Fuhrman's racism, Darden argued before Judge Ito, and seemingly to the world, that the African-American jurors would be so blinded by the epithet that they would be unable to evaluate the evidence rationally. If testimony that Fuhrman had used the epithet were admitted, Darden argued, "It [would] blind this jury. It [would] blind them to the truth. They won't be able to discern what is true and what is not. It [would] affect their judgment. It [would] impair their ability to be fair and impartial."[37]

This thinking prompted Richard Yarborough, an English professor at UCLA, to comment, "To suggest [that] black people are so sensitive to the term they are disabled is extraordinary."[38]

In replying to Yarborough's observation, Darden explained:

Yes, that was extraordinary. And it wasn't what I said. I had to argue that jurors would lose focus, that the case would turn into a race case, that the entire trial would be diverted from Simpson to Fuhrman. And, as far as I could tell, that was exactly what happened.

However, Darden's own statement supports Yarborough's analysis. Arguing that the jurors would "lose focus" merely upon hearing a racist epithet is tantamount to arguing that they would be disabled. Moreover, Darden's logic explicitly delegitimized black subjectivity where it diverged from that of whites, thereby anticipating the disparaging postverdict attack on the jury after the verdict. Yet, despite Darden's deployment of a racially derogatory contention designed to facilitate the prosecution's interests, Darden was not condemned as playing a race card by pundits and critics. Instead, some pundits viewed his argument as a heroic attempt to save the case from the threat of black irrationality, or an emotional "acting out."

In making this argument, Darden managed to gain credibility as a black insider while crossing the very boundaries that he claimed other African Americans could not. He directly invoked his own identity as an African American to authorize his claim that blacks just can't see straight when they hear the word "nigger." Yet he, apparently, was immune to this group-based impairment, perhaps due to some special knowledge or a higher moral commitment to justice. Indeed, Darden reveals that he assumed the mantle of the truth-telling insider who alone could decode and thwart the defense's attempt to send a secret message to the jury. In Darden's view, it was his willingness to call a spade a spade that contributed to Cochran's unprincipled assault on him. "I had truth on my side, all right. That's why the defense had to come after me. I was standing up alone, screaming, 'This is going to be a race case.' "[39] Indeed, the tragedy, as told in Darden's account of the trial, was that despite his heroic efforts he was unable to save justice from being devoured by uncontrollable racial sentiments unscrupulously released by Cochran and company.

Darden's heroism as the lone black defender of justice was further invoked in his portrayal of a jury so revealed racially myopic that they could not begin to empathize with the victims. Said Darden, "Throughout, we read in their faces a lack of sympathy for Nicole Brown. We were reminded every day that idealism and tolerance aren't always welcome in the real world."[40] As evidence of this hardened attitude he complained that when the graphic crime-scene photos were displayed, "O.J. Simpson turned away. Denise Brown wiped her eyes; Tanya Brown covered hers. Kim Goldman began crying. The jurors looked on impassively."[41]

Darden unwittingly revealed his own compromised position as he wrapped himself up in a discourse of justice, unaware that his simultaneous behind-the-scenes commentary revealed that his journey to justice is perfectly compatible with propping up perjuring police officers, insulating them from attack, and building a case on their testimony. In order to prevail, Darden had to rely on, indeed, even hope for, success in presenting untrustworthy cops as credible. He thus participated in the very institutionalization of police dishonesty that compromised the integrity of the case against Simpson. Darden seemed to jettison his personal and professional concerns with such dishonesty. Commenting on Clark's temporarily successful presentation of Fuhrman as an honest cop, Darden confessed, "We all felt great. The day was almost over and Fuhrman was handling F. Lee Bailey easily."[42]

Darden was fully aware, however, that allegations about Fuhrman's racism were probably true. Although it was a truth he was prepared to suppress in the courtroom, it was one that he was willing to toy with outside the purview of the jurors.[43]

> The detective sat leaning against the jury box during a recess. I whispered to Marcia, "Follow my lead." I put my arm around her shoulder and pulled her head to rest on my chest, and we walked in Fuhrman's direction. His face turned bright red and he stared at us.
>
> "What are you doing having that guy hanging all over you like a cheap suit?" Fuhrman asked Marcia after I'd left. I took it very seriously; perhaps Mark Fuhrman hadn't changed after all.[44]

Yet nothing about this encounter prompted Darden to reassess the propriety of attempting to whitewash a person whom both Darden and Clark knew to be racist.[45]

Despite Darden's past efforts to challenge both the dishonesty and the racism within the LAPD, the institutionalized expectations and the particular hand he was dealt in this case proved to be difficult for him to negotiate. In this sense, one could construe Darden as having been institutionally entrapped. Caught on the one hand between the institutional expectations that he would perform "as if" colorblindness and constitutional proceduralism prevailed and on the other hand, a profound and troubling recognition that there were dimensions of this case that clearly belied this claim, Darden was understandably frustrated.

Although Darden's very public entrapment was obviously quite difficult to negotiate, his position was not unlike that of any number of African-American professionals subject to the demands of being a team player within institutions where the rules of the game seem to require a painful silence about the racial dynamics of the institutional project. Yet empathy for

Darden's difficult position ends precisely where he reduces the complexity of the case and his role in it to a singular and simplistic attack on the black jurors. To be sure, Darden's disappointment in the verdict was to be expected given his sincere belief, shared, in fact, by many other African Americans, that Simpson did murder Nicole Brown Simpson and Ronald Goldman. Others—including some of the much maligned black jurors—understood the verdict as reflecting not so much Simpson's innocence but serious prosecutorial problems produced by slipshod investigatory practices and incredible police testimony. Yet Darden heaped the entire responsibility for the disappointing outcome on the easiest target—the largely black, female jury. It is as if Darden dished up a meal with an obvious contaminant in it and hurled insults at the jury for their refusal to swallow it.

Darden's crusade against the putative black bias that corrupted the verdict is not only unfortunate, it is also wide of the mark. One would have hoped that given his unique position as a prosecutor intimately familiar with two basic realities in criminal law—that money talks and that police do not always do what they are supposed to do—he would direct his energies toward working for the institutional reforms more likely to instill confidence in the police across all sectors of American society. One doesn't need the discourse of "empty payback" and unresolvable racial divide to push this agenda forward. Indeed, it seems hard to fathom why Darden, given the misfortune of his own institutional entrapment, would not seek to explain to those who were similarly disappointed by the verdict that this outcome constitutes further evidence that the system desperately needs fixing. And rather than positioning the black jurors as irrational racialists, he could effectively amplify the argument made by Dershowitz and others that the problem cannot go away as long as prosecutors and other actors in the criminal process continue to hide behind dubious courtroom performances.

Re-racing: "Ideological Re-envisioning and the White Riot"

The intense emotional reaction to an apparently unexpected verdict prompted a critique of the jury that was articulated in terms that recall formally rejected antiblack stereotypes. Experts, commentators, and laypersons alike described the jury as lawless, immature, emotional, and irrational. As George Will revealed:

> There was condescension, colored by racism, in some of the assumptions that the jurors would be incompetent jurors and bad citizens—that they would be putty in the hands of defense attorneys harping on race, that they would be intellectually incapable of following an evidentiary argument, lack the civic conscience to do so. But those assumptions seem partially validated by the jury's refusal to even deliberate.[46]

In reproducing these racial stereotypes, it appeared that the formal rejection of white supremacy's racial binarisms, along with Simpson's acceptance in the "neutral" world of white culture, was conditional and ultimately revocable.

Chris Darden's denunciation of the jury in similar terms was all the more damning (and self-elevating) due to his racial insider status:

> Should I say that, above all, I was ashamed of a jury that needed just four hours to dismiss the lives of two people

and a year's work, a jury that picked a dreadful time to seek an empty payback for a system of bigotry, segregation, and slavery?[47]

Darden's own mistakes, although readily admitted, did little to temper his criticism of the jury. He continued:

What could I say to Nicole and Ron? That I was sorry their murderer went free because of the deep chasm that racism and slavery have carved in this country? That I was sorry that Johnnie Cochran had dragged them into that dark pit? That I was sorry about the gloves and the other mistakes I had made?[48]

These very mistakes that so distressed Darden did little to dissuade him from ultimately laying responsibility for the acquittal at the feet of jurors. Marcia Clark echoed the same theme, broadening her attack on the jury to include even colorblind liberals. In her own version of racial realism, she complained, "Liberals don't want to admit [that] a majority black jury won't convict in a case like this."[49]

Much of the reaction was organized around paternalistic themes that sounded the note of disapproving parents of irresponsible children. Stock racial images grounded antidemocratic sentiments that blatantly condoned the circumvention of black decision making and anticipated the "correct" decision of a more reasonable (and white) Westside jury. Like juveniles, African Americans were to be divested of discretion until they learned how to exercise authority responsibly.

The level of apoplectic outrage was remarkable in light of the sober warnings throughout the trial that the verdict could go either way. Yet postverdict harangue against the jury continued to rehash what the prosecution had claimed to be a mountain of evidence that should have proved Simpson's guilt beyond a reasonable doubt. Indeed, as even Darden admitted, the prosecution was hoping for a few holdouts; conviction was by most accounts highly improbable. The prosecution's chief strength was an impressive array of scientific evidence—DNA tests confirming that Simpson's blood was found at the Bundy address, and that Goldman's and Brown's blood were found in Simpson's Bronco and on socks and gloves recovered from Simpson's estate. Yet despite claims that this apparently solid evidence rendered any doubt about Simpson's guilt simply unreasonable, pundits warned long before the jury retired that the evidence was convincing only to the extent that the jury had confidence in its integrity. There were, of course, weaknesses in the prosecution's case. Taking into consideration an unconvincing and credibly contested time line that the prosecution seemed (unnecessarily) wedded to, an incomplete narrative of domestic violence that was abandoned early in the case, the inexplicably varying concentrations of DNA in Simpson's blood, found at the crime scene, the presence of preservatives found in the disappearing/reappearing socks, the unauthorized transportation of Simpson's blood back to Rockingham, recorded irregularities in the harvesting and preservation of blood samples, the last minute explanation for Simpson's missing blood, and, of course, a glove that didn't fit, the proof of Simpson's guilt beyond a reasonable doubt was, as the experts acknowledged, not as open and shut as laypersons might have believed. Indeed, although some commentators attempted to maintain an objective attitude about the case, the most common prediction was that the jury would wind up deadlocked.

Yet despite the pundits' sportslike commentary on the strength of the prosecution's performance throughout the trial, (touchdowns, home runs, and knockouts were frequently used to keep score), trial watchers joined many Americans in expressing shock and outrage at the not-guilty verdict. Lambasting the jury for what many regarded to be a "racist decision," critics readily reduced the value of Simpson's million-dollar defense to the simple playing of the now familiar "race card." This racial interpretation, however, flies in the face of numerous facts, the least of which is that if the jurors' reaction was as simplistically race-based as some of the more outraged critics seemed to suggest, then Simpson grossly overpaid his many expert lawyers. Such simplistic criticisms failed to acknowledge that it was Simpson's resources that allowed him to capitalize on the state's mistakes. Even critics of the verdict agree that Barry Scheck and Peter Neufield's masterful dissection of the state's blood evidence was damaging. Moreover, simplistic racial explanations fail to account for the rather unremarkable fact that black juries regularly convict black defendants. Equally troubling is the rejection of numerous factors that would complicate the easy resort to racial scapegoating as the sole explanation for Simpson's acquittal. Not only were prosecution mistakes elided in this narrative of racial revenge and injustice,[50] so too was the participation of the three nonblack jurors. If the verdict was truly about black revenge for white injustice, what then explains the apparently zombielike response of the white and Latino members of the jury? As Pat Williams mused, "it's almost as though . . . the white jurors must have been mugged by the black jurors—this is clearly only racial passion."[51] Moreover, what can be said about the millions of white Americans—twenty-five percent of the white population; more whites than the *total* number of African Americans in the nation—who also agreed with the verdict? If it is implausible to believe that the three nonblack jurors—and the millions of whites and other nonblacks who were similarly unconvinced about Simpson's guilt—were acting out racial revenge rather than reasonable doubt, then we must question why similar doubts, when articulated by black jurors, were immediately denounced as biased, irrational, and lawless.

The verdict apparently caught many commentators with their color-blind shades off, for the otherwise sober voices of reason almost reflexively reproduced the very racial polarity that they had worked mightily throughout the trial to suppress. In the venting that followed the verdict, commentators not only claimed white opinion as the "public" opinion, it defined whites who supported the verdict out of the category. *Newsweek*'s Mortimer Zuckerman, for example, proclaimed in the aftermath of the trial that "(a)lmost at once it became clear that while Simpson had won with the jurors he had lost with the public—or most of it." To put a finer point on his claim, Zuckerman opined, "The white community, along with some blacks, has done what the jury failed to do: it has ostracized Simpson."[52]

To draw an analogy from America's miscegenation rules, one drop of reasonable doubt apparently makes whites black. Simultaneously, a few "responsible" blacks who did not support the jury's verdict can be figured as "right-thinking white."[53] Whites with reasonable doubts about the prosecution's case are apparently excluded from the "white reaction," or from what the public thinks.

The reaction and coverage of the reaction reveal even more about the process of racing. For example, cameras trained on blacks and whites for a "reaction" missed other possible dichotomies, particularly between men and women, or professionals and working-class people. Hence, in studying the media readings of the Simpson story we can discern how racialization occurs at the *moment* of reading itself. Additionally, the media's "racial narrative" of the events instituted itself as the discursive real, in part by subordinating other social nodes of meaning such as gender onto an overdetermined and monolithic racial narrative. There were many more factors that simultaneously operated to structure public opinion around the case than could possibly have been captured by race alone. Indeed, many of these alternative factors, such as gender and class, had been deployed earlier to mark what this case was really about; yet in the final analysis, all were abandoned in a headlong rush toward racial recrimination. The nip and tuck necessary to fit the entire picture into the narrowest of racial narratives facilitates re-racing and the vilification of the jury's verdict as the illegitimate product of a black subjectivity. Indeed, this reduction of a complex set of factors into one simplistic racial plane arguably presents precisely the evil of "playing the race card" that so many had bemoaned throughout the course of the trial. Critics might have regarded this postverdict "racing" as the most powerful of "race card" plays, devastating because few recognize the sleight of hand that shifts from the purportedly high ground of color-blindness to an old-style practice of racial blame. Yet in keeping with the redeployment of race consciousness as a discourse about black pathology and irrationality, racing reemerges in the aftermath of the trial of America's most race-neutral black, an "honest" assessment of a racial reality.

The temptation to lambaste the jury was apparently difficult for critics to resist, even for those who firmly believed that the prosecution's poor performance and judgment was inexcusable. For example, Vincent Bugliosi, the prosecutor who successfully prosecuted the Charles Manson case, was scathing in his criticism of the prosecution.[54] Yet his harsh critique of prosecutorial incompetence paled in comparison to his characterization of the jury's misdeeds. According to Bugliosi, a white jury could have compensated for the prosecution's mistakes and would have done the right thing.

Bugliosi may be correct in assuming that a white jury would have convicted Simpson, yet he fails to acknowledge that such a verdict might have itself constituted bias for the prosecution, especially given the prosecution's weak performance. Other commentators routinely compared the Simpson jury's verdict to what a more responsible Westside jury would have done without even vaguely acknowledging that the putative difference between the two not only does not render this jury's decision inherently suspect, but to the contrary, may render suspect the fictional Westside jury. Indeed, it is fair to ask why so much more criticism has been directed against black jurors (and blacks in general) for closing their minds to the possibility that Simpson might be guilty than against whites for closing their minds to the possibility that the police might have planted evidence against him whether he was ultimately guilty or not. Indeed, the largely black jury may compare favorably to the putative Westside jury. If the abysmal performance of the prosecution and the LAPD was typical, the Simpson jury might be credited for imposing higher standards on police and prosecutorial performance. As Alan Dershowitz acknowledged, "The jury is our only realistic protection against police perjury, and if black jurors are more likely than whites to be open to finding police perjury, then that is a racial 'bias' that promotes justice."[55] Elsewhere he notes:

> We were pleased that we had a largely black jury, which might be more open to arguments about police perjury, evidence tampering, and so on—arguments we believed were correct. If that is playing the race card, then the race card should be played because the fact is that police do routinely lie and do sometimes tamper with evidence, and

it is good that juries include people whose life experiences
make them receptive to these possibilities . . .[56]

Thus, as Dershowitz allows, racial difference is not inherently problematic. Moreover, difference itself is symmetrical: if
blacks and whites do interpret the evidence differently—and as
discussed above, it is easy to overstate the role that race might
have played here—white views and black views are nonetheless
equally different from one another. The distance one must travel
between the two is the same no matter the end from which one
starts. Yet in the discourse of the white riot, black subjectivity is
not only rendered as bias or a distortion that effected this particular jury, it is a problem that requires prophylactic measures
effecting the broader community.

Expressions of white outrage in the wake of the verdict
revealed the utter contingency of white commitment to the color-
blind ideal. White anger at the expression of what appeared to be
a distinctively black subjectivity apparently justified their own
rejection of colorblindness. This break with the color-blind performance was probably not surprising to many African Americans.
The tension between the high moral position of colorblindness
and the ubiquitous presence of the racially encoded discourse
around the trial was present from the start; many black commentators had acknowledged as much. Indeed, perhaps the most significant "difference" in racial attitudes concerns the differing
degrees to which the conradictions in color-blind discourses are
recognized or denied.

Yet the white riot not only marked the collapse of the
color-blind performance, but also reflected a broader receptivity
among elites to a racially explicit discourse positioning blacks as
a problem population. The reactions ranged from the moderate
proposal of black circumvention to a more reactionary response

of censure and punishment. These responses might be seen as a replay of an earlier debate concerning African Americans that was framed in the language of benign neglect on the one hand and aggressive discipline and containment on the other.

The case for circumvention was grounded in criticism of the prosecution for trying the case in a locale that was likely to produce a largely black jury. Darden himself contributed to this critique by acknowledging that "downtown" juries, by virtue of their race and class makeup, were notoriously different from Westside juries. Rather than undertaking the more difficult task of addressing the conditions that create the differing racial sensibilities that apparently contributed to the verdict, critics called for reforms to circumvent the black community. Reforms such as a nonunanimity rule were offered along with proposals to limit the discretion of prosecutors to try a case outside the jurisdiction in which the crime occurred, and proposals to ban the use of "political appeals" in closing arguments. The black circumvention theme was similarly expressed when attorneys for the Brown and Goldman families assured an angry white public that chances for a conviction in the civil trial were higher given their strategic decision to file their suit in the largely white city of Santa Monica, thereby avoiding the pesky problem of biased black jurors.[57]

The circumvention theme is not new in the repertoire of responses to white concerns about black bias in the context of certain racially charged cases. Circumvention was clearly afoot when the first Rodney King trial was moved to Simi Valley. Indeed, across the country, many of the cases involving controversial acquittals of police officers accused of unjustifiable homicide have been removed to white suburbs, effectively circumventing nonwhite decision making. Over the course of just a few weeks in November of 1996, three separate cases of police abuse involving people of color resulted in a vindication of the officers involved. In none of these cases did the aggrieved communities take part in the judgment. Responsibility for the deaths of Johnny Gammage in Pittsburgh, Pennsylvania, TyRon Lewis in St. Petersburg, Florida, and Anthony Baez in Bronx, New York, was determined by white decision makers whose distance from the "problem" was thought to render them nonbiased.[58]

The circumvention discourse following the Simpson case was unique, however, in its explicit invocation of race as the legitimate justification for the proposed actions. By contrast, the articulated rationale for the removal of the first Rodney King trial was a concern that too much pretrial publicity had compromised the officers' right to a fair trial. Of course, this argument was utterly transparent given the absolute saturation of the airwaves with the tape of the King beating. Moreover, under this argument, it would seem that the Simpson civil trial would, at minimum, have to be postponed, since any person who has not been affected in some way by the omnipresence of the Simpson trial over the last few years might be a bit too removed from the events of the day to be a useful juror. Yet at least in the King trial, as well as in the Gammage and Lewis trials, there existed a background sensibility that required that the articulated reason for the removal invoke concern about pretrial publicity rather than the avoidance of black decision making.

The color-blind justification for circumvention, as unbelievable as it was in the King, Gammage, Lewis, and Baez cases, gave way in the aftermath of the Simpson verdict to a "racial reality" bite. The frank talk supporting circumvention seems to be: "If it's gonna be done right, it's gotta be done white." The frankness of the circumvention discourse is useful in revealing the failure of the color-blind paradigm to dislodge the (usually) submerged norm of whiteness and the power relations it grounds. Difference measured from this hidden norm is marked as illegitimate bias; difference measured from black subjectivity is objectivity. In these terms, the circumvention is not regarded as an expression of sheer power; instead, it is an exercise of rationality. Difference, of course, is not inherently problematic. It is partly in recognition of the value of difference that juries are meant to be drawn from a cross section of the community. Yet difference strains at the logic of the color-blind paradigm that casts a suspicious eye on assertions and enactments of racial differences. Aggregate divergences between black and white opinion cannot be comprehended as normative within this paradigm, and thus subjective divergence is marked as bias. Because of the dramatic divergence in perspective—not explainable under a formal color-blind paradigm, it appears as bias rather than normatively—acceptable differences in viewpoint are negated. Indeed, the association between this framing of black subjective divergence with bias and lawlessness was so significant that some critics went as far as to equate the Simpson jury with the twelve white men who acquitted the murderers of Emmett Till in 1955, and the murderers of the three civil rights workers in 1964. Critics seem wholly unable to distinguish between white approval of racist murder and the presence of reasonable doubt. Yet this difference was seamlessly woven into a discourse of deviance in the postverdict recriminations.

The most troubling dimension of the postverdict racial discourse was not the collapse of the color-blind performance, but rather the manner in which the abandonment of colorblindness morphed into old-style forms of disciplinary zealotry not entirely disconnected to a lynch mob sensibility. For example, columnist Ben Stein opined that "the whites will riot the way we whites do: leave the cities, go to Idaho or Oregon or Arizona, vote for Gingrich . . . and punish the blacks by closing their day care programs and cutting off their Medicaid."[59] Another columnist reported in grave tones that a Hollywood executive planned to teach blacks a lesson by firing them from their jobs as cooks, janitors, and the like: "Let them see what Cochran can do for them," he intones. The actions of the "white rioters" were duly reported under the cover of notable and legitimate commentators who sternly reported how whites were reacting to the verdict. Such "reports" were often devoid of any critique: the transmission of the message to both blacks and whites was facilitated by the apparent disinterest of the reporter. The messenger bore no personal responsibility for the content of the message, while the speakers—the racial actors who would carry out the racial revenge—were shielded from view. The media thus became the medium for chilling racial threats that were articulated as mere descriptions of the sentiments of others. The racial backlash was presented as the sobering consequences of the verdict, facts of life that blacks now would have to confront.

In both the circumvention and the punishment discourses, black divergence from colorblindness serves to ground the legitimacy of the white reaction. This points to the ways in which the narrow vision of power underlying colorblindness facilitates reactionary politics that would no doubt trouble the elites who put the paradigm into play. This is not to say, of course, that a broader, more dynamic view of racial power would have cut such responses off at the pass; one could imagine a white riot taking place under a regime organized around a different paradigm of racial justice.

Yet the emphasis on colorblindness sets progressives back a move, as it did in the discourse surrounding the Simpson trial. Rather than beginning with an honest recognition of existing power relations and proceeding to an analysis on whether and how those relations would shape the dynamics of the case, colorblindness marginalizes progressive responses by centering the color-blind paradigm as neutral and decrying all discussions of race whether conservative or progressive as racism.

"All the Women Are Mad, and All the Blacks Are Happy . . . and Haven't We Done This One Before?"

Lurking beneath the general white riot was a gender specific discourse which added an additional element to the indictment against the verdict. Like other participants in the diatribe against the black jurors, the purported absence of color-blind justice was the offense, but among those who marched under the exclusive gender banner, the failure of the jury was not simply a wrong against "neutrality." It was specifically a wrong committed against women—in particular, victims of domestic violence. The divergence between race and gender which marked the early discourses concerning the trial was reproduced most aggressively among those who claimed that the jury's color consciousness precluded their ability to see what this case was really about, that is, violence against women. Paradigmatic of this sentiment was Tammy Bruce, president of the L.A. chapter of NOW, who, invoking "the bodies of Ron and Nicole . . . rotting in their graves," claimed:

> This case was not about race. It was about domestic violence . . . This jury decided to not do what it was impaneled to do. They decided these two lives were expendable, and they decided to move through the hatred and bigotry

that Johnnie Cochran asked them to. And they are ... an embarrassment to this city. ...

They became a jury of Mark Fuhrmans, of people who cared nothing for justice.[60]

Bruce did not stop there. In a later discussion on *Nightline*, she asserted, "what we need to teach our children is ... not about racism, but is about violence against women." A focus on domestic violence would, moreover, provide, "a needed break from all that talk of racism."[61]

To NOW's great credit, President Patricia Ireland condemned Bruce in stern terms:

> These statements have blotted NOW's otherwise impressive record of committed activism in the fight for racial justice and equality. It pains me that these unfortunate and unwise comments have tainted NOW's reputation and our relationships with people of color and our social justice allies.[62]

Despite the specific censuring that Bruce received, and the rather obvious tone of her later gaffe—a comment that she did not have the time to discuss domestic violence "with a bunch of black women"—Bruce believes that her crusade is grounded in a legitimate and defensible color-blind vision. Refusing to apologize for her remarks, Bruce stated, "There is nothing to retract. I have made it clear that this issue affects all women, including women of color. Of course, this issue is colorblind."[63]

While Bruce was certainly the most inflammatory of the feminist critics, she was certainly not alone in expressing absolute bewilderment at what was presented as the inexplicable blindnesses of black women. Columnist and law professor Susan

Estrich, for example, found the celebration of black women "unbelievably troubling."

> I mean, I watched pictures of black women cheering this verdict, and I thought to myself, how can they cheer. Don't they know that they will be and they are on the receiving end of this kind of garbage?[64]

The Bruce narrative, along with more moderate feminist objections to the pro-Simpson black women, exemplifies how the absence of an intersectional orientation regarding race and gender can produce politically counterproductive discourses. These responses to black women's support of Simpson raise problems on at least two levels. First, at a rhetorical level, they completely reinforce the standard polarizations of race and gender that proved so unproductive in the Thomas/Hill hearings. By this account of the Simpson case, race and gender were locked in a zero/sum game in which a win for blacks was a loss for women, and vice versa. Of course, the second problem is obvious: this vision either erases black women, or alternatively, positions black women as simplistically and unjustifiably race-conscious.

Within the context of the Simpson verdict, the race consciousness among African-American women, rather than the institutionalized practices of marginalizing women and domestic violence, authorized this affront to women. While the jurors' verdict itself bore no inherent dimensions of black women blindly loyal to the home team, critics wedded images of battered black women celebrating Simpson's release to the fact that the jury that acquitted Simpson was largely black and female to support a claim that black women "just don't get" gender. Thus, black women became the target of *some* expressions of white female rage.

On one hand, this expression of frustration leveled against black women should come as no surprise. Feminists—white and African American—have been discussing and debating the nature of the tension between black and white women for years. There is, however, a subtle difference in the register and the direction of the articulation of this tension in the aftermath of the verdict. It is almost a common expression to hear African-American women say to white women, in one way or another, "you don't represent us." The standard response, politely but sometimes dismissively articulated, is usually, "why we certainly intend to, and we will make every effort to be more inclusive in the future." In this context, however, the dialogue is a bit more like white women declaring to the black female jurors, "You didn't represent us!" and the black women saying, "We never said we would!"[65]

This admittedly reductive account obviously belies enormous complexities not only in what the verdict represented, but most important, in what the raced *and* gendered reaction to the verdict reveals. Indeed, it is simply not news to say that there is and has been a gulf between black women and white women, a gulf that extends to those white feminists who invoke "all women" as their constituency and black women who do not connect with the standard white feminist agenda. But the Simpson case and its aftermath raise important questions about how the gulf is constituted and what its implications are with respect to ongoing efforts to ground antiracist and feminist politics in a manner that emphasizes the intersections of systems of power rather than one that endorses notions of mutual exclusivity. White feminists often agree with African-American feminists on this point in principle (which is frankly more than what can be said of African-American male leadership), but in the messy trenches of real politics, that vision is easily obscured. The difficulty is complicated, moreover, by the obvious fact that there is something behind the reluctance of many African-American women to endorse feminism; but that something is certainly more complex than the simplistic and self-promoting discourse forwarded publicly by Bruce and, more than likely, endorsed privately by others.

In order to validate the targeting of Bruce's rage against the black female jurors, one would have to believe that it was widely understood that this case was really about domestic violence, other juries not blinded by race would have seen it that way, and that this jury's refusal to convict Simpson was simply an inexcusable act of choosing race over gender. Under this view, the role of broad institutional patterns of marginalizing women fade, and black people end up being the source of resistance against the urgency of addressing the tragedy of domestic violence.

These premises are faulty.

First, even those closest to the prosecution's case did not, initially, understand this case to be about domestic violence. None other than Denise Brown, Nicole's sister, who later testified to witnessing several episodes of spousal abuse between the Simpsons, told the *New York Times* that Nicole "was not a battered woman. My definition of a battered woman is somebody who gets beat up all the time. I don't want people to think it was like that. I know Nicole. She was a very strong-willed person. If she was beaten up, she wouldn't have stayed with him. That wasn't her. Everybody knows about 1989. Does anybody know about any other time?"[66] Denise was not alone in doubting the relevance of domestic violence in the murder. Lead prosecutors Clark and Darden initially approached the case as a standard murder without any domestic violence overtones. As Darden tells it, in the hustle and bustle of the formative period in building the prosecution's case, the district attorney's domestic violence experts waited for days to lobby the head prosecutors to focus on domestic violence. In the end, they literally camped out in Darden's office to win an audience with Clark and Darden.

Of course, Brown, Clark, or Darden should not be singled out for their initial failure to conceive of Nicole Brown Simpson as a battered woman. This failure to perceive battering is itself a feature of this pressing social problem. Indeed, Hertz officials might well have been speaking for the majority of Americans when it proclaimed that "[w]e regard it as a private matter to be treated as such between O.J.'s wife and the courts."[67] This tolerant approach to Simpson's battering was a reflection not only of his celebrity status, but also of a broader societal attitude which was reflected in the criminal disposition of this case.

Thus, if black female jurors approached the case with an orientation that was unsympathetic to the prosecution's efforts to tie the murders to domestic violence, they certainly were not alone in this regard. Yet the rhetoric of blame would suggest that the jurors rejected the domestic violence frame as a reflection of a simplistic racial disposition against it.

The indictment against the jury also overlooks obvious weaknesses in the prosecution's presentation of the domestic violence evidence. Indeed, these jurors saw little that would have significantly altered any predisposition to see the domestic violence incident from 1989 as marginal to the case. Even Darden admits that the domestic violence evidence was not convincingly presented. Coming in essentially as an afterthought, the prosecution then led with the history of abuse, organized around the metaphor of a long fuse that eventually exploded on the night of June 12. From the jury's vantage point, however, the fuse fizzled out, as much of the evidence promised was never introduced to the jury. The prosecution's case was further weakened when

Judge Ito sanctioned the prosecution for failing to meet their obligations to turn over their witness list to the defense. They were then forced to hold their domestic violence witnesses until the end of their case. By that time, the case had dragged on too long and Darden, who would have been the lead counsel on this issue, had already lost considerable credibility within the prosecutorial team in the aftermath of the failed glove demonstration.

The tremendous outpouring of support for the prosecution and the harsh criticism against the verdict can be marshalled as evidence that the case dramatized to an uneducated public the magnitude of domestic violence. Tammy Bruce rode high in the saddle of this rage, declaring that Simpson was not welcome in Los Angeles and was not welcome "in our culture." To be sure, many Los Angelenos did in fact isolate Simpson, and those who could *did* drive him out of their milieu. But it is doubtful that the rejection of Simpson stands as a statement of society's intolerance of batterers. Indeed, the flames of this reaction seemed to be stoked less by concerns about domestic violence per se, and more by the strong belief among many that a guilty man went free and used his race (and money) to do it.[68]

The case was not, therefore, a massive teach-in about domestic violence, despite the number of people who are convinced of Simpson's guilt. Clearly, millions of Americans thought Simpson guilty, but it is doubtful that their beliefs were informed by a new understanding of domestic violence. The case remains amenable to any number of narrative frames that are only remotely enlightening with regard to domestic violence. For example, older man/younger woman, "has-been" sports hero/woman in her prime, Othello/Desdemona—all these long-standing narratives figured in various accounts of the case, yet none of them necessarily reflects any substantial shift in the public perception about domestic violence.

The polarization between the racial solidarity line and the domestic violence line as an overlay for pro-acquittal versus pro-conviction opinion is further refuted by the fact that among those who also supported the verdict were no doubt millions of whites whose support has little to do with blind racial solidarity. In fact, there are probably many men of all races who probably sympathized with Simpson's rage at the thought of losing his young wife to a man half his age. One writer captured this male rage in a friend's reaction to Simpson's initial arrest:

> "THAT ... THAT ... THAT ... (expletive)," he shouted about Nicole Simpson. "Look what she's done to O.J., spending all his money, letting that young guy drive Juice's Ferrari. How'd she think he'd react? What did she think would happen?"[69]

Thus, critics who frame the verdict in terms that position the jury's lack of colorblindness against the preferred vision of gender consciousness are themselves engaged in an interpretive process that simply collapses complex issues of gender into a singular dimension of race. Ironically, this is precisely what they have claimed the jury has done.

A more complicated and useful analysis can, however, proceed from the claim that black women deliberately and self-consciously chose race over gender. Many black women did credit Simpson's potential victimization by police more readily than Nicole Brown Simpson's victimization by Simpson. This race over gender line, of course, is not new. But the problem—and the solution—is far more complex than some exasperated white feminists would admit.

As an initial matter, the analysis must move beyond the reductive dimension of the "race over gender" rhetoric which obscures more than it illuminates. This oft-repeated claim distorts the fact that race and gender figured on both sides of the acquittal-conviction debate. It is thus simply unrevealing to say that the black women who celebrated Simpson's acquittal were chosing race over gender. To the extent that the reactions of some African-American women can be read as signaling something deeper than celebrating the acquittal of a man they believed to be "not guilty," they were expressing an identification of interest with a particular configuration of race and gender over a different one. To fail to acknowledge the intersection of race and gender in shaping the symbolic appeal of Simpson on the one hand, and Nicole Simpson on the other, is to take black maleness as representing "race" and white femaleness as representing "gender." This conceptual and political mistake simply replicates the domination within race and gender discourses of black men and white women, respectively.[70]

This reductive framing also obscures the extent to which the choices presented marginalize black women from the very start. From the celebrants' vantage point, their *own* configuration of race and gender—that of a black female—provided no subject position or narrative structure to choose. Thus, identification with the figure that most closely symbolizes their sense of shared oppression was almost inevitable. Among those who made a choice, the identification with Simpson was far from inexplicable.

My goal here is not to glibly explain away the battered women who cheered Simpson's acquittal. Instead, it is to bring into sharper relief the suppressed dimensions of "race versus gender" construction in order to replace with more sober analysis the widespread pejorative denunciation of many black women's political allegiances. The "they don't get it" critique of black women presumes that there is a clear answer to the ques-

tion of whether black women should align themselves with black
men or white women in matters relating to sexual abuse and violence. This is, however, an enormously complicated issue in
which the better option of black women identifying with themselves is marginalized from the very beginning. The debate is also
off center in that it equates the frequently distinct practices of
racism and sexism. For example, racial oppression involves state
repression and policing that has historically incorporated within
its logic specific narratives connecting black criminality with
deviant sexuality. Racism has thus been exercised and constituted
through expressions of state power, often through the police and
the courts. The logic of patriarchy works to marginalize domestic violence and other forms of sexual abuse through a discourse
of privacy. Thus, the state's relation to gender power has traditionally been expressed through a failure to intervene against
patriarchal power expressed in the putatively private sphere.

In the absence of discourses that center specifically on
black women, an important and unresolved question is whether
the oppression of black women is more closely linked to the
policing of black men within the public sphere or the marginalization of white women within the private sphere. Gender solidarity with white women requires a primary identification with
the private and personal over the public and collective group
struggle. When forced to choose, it is not entirely clear which is
the primary locus of black women's disempowerment.

The reality is that both dimensions of disempowerment
shape the lives of African-American women. When these analyses are not readily intersected, or when the symbols which render
them mutually exclusive remain stubbornly resistant to representation, it is neither irrational nor morally reprehensible for
African-American women to choose primary identification with
one configuration over the other.

This analysis is not meant to deny the presence of varying degrees of hostility between black women and white women. Moreover, this tension is likely reflected in some of the attitudes held by some black women against Marcia Clark as well as Nicole Brown Simpson. The "Angels Wings" representation of Nicole probably struck a particular sour note among some black women in that its construction of Nicole as an essential innocent is belied by the fact that Nicole first came into Simpson's life as the teen-aged "other woman" who eventually replaced Simpson's African-American wife.[71] Other factors may also have distanced black women from Nicole. Evidence that Nicole was violent toward her domestic help certainly did little to seal any gender bond between Nicole and many black women, nor to support the impression of Nicole's essential innocence. Moreover, Nicole's casting in many media as "stunning blond," half of a "dazzling couple" made palpable to many the tyranny of racially skewed aesthetic standards that predetermined that most African-American women not be similarly regarded.

This rejection of the angelic positioning of Nicole in death is by no means an endorsement of her murder. Instead, it is simply a recognition that many African-American women may be less likely to allow the tragedy of her death to work backward to sanitize her life. Nor were they likely to identify with her solely on the basis of a shared identity as women. It seems therefore undeniable that Nicole's whiteness had some bearing on the likelihood that black women would take up the implicit invitation to read themselves into the tragedy as stand-ins for Nicole. They were more likely to relate to the narrative in a number of other ways. The reasons for this, however, are more complex than the simple frames of "racism" or "blind loyalty" reveal.

To read this case as indicative of whether black women "get" gender also participates in the same color-blind perfor-

mance that suppressed and distorted so many other dimensions
of the case. Irrelevant in the color-blind field of vision are obvious historic and social factors that tell much more about why
many black women identified primarily with Simpson. When
one squarely confronts the fairly different narrative frames of
first, "the black man caught within a potentially racist criminal
proceeding" and second, "the white woman brutalized by her
black obsessor," it seems obvious why one appears to be more
compelling than the other. This choice thus should not be cast
to support a definitive inference that black women are neither
engaged with nor concerned about gender domination.

There are, however, other high-profile cases that do suggest
that the many black women approach gender politics hesitantly,
and may well be overly loyal to black men by virtue of the "black
man caught in the racist criminal justice" frame. The gendered
deployment of racial solidarity has led many African-American
men and women to support Mike Tyson, Mel Reynolds, and
Clarence Thomas.

The Simpson case, however, did not produce the same
explicit articulation of a male-centered racial solidarity that
characterized debates within the community around the Tyson
rape trial or the Thomas confirmation hearings. In those earlier
cases, the presence of a black woman in both dramas forced
those who sought to defend the men in the name of racial solidarity to articulate exactly why the women were not also deserving of black support and concern. Racial solidarity, when
invoked in cases involving contests between black men and black
women, has tracked familiar patterns of privileging males even
in cases involving black men and black women. In these contexts,
a vision of a common struggle against racism was evoked that
typically focused on black male victimization by judicial and
extrajudicial practices while completely marginalizing the strug-

gles of black women against violence, both intraracial as well as interracial. The repetition of these male-centered narratives in African-American political memory contrasts with the relative absence of clear symbols of the particular dynamic of the oppression of black women.

The Clarence Thomas/Anita Hill, Mike Tyson/Desiree Washington, and Mel Reynolds/Beverly Heard controversies are thus texts that present a clearer basis for revealing and politicizing black women's orientation toward gender in that they present the possibility of identification with a race and gender configuration that does not elevate maleness or whiteness over black femaleness. A critique of gender consciousness within the black community generally, and an effort to politicize gender among black women in particular, would be far more productive if grounded in these contestations rather than in the context of a highly charged trial that features virtually all of the symbols of racial injustice that have shaped antiracist resistance discourses for generations.

White feminists are not without their own need to interrogate the way race may have mobilized sentiment and shaped identification with Nicole within the white community. The unrelenting references to Nicole as being the victim of "Othello's" rage suggest repeatedly that a driving feature of the white public's fascination and outrage was linked to the specter of interracial sex and death.[72]

Indeed, it may be that the racial dimension of the verdict shaped not only the response of the general public, but also the reactions of those more intimately associated with domestic violence. The media's report of widespread panic among victims of violence and some of their advocates seemed at some level to contain a racial element. Among some, it seemed that the outrage was not simply that a batterer may have gotten away with

murder, but that this particular batterer had gotten away, send-
ing an amplified message. This "message" was evidenced in one
paper that found it so compelling that it became the lead in a
story about how battered women's shelters were coping with the
"blow" of the verdict. The story invoked the harrowing tale of a
doctor's wife, a woman "who wore the clothes of upper-class
affluence—and the lumps and scars of classless victimization"
who reported that her husband had declared: "If that N____R
football player got away with it, I can do anything I want to
you."[73] The Simpson verdict, of course, did not fundamentally
alter what this white doctor could and could not get away with,
which most domestic violence advocates probably understand.
Yet the doctor's purported comments, as well as the presumed
newsworthiness of them, probably speaks volumes about both
the outrage and panic that were produced by the verdict.

    Thus, it may well be that the heightened interest in domes-
tic violence prompted by Nicole Brown Simpson's murder may
have far more complicated dimensions than the Tammy Bruce
cohorts are willing to admit. Yet the racial politics of gender violence is evident within the African-American community as well.
It goes without saying that numerous rapes have occurred involving African-American women over the past several years. Yet
only two African-American women who reported being raped
managed to galvanize the black community in response: Tawana
Brawley and the black student at St. John's. The common de-
moninator in both cases: the alleged assailants were white.

    Of course, most rapes and other gender-related violence
are intraracial. Yet, until the public discourse on these issues is
explicitly recentered around this fact, efforts to politicize gender
violence will continue to be remain subsumed—either implicitly
or explicitly—within the discourse of race.

White women have as much of an interest in contesting the terms of the Simpson aftermath as do African Americans. Whether this case ended in a conviction or not probably has little bearing upon individual women or the national debate about domestic violence. The fact of the matter is that the high-profile nature of this case and its aftermath is probably contingent upon the interracial dimension of the case. Indeed, just as sexual abuse of black women becomes a political issue within the black community when the assailant is white, sexual abuse of white women garners far more public attention when the assailant is black. These vestiges of nineteenth-century patriarchy are not difficult to discern in other cases as well. Consider, for example, how quickly the story of a Boston couple, allegedly shot by a black man in a jogging suit, created a national media frenzy, especially after the mother and her fetus died. Consider as well how quickly public interest in the story collapsed once it was revealed to be a tragically routine story of intraracial marital homicide. The case still stands as a telling illustration of the role race plays in elevating the few interracial white victims of abuse and violence over the vast majority of others who are routinely assaulted intraracially.

If it is true that the racial dimension of the case contributed to its high profile, then most white women who, like black women, are more likely to be abused intraracially rather than interracially, have every reason to question the terms of the postverdict debate and to demand greater accountability on the part of police departments, as well as communities, employers, families, and the like.

A feminist antiracist politic would not only join the condemnation of police and prosecutorial practices that privilege some victims over others, but also to demand more reliable investigatory and prosecutorial practices. Whatever one thinks about the role that racism may have played in the events of June 12, it is clear that the inability of the LAPD to weed out cops like Fuhrman and to institute procedures and practices upon which juries can rely compromise any attempt to use the criminal justice system to vindicate and protect the interests of women across the board. As Patricia Ireland cogently argued:

> We say that the racism and the sexism in the LAPD was part of the problem and that if they'd implemented the Christopher Commission findings that said they should have more women and people of color on the force, it might have had a different result for lots of women whose names we don't know. And for lots of men who don't see any justice there.[74]

It is thus appropriate for organized women to incorporate within their politics a firm stance against racism and business-as-usual incompetence within the criminal justice system. While it may appear momentarily advantageous for white feminist groups to join the anti-Simpson bandwagon, that mission is likely to reveal itself to be much more grounded in racial polarization than in gender enlightenment.

The task at hand is to develop political discourses that reject the reductive either/or framing that surrounds the Simpson trial and other social controversies involving such vexed categories as race, gender, and class. Such cases call for an intersectional politics that merges feminist and antiracist critiques of institutional racism and sexism. While both feminists and civil rights activists have developed useful critiques of the issues played out in the Simpson case, there was no readily accessible framework that allowed the critiques to be aligned in a complementary rather than implicitly oppositional fashion. Feminists have long criticized institutionalized police practices, including the reluctance of police officials to take domestic violence seriously, and African Americans have consistently politicized the ways in which racist police and prosecutorial practices are normalized with the criminal justice system. These discourses, however, fell into opposition both during the trial and in the verdict's aftermath, and the mutual exclusivity of these various narratives is ultimately tied to the centrality of a paradigm that produced an ultimately flawed vision of what this case was about.

Conclusion

I am, of course, mindful that a likely response to the issues discussed herein is that none of this changes the fact that Simpson may have killed his ex-wife. Similarly, the fact that Simpson may very well have killed his ex-wife does not change the issues that I have explored herein. Indeed, this project is not animated by a belief in Simpson's factual innocence but instead by a notion that the framework through which the racial issues in this case were framed has played a central role in inaccurately constructing the jury's verdict as racial payback and a travesty of justice. In this regard, the dominant understanding of this case as the nefarious consequence of an unjustified departure from color-blindness reduces complex issues of institutional power, racially divergent subjectivities, intersections of race, gender, and class, and a host of other issues all onto a flattened plane of race. In this sense, the charge of playing the race card is itself revealed to be a race card, one that reflects a particular consciousness about race rather than a transcendence of all consciousness about race.

The reverberations of the O.J. Simpson trial will surely persist for decades, particularly given the civil suit that is pending in Santa Monica as this book goes to press. A different outcome there is likely to reinforce elite commitment to paradigms that permit mere performances of colorblindness, police accountability, and the like to serve as stand-ins for a more substantive engagement with the terms of social power in American society. In order for American society to learn from these tragic events, we must take the risk of reimagining both power and politics as they are informed by race and gender, a task that will become increasingly difficult the longer we evade its challenges.

Notes

I would like to extend my gratitude to several people who provided the research, comments, criticism, and general encouragement that made this project possible: Katherine Chung, David Cohen, Marian Crenshaw, Duncan Kennedy, Chandan Reddy, Richard Yarborough, and, of course, Toni Morrison.

1. While this is certainly not the exclusive interpretation of the Simpson verdict, it is certainly a dominant one, reproduced both in contemporaneous news coverage of the case and in the many postverdict books and retrospectives that flooded the market in the year following the criminal acquittal. Even those texts that offer a counternarrative implicitly acknowledge the dominance of the travesty critique by organizing their opposing arguments in an essentially defensive posture. Alan Dershowitz, for example, argues that his book defending the verdict is intended for "the majority of thoughtful observers who sincerely and understandably believe that O.J. Simpson killed Nicole Brown and Ronald Goldman and that the jury's verdict of 'not guilty' was therefore a miscarriage of justice." Alan Dershowitz, *Reasonable Doubts: The O.J. Simpson Case and the Criminal Justice System* (New York: Simon & Schuster, 1996), p. 16. This defensive posture is suggested in the very title of the book *Madam Foreman: Rush to Judgment?* featuring the accounts of three of the Simpson jurors.

2. Neil Gotanda, "A Critique of Our Constitution Is Colorblind," 44 *Stanford Law Review* 16 (1991).

3. Gary Peller, "Race Consciousness," *Duke Law Journal* 560 (1990), reprinted in Kimberlé Crenshaw et al., *Critical Race Theory: The Key Writings That Formed the Movement* (New York: The New Press, 1995).

4. I'm using this term to identify both the "outing"—the summoning and undiscovering of race—and its suspension.

5. Kimberlé Crenshaw, "Race, Reform and Retrenchment: Transformation and Legitimation in Antidiscrimination Law," *Harvard Law Review* 101 (1988), reprinted in Crenshaw, *Critical Race Theory*, p. 103.

6. Alan Freeman, "Antidiscrimination Law: A Critical Review," *Politics of Law* (New York: Pantheon, 1982), pp. 109–14.

7. For an excellent analysis of how whiteness has been constructed and privileged by law, see Cheryl Harris, "Whiteness as Property," 106 *Harvard Law Review* 1707 (1993), reprinted in Crenshaw, *Critical Race Theory*, p. 276.

8. For a similar use of the term "racial realism," see Derrick Bell, "Racial Realism," 24 *Connecticut Law Review* 363 (1992). Racial realism, Bell states, is a "mind-set or philosophy [that] requires us to acknowledge the permanence of our subordinate status. That acknowledgment enables us to avoid despair, and frees us to imagine and implement racial strategies that can bring fulfillment and even triumph." *Ibid.*, pp. 373–74.

9. Richard J. Herrnstein and Charles Murray, *The Bell Curve: Intelligence and Class Structure in American Life* (New York: The Free Press, 1994).

10. Matt Spetalnick, " 'Race Card' Stirs Controversy in Simpson Case," *Reuters*, October 24, 1994.

11. Along these lines, a personal favorite is "flesh tone," which is invariably white.

12. Ellis Cose, "Caught Between Two Worlds," *Newsweek*, July 11, 1994, p. 28.

13. Ron Borges et al., "O.J.—Trouble Under the Surface," *Boston Globe*, June 23, 1994, p. 1.

14. Or as one "political" observer rather inelegantly put it, "I always thought [the case] was going to be race-neutral. I thought that if anyone was going to be considered kind of a generic person rather than a—a person of color—an African American, a black person—whatever, I thought it would be O.J. Simpson. Apparently I was wrong." Geraldo Rivera, *Rivera Live*, August 17, 1994.

15. (Emphasis added.) Peter Gelzinis, "O.J. May Not Rise After His Hard Fall from Grace," *Boston Herald*, July 7, 1994.

16.   Borges, *supra* note 13.

17.   *Ibid.*

18.   *Time*, June 27, 1994. *Time* defended the photo, stating that "no racial implication was intended, by *Time* or by the artist." "Cover Wasn't Racist, *Time* Magazine Says," *Chicago Tribune*, June 25, 1994, p. 8.

19.   Not all commentators have criticized the *Time* cover. Jeffrey Toobin argued that it was blacks who made the association between the darkened picture and criminality. This rather remarkable observation is strikingly similar to the Supreme Court's observation in *Plessy v. Ferguson* that African Americans who claimed to be affronted by racial segregation were suffering from a self-inflicted injury. The *Plessy* decision attempted to turn the table on black claimants by ignoring the social circumstances that dissenting Justice Harlan said "no one should be lacking in candor to admit." Toobin similarly frames the close association between darkness and criminality as simply a black fantasy. Like the nineteenth-century justices whom Toobin echoes, one would have to be totally lacking in candor to deny the deep associations between blackness and crime to sustain Toobin's argument. Jeffrey R. Toobin, *The Run of His Life* (New York: Random House, 1996).

20.   Meri Nan-Ama Danquah, "Why We Really Root for O.J.: The Superstar Suspect Embodies the Illusion of a Colorblind America," *Los Angeles Times*, July 3, 1994. "News articles about Americans' need to create heroes paint only half of the picture. The other half perhaps is that O.J. Simpson, more than any other black hero or celebrity, embodies the idea, the dream, the illusion—call it whatever you want—that we as a nation have transcended race."

21.   The following comments on African-American responses to the O.J. Simpson "event" are purely speculative on my part and are not emperically proven. My comments are not intended to homogenize the multiplicity of responses found within African-American communities. Rather, I am attempting to understand, as I see it, the simultaneous distance many black people established with O.J. Simpson and the keen interest they showed in viewing the daily saga. As a speculative analysis, then, I would urge further inquiry into African-American interests in black celebrities in general, and how this interest shaped responses to Simpson in particular.

22.   Donn Esmond's exasperated tone was typical: "Prior to the slaughter of two people, O.J. Simpson didn't stand for much of anything in the

black community. If anything, he rendered America color-blind—admirably so. So how did he become a symbol for centuries of racial injustice? The guy was more comfortable golfing with CEOs at a private country club than I'd be. Now, to much of black America, he's a hero." Donn Esmond, "Celebration Seems Inane in Glare of Two Murders," *The Buffalo News*, October 5, 1995, p. 7A.

23. Ellis Cose, explaining why African Americans were invested and hopeful that Simpson was innocent, said, "A number of [African Americans] felt, in effect, that when you have a very visible black male who is accused of a heinous crime ... This somehow reflects on the race as a whole." *Charlie Rose*, July 7, 1994. Although he dismissed this concern as absurd, indeed, the negative reaction to the verdict does seem to suggest that there is something to the concern that the sins of some will be visited on all.

24. Jeffrey R. Toobin, in "Incendiary Defense," *The New Yorker*, July 25, 1994, p. 56.

25. *Nightline*, July 22, 1994.

26. See, e.g., Debra Saunders, "Being Branded," *Times-Picayune*, September 3, 1994.

27. See "The Simpson Legacy: Just Under the Skin; Pushed by Change, Pulled by the Past; as the LAPD Pursues Community-Friendly Policing, a Paramilitary Tradition Dies Hard," *Los Angeles Times*, October 10, 1995.

28. *California v. Simpson*, Record No. BAO 97211, 1994 WL 575824, p. *8 (Oct. 19, 1994).

29. See, e.g., Armanda Cooley et al., *Madam Foreman: A Rush to Judgment?* (Los Angeles: Dove Books, 1995), p. 100.

30. Doubts about the credibility of the police testimony were shared by nonblack jurors as well. White juror Anise Aschenbach—the juror who prosecutors probably hoped would, at minimum, give them a hung jury—indicated that she did not believe Vannatter was "playing it square." This and other doubts about the integrity of the police investigation gave her reasonable doubts. *Ibid*, p. 85. Dershowitz, *Reasonable Doubts*, p. 97. See "Why Do So Many Police Lie About Searches and Seizures? And Why Do So Many Judges Believe Them?" *Ibid.*, pp. 49–68. Dershowitz's comments, published as a *New York Times* op-ed article, were supported by numerous studies and commission reports. Yet the reaction to his op-ed was predictably "swift, vociferous, and well-orchestrated." One of the most vocal critics was Detective Van-

natter's boss, LAPD Police Chief Willie Williams, whose staged out-rage actually confirmed Dershowitz's claim that testilying is at least tolerated from on high. On the other hand, William F. Bratton, police commissioner of New York, acknowledged the institutionalization of the problem in terms that illuminated the contributing role of prose-cutors. "When a prosecutor is really determined to win, the trial prep procedure may skirt along the edge of coercing or leading the police witness. In this way, some impressionable young cops learn to tailor their testimony to the requirements of the law." *Ibid.*, p. 63.

31. "I watched all the other deputy D.A.'s smile and agree that he would make a very good witness. But I was sick. There was something about this guy." Christopher Darden, *In Contempt* (New York: Regan Books/HarperCollins, 1996), p. 199.

32. *Ibid.*, p. 188.

33. *Ibid.*, p. 189. Of course, Darden's instincts were correct. As one of the jurors recalled, "I remember thinking he was there as a token because the jury was predominantly black. I thought the prosecution felt they need this particular balance. To me this was the first race card, as it has come to be called, and it was played by the prosecution. It didn't fool me and it didn't fool a lot of other people on the jury either." See, e.g., Armanda Cooley et al., *Madam Foreman: A Rush to Judgment?* (Los Angeles: Dove Books, 1995), p. 88.

34. "One of the other clerks suggested that Marcia was dumping the worst witnesses and taking the clean ones for herself. I didn't think so. I watched how hard she worked, and knew she wouldn't back down from any witness." Darden, *In Contempt*, p. 188.

35. Darden's reaction to the jury's verdict virtually ignores the possibility that the jury simply didn't find key elements of the investigator's story credible. Instead, he fully condemned the jury, despite his own recog-nition that the case was substantially weakened by their reliance on Fuhrman. According to Darden, the verdict was simply a misplaced act of racial revenge. See the discussion on page 284.

36. "We'd done all we could to keep out the nasty baggage that he carried, to allow the jury to focus on the murder and not Fuhrman's past. We'd managed to keep out of the trial: a political cartoon from Fuhrman's desk showing a swastika rising from the ashes; unfounded allegations that he'd planted evidence; the 1980 and 1981 psychiatric reports; and a rumor that he had made a comment to a colleague about seeing Nicole

Brown's augmented breasts before she was killed. . . . Marcia was masterful with him, gentle enough to calm him down when he was jittery early in his testimony, firm enough on the details to leave no room for the defense to claim he planted evidence. It was a sharp contrast to the mistrust and discomfort with which I would have questioned Fuhrman." Darden, *In Contempt*, p. 284.

37. Darden, *In Contempt*, p. 202.

38. Lisa Resper et al., "Blacks Debate Issue of Race in Simpson Case," *Los Angeles Times*, January 15, 1995, p. 1.

39. Darden, *In Contempt*, p. 211.

40. *Ibid.*, p. 266.

41. *Ibid.*, p. 239.

42. *Ibid.*, p. 288.

43. Darden admits that "Cochran warned me three or four times. I knew they must have something on Fuhrman, but what could it be? That he had been a racist? a Nazi? Unfortunately, that wasn't enough to keep him off the stand" (Darden, *In Contempt*, p. 274). Yet a poor performance on the autopsy certainly kept the coroner off the stand. More complicated reasons for Darden's ambivalence about Cochran is suggested by the following: "I think he was honestly trying to warn me away . . . I was just as serious; I wasn't going to be limited by my race. And I wasn't going to leave Marcia in a position like that." Darden, *In Contempt*, p. 272.

44. Darden, *In Contempt*, p. 288.

45. *Ibid.*

46. George F. Will, "Circus of the Century," *Washington Post*, October 4, 1995, p. A-25.

47. Darden, *In Contempt*, supra note 25, p. 10.

48. *Ibid.*, p. 11.

49. William Claiborne, "A Majority Black Jury Won't Convict in a Case Like This," *Washington Post*, October 6, 1995, p. A-4.

50. Dershowitz gives his account of why and how the jurors probably found reasonable doubt. He first notes that the jurors simply did not believe Vannatter's statement that the police initially did not believe Simpson to be a suspect. "The jury thus started out with the realization—new, perhaps, to some; not so new to others—that these policemen were prepared to lie to them and to cover for each other, at least as to certain aspects of the case." Dershowitz, *Reasonable Doubts*, supra

note 29, p. 73. "Any reasonable juror who believed that several police officers might have lied to them about some of their actions and tampered with some evidence could not simply ignore those beliefs in assessing the rest of the evidence. All the police evidence and testimony would now come before the jurors bearing a presumption, or at the very least a suspicion, that it had been corrupted. Perhaps the prosecutors could have overcome that presumption or suspicion, but it would not have been easy. After all, policemen who are deemed willing to lie and tamper with respect to some evidence should not be deemed unwilling to lie and tamper with respect to other evidence" (p. 87).

51. The MacNeil/Lehrer NewsHour, October 4, 1995, p. 15. Transcript #5368. Educational Broadcasting and GWETA.

52. Mortimer B. Zuckerman, "The Sad Legacy of 1995," *U.S. News & World Report*, January 15, 1996, p. 68.

53. *Ibid.*

54. Vincent Bugliosi, *Outrage: The Five Reasons Why O.J. Simpson Got Away with Murder* (New York: W. W. Norton, 1996), pp. 91–226. (See especially two chapters entitled "The Trial: The Incredible Incompetence of the Prosecution" and "Final Summation: The Weak Voice of the People.")

55. *Ibid.*, p. 124.

56. *Ibid.*

57. For example, the *Los Angeles Times* both explicitly and implicitly suggested that jurors at the Santa Monica courthouse would be more sympathetic to the prosecution than the downtown jurors because of their different racial composition: "Juries drawn for the Santa Monica courthouse are more affluent, better educated and have a different ethnic mix than those at the Downtown courthouse. A Westside jury in the Simpson double-murder trail, legal experts say, would have been much more receptive to the prosecution's case." Of course, untouched is the question of whether a jury more "receptive" to the prosecution's case necessarily makes them a better rather than a weaker and less careful jury. Please see Miles Corwin, "Location of Trial Can Be Crucial to Outcome, Experts Say," *Los Angeles Times*, November 27, 1995.

58. For discussions of the Gammage incident and postverdict responses, see Robyn Meredith, "In Pittsburgh, White Officer's Acquittal Brings Protest March," *New York Times*, November 15, 1996; for discussions of the TyRon Lewis incident and postverdict responses, see Mike Clary, "Officials Remain on Alert in Riot-scarred St. Petersburg," *Los Angeles*

Times, November 15, 1996; for discussion of the Anthony Baez incident, see David Stout, "Judge's Hypothetical Question Is Cited in Bronx Officer's Acquittal," *New York Times,* October 11, 1996. Importantly, the New York case, in which Officer Livoti stood trial for the murder of Anthony Baez, was decided not by a jury but by a judge at the request of the defendant, Officer Livoti. Although defendants always have a constitutional right to choose trial by a jury, they can choose to be tried by a judge. The trial of Officer Livoti was conducted at the Bronx Criminal Court where there is a large African-American and Latino jury pool. Hence, there is little question as to why Officer Livoti chose to relinquish his constitutional right for a trial by jury.

59. Quoted in Frank Rich, Op-Ed, *New York Times,* October 4, 1995, p. A-21. See also Susan Estrich.

60. "Tammy Bruce of NOW Feels Strong About Simpson Case," CNN, Oct. 3, 1995, transcript # 1258-6.

61. Marc Lacey, "NOW Condemns Leader of Its L.A. Chapter," *Los Angeles Times,* Dec. 7, 1995, Part B: p. 3.

62. "Women's Group Apologizes for Member's Racial Remarks," *Reuters,* Dec. 6, 1995.

63. Lacey, *supra* note 61, p. 3.

64. CNN & Company, Oct. 5, 1995, transcript # 685.

65. As forewoman Armanda Cooley put it, "When I signed up for jury duty, I didn't see the State of California versus NOW, the State of California versus Racism...All I saw was the State of California versus Orenthal James Simpson...Out of this, we got political wars. We got wars with battered women's organizations...We're hearing that we set this world back on its toes from square one. The hell if we have. These things have always been here. They have always been here camouflaged. Don't blame us." See Cooley et al., *Madam Foreman,* pp. 140–41.

66. Sara Rimer, "The Simpson Case: The Victim," *New York Times,* June 23, 1994, p. 1.

67. James Ryan, "O.J. Simpson Sentenced to Probation in Wife Beating," *United Press International,* May 24, 1989.

68. Although it was clearly Simpson's money that allowed him to mount an effective defense, it is doubtful that much of the anger concerning Simpson's acquittal is about the obvious class privilege he exercised. At least among the elite, it is unlikely that any moves are afoot to equalize

resources among defendants, or to limit wealthy defendants' ability to
use all their resources to defend themselves.

69. Danquah, *supra* note 20.

70. As I note elsewhere, [t]his focus on otherwise privileged group members creates a distorted analysis of racism and sexism because the operative conceptions of race and sex become grounded in experiences that represent only a subset of a much more complex phenomenon. I expand on this problematic in an earlier work, "Demarginalizing the Intersection of Race and Gender in Antidiscrimination Law and Politics," *Chicago Law Forum* 140 (1989). I explore this problematic in the specific area of violence against women in "Mapping the Margins: Intersectionality, Identity Politics and Violence Against Women of Color," 43 *Stanford Law Review* 1241 (1993), reprinted in Crenshaw et al.

71. Angel-shaped lapel pins were worn by supporters of the victims' families. Marcia Clark attempted to wear such a pin in the courtroom, but Judge Ito ruled that it was improper. See Matt Krasnowski, "Angel-Pin Protest Is New O.J. Sideshow," *San Diego Union-Tribune*, Feb. 13, 1995, p. A3.

72. See, e.g., "Simpson Verdict Shakespeare, Not Justice," *The Herald Sun*, Oct. 4, 1995, p. A12. "If this country has ever had an Othello, he walked out of a Los Angeles courtoom Tuesday, acquitted of double murder by a jury of his peers.... [T]he trial revealed for all to the world to see that beneath the seemingly personable juice was a tormented soul— Othello, again—capable of unleashing the most dreadful domestic violence on Nicole Brown."

73. Jacquin Sanders, "Spouse Abuse Shelter Felt the Blow of the O.J. Verdict," *St. Petersburg Times*, Oct. 26, 1995, p. 1.

74. Teresa Moore, "Taking NOW Into the Future," *The San Francisco Chronicle*, April 21, 1996.

Bigger and O.J.

Ishmael Reed

In Richard Wright's *Native Son*, Bigger Thomas, a part-time hoodlum and welfare recipient, lives in the slums of Chicago with his dysfunctional family. He gets a job in the rich household of the Daltons, a wealthy white family, whose philanthropic patriarch is also a slumlord. His wife is blind, and his daughter flirts with radical politics and has a radical lover. After driving the drunken daughter Mary home one night, he tries to put her to bed, all done in innocence, but so as to avoid detection by her blind mother, who enters the room, he suffocates Mary. The narrator calls this an accident. The rest of the novel covers Bigger's flight from justice, capture, and imprisonment. Unlike today's middle-class writers who write about underclass characters, the Boyz in the Hood, Richard Wright knew what he was talking about. Not only had he been poor but as a youth worker he got to know many Biggers and, on the basis of this experience, was able to draw a character so convincing that Bigger has become an archetype for the inner-cities' disaffiliated youth.

During the O.J. Simpson trial, Simpson was compared to Shakespeare's Othello, which seemed stretched, since it is apparent that while Othello was a naive patsy, O.J. Simpson's cunning and intellect contributed to his legal team's overwhelming one of the most formidable adversarial armadas ever assembled: forty prosecutors, an international police force, including Interpol, the FBI, and media investigation teams so biased as to appear as operatives for the prosecution. In addition, a hi-tech paradigm constructed by a Silicon Valley computer, which concluded that Simpson was the killer, was used by the prosecution. Moreover, Nicole Simpson was no Desdemona.

On other occasions, Simpson was compared to Bigger Thomas. On the surface, the two have little in common. Bigger Thomas was a poor, rootless slum-dweller whose opportunities were slight. O.J. Simpson, though of humble origin, graduated from college, became a football star with the Buffalo Bills, a celebrity salesperson for Hertz Rent A Car, and a movie actor. While Bigger Thomas was one who used violence to communicate with his associates, O.J. Simpson is highly articulate. I saw him deliver a stand-up monologue on *Saturday Night Live.* It was flawless.

O.J. was comfortable in a world of whites, while Bigger remained in a psychological and mental slum, even though the hand of white philanthropy reached out to him. What Bigger and O.J. Simpson do have in common is that both were arrested for the murder of blond white women, both were subjected to a mob-rule public opinion that convicted them before all of the evidence was examined, and both were tried in the media, which, instead of serving as an objective reporter of the facts, inflamed the situation and contributed to a racial divide. (A caller into NPRs "Talk of the Nation" on March 28, 1996, asked why the media never repeated its showing of a split screen that showed both an all-white bar in Buffalo, New York, and a gathering of blacks, cheering the announcement of the acquittal. Christopher Darden, the show's guest, agreed with the caller that the media contributed to a racial divide by depicting all whites in favor of a guilty verdict, and all blacks favoring an acquittal.) This wouldn't be the first time. A book titled *The Betrayal of the Negro* by Dr. Rayford W. Logan documents how, historically, the American media have contributed to racial discord and riots between whites and blacks. For example, the Carnival Riot that took place in New Orleans in 1900 was the result of a newspaper publisher's agitation, both public and editorial.

Richard Wright's book also indicates that the relationship between African Americans and the racist criminal justice system hasn't changed since Richard Wright wrote *Native Son.*

The views of the characters and the narrator about politics, class, race, gender, religion, economics, and the media also have a contemporary ring.

Bigger's arrest, imprisonment, trial, and execution provides Wright with an opportunity to explore racism in the criminal justice system, which is still an issue—especially when black youth are five to ten times more likely to be incarcerated than white youth for committing the same crime, and when blacks are receiving mandatory five-year sentences for possession of crack cocaine while white crack possessors are not, and when there exists a disproportionate number of black prisoners on death row. My examination of Uniform Crime Reports (U.C.R.), a system that critics accuse of being flawed, leads me to conclude that blacks don't commit more crimes: they're arrested more.

The institutions that manipulate the crime figures are often institutions whose racist attitudes toward blacks have been documented. The police departments and the FBI have been investigating and often smearing black celebrities and political leaders at least since 1919. In the Simpson case, it was obvious that the police were willing to lie in order to convict a black defendant, and the FBI's role was also designed to benefit the prosecution. In fact, during the last phase of the trial, a witness was ready to testify about an FBI scientist's willingness to produce results favorable to the prosecution. The FBI agent in question agreed with the defense about some crucial sock testimony but, after being contacted by the prosecution, changed his testimony.

Bigger travels through the novel complaining about his lack of freedom in a white society that controls him and orders him around. After the Simpson verdict, Tammy Bruce, head of Los Angeles NOW, proposed that Simpson leave the country and be removed from the culture. Media commentators like Geraldo Rivera urged that he be ostracized. Both Rivera and Bruce were attempting to restrict Simpson's movements, to control him. Nothing could be more revealing of the attitudes of some whites toward African Americans than Jeffrey Toobin's remark that Simpson was now treated like a "pariah." Obviously, Simpson has been greeted very warmly by African-American audiences. For Toobin, being a pariah means ostracism by the wealthy whites of Brentwood. Where do pariahs go? To the African-American community, which, for Toobin, is occupied by intellectually inferior lepers. Professor Dennis Schatzman described the Toobin book as the second bell curve in which blacks are characterized as stupid and incapable of understanding hard evidence. Though he found no evidence to accuse Colonel North of drug dealing, Toobin is convinced of Simpson's guilt. It figures. Mr. Toobin's ideas about blacks are consistent with his employer's, *The New Yorker*, attitudes toward blacks. Its founding editor, Harold Ross, characterized "negroes" as "dangerous or funny." The soft treatment accorded Toobin by the media was typical of how pro-prosecution writers and pundits were coddled and nurtured. Former Los Angeles Police Chief Darryl Gates told the networks that he never used the "N" word. However, former Chief of Police of San Jose Joseph McNamara, now a fellow at the Hoover Institute, said that he had heard Gates use the word "nigger" frequently. When I called a local television station to ask McNamara, a guest on the show, to elaborate, the screener said that she didn't think the question important.

Bigger tells his lawyer, Max, "... a guy gets tired of being told what he can do and can't do. You get a little job here and a little job there. You shine shoes, sweep streets; anything..." Elsewhere he mentions the penal-like condition of African Americans. "Not only had he lived where they told him to live, not only had he done what they told him to do, not only had he done these things until he had killed to be quit of them; but even after obeying, after killing, they still ruled him. He was their property, heart and soul, body and blood." Like Bigger, Simpson became a commodity, making fortunes for television networks and publishers, rescuing careers, and even providing a man who hated him, Chris Darden, with an opportunity to make more money than he ever would have had he remained an obscure Los Angeles prosecutor; and his fellow prosecutor, Marcia Clark, received the third highest advance in history to write a nonfiction book about the case. Geraldo Rivera's show was about to be dropped, which would have jeopardized his $500,000 per year income, before he began to do hundreds of shows about Simpson. The ratings of CNN were described as "languishing" before the onset of the Simpson trial. Afterwards its ratings increased sevenfold and put Ted Turner in a position to bargain with CBS and Time Warner. Though journalists and politicians complained about the $13 million that the Simpson case cost Los Angeles, they rarely mentioned the millions made by the city as the result of it being the site of the trial, including $400 million in hotel taxes.

Moreover, an industry of mostly white pundits and commentators, some of whom didn't even follow the trial yet had opinions, was generated as a result of the trial. CNN's Greta Van Susteran and Roger Sessions and Entertainment TV's Kathleen Sullivan deserve congratulations for their fair and unbiased coverage of the trial. *Newsday*'s Shirley Perleman also deserves kudos for her avoiding the lurid stampede toward the tabloid exhibited by many journalists covering the case, but in their general coverage, the media were on bended knees before the prosecution. Katie Couric, Geraldo Rivera, and Gloria Allred became little more than advocates for the Brown family, abandoning any pretense of objectivity.

Steve Brill's Court TV, which has been accused of commercializing and tabloidizing the criminal justice system, ran ads for the O.J. trial, and Brill was quoted by *The New York Observer* as saying that he was the happiest man on the planet when O.J didn't commit suicide, a quote that Brill denied having made. At one point, the amount of money made by some businesses from the O.J. phenomenon totaled $300 million, more than the economy of Grenada; yet, when Simpson attempted to earn money by promoting a video that explained his side of the case, he was chastised by others who were making money from the case themselves, including Dominick Dunne, who expressed his disgust about Simpson marketing his video, even while writing his own book about the case. Mr. Dunne, one of a number of commentators who pronounced Simpson guilty before the defense began its case, wrote vicious, gossipy articles in *Vanity Fair* (published by a tabloid-happy import named Tina Brown). Dunne called the jury, which included nine African-American women, stupid for acquitting Simpson; yet he was also used by NBC as an objective reporter about the trial.

Of whites, Bigger says, "They choke you off the face of the earth . . . they don't even let you feel what you want to feel. They after you so hot and hard you can only feel what they doing to you. They kill you before you die."

In another section Bigger says, "We black and they white. They got things and we ain't. They do things and we can't. It's just like living in jail. Half the time I feel like I'm on the outside of the world peeping in through a knot-hole in the fence. . . ." This remark by Bigger expresses the feeling that many African Americans, Hispanics, Asian Americans, and Native Americans have when viewing a media that's fifty years behind the South in their efforts to diversify. Having their points-of-view excluded from a media discussion during which their enemies often discuss their lives and culture contemptuously and without risk of rebuttal is for African Americans and others like peeping into the world from a knothole in a fence. During the recent protests over Hollywood's lack of black Oscar nominees, it was revealed that the number of black writers who are members of the Screen Writers' Guild totals two and a half percent. Minority representation in newspapers and television is slightly higher, and so the dialogue regarding race in this country is monopolized by white males, who are ignorant of black history and culture, talking to each other, or to themselves. This characterized the media discussion in the Simpson case. *The New Yorker*'s Jeffrey Toobin, who carried on like a prosecution plant, even went so far as to serve as a consultant to other white journalists about the mores in the African-American community. Because he presumably was able to read the minds of the mostly black female jury, he predicted, the night before the acquittal, that they would convict Simpson. Shortly before the verdict another white male expert on black psychology predicted that the black women would vote for conviction because black women can tell when black men are lying.

The most conspicuous representative of white society for many blacks, and the only whites whom they may see on a day-to-day basis, are the police, who are often viewed as members of an invading force, which arrives in the community to impose brutality and engage in illicit activities. This image is reinforced by the large percentage of policemen who don't reside in the inner city. In Oakland, California, where I live, eighty percent of the police reside outside of the city, including one officer who commutes from Denver, Colorado. Every time the citizens of Oakland attempt to change this situation, they are opposed by the policeman's union.

As in the case of the 1992 Stuart case in Boston, in which a white man claimed that his pregnant wife was murdered by a black man, and the 1994 Susan Smith case, in which a white woman accused a fictitious black figure of murdering her children, the murder of a white person, especially a Nordic-appearing white woman, as in the Simpson case, puts the entire black male population under suspicion. Police suspend with the Bill of Rights and employ the kind of tactics that the United States says it despises in totalitarian regimes. In *Native Son,* the police and the vigilantes search every black home under a blanket warrant from the mayor. The police in the Simpson case were accused by the judge of a reckless disregard for the truth when they concocted a probable cause for entering Simpson's property without a warrant.

After it is discovered that Bigger is responsible for Mary Dalton's death, thousands of police and vigilantes throw a cordon around the Black Belt. For whites, all blacks become culpable for the actions of one black and must be punished. Since the Simpson case, America's yellow journalists, who feed upon racial psychoses for profit, have been speculating about how whites are going to pay blacks for the verdict. Will affirmative-action programs be curtailed? Will welfare policies become more stringent? Some have suggested that this is how whites riot—economically—though whites still engage in physical riots as well. Thirteen percent of those arrested during the 1992 riots that took place after the Rodney King verdict were white (and probably from two-parent households), yet no black or Latino mob has given as good a riot as Irish Americans did in New York in the late 1800s. The *Wall Street Journal* and Los Angeles mayor Tom Bradley said that whites were responsible for burning down restaurants in Koreatown.

Since the typical recipient of both affirmative action and welfare is white, this retaliation will affect whites as well. Mob psychoses cause one to cut off one's nose to spite one's face. Self-maiming is the kind of action that results from a psychosis.

In Wright's time, the whites perpetrated physical assaults upon African Americans when a black man was accused of a heinous crime against a white. After Bigger has escaped, black men are beaten and the homes of black people are assaulted. One thousand homes are raided. The *New York Times* of October 25, 1995, reported that interviews conducted with students on American campuses revealed an anger among whites about the outcome of the Simpson trial. Oprah Winfrey reported that tips given black doormen declined after the Simpson verdict. (A week after Ms. Winfrey made this remark, the black doormen at New Orleans's Fairmont Hotel told me the same thing.) Eco-

nomic reprisals were also visited upon blacks after Bigger
Thomas's escape. Bigger reads a newspaper that reports "several
hundred Negro employees throughout the city had been dismissed from jobs. A well-known banker's wife phoned a newspaper that she dismissed her Negro cook "for fear that she might
poison the children." Just as, in some instances, groups of Native
Americans were slaughtered because of the actions of one or
two, and the German Jews paid with Krisstalnacht after a Jew
assassinated a high-ranking Nazi official, the fact that all blacks
are still blamed for the actions of some blacks is an indication of
how much racism in this country persists. In fact, freedom can
be measured according to the degree of anonymity that the society offers to members of a particular group. Though Irish-
American Andy Rooney offered a reward for the capture of Ron
Goldman and Nicole Simpson's killers, no one in the media
blames Andy Rooney for the actions of Irish-American Timothy
McVeigh, who is suspect in the bombing of the Oklahoma City
federal building, nor were Irish-American leaders like Daniel
Moynihan required to condemn Irish-American extremists like
Pat Buchanan. (In fact *Newsweek*, which ran a scurrilous article
about Simpson, presented what for some was a sympathetic portrait of Oklahoma bombing suspect McVeigh and *Time*, which
issued a controversial cover portrait of Simpson, printed a
benign one of McVeigh.)

As soon as Bigger encounters the police he is accosted with
"N" words, "A" words, and "B" words. He's an animal, a black
son of a bitch. The "array of faces, white and looming," threaten
to kill him, to lynch him. After the Simpson verdict, a white
woman called one of the talk shows and said that the people in
her town were saying that the "nigger" ought to be lynched, that
the "nigger" ought to be burned. For me, the low point of the
ugly and racist journalism in the Simpson case occurred when

A.J. Benza, a reporter for the *Daily News,* appearing on Entertainment Network's *The Gossip Show,* encouraged Fred Goldman to shoot Simpson.

In *Native Son,* Bigger is called a black ape. Black men are animals, and the inner cities are the jungles that we inhabit. Bigger is described as a "rapacious beast who is driven from his den into the open. He is a beast utterly untouched by the softening influence of modern civilization. He seems out of place in a white man's civilization, according to the *Tribune,* the rabble-rousing newspaper that carries the story of Bigger's flight, capture, imprisonment, and trial. Such descriptions of African Americans are not limited to contemporary ultra-right publications; but they are the kinds of things one might read in the *New Republic,* where *The Bell Curve* was favorably discussed, or *The End of Racism,* where an imported demagogue named Dinesh D'Souza (who was once associated with the anti-black, anti-Semitic *Dartmouth Review,* and who is backed by powerful interests, including William Simon, a former cabinet member, The Olin Foundation, and the American Enterprise Institute) writes that blacks have a civilization gap. Mr. Dinesh D'Souza suffers from the same historical amnesia as the Irish police captain who is quoted in the same *Tribune* article in Wright's novel describing Bigger as a beast, a man without civilization. A governor general of India said that Indians had the intelligence of a dog, and the British said that the Irish were the earlier missing link in the human species, which matches the description of Bigger in the novel. It has been noted that in the United States, the former victims of racial oppression practice racist oppression against blacks.

Animal imagery was also used to describe Simpson. A savage. A beast. The networks kept rubbing the 1993 tape recording in the public's face, without informing them that during the time period of this tape Simpson didn't strike Nicole Simpson. Pho-

tos of her bruised face were shown to worldwide audiences without the media stipulating that there was no proof that Simpson
was responsible for inflicting these bruises. In one of a number of
salacious *Vanity Fair* pieces about the case written by Dominick
Dunne, Nicole Simpson's reference to Simpson as an animal was
gleefully highlighted in bold type. In a phone call to the Larry
King Show, Louis H. Brown, Nicole Simpson's father, a man who
has benefited from Simpson's largesse, called Simpson an animal
when it was suggested that the defense might call Sidney Simpson
as a witness. Whether Brown expressed indignation at the actions
of his daughter Dominique is not known; she sold pictures of a
topless Nicole, and of the Simpson children, to tabloid publications for $100,000.

While Wright mocks the novel's journalists with scathing
gusto, these early journalists behave like Freedom Forum Fellows
in comparison to today's journalists, those who work for outfits
whose ambition is not to create good journalism but to make
money. So sleazy was the coverage of the Simpson case that
when the editor of the *National Enquirer* appeared on ABC's *Nightline* to discuss the case in the company of some prominent mainstream journalists, he seemed right at home. In the Thomas case,
as in the Simpson case, the media behaved as a sort of public
relations department for the police and for the prosecution,
inflaming the public with sensational copy unfavorable to the
defendant. From the time of the Simpson arrest, the police and
the media began a partnership—the media doing its part by
leaking damaging information, much of which was false.
Remember the ski mask and the scratches on O.J.'s body? Five
days after Simpson's arrest, CBS ran a poll to which respondents
were asked whether, if convicted, Simpson should receive life
imprisonment or death. There was no question in CBS's mind
about Simpson's guilt.

A gullible American public, which reveals its ignorance about the world in poll after poll, is an easy prey for manipulation by the media that keeps them confused and naive. A white public, large segments of which expresses shock frequently when some outrage upon the black community is exposed, is fair game. They're shocked that the CIA is cooperating with drug dealers who've been selling drugs in Oakland, San Francisco, and Los Angeles. They're shocked that Susan Smith lied about blacks kidnapping her children. They're shocked that the government permits plutonium injections upon unsuspecting blacks. They're shocked by the brutal beating of Rodney King. They're shocked by Mark Fuhrman's testimony about the kind of torture and cruelty practiced against blacks and Latinos in police stations throughout the country. Even the pundits and the commentators showed themselves to be as naive as the average white about the police's attitudes toward black Americans. Jack Ford, who was then a commentator for Court TV (before his looks got him a job on NBC), said that the idea of the police planting evidence was absurd. Vincent Bugliosi told CNBC commentator Charles Grodin that to suggest that police plant evidence is "blasphemy." The white commentariat and segments of the white public also expressed a naïveté about how the drug trade works in California. Willard Scott hinted on the *Today* show that cocaine is the drug of choice among media personnel, and so they must reside in a world where the drug dealers extend unlimited credit and make appointments before arriving to slay deadbeats. The white public dismissed the theory that drug kingpins murdered Nicole Simpson and Ron Goldman, yet Colombian nationals are regularly arrested for drug dealings in California. Many whites showed their naïveté about how the criminal justice system effects blacks when they were seduced by Mark Fuhrman's testimony. Even the media lavished praise upon Fuhrman. He became a hero to many whites and had the McKinny tapes, during which he revealed his hated of blacks and Mexicans, not come to light, it's quite possible that he could have become a powerful political figure, running on a fascist platform. Not only did Fuhrman express a bias toward Mexican Americans and African Americans, but he also displayed Nazi paraphenalia. In addition, two Jews told *Hard Copy* that Fuhrman beat them up.

This early trial by leak, and the subsequent siding with the police and prosecution by the media, its pundits, and pro-prosecution commentariat, did much to influence the polls that saw the majority of whites convinced of Simpson's guilt long before evidence had been introduced and the defense had begun its arguments. I followed the case on a daily basis and found the media coverage to be full of errors and a pro-prosecution bias. Those seven thousand daily callers, who followed the trial, instead of relying upon news reports, and who were polled daily by Entertainment network, consistently favored the defense in their voting, and at the end of the case voted overwhelmingly for acquittal. Whites telling white pollsters that they believed in O.J.'s guilt may have been a result of their desiring to express solidarity with pollsters belonging to the same race. When they voted by phone and were able to be anonymous, those who followed the case on a daily basis voted for the defense. If the majority of whites do believe in Simpson's guilt, it could be the result of the media siding with the prosecution. In taped network news reports which were blatantly of such a nature, often the networks failed to even cover the defense's arguments. When Johnny Cochran attributes the animus toward Simpson to pontificating pundits and biased wrapups, he has a point. Alan M. Dershowitz pointed to one glaring example of media bias when he mentioned a report on the case by *The New York Times*, whose copy

was consistently pro-prosecution and whose reporter, David Margolick, seemed to spend most of his time hanging out with Faye
Resnick. After the glove demonstration, Margolick said that
the gloves fit "snugly" even though he didn't witness the demonstration. During an exchange with a black lawyer, Margolick
pompously ridiculed the legal profession. Pundits like Jeffrey
Toobin also raised questions about the ethics of the legal profession. Toobin works for *The New Yorker* magazine, whose editorial
policies are being influenced by Roseanne Barr, a Denise Brown
confidante, leading to the resignations of some of its finest writers. Certainly the legal profession could use some reform, but so
could the media. But we won't hear about it because the media
resent criticism. They can dish it out but they can't take it. Their
attitude toward Simpson is typical of their attitude toward black
people in general, which hasn't changed since the time of Wright's
novel: Blacks are guilty until proven guilty. CNBC's Jay Monahan,
expressing regret that the public will have to rely upon media
reports of the civil trial instead of being able to watch it on television, said on October 3 that "the bad reporting and bad commentary which characterized the media's treatment of the first trial
contributed to the polls which saw the majority of whites convinced of Simpson's guilt, while those who actually followed the
trial came to the opposite conclusion." He also questioned the
methodology of the polls.

Bigger's lawyer accuses the press of being part of a conspiracy to
kill not only Bigger but the Communist party in the hearts of its
readers. The press then, as now, reaps revenues by whipping up
irrational fear on the part of the white population, and being
used as a weapon against minorities and unpopular beliefs. And
instead of engaging in serious debate with one's opponents, slo-

gans are substituted for thought. Those who disagree with media pundits are politically incorrect or out of touch with reality. Bigger's lawyer says, during the trial, "The hunt for Bigger Thomas served as an excuse to terrorize the entire Negro population, to arrest hundreds of Communists, to raid labor union headquarters and worker's organizations, indeed the tone of the press, the silence of the church, the attitude of the prosecution and the simulated temper of the people are of such a nature as to indicate that more than revenge is being sought upon a man who has committed a crime." The media, in the Simpson case, was used as lynch-mob leader just as it was used against Mike Tyson and Clarence Thomas.

The behavior of some media feminists in the Simpson case confirms my suspicion that some elements in the white feminist movement, and their African-American surrogates, pose the most serious threat to African-American men since the Klan. Michelle Carouso, of the *Daily News,* said on *Larry King Live* that she was glad that there were eight women on the jury, implying that she was hoping for a conviction, and Leslie Abrahamson and Gloria Allred recommended the death penalty for Simpson—yet both were hired by ABC and CNN to be objective consultants on the case. Ms. Allred was even accused by one defense witness of phoning her and trying to badger her into revealing her testimony. *The Nation* printed an article about how the white women who ran for office as Anita Hill feminists abandoned women's issues and voted with their male colleagues. During the Simpson trial, Ms. Hill was used as a prosecution prop, putting her on the side of a team that gave Mark Furhman a clean bill of health, possibly planted evidence, had the defense teams' experts followed and harassed, and withheld exculpatory evidence.

The Simpson case also provided some high-profile white male journalists and pundits who hypocritically posed as women's rights advocates with an opportunity to posture. They included Geraldo Rivera, who admitted in his autobiography that he abused his first wife, Edie Vonnegut, causing Kurt Vonnegut to refer to Rivera as the vilest human being he knows; a talk-show host who was accused of sexual harassment by a woman employee, and a former attorney general who functioned as a consultant on the Simpson case for different networks. This man's use of women to entrap a black mayor was termed pandering by a *New York Times* columnist, yet he wasn't subjected to the sort of feminist harassment to which black men have been subjected, portrayed as poster-boys for sexism by women who are silent about such practices that occur in their ethnic groups. The case also revealed a split between white feminists and black women. After the jury came back with the not-guilty verdict, a prominent feminist appeared on television to denounce the verdict. She said that this verdict arose from black women being accustomed to abuse by black men. Yet statistics show that the rate of black men murdering black women and black women murdering black men is about the same, due to the tendency of black women to retaliate.

Also never mentioned in places like *The New York Times, The Village Voice*, and NPR, where misogyny is viewed as an exclusively black male problem (but where we never learn how women, who share the ethnic backgrounds of the men who direct these media outfits, are treated), are statistics which show that the murder of black women by their husbands and boyfriends has declined by 40 percent since 1976. The split between white feminists and black women, exemplified by the racist comments of Tammy Bruce, the grand dragon of the feminist movement, continues. In a review of journalist Jeffrey Toobin's *The Run of His Life*, *Times* critic Wendy Kaminer came to Marcia Clark's rescue by rebutting characterizations of Ms. Clark which Kaminer considered sexist, but failed to defend her black sisters on the jury from Toobin's assault upon their integrity. Mr. Toobin said that these black women were swayed by the demonic negro oratory of Johnnie Cochran to vote for Simpson's acquittal, but the jurors themselves said that they were more impressed with Barry Scheck's testimony than with Cochran. During his book tour none of his interviewers, including Bryant Gumbel, asked whether the two white and the one Hispanic juror were enchanted by Cochran's spellbinding Negro oratory. Just as Bigger Thomas was used by the establishment to smear all blacks, O.J was used to signify on all black men, and the black women jurors were used to do the same for black women. Indeed, for some white men and white women in the media, Faye Resnick, whose wretched past has been exposed in Joe Bosco's new book, had more credibility than the black women jurors.

Though the criminal justice system and the media are treated in Wright's novel, the theme that gives umbrage over all others is the theme of miscegenation. (Though Johnnie Cochran and Robert Shapiro have both been accused of playing the race card, one could argue that Christopher Darden introduced the race card when he accused Simpson of having a fetish for blondes, an accusation he would never have used against a white man). The high-priced model of international capitalism is the white woman, preferably Anglo-looking and preferably thin. Her face and body have launched millions of products. She is the icon that adorns the motion-picture screens and the fashion magazines. Black fashion models complain that they can't find work and that there's racism on the runway. Though many claim that the enormous attention paid to the O.J. Simpson case was a result of Simpson being a celebrity and a presence for many years in every living room due to his role as an NBC sportscaster, the miscegenation angle is what excited many viewers, just as Nazi newspapers like *Der Stuermer* and magazines like *Jugend* fascinated their readership by printing sensational stories about relationships between Jewish men and Aryan women. But many wondered whether such attention would have been paid if the murdered woman in the case had been a black woman. In *Native Son* the murder of the white woman by a black man excites more interest than the murder of a black woman, Bessie, by Bigger. Moreover, when Richard Goldstein of *The Village Voice* sought to discover whether as much attention had been paid to black and Latino women who were murdered in Central Park as there was to the highly publicized crimes against white women, he complained that the New York authorities gave him the runaround. (Gerry Spence, who received an education about race during the trial, said that many whites believed that Simpson had taken something that belonged to them. Their property—our woman.) The commentary on *Native Son* and even the narrator says that Bigger's murder of Mary was an accident. But a closer examination of the text reveals that Bigger has a motive. He kills Mary because he doesn't want to be caught in the bedroom of a white woman. Black men have been lynched for less. Black men have been arrested for recklessly eyeballing a white woman. During the Simpson trial Kathleen Bell testified that Fuhrman told her that he'd arrest a black man driving in the company of a white woman. Deeply embedded in African-American folklore is the notion that a black man shouldn't be caught dead coming into contact with a white woman. There are tall tales about black men walking up the side of buildings so as to avoid passing a white woman who was approaching them on the street from the opposite direction. But like many taboos the possibility of black

men and white women sharing intimacy raises excitement, some
of it sexual. When Bigger is captured by the police, they want
him to simulate his raping of Mary. They desire to get their
kicks by having this entrapped black man tell them how he did it
to a white woman. How many commentators about the Simpson
case revealed a similar voyeuristic attitude? A San Francisco
attorney sought to answer those who believed that Mark
Fuhrman planted the infamous bloody gloves by suggesting that
Fuhrman could not possibly have done so because he didn't
know whether Simpson had an alibi. *He could have been in bed with
Paula Barbieri*, he explained on several occasions. Was this commentator thrilled by the prospect of Simpson being in bed with
one of his bimbos? Would he have liked to have been in some
creepy corner of the bedroom, in the dark, panting heavily and,
perhaps, manipulating himself?

One of the most vicious attacks on Simpson, the prosecution, and the defense team has come from Mark Fuhrman
defender Vincent Bugliosi, former Los Angeles district attorney.
He told talk-show host Charles Grodin, whose flagging audience appeal was lifted by one-sided pro-prosecution commentary, and panels that were hostile to Simpson and the defense,
that to believe police would plant evidence was "blasphemy." He
is the author of *Outrage*, a book that the publisher, Norton,
described as putting the "noose around Simpson's neck."
Christopher Darden, who was criticized in the book, said on
June 12 that Bugliosi hadn't even read the transcripts of the trial,
or watched it on television. Moreover, he said that Bugliosi
hadn't tried a case in thirty years, and was out to cash in on the
case. The book's arguments were demolished by Alan Dershowitz, who debated Bugliosi on June 11, reducing him to a rub-
ble of sputtering invective. Previously appearing on the Geraldo

Rivera show, Bugliosi complained about Simpson's returning from Bermuda with "lipstick all over his face."

For her part, Ms. Barbieri told interviewer Diane Sawyer that her father warned her that if she were ever raped by a black man, she shouldn't come home, which is what an Anglo father may have said to an Anglo woman about associating with Italian-American men—about thirty years ago. In a review of Spike Lee's film *Jungle Fever*, Professor Lawrence Di Statsi said of this movie (about a relationship between an Italian-American woman and an African-American male) that taking white women was the charge originally made against Italians. Other commentators said that if Simpson were let out of prison, he'd be at the Riviera Country Club with white women. Geraldo Rivera, who revealed his homoerotic yearnings for Mick Jagger and Rudolph Nureyev in his autobiography, *Exposing Myself* (yet referred to Simpson as a "punk"), seemed particularly aroused over the prospect of Simpson appearing on the beach in the company of white women. During the trial, the Entertainment network announced a poll that revealed most women would rather watch the O.J. Simpson trial than have sex.

Even the most progressive and intellectual people have bought into the myths surrounding black men and white women. Some highly educated African Americans, including those who can figure out what on earth Foucault and Derrida are driving at, sound like your typical backwoods peckerwoods when discussing miscegenation. Those who make a career out of scolding folks about their sexism, homophobia, and misogyny also get steamed up when the discussion of miscegenation is brought up. Today, as in Bigger's day, the eerie sexual fantasies that revolve around the black male presence in the United States present a danger to black men in everyday life.

Even feminists like Susan Estrich, who is beginning to sound more like the late Lee Atwater with each new column, have bought into myths about black men and white women. In a column, she warned white women about coming into contact with black men, and justifies this on the basis of crime statistics (even though interracial crime is rare). Young professional black men often complain that white women are scared to ride in the same elevator with black men. Well, if a woman is usually raped or killed by somebody she knows, then white women should be fearful of riding elevators with white men. If Jesse Jackson is fearful of walking down the street at night with a group of blacks following closely behind, then why, given the fact that 70 percent of the violent crimes committed against whites are committed by other whites, aren't whites afraid of walking down the street while being trailed by other whites? Though sexual contact may have been in Bigger's thoughts, there is no sexual contact between Bigger and Mary Dalton when he "accidentally" murders her. Yet from the very beginning of the case, the newspapers charged Bigger with rape. One headline reads, "Troops Guard Negro Killer's Trial, Protect Rapist from Mob Action"—this being the kind of singling out of blacks for crime, especially when the victim is a white, that we read in the newspaper daily. The narrator of the novel says, "To hint that he had committed a sex crime was to pronounce the death sentence; it meant a wiping out of his life even before he was captured; it meant a death before death came, for the white men who read those words would at once kill him in their hearts."

There's something crazy about thinking about race in this country, and Richard Wright was among the first to point out the ironies and paradoxes of the American racial situation. Maybe the question of race shouldn't be left to a crime system that buys into the logic of race, or a media devoted to zebra journalism that only exacerbates the problem by photographing only those whites who were disappointed about the Simpson verdict but providing no photos of those who cheered, and by photographing blacks who cheered but editing out pictures of blacks who were disappointed. Maybe the question of race shouldn't be left to academics in disciplines that require little empirical proof, the kind of field where demagogues with P.h.D.s are allowed to run wild, such as members of the African-American literary tribal council who are attempting to disappear African-American male writers, including Ralph Ellison and Richard Wright, with the charge of misogyny, which is like calling somebody a Communist in the 1950s. They object to Wright's treatment of Bigger's mother and his girlfriend but are silent about his treatment of the black males in the novel, Bigger's associates and even Bigger himself.

Maybe it's time to bring the question of race into the clinic room or the emergency room and treat it for what it is: a public-health crisis. Miscegenation has made people hysterical. Joel Williamson reports in his powerful book *The Crucible of Race* (1984) that one of the causes of the Atlanta race riots was a rumor that black men were drinking from a bottle with pictures of white women on them, and a great black Cajun singer was murdered by white men because he used a handkerchief given him by a white woman to wipe the sweat from his face. Miscegenation is also an issue that hovered over the Simpson trial, yet Americans, black and white, though often feigning repugnance at the mixing of the races, are more familiar with this demon than anyone might admit. In fact, interracial sex may be the taboo that millions of Americans have enjoyed the most. There is a saying in the South that white men didn't know that white women could have sex until they got married. While visiting Memphis, I was told by Professor Brett Singer, the niece of the great Yiddish writer Issac Bashevis Singer, that she asked her classroom of whites how many had engaged in sex with a black person. Everybody raised their hand. (I also asked her why feminists belonging to her ethnic background ignore the copiously documented misogyny—spousal abuse, battery—that occurs in their community, while blaming all of the world's sexism on Simpson and black men. She said that she was taught by her father to keep the sins of her community a secret.)

The parallels between the racial climate of Wright's novel and that of the Simpson case are endless. Nineteen nineties California, where the criminal trial took place and the scene of the civil trial, very much resembles the Jim Crow Chicago of Wright's novel. Scene of a drive against affirmative action, financed by ultraright forces and led by a governor who ties his career to wedge issues, and a right-wing legislature, a number of what might be called Negro laws have been introduced, including the notorious Three Strikes Law, which affects black defendants disproportionately. These laws have been advocated by the same attorney general, Dan Lungren, who negotiated a plea bargaining deal that let Mark Fuhrman, a white policeman, off with a light $200 fine and three years probation, shocking even Melanie Lomax, the Simpson prosecution's best friend and the darling of the "lynch Simpson" media. Tough on crime for Lungren apparently means tough on the poor and the black. These racist laws follow the historical pattern in which, at one time, Chinese Americans and Japanese Americans were excluded from California. During one nineteenth-century legislative session, called The Legislature of a Thousand Drinks because most of its participants were drunk at the end of the session, blacks were nearly excluded. Proposition 187 indicates that such enmity toward nonwhite immigrants still exists since the over one hundred thousand illegal European immigrants reasiding in California are never mentioned in the debate. And so it's not surprising that the California legislature has intervened three times in the Simpson case, most recently in an effort to change the rules of evidence so that Nicole Simpson's diary could be admitted, a diary that would usually constitute hearsay. Previously, another get-a-Negro measure, a terms limit proposition, was passed as a way of ridding the assembly of Willie Brown, who California racists considered too uppity. Given California's attitudes toward Asian Americans and the rising number of hate crime against Asian Americans, it's not surprising that two Japanese-American judges would side with the prosecution so as not to raise anxiety among some whites about Japanese Americans who were interned during World War II. Republican appointee Judge Lance Ito, in the minds of the media and many whites, failed to do the job, even though he did his damnedest to convict Simpson, consistently siding with the prosecution in his rulings. His failure has put pressure on the new Japanese-American judge, Hiroshi Fujisaki, who has to prove to the media and many whites that he can deliver a verdict holding Simpson liable for the wrongful deaths of Goldman and Nicole Simpson. Apparently he is doing a good job. The media are congratulating him as being no nonsense, and praising his toughness with Simpson's team in the civil case. As of this writing Judge Fujisaki has gutted the defense's arguments and has permitted the plaintiffs' attorneys to dismiss fifteen prospective black jurors who had doubts about Simpson's guilt, while keeping white jurors who expressed belief in his guilt. One observer, the law partner of the late William Kunstler, was right to term this civil trial "the revenge of the white establishment."

The media lynching of Simpson by prominent feminists, lawyers, intellectuals, and journalists, without exploring the evidence, has not only been disgraceful but should be alarming to black men. Not only was the defendant lynched but also his lawyer has been subjected to media-inspired hatred. A *New York Times* feminist referred to Johnnie Cochran as "odious."

Bigger Thomas gets into trouble because this poor black stepped out of the box that society had created for him. While his friends are petty thieves, he gets a job working as a chauffeur, which, in view of what was expected of him, was a step up. He is surrounded by liberals who are interested in his welfare and who give him lectures about self-improvement. Stepping beyond his bounds was the kind of adventure that got his creator, Richard Wright, into trouble. When he left the themes that made him famous—the conflicts between white and black Americans—and abandoned the United States for Europe, Wright was written off by the critics and dismissed as a one-novel writer, that novel being *Native Son*, when *The Outsider*, written in exile, might have been his best novel.

Simpson's troubles may have also arisen from his transcending the fate that awaited him had he not been a talented athlete: imprisonment, death, or a slave to a low-paying service job. On a recent trip to Los Angeles, I passed by his Rockingham estate and found it to be the kind of residence that kings and presidents possess in many countries. He associated with the high and the mighty and dated women with international reputations for their beauty. This was too much for some whites—those who couldn't wait for him to fall, like the four policemen who told us that they all abandoned the crime scene just to inform Simpson of his wife's death, even though he wasn't the next of kin; those who told us that they were so worried about Mr. Simpson's health that they climbed over his wall without a search warrant. One detective, Philip Vannatter, in a remark that the white commentariat overlooked, said it all when asked about the activities of Simpson's maid on the night of June 13. Mr. Van-natter said wryly, "I don't have a maid."

Both Wright and Simpson have been accused by those who still wish to play the racial extortion game of abandoning the "black community." But if all Wright had done was to write *Native Son*, he contributed to the African-American community immensely by exposing the racist forces that are arrayed against black achievement, and he did it in a manner that was artful, pro-found, and with an acid sense of humor. Whatever dues Simp-son owed to the community have been paid because never before has the deeply rooted hostility toward African Americans by the police, prosecutors, and other components of the criminal jus-tice system been revealed to the whole world as they were in the Simpson case.

Native Son excels as a novel in my mind because, though published over fifty years ago, the issues that are addressed by the author still exist. A classic is a book that though written decades or even centuries before the present time could have been written today. Thus, *Native Son* is a classic novel, as true now as it was when it was published on March 1, 1940, and its truth was certi-fied in 1995, the year of the trial of the century.

"Hertz, Don't It?"

Becoming Colorless and Staying Black in the Crossover of O.J. Simpson

Leola Johnson and David Roediger

"Look at the unprecedented market presence that black athletes have today, what they're called upon (or allowed) to symbolize. Jackie Robinson never made it onto a box of Wheaties."

—Henry Louis Gates, Jr.

Twenty years ago, O.J. Simpson told of his strategy for responding to racial taunts. It consisted of a sharp jab to the offender's chest, followed by a literal punch line: "Hertz, don't it?" The humor rested on the bitter contrast of Simpson's tremendous success as an athlete crossing over to become a corporate icon with his continued facing of racial hurts and desiring to strike back against them. In anticipating the "Hertz/hurts" punning that now is repeated endlessly on "O.J. Jokes" web sites, Simpson surely knew that he briefly stepped out of character. He followed the remark with laughing reassurances that such jabbing was of course unnecessary. Referring to himself in the disturbing third-person manner common to toddlers and Republican presidential hopefuls, he pointed out that "the Juice" so transcended white racism that he scarcely faced bigotry. He then shifted discussion to the troublesome African-American women who criticized his acting out interracial romances in films and to the insecure African-American militants who had tried to draw him into their own wrestling with racial identity. In general, despite the occasional line regarding country clubs flying their flags at half-staff on the days he was their guest, Simpson's pre-1994 self-presentation was as someone for whom racism was not a problem. As early as 1969, he triumphantly reported that O.J. was thought of as a "man," not an African American. Although he professedly retained a healthy sense of African-American consciousness, he later told reporters, the American public happily saw him as "colorless." In making the latter claim, Simpson also invoked Hertz. The marketing division of the firm, he observed, had generated data proving his transcendence of race.[1]

As this is being written, lawyers and trademark bureaucrats are deciding a bizarre conflict regarding who owns the initials "O.J." They are deciding whether, after all, Simpson still might be a colorless commodity rather than a racialized body. Amidst much bad financial news, Simpson has recently prevailed on the orange juice lobby to give up its disputing of his claim to be O.J. Perhaps reflecting a desire not to be much associated with Simpson, the juice industry has ceded claims to the initials, save in direct reference to their product. If the claims of the clothing manufacturer Outer Jock are disposed of, O.J. Simpson will be O.J.® He hopes to market a range of products—from apparel to toys—under that trademark. Such connections of Simpson to the sale of things are longstanding and wide-ranging: razors, boots, books, videos, juice, clothing, soda, combination juice and soda, sunglasses, televisions, films, dolls, cars, sneakers, sporting goods, chicken, cameras, aftershave, rental cars, and, as both he and others have long observed, his own "image" and "personality." The length of the list suggests why Simpson could still imagine that the white public might see him as without race.[2]

This essay examines the role of race and the claim of colorlessness in O.J. Simpson's life prior to the 1994 murders of Nicole Brown Simpson and Ronald Goldman. It seeks to understand why Simpson became the first black sports star to massively cross over from athletic hero to corporate spokesman and media personality. We argue that however tragically Simpson believed that such crossover also involved a movement beyond race, his success rested on appeals rooted strongly in his race, in the presence of movements for racial justice, and in the history of race and gender in the U.S. While there can be no doubt that Simpson's image became a valuable commodity, commodity and color were consistently imbricated in his appeal.

We address these pre-1994 realities as critical in their own right, murders and trials aside. However, we also realize that all thinking about Simpson now is read as reflecting on "the case"— that books on him are now not in sports or business aisles but in the "True Crime" sections of bookstores. Our writing here obviously intersects with one of the enduring fascinations of that case: the terrifying juxtaposition of slashed, maimed, and lifeless bodies of the victims with the feverish rush of media and markets to sell, and of the public to buy, any and every commodity related to the tragedy. The awful fact that the sales of white Broncos skyrocketed alongside those of the type of stiletto once thought to be the murder weapon, the obscene sensationalizing by the tabloid and mainstream media, the paid-for interviews with witnesses, the seven-figure book contracts, the auditioning for further parts from the witness stand by Kato Kaelin and the nude photo spread of a Simpson "juror with a difference" in *Playboy*— all these provoked horror precisely because they showed how quickly and fully the pursuit of dollars displaces and desecrates the memory of the dead. O.J. Simpson, selling his own image from jail (signed, on football cards), hawking books, videos, medallions, interviews, and even photographs of his children, focused this outrage. Indeed, the prosecution's appeals, from Christopher Darden's warnings against being taken in by high-priced Dream Teamers to Marcia Clark's closing slide show of the victims, offered jurors an opportunity to rescue dead bodies from the lively rush to profit.[3]

The deeply gendered connections of house, home, and community in Simpson's commercial success, which we likewise will explore, underpin another major narrative regarding the case, one especially found in black reflections on it, from the neighborhood where Simpson grew up to the speeches of Louis Farrakhan. According to this narrative, which has some force, Simpson progressively concerned himself less and less with African-American life, yet was nonetheless unable to transcend racism, and ironically found significant support within a community he had left behind. Simpson's own writing on the case details a growing horror at having to "see race" after a life he characterizes as entirely lived on merit. Understanding O.J. as a seemingly colorless but fully racialized commodity, brilliantly positioned to be marketed to middle-class white men, is thus vital to comprehending his and the public's reaction to the trial.[4]

The Un-militant: Black Revolt and Simpson's Success

So familiar is Simpson's commercial success, and that of the few African-American athletes who followed him to advertising superstardom, that it is difficult to recall how spectacularly improbable such celebrity was. No black athlete, no matter how great, had ever crossed over with anything like such success. In the late 1960s, endorsements remained unavailable to those with substantial professional careers as the greatest in their sports under their belts—not Willie Mays, not Hank Aaron, not Bill Russell, not Oscar Robertson, not Wilt Chamberlain, not Jimmy Brown, and, above all, not Muhammad Ali. Nor were African-American stars who might have been marketed for their excellence and their youth deluged with offers—not Lew Alcindor, not Lou Brock, not Arthur Ashe, and not Tommie Smith, who in the late 1960s had perhaps the broadest claim ever to the title "world's fastest human." Superstars like Russell and Bob Gibson faced slights and exclusion even in the relatively paltry local markets in which they were the dominant sports figures. Advertising firms, reacting to research demonstrating that commercials overwhelmingly focused on and appealed to whites, stridently maintained that ads should not "look like America" but should look like what advertisers thought white mainstream audiences thought America should look like. They listed products, such as razors and razor blades, for which African Americans were perceived as being too different-looking to ever endorse in ads pitched to those outside the black community. More broadly, as Anne McClintock's work in cultural studies points out, mass advertising since 1900 or before had consistently used racist and racial imagery to sell to white markets. Black images on products were not unknown, but they were often demeaning, servile, and anonymous: Aunt Jemima, the Cream of Wheat man, Uncle Ben, the Gold Dust twins, and so on. Indeed, McClintock tellingly shows that such "commodity racism" was not just reflective of how the broader society's racism showed up in ads but deeply constitutive of the very ways whites connected race, pleasure, and service.[5]

And then O.J. Simpson, two years out of junior college and not having played a down in the NFL, suddenly entertained so many offers from advertisers that he could turn down any proposals that he appear in individual commercials, insisting on contracting only as an ongoing spokesperson for products. Money poured in from GM, from Royal Crown Cola (for whom Simpson had worked as a deliveryman until shortly before moving to USC), and from so many other sponsors that, as one *Sports Illustrated* writer put it, he was busy just cashing checks. ABC made him a network sportscaster. He soon would impress Schick as not so different as to rule out his appearances in shaving ads. By 1977, he would win polls as the most admired person among U.S. fifth to twelfth graders and as the "most watchable man" in the world. He would garner *Advertising Age*'s "Oscar" as the top celebrity spokesperson in the U.S., and he would receive coverage not just as the most successful black athlete in attracting money from beyond his sport but as the most successful athlete of any color.[6]

That this phenomenal success began in 1969, after Simpson's Heisman Trophy-winning season, not in his record-breaking 1973 NFL year, is crucial in beginning to explain his crossover appeal. Then, as now, winning the Heisman had little relation to future professional success, but corporations and the media took a chance on O.J. The sunlit 1968 season of Simpson's Heisman "campaign"—he had chosen Southern Cal in large part because its campaign machinery had functioned so well when Mike Garrett won the trophy—stands out anomalously against the other dramas of that eventful year. But those stormy events constitute an indispensable context for any explanation of Simpson's commercial crossover. His triumph—not in the Heisman race where he had no close rivals, but in the corporate world—lay in the distance Simpson put between himself and

those momentous events, quite as much as in the ground
between him and would-be tacklers.[7]

Simpson's reception during and after his Heisman campaign unfolded amidst revolt and repression. In 1968, from Paris
to Prague to Mexico City to Chicago, protesters faced guns,
clubs, and tanks as they campaigned for nothing less than a new
society. Vietcong military campaigns reached their turning point
in the bloody Tet offensive. The U.S. presidential campaign saw
the assassination of Robert F. Kennedy and police riots at the
Democratic national convention. Richard M. Nixon won the
White House, skillfully deploying a "southern strategy" of
appeal to white backlash. The campaign of Memphis sanitation
workers for dignity and trade union rights moved Martin Luther
King, Jr., to that city and to his death.

Students, African Americans, Californians, and, to an
unprecedented extent, athletes played central roles in the struggles of 1968. Thus, Simpson's glorious Saturday afternoons, his
disdain for "politics," his ability to socialize one moment with
Bill Cosby and the next with John Wayne, and his smiling California and American dreaming stood out in sharp contrast to
other televised images and realities of campuses, of the Bay area,
of southern California, of black America, and of the world of
sports. Decathlete Rafer Johnson disarmed the assassin of
Kennedy, who was shot as he celebrated victory in the California
primary. The Black Panther Party, whose roots lay in the Bay
area, also became a significant force and a victim of savage
COINTELPRO police repression in southern California. California's campuses continued to be symbols of student revolt,
especially in the Bay area and Los Angeles. California's Governor
Ronald Reagan, Senator George Murphy, and San Francisco
State University administrator S.I. Hayakawa joined Nixon, yet
another Californian, as the most visible figures capitalizing on

opposition to campus protests. So extensive was politicization across the ideological spectrum that even Nixon had an African-American superstar as an active supporter. Wilt Chamberlain, drawn to Nixon's advocacy of black capitalism, was the tallest delegate at the 1968 Republican convention.[8]

In sports, two symbols dominated what the sociologist and activist Harry Edwards called the "revolt of the black athlete." The first, Muhammad Ali, faced jail in 1968 and suffered suspension from boxing for his refusal to regard the Vietcong as his enemy and to be inducted into the military as a draftee. Pretty, poetic, and seemingly invulnerable in the ring, Ali clearly enjoyed greater recognition, nationally and internationally, than any other American athlete. Just as clearly, he had what the advertisers and pollsters call "high negatives."[9]

The second symbol of black athletes' revolt—the protests surrounding the 1968 Mexico City Olympic games—hit far closer to home for Simpson. The entire summer games carried an immense political charge, from Cold War medal-counting to the gunning down of protesters, which, more tellingly than the lighting of the Olympic torch, marked the beginning of the competition. The struggle over participation in South Africa's reentry to the games invigorated international antiapartheid protest. Fighting for a host of demands, the topmost of which was an end to Ali's victimization and at the center of which were the rights of collegiate athletes, California's Edwards and others built the Olympic Project for Human Rights, which counted Dr. King among its supporters. For a time, the threat of an African-American boycott of the games loomed. Lew Alcindor, Lucius Allen, and Mike Warren of UCLA's outstanding basketball team all declined to try out for the U.S. team. Alcindor's gracefully worded demurral did not stop threats against his life. Although he would not adopt the name Kareem Abdul-Jabbar until later,

Alcindor converted to Islam in 1968. In Mexico City, California-based sprinters Tommie Smith and John Carlos, both of San Jose State University, protested most visibly, famously clenching their fists in Black Power salutes on the victory stand after the 200-meter race. Simpson, who had run a leg on a world record-setting 4 by 110 yards sprint relay team earlier in 1968, might well have competed at Mexico City had he concentrated solely on track. Back in California, he publicly denounced the Olympic protests. This denunciation was of a piece with Simpson's generally oppositional stance vis-à-vis the revolt of the black athlete, though his frequently noncombatant response of simply ignoring freedom struggles and his ability to tap into certain aspects of Ali's cultural style and of Chamberlain's black capitalism also are vital in accounting for Simpson's ability to cross over.[10]

Southern Cal, in contrast to UCLA's limited but real progressivism, had an abysmal record of race relations. Even the *Sports Illustrated* reporters there to write on Simpson's football exploits commented on the tense, besieged-by-the-city whiteness of the campus. Dean Cromwell, the legendary track coach who engineered many of the school's most significant pre-Simpson triumphs, explained in the 1940s that "the Negro excels in the events he does because he is closer to the primitive than the white man." In the late 1960s, the school's enrollment of nonathlete black students was tiny, a fact the student newspaper complacently explained by noting that this was because tuition was so high. At a time when football success had passed overwhelmingly to large public universities, USC was an oddity: an elite (in terms of tuition) college football power. When a necessarily small black student movement took shape at Southern Cal, Simpson denounced it. He argued that its leaders were rich "Baldwin Hills" kids agonizing over a black identity that they had just discovered, but one that he was "born with" by virtue of his poverty.[11] Whatever the doubtful merits of this analysis of USC's movement, it deserves noting that origins among the working poor hardly kept such leading figures as Ali or Tommie Smith away from protest. Simpson's main competitor for the Heisman, Purdue running back Leroy Keyes, proudly told reporters of his role in militant protests, including the hanging of a banner reading THE FIRE NEXT TIME. Simpson emphasized his "own philosophy" of positioning himself to be able to make charitable contributions and to offer himself as a role model of financial success to black youth.[12]

Simpson carried into the professional ranks an animosity to "politics," which meant for him both endorsing candidates and supporting protests. He offered to stay out of politics as long as politicians stayed out of football. At the time, as Nelson George puts it, "Brothers [in sports] were sporting huge Afros, bell-bottom pants and gold medallions. They were reading Eldridge Cleaver's *Soul on Ice*, listening to the Last Poets and smoking marijuana instead of drinking beer." Simpson meanwhile disavowed drug use, kept private his feeling that it would be "crazy" to go to Vietnam, and made fun of bearded acquaintances to reporters, referring to them as H. Rap Brown. Buffalo's team had a hair and grooming code during his early career. That Simpson complied made him look different from many athletes of the time. He again connected beards and politics in the late 1970s, in a remarkable, highly public campaign to have Robert Altman cast him as Coalhouse Walker, the black entertainer-cum-revolutionary in the film version of E. L. Doctorow's *Ragtime*. Not only did reporters note his sudden interest in African-American culture and politics and his new, bearded look, but Simpson himself repeatedly announced that he was changing his image in a frank bid to get a role that would enable him to realize his central acting goal: to become a "bankable" star.[13]

Simpson also weighed in during the mid-seventies on an issue of great concern among antiracist sports activists, the near total absence of black quarterbacks in an increasingly African-American National Football League. Coaches continually steered black quarterbacks to other positions—those for which speed and power, rather than intelligence and leadership, figured most prominently in the job description. Discouraged by many college coaches, black quarterbacks were infrequently drafted as professionals and, when they were, needed to deliver solid results much more quickly than white signal callers. James Harris, a young black quarterback who had performed successfully and won no steady starting job, became a focus of the debate. Simpson provoked strong opposition in the black press in 1977 when he unaccountably offered the opinion that an aging and injured Joe Namath could better quarterback the Rams than could Harris, who for a time played on the Bills with Simpson.[14] Only on the issue of freer movement between teams for professional athletes did Simpson flirt with protest movements. But even on this matter his retreats, and the grounds for them, were more spectacular than his advances.

In 1969, Simpson made plans to sue the National Football League—even before he had ever played a down in it. Fresh off of his Heisman Trophy-winning 1968 season at Southern Cal and drafted by the Buffalo Bills, Simpson badly wanted to avoid going to a frigid city with a poor team and a small market. He came within an eyelash of emulating baseball's Curt Flood and risking his career to challenge restrictions on the free movement from team to team by players. Like Flood, a gifted St. Louis Cardinal centerfielder much influenced by the black freedom movement, Simpson sometimes cast his personal contractual situation within a broader civil rights framework. His large contracts with General Motors and other corporations, Frank Deford observed in *Sports Illustrated*, made it possible for Simpson to finance legal action and to survive a delay in signing. But the corporate endorsements cut two ways. The negotiator for the Bills, an ex-union lawyer, appealed to Simpson to realize that the real money coming his way would be provided by advertisers, not football owners, and that such endorsements could only continue if he remained in football's limelight. Chevrolet, the negotiator argued, would not fork over another quarter million dollars to a holdout. After much hesitation, Simpson signed for far less than he had demanded. He admitted that the agreement was a capitulation on his part, but he embraced the logic that his real future lay in advertising and "image." Looking around at all the things he had acquired, particularly his new home, and glorying in his relationship with Chevrolet division head John DeLorean reassured O.J. that he had done the right thing. He would again threaten legal action against the League in the middle 1970s when he charged the NFL with placing itself above the Constitution and supported the 1974 players' strike; he also predicted cooperative ownership of all franchises. But his flirtations with open challenges to the League typically stopped short of decisive action. Simpson's first year with the Bills would be the subject of a book, written with the football journalist Pete Axthelm. Despite his disappointing contract, its title, *Education of a Rich Rookie*, was apt and significant.[15]

Locating Simpson's crossover success within the era of the revolt of the black athlete illuminates two critical ironies of that crossover. The first is that militants in and out of sports both established the preconditions for the advertising and media success of a Simpson *and* ensured that the first athlete to cash in on new possibilities would be anything but a militant. Black Power, as Robert Weems has shown, brought sharply rising interest in African-American markets among advertising executives: the ferment of 1968 in particular brought an unprecedented escalation in civil rights lobbying against racism in advertising; mass pressure encouraged sports, media, and marketing elites to search energetically for role models and to trumpet the myth of sport as a "level playing field" so loudly as to deflect attention from inequalities within athletics and from the realities of who owned and ran the industry. The second irony is more subtle. In making his historic crossover breakthrough, Simpson's seeming transcendence of color rested squarely on his racial identity. The epithet "white man's Negro" is noteworthy in this connection, even though we are far more interested in why Simpson's image sold, and in what he bought into, than in the question of whether he sold out. Even the most assimilative crossover strategies rested not only on just pleasing the white (in Simpson's case mainly male) public but in pleasing that public as a "Negro." Being a cheerful athlete who deflected attention from black revolt worked so powerfully in Simpson's case not because he crossed over from black to white. Instead, those attributes had meaning largely because he remained an African American as they enabled him to cross over from athlete to advertisement.[16]

Buying and Selling Houses: Home and the Traffic in Style

Simpson's wealth underwrote a Southern California existence that took him far from his roots in inner-city San Francisco to fabulous homes in overwhelmingly white areas. His lifestyle-of-the-rich-and-suburban image reinforced his seeming transcendence of color in a nation in which upper-class whiteness is often cast as the normative experience. However, not only did Simpson's pride in grand homes grow out of his past, but white fascination with his lifestyle and with what flavor he could bring to suburban blandness fundamentally hinged on Simpson's racial identity. At fifteen, and just out of a short stay at a youth detention center, O.J. Simpson got to spend much of a day with the Giants' centerfielder Willie Mays. During this adventure, Simpson later and often related, he was not awed. But the ease of Mays's manner and the absence of any preaching regarding staying out of trouble deeply impressed Simpson. Equally impressive was simply viewing Mays's house and possessions. This visit convinced Simpson of what success could bring. He worshipped Mays not simply for being a great player but for having "a big house to show for it." Fiercely defensive of Mays when the latter was said to pay insufficient attention to using his fame to further African-American causes, Simpson argued that his teenage encounter with superstardom provided a model for celebrity role modeling. In Heisman-year interviews and after he emphasized not only a desire to fund a boys' club in the "old neighborhood" of Potrero Hill but to build an impressive house for himself outside of it. He cast *both* acts in terms of aiding black youth. "I feel that it's the material things that count," he told reporters when explaining how to impress lessons on young people. To accusations that he played the "Establishment game" to acquire "the money ... the big house," he replied that such acquisitions would "give pride and hope to a lot of young blacks." From his early *Sports Illustrated* interviews to the video he has sold after acquittal, Simpson has toured America through his houses. Indeed, prosecuting attorney Christopher Darden has recently complained that Simpson gave such tours when the jury in his murder trial visited his Rockingham home.[17]

Simpson's passion for houses and homes as the symbols of success was not surprising, given his own youth as a resident in housing projects built as temporary shelter for World War II

shipyard workers in the Bay area and his father's absence from
the family. Simpson could enthuse, in an interview with *Playboy*,
over the projects as "America the Beautiful," and a "federally
funded commune," but he seldom looked back after his move to
Southern Cal. Although *Time* referred to him as "molded by the
slums," reporters and biographers showed little interest in the
facts of his youth. (The mainstream press spelled Potrero Hill
no less than four different ways, and usually wrong. His own
autobiography, with Pete Axthelm doing the writing, offered the
least plausible misspelling.)[18] The "old neighborhood" became,
not just for Simpson but for the press, a source of a handful of
legends, spun out as the occasion required and with much of the
ambience of *West Side Story*. Almost all the accounts centered on
whether the "gangs" Simpson joined, and sometimes headed,
were or weren't tough and criminal. To a remarkable extent,
Simpson managed to portray his gang activity as both hard and
masculine, and as playful and harmless. Even when he referred to
cohorts as a "bunch of cutthroats," the half-seriousness of his
account perfectly struck a chord allowing readers to see his youth
variously. He described his teenage encounter with marijuana
with similarly wonderful ambiguity. Long before President Clinton professed to have "not inhaled," Simpson offered virtually
the same account of what happened when he was offered a joint
after the "hippie invasion" of San Francisco. Like Clinton, he
told the story with a savvy that mixed blamelessness with intimations of a thorough knowledge of the drug culture.[19]

But in the main, Potrero Hill functioned simply as a backdrop to Simpson's real life of stardom. Even when he was just a
year out of San Francisco, *Ebony* wrote of Simpson as a "once-
tough youngster" who had become "a model of deportment, a
B-minus student, a dedicated husband, and an interviewer's
dream." Simpson's collaborator on his 1970 book described him as

having succeeded in "running from the traps of his ghetto upbringing . . . towards new dreams and images of himself." Simpson married his high school sweetheart and hung out consistently at Southern Cal and elsewhere with Al Cowlings, a high school teammate. But his visits to Potrero Hill were increasingly infrequent. When publicized, they were mediated by charitable contributions and commodities—most spectacularly when Simpson publicized juices with ads revisiting his youth.[20]

The most significant erasure in accounts of Simpson's youth is that of the 1966 rebellion against San Francisco police violence after Matthew Johnson, a black teenager, was shot dead by a white patrolman in the Hunters Point/Potrero Hill area. For more than five days, "soft" and "hard" antiriot tactics failed to quell the defiance, looting, arson, and vandalism. Damage caused by the rebellion was limited, but police intimidation of the community was not. The authorities' attempts to enlist the aid of ex-gang leaders—the leading study of the neighborhood insists gangs "no longer existed" in Hunters Point in the mid-1960s—failed dramatically. So too did efforts to bring in middle-class "community leaders," largely from other neighborhoods. Police so aggressively "herded" blacks from other public spaces in the city to Hunters Point that "moderate responsible" adults feared that a plan was being implemented in which an aircraft carrier passing in the Bay would stage massive bombings of the neighborhood "like," as one resident put it, "they do in Vietnam." These extremely bitter relations with the police, and the passionate denunciation of "Uncle Toms" and "white Negroes" on Potrero Hill during and after the 1966 events, figure nowhere in accounts of Simpson's youth, though they are vitally important as context to both his triumphs in the sixties and trials in the nineties.[21]

Far more remarkable than the desire to escape poverty, enjoy the fruits of achievement, and secure privacy, which led Simpson to concern himself so passionately with house and home, was the extent to which his hunting for both became a hugely publicized story on America's sports pages. The larger society's obsession with his personal obsession is another key to his crossover appeal and demands an explanation set in the context of the larger racial politics of the period. When Simpson showed reporters his first home going up in Los Angeles's Coldwater Canyon, the focus was on color and housing, but in a way strikingly unfamiliar to readers. At a time when such idols of Simpson's youth as Bill Russell and, significantly, Willie Mays, had recently suffered through highly publicized incidents of racial discrimination in housing in California, and when NFL teams had just begun to break the color line in rooming assignments, Simpson's concern centered on the orange color of Los Angeles's smoggy air. His solution was a fully private one. The house sat, he proudly noted, above the "smog line."[22]

This same sense of the transcendence of concern about race via class mobility ran through the long-running drama of Simpson's attempts to get out of his Buffalo Bills contract and to play at "home." From the start of his pro career, the preferred home was a wealthy section of Los Angeles, not his longtime boyhood home. Simpson's image was not just that of a Californian, but of a wealthy southern Californian. His world was warm, cosmopolitan, lavish, and upscale. Buffalo, known as ethnic and working-class as well as cold, had a team run as a "rinky-dink" operation, and it was a city with nothing going on. Its grime and grit contrasted with L.A.'s splendor and sparkle in a drama in which Simpson's race seemingly mattered little and his class and regional loyalties much. Indeed, in describing what made Buffalo rinky-dink, he told *Playboy*, "In college, I'd played at L.A. Coliseum, which you can see from half a mile away. In Buffalo, you'd be walking through a black neighborhood and suddenly, sixty feet in front of you, you'd see this old, rundown stadium."[23] Simpson so consistently criticized Buffalo that when his salary reached a (mis)reported $2.5 million annually, Johnny Carson joked that the half million was for playing football, the balance for living there. His decisions to renege on refusals to go back to the Bills consistently turned on dollars and on supporting his Bel-Air lifestyle. In 1973, he returned to Buffalo, for example, after a hard look at "the material things that I have" in Bel-Air. His symbolic value here went quite beyond providing a hopeful scenario regarding fame and wealth as antidotes to racial division. Embodying and very visibly championing the lifestyle of the white upper-middle class in the very region in which its growth and pretensions were most spectacular, Simpson reassured a vital segment of audiences that what they had and wanted, along with the ways in which they related work to consumption, were everybody's dreams, the profound questions raised by the black freedom movement, by hippies, and by the sixties generally notwithstanding. Simpson's race, even and especially when unmentioned, mattered greatly in his providing of this reassurance.[24]

A subplot of the "let's rescue O.J. from Buffalo" melodrama more directly focused on race. Almost all of the many stories of his migrations and his threats to stay put mentioned his thorough consideration of family in all decisions. Since Marguerite neither liked Buffalo nor wished to uproot the children twice a year, joining and rejoining the Bills meant extensive separation from his nuclear family (such separations from his mother and other extended family members went largely unremarked). Coverage consistently stressed Simpson's role as a model father and husband who anguished over the decision and recalled his own father's estrangement from the household as Simpson grew up. "Home is always where the heart is," *Parents' Magazine* headlined in a Simpson profile, which allowed that it was often not where he was. The utter responsibility of O.J.'s decision contrasted sharply with the father's apparently unconsidered decision, as did the tremendous financial reward O.J. gained with the lack of support provided by his father. At a time, like ours, when single mothers and absent fathers were indicted as the keys to the "pathology" of black families and communities, the "O.J., L.A., and Buffalo" stories did more than offer a positive role model. They portrayed African-American success as overwhelmingly hinging on male responsibility, so that Simpson and not Marguerite became the model family member, even as Willie Mays often crowded Simpson's mother out of the success story of O.J.'s youth.[25]

However much Simpson marginalized racism and claimed a colorless appeal, his crossover success very much rested on his race. This was true not only with regard to his anti-Black Power, suburban homeboy positioning, but also with regard to his ability to resonate with familiar racist marketing images and to sell new images of black style. Although his later advertising image came more or less strictly out of the country club, Simpson's early appeals very much drew on the marketing of black athletic style for crossover purposes. He did so at a time when African-American "aesthetics" had begun to dominate images of professional basketball, when Maury Wills and Lou Brock had revolutionized base running, and when Muhammad Ali had brought to the public new styles in boxing and voluble reflections on those styles.[26] Simpson's claims to symbolize stylistic innovation came from a relatively weak position, especially compared to basketball players, since football was not a game nur-

tured on playgrounds to anything like the extent that basketball was. Played mostly, at least after high school, before white
coaches with white quarterbacks calling the signals, football was
not so dramatically transformed by African-American athletes,
though running back was the most changed position. Nor, of
course, was Simpson's style anything like as distinctive as Ali's.
With neither the power of Jimmy Brown, who more than dou-
bled Simpson's professional touchdowns in a significantly
shorter career, nor the breakaway creativity of Gale Sayers,
Simpson was a brilliant back largely because of his combination
of gifts. But that combination did not rival Brown's.

Nonetheless, Simpson, profiting greatly from increased use
of slow-motion photography in sports, did successfully cultivate
public interest in his style, which he linked to African-American
expressive behavior. Although his Heisman campaign stressed
the standard elements of grit, aggression, power, and speed,
Simpson quickly developed a more distinctive rap about his
style. Reporters referred to his "jive patter" regarding descriptions of his own running, replete with references to music and
dance. While other backs slashed and ground out yardage, his
game plan involved fakes and feints—"juking the tough guys," as
he put it, using in "juke" a term that referred to dance halls and
evasive swerving as well as to sex. He told *Playboy* that "setting a
cat down" with a convincing open-field fake and cut was his
greatest football thrill. Stressing his own studied invulnerability,
he claimed to have learned to tell the place on the field of all
defenders as plays unfolded so that he could avoid crippling hits.
Nor, he bragged, even during the hard early years in Buffalo, did
he hesitate to go out of bounds to avoid punishing tackles. He
never let critics force him to squirm for the last bit of yardage
and therefore offered star defenders like Dick Butkus (the line-
backer Simpson most delightedly talked of frustrating) slim

chances to hit him squarely. On his own description, he hit holes "like a coward" searching for seams.[27]

In his caginess, in his claims of an invulnerability born of intelligence and instinct, and in his ability to evoke comparisons with dancers, Simpson called to mind the ways in which Ali marketed his style. Like Ali, Simpson made individual claims to redefine and transcend his sport. Sportswriters accepted Simpson's claims and the connections to Ali. One major account argued that Simpson's appeal lay in his daring demonstration that "a man can play football just the way he lives." As early as 1968, *Senior Scholastic* clearly made the links to Ali, claiming that Simpson "changed direction like a butterfly and hit with the power of an oil truck."[28]

Echoing the champ's penchant for rhyming self-promotion, Simpson named his deceptive repertoire of fakes, shifts, starts, and pauses as the *okey-doke*, again popularizing "jive" black speech. The press bit hard on the term. His 1973 season, *Time* headlined, was the "Year of the Okey-Doke." When Simpson shared a story of fooling high school administrators with playful lies, he was portrayed as perfecting the "verbal *okey-doke*." Like Will Smith in the recent television comedy hit *Fresh Prince of Bel-Air*, Simpson safely brought sprinklings of "the other's" slang to white Americans. He may also have had a sly, complicated laugh of his own in the case of *okey-doke*, which not only meant a "con game" but also sardonically referred to "white values."[29]

Simpson's nicknames offered a further opportunity for white fans to consume the "other." In reflecting on Michael Jordan, breakfast cereal, and McDonald's (which once named a sandwich after Jordan), Michael Eric Dyson has recently argued that the historic consumption of black bodies by Western capitalism is recapitulated in a very different form today via athletics and athletic endorsements.[30] In Simpson's case, the tie between older and newer forms was greatly facilitated by his nicknames. Called O.J. rather than Orenthal James since his youth, Simpson was, according to one journalist, nearly as famous for being dubbed Orange Juice as for his running at Southern Cal. "The Juice," connoting energy, appears to have been generated in Buffalo, where Simpson's blockers were the "Electric Company." As Orange Juice, Simpson came prepackaged as a breakfast staple, recapitulating the impressive history of black advertising icons invited into homes to serve morning pleasure. The Orange Juice image not only contributed to the sunny, cheerful "Southern Californiazation" of Simpson. It also connected him to Aunt Jemima and to the Cream of Wheat man and offered, a la the McJordan sandwich, a direct opportunity for Simpson to be consumed. His runaway fame eventually made "O.J.," originally a "lunch counter" abbreviation, more popular as the familiar reference to orange juice. His earliest and some of his most lucrative endorsements came from juice contracts, especially the "teaming up of two great juices" in Tree Sweet ads. If his big contracts broke with advertising's powerful tradition of "commodity racism," his image was also very much a part of that tradition.[31]

Media-Made O.J.: Race, Speech, and Slow-Motion Supermanhood

As early as 1968, media projections of O.J. Simpson so insistently pegged him as Superman that his first wife, Marguerite Simpson, felt the need to remind the press that there's no such thing.[32] If not quite interplanetary, Simpson's aura of greatness and goodness was distinctly Supermanly, and that aura suffused accounts of his image as being above the racial fray. In his reflections on the trial, none of Simpson's anger runs more deeply than that directed against the press, which he portrays as suddenly seeing him in terms of race, and making him regretfully see race in everyday life. The contrast that Simpson notes was stark. Before 1994 he enjoyed adulation from the sports media's star-making machinery and a quarter-century's work as one of the boys in the booth of television sportscasting. After 1994, he became (literally in the case of *Time* magazine's famous cover) a blackened figure. Executives, who had earlier held that his jobs would likely be waiting for him if a "not guilty" verdict came in, made no gestures toward such reemployment.[33] But to see such dramatic changes as simply a movement from colorless acceptance to race thinking misses the large extent to which Simpson's Superman image was itself about race and the extent to which he remained the black guy in the booth as well as one of the boys there.

Simpson's media image clearly derived from long-standing journalistic traditions and modern television innovations that influenced the public's view of both white and black athletes, though in differing ways. When Los Angeles *Times* sportswriter Dwight Chapin flatly proclaimed "Superman is Orenthal James Simpson" in 1968, he followed a tradition of monumentalizing football heroes dating back almost a century. An 1891 New York *World* football story caught the spectacular flavor perfectly:

> Surely, here were the old Roman kings circled about in their clattering chariots gloating over the running fight, and satiated with death.... Here were the lovely maidens of ancient days, turning down their pretty thumbs with every mangling scrimmage, and shrieking with delight at every thrust and parry ... Think of Ulysses, as a center rush, of Menelaus as a guard or of Paris as a quarterback.[34]

The early twentieth century's Walter Camp-inspired reportage on All-American football role models, mostly from elite colleges, coexisted with, and by the 1920s gave ground to, emphases on spectacle, violence, and the alleged racial and ethnic characteristics of minority players. Nor did decades of print journalism on football decide the tension between dwelling on manly, individual heroism or the competing and equally masculine narrative of teamwork and male bonding in the trenches. Simpson—a ghetto kid at an elite private school and the breakaway Juice in the open field, as well as a back depending on the blocking and loyalty of the Electric Company line in front of him—became the focus of these tensions and traditions, especially in *Sports Illustrated* reporting. Nowhere did his distance from the 1968 protest help him more than among sportswriters, whose opposition to the Olympic boycott was broad and angry.[35]

Ironically, the media's fascination with Simpson's supermanly body and spirit coexisted with emphases on the abuse that body took from tacklers and on the inevitability of injury. The "Superman for a day" narrative of so much media coverage of modern sports finds its best expression in highlight films of football, showing bodies that "can fly," but which also collide, writhe, and break. Not incidentally, these bodies are increasingly black and the audience consuming images of their triumph and destruction is overwhelmingly white.

Growing up with a largely untreated case of rickets, leading to childhood taunts as "Pencil Pins," Simpson was acutely aware of disability. Sportswriters and opposing coaches often commented on his practice of getting up very slowly after being tackled, looking absolutely unable to continue, and then fully bouncing back. This habit, reminiscent of Jimmy Brown and designedly disheartening to defenses, dramatically suggested Simpson's vulnerability. His early Ali-like boasts regarding invincibility backhandedly raised the same concerns. In his many interview references to endorsements and films as necessary to ensure a career after football, Simpson increasingly broached the issues of the inevitable brevity of his career and of the peril to his body. Sportswriters played on the same theme. Predictably enough, Simpson was in fact chronically hurt by his later years in the NFL. His murder trial's references to his joint problems only continued a long-running pattern of press coverage regarding the results of the "sacrifice" of Simpson's body. Nowhere was the obsession better reflected than in the *Naked Gun* film series, in which Simpson's acting career came pitifully to rest on the repetition of injuries, culminating in a pratfall from a wheelchair. If part of the humor here arose from the contrast with Simpson's slow-motion grace in the field and in Hertz commercials, the gags also recalled his long career of risking and receiving crippling injuries, of "sacrificing his body" before white audiences.[36]

Print journalists, who consistently emphasized his "mild, warm, and talkative" nature as against the moodiness of Bill Russell or the cerebral qualities of Kareem Abdul-Jabbar, helped Simpson toward crossover salability by making him known as an affable and "inoffensive" football superstar.[37] But it was television coverage and corporate sponsorship that contributed most decisively to the polishing and preserving of his image of easygoing Supermanhood. Both as the football-playing object of the television camera's attention and as the sportscaster covering football and the whole "wide world of sports," Simpson's fortunes consistently intertwined with those of the producer Roone Arledge. Arledge's technical innovations in the filming of sports and his studied blurring of the lines between journalism and entertainment helped to make a spectacle of Simpson.[38] His reliance on Simpson as a broadcaster helped to ensure that O.J. would not leave the spotlight and would function as one of the boys in sports journalism, largely insulated from serious criticism.

The story of dramatic and seemingly race-neutral technical innovations in the world of televised sports is largely Arledge's story. Arledge began the transformation of television sports coverage seven years before Simpson entered USC. Hired at ABC's sports division in 1960, he immediately set out to cover sporting "events"—as sets of spectacular happenings—off as well as on the field. In 1966, when ABC signed a contract with the NCAA, granting it exclusive college football coverage, Arledge pioneered in the introduction of instant replay during live telecasts. He combined this technique with the extensive incorporation of slow-motion photography. The latter technology, applied to the screening of sports since the early twentieth century and used most effectively by the Nazi director Leni Riefenstahl in the 1930s, had become a staple of Arledge-produced sports telecasts by the time Simpson played his most touted games at USC.[39]

The combination of slow motion and instant replay—along with Arledge's increased use of close-ups, stop action, and sidebar stories on individual athletes—transformed the ways in which sports, and Simpson, were seen. It suddenly became arguable that television viewers could take in more of the action than those at the event. So thoroughly did Arledge come to regard the game as only the raw material from which he would fashion a "show" that his *Wide World of Sports* often featured esoteric sports, with little worry that viewers would be lost.[40] Simpson profited greatly from Arledge's innovations. He smiled not only engagingly, as other athletes had, but in stop action, as they largely had not. Above all, Simpson was among the first great backs to play his full college career with slow-motion instant replay in full use. The effect of such replays cut in two directions. On the one hand, it made couch-bound athletes of all races able to imagine themselves "in his shoes," seeing the holes in the defense and the coming of contact in ways live action precluded. Hertz advertisers appreciated as much in transforming Simpson to a slow-motion rusher through airports. On the other hand, slow-motion replays became vital in the popularizing and even the naming of specifically African-American sports performance styles such as the one Simpson marketed with his "jive talk." As Riefenstahl appreciated, slow-motion photography let viewers linger over the "natural" bodies of athletes, making it an effective vehicle for her monumentalizing of Aryan supermen in sports. Before Arledge, slow motion had most frequently been used in the filming of boxing matches, contests in which racially and ethnically typed bodies contested most nakedly and openly.[41] Slow motion also, as Arthur Ashe brilliantly observed, provided the medium that could best showcase highly improvised and visually exciting running styles increasingly seen as hallmarks of African-American players, especially Simpson. So thoroughly were race, body, and style entwined in viewers' perspectives that the extent to which intelligence and judgment undergird such rushing went almost unremarked. Instead, the style was seen as natural and Simpson as not only Superman but "supernatural."[42]

Beyond technical innovations, Arledge typified two other important trends in sports television, changes that would influence both coverage of Simpson as a player and by Simpson as a reporter. The first centered on his further blurring of the line between sports journalism and entertainment. Famously illustrated by Howard Cosell's bitter writings on the battle between professionals (i.e., Cosell) and "jockocrats" (everyone else) on Arledge's *Monday Night Football*, the threat to standards posed by Arledge's allowing stars to report sports was undoubtedly overblown. Ex-athletes had long announced games, and Cosell himself used celebrity rather than qualifications to branch out into reporting on sports about which his expertise was much in doubt. When Arledge's entertainment-first philosophy won him promotion to heading the news division, Cosell steamed because he was not hired to work on the news side, alongside such Arledge discoveries as Geraldo Rivera. Print journalism's standards of objectivity in sports reporting hardly provided an impeccable professional model for television. The broader ethical problems of the cozy, contractual, and mutually rewarding relationships between the networks and the leagues, and between the networks and sponsors who used celebrity spokespersons who were being reported on during the games, raise much more troubling issues than the presence of jockocrats. Nonetheless, Arledge's use of "jocks," including active professional athletes, on telecasts clearly set the stage for Simpson's crossover into media and abetted the sort of nonreporting that caused fraying in Simpson's Superman cape to go unremarked.[43]

The fraternity of jockocrats that Cosell ultimately hated was part of a second contribution of Arledge as a producer. He popularized a sports television style that crafted an appeal designed mainly around gender rather than race or class. Comparing football to bullfights and heavyweight boxing, he hoped to capture some interest from women, but not because they appreciated either the subtleties of football or even the "deftness" of an athlete generally. Instead, he hoped women would tune in to "see what everyone is wearing [and] watch the cheerleaders." He filmed the latter from "a creepy, peepy camera," knowing that "very few men have ever switched channels when a nicely proportioned girl was leaping into the air."[44] Before coming to sports programming, Arledge had hoped his pilot of *For Men Only*, described as a network version of *Playboy*, would move

his career beyond the producing of *Hi, Mom,* Shari Lewis's pup-
pet show. Much of his football programming could have also
carried the "for men only" tag. Male camaraderie was especially
at a premium in the antics of the "teams" of broadcasters, especially the road warriors covering *Monday Night Football.*[45]

Simpson joined the boys on ABC telecasts quite early in
his career, very much as both a jockocrat and as a black voice. As
in advertising, his crossover from the football field to television
reporting was precocious and virtually without precedent. He
had just left USC when Arledge signed him to a 1970 contract as
a very visible freelancer with *Wide World of Sports.* That role, and his
reporting on the 1972 Olympics, cast Simpson as an American,
abroad and often at sea in the confusing variety of international
athletic competitions.[46] But far from colorless, Simpson's easygoing presence as a *Wide World* correspondent bespoke efforts to
forget, and to make the world forget, the 1968 Olympics. His
more durable career as a "color man" on football telecasts
unfolded squarely within a context of race. He succeeded where
other great black athletes, such as Bill Russell, floundered.
Racism plagued Russell's brief tenure as a superb network basketball commentator and was charged when Fred Williamson
was removed after a few pioneering *Monday Night Football* telecasts.[47] However, that Simpson prospered, and became the first
African American to work regularly on Monday night games,
hardly suggests his transcendence of race. His nonstandard English, so endearing to print reporters, became the object of a
running dialogue among critics, who constantly anticipated
improvement. During his bitter 1983 feud with Simpson, Cosell
began to doubt that his partner's "deplorable diction" and
"locution problems" would ever be remedied.[48] Critics also
noted his bobbing head, mechanical delivery, and forced smile,
but Simpson's highly publicized announcing problems centered

on his language, which was heard as insufficiently white English. His 1985 demotion to pre- and postgame coverage of the Super Bowl brought a rare example of contact between Simpson and a civil rights group, with the NAACP vigorously lobbying ABC on his behalf.[49]

Nor was race absent in the highly gendered and economically driven dynamics that led to the failure of the press to investigate and cover stories regarding Simpson's abuse of women and his use of drugs. After the murders, long-standing reports of Simpson's cocaine use, possible violence toward Marguerite Simpson and women at USC, and allegedly compulsive sexual conquests came to light.[50] That these stories had by and large never seen the light of day, or been subjected to scrutiny, caused no significant self-criticism. (Indeed, recent accounts of sports reporters *buying* drugs from New York Giants players in the 1980s have also created little stir.)[51] We raise this issue of nonreporting not out of a commitment to more sensationalist, censorious news about the personal lives of athletes; we would rather prefer less. But in light of the constant stories on Simpson as family man and role model, the quite negative press on other athletes, and the mania for reporting anything and everything about Simpson after 1994, his insulation from bad press regarding violence, sex, and drugs requires some scrutiny.

That insulation clearly reflected Simpson's role as a commodity valuable to his teams, the NFL, the networks, and major corporate sponsors of games and much else on television. Preserving his image served also to protect the images and profits of powerful interlocking forces. The silence of the press on the difficult, complex relationship of football to male supremacy and to the battering of women suggests how the media and the game protect each other. In Geraldo Rivera's remarkably persistent attempts to combine utter sensationalism with worn-on-the-sleeve concern about domestic violence, you won't hear, for example, the nuanced analysis of gender and football provided in James McBride's *War, Battering and Other Sports*.[52]

Simpson likewise benefited from a more intimate form of journalistic self-protection. When he interrupted filming of a sidebar story on "nightlife" and football to have semipublic sex in the backseat of a car, or when he sought out one-night stands during his marriages, Simpson hardly outraged the norms of sports journalism. Arledge had married the personal secretary of RCA head David Sarnoff in 1953. She typed Arledge's proposal for a pilot on Sarnoff's letterhead and forwarded it to the president of NBC, then an RCA subsidiary, as if it came from on high. This "different brand of cunning" failed, as did the marriage, when Arledge left his wife while on vacation. He subsequently married his secretary, a former Miss Alabama, seventeen years his junior.[53] Cosell, the professional on *Monday Night Football,* "joked" with network secretaries by unbuttoning their blouses "playfully." More broadly, the ABC network had precisely one woman in an executive position.[54] Sexism at the top was neither news nor a topic to be investigated with relish.

But as thoroughly structured by male supremacy and economic self-interest as the nonreporting on O.J. was, the dynamics by which his image was propped up were hardly colorless. The black-star-as-role-model and black-star-as-thug-on-drugs images grew up absolutely in tandem in the press in the last twenty-five years, so that there was little room to cast Simpson in a middle position. Reporters and athletes did not just fraternize via shared drugs, sex, and secrets, but such vices often specifically lubricated more extensive interaction between African-American athletes and white journalists. And, of course, the black Superman media image of the 1970s was also Superspade and Superfly, one in which violence, sex, and drugs were assumed to be prominent. Indeed, so important is the extent to which recent discourses on the common manliness of white and nonwhite men has assumed, expressed, and reinforced racial stereotypes that we conclude with an examination of Simpson, gender, and race that extends beyond the coverage of sports.

Hertz and the Buying of O.J.: Company Man, Real Man, Black Man

In a 1994 *Business Marketing* article describing Simpson's genius, a top Hertz executive credited him with having transcended mere sport and "really taken on the persona of a businessperson," impressively "capable of speaking to another businessperson." Aside from its noteworthy assumption that moving from being among the greatest athletes of one's generation to being a "businessperson" represents a steep ascent, the executive's observation is of interest for its framing of Simpson's crossover as one from sports to commerce in a way which both ignores race and renders Simpson's rise in gender-free language.[55]

Such a claim both captures and obscures large parts of Simpson's appeal to the independent entrepreneurs and the corporate salesmen targeted by Hertz's rental car ads. Simpson consistently emphasized his desire to own businesses and to invest. In his initial Buffalo contract negotiations, the one significant concession he did manage to secure was a large bonus for investment purposes. He not only made films as an actor but also as the owner of a production company. His switch from ABC to NBC was much publicized as resulting from a desire to be a producer.[56] He acquired stakes in many of the corporations he endorsed—enough, as he put it, to be "a player." As time went by, his commitment to being an entrepreneur was increasingly colorless, divorced from any claims to his being a specifically African-American role model in this realm, let alone from the sort of ideologically nationalist commitment to black capitalism so much a part of Jimmy Brown's ongoing projects.[57]

By all accounts constantly busy, always moving about along with other men, risking family relationships amidst anguish in order to be a good provider, Simpson served as a perfect symbol with which the business traveler could identify. However, given the fact that his business ventures were plagued by failures born of incredibly bad timing, and given his great prominence as a spokesperson for Hertz and a host of other corporations, Simpson likely wore the label "company man" more fittingly than "businessman." One of the nation's most sought-after motivational speakers at corporate dinners, Simpson could convincingly address his audiences on the importance of being a "team member" in the corporate world. Appealing to both the independent businessmen and to the company men who constituted the bulk of the rental car market, Simpson sent Hertz's sales and recognition skyward.[58]

But even Simpson's appeal to white men in meetings, airports, and offices ultimately turned on his status as an acceptable and exemplary black man, not as a colorless fellow worker. In this connection the recent study of race, gender, and sport by Lisa Disch and Mary Jo Kane especially succeeds in illuminating how the notion of upper middle-class white masculinity both fantasizes important connections with black athletes and retains prerogatives to judge, type, and distance itself from such stars. Employed largely in physically passive jobs, such men cannot claim maleness based on a working body and therefore base such acclaim to an unprecedented extent on the "sovereign masculinity" of sport.[59] Thus the golf course's male foursome beckons as the reward for choosing Hertz's faster service. The quite passive experience of flying becomes an open field dash through air-ports. Sporting performance by a few professionals becomes the property of many. As one white male professional puts it in a study by the sociologist Michael Messner, "A woman can do the same job as I can do—maybe even be my boss. But I'll be *damned* if she can go out on the football field and take a hit from Ron-nie Lott." Forging pan-male unities, athletic striving particularly shores up male dominance in periods of forward political and economic motion by women so that women's liberation move-ments as well as Black Power form a critical context for Simp-son's rise in the late 1960s.[60]

The view that every male middle manager could "take a hit" from Lott is on one level ludicrous, but such a view expresses in shorthand the very real fact that professional team sports are places where women can't play either on the field or, by and large, participate in ownership and management. For black men, during Simpson's career, sports were one of the few realms in which it was possible to be a "player," though the bars to managerial roles, let alone ownership, remained virtually com-plete. Sport has functioned as a spectacle in which the male body and the white mind are at once exalted, and in which white men feel especially empowered to judge, to bet on, and to vicariously identify with African Americans. Thus, when Simpson, as early as 1969, boasted that his triumph lay in being seen as a "man" and not black, he was half right.[61] The white male target audi-ence had a great interest in claiming his footloose power as male. But in so doing, they could also reserve the right to view his abil-ities as the natural, easy, and elemental traits of what Messner calls the "primitive other." Time and again, sportswriters, execu-tives, and middle-level managers would credit him as a "real man." From fans at corporate dinners to the television executive commenting on why Simpson's "diction" did not get him fired, to the network official who explained why his 1989 domestic violence case did not finish his broadcast career, the judgment was that he was also a "nice guy." Such accolades, we argue, were not colorlessly conferred. At the height of his acceptance, Simpson was a "real black man" and a "nice black guy."[62]

Simpson's crossover success offered white viewers the opportunity to sit in judgment of black manliness at the same moment when they claimed to have gotten past racial thinking. The more marketable appeal was not Simpson's supposed transcendence of race but rather the alleged transcendence of race among his audiences. The terrible force of much white reaction to the trial and to the verdict grows in no small part out of the dynamics described in this article. Such is most obviously the case with regard to the ease with which Simpson's image as a black man could fully accommodate the recrudescence of racist stereotypes. But perhaps more telling has been the outpouring of white rage against the "injection" of the issue of race into the trial—a rage that has consistently blamed a black attorney rather than white police for race's presence in the courtroom. Despite the wholesale change in attitudes toward Simpson himself, his image has remained a vehicle through which white racial ideologies, and the pretense of their absence, can be spun out together.

Notes

Assistance from Tiya Miles, Tom Sabatini, Rachel Martin, and Marjorie Bryer greatly improved this article.

1. The epigraph is from Henry Louis Gates, Jr., and Cornel West, "Affirmative Reaction," *Transition* 68 (December 1995): 180. See also Rob Buchanan, "18 Holes With O.J. Simpson," *Golf,* December 1990, pp. 100, 106; Lawrence Otis Graham, *Member of the Club* (New York: HarperCollins, 1995), p. 17; Joe Marshall, "Now You See Him, Now

You Don't," *Sports Illustrated*, October 19, 1973, pp. 30–43; Marc Cerasini, *O.J. Simpson: American Hero, American Tragedy* (New York: Windsor Publishing, 1994), pp. 196, 226–27; Beth Ann Krier, "What Makes Simpson Run?" *Ebony*, December 1981, p. 109; Teresa Carpenter, "The Man Behind the Mask," *Esquire*, November 1994, pp. 84–90; "Harsh Realities Haunt Simpson," Columbia (MO) *Daily Tribune*, June 25, 1994, p. 3-B; and especially, "*Playboy* Interview: O.J. Simpson," *Playboy* 23 (December 1976): 92–94.

2.   Melanie Wells, "O.J. Agrees to Share Rights to His Initials," *USA Today*, February 22, 1996; Cerasini, *Simpson*, p. 192; *Michigan Chronicle*, July 16, 1977, p. B-1; Louis J. Haugh, "O.J. Tops Year's Star Presenters," *Advertising Age*, June 20, 1977, p. 1; "The Juice Joins the Soda Wars," *Fortune*, September 30, 1985, pp. 9–10; Jack Slater, "O.J. Simpson: The Problems of a Super Superstar," *Ebony*, November 1976, p. 164; Richard Hoffer, "Fatal Attraction," *Sports Illustrated*, June 27, 1994, pp. 22, 31.

3.   See, for example, Hugh Pearson, "Trial by T-Shirt," *Wall Street Journal*, August 12, 1994; "*MAD's* O.J. Pog Schtickers," *MAD Super Special* 105 (July 1995): 31–32; "Enough to Open a Library," *Newsweek*, March 25, 1996, p. 53; Clifford Linedecker, *O.J. From A to Z* (New York: St. Martin's Griffen, 1995), p. 37; "Cashing in on O.J., Reluctantly," *Harper's*, October 1994, p. 21; Adam Hochschild, "Closing Argument," *New York Times Book Review*, April 28, 1996, p. 14.

4.   "The Pack in Search of O.J.'s Roots," *San Francisco Chronicle*, June 25, 1994, p. A-24; Greg Krikorian and Eric Lichtblau, "A Rising Star," *Los Angeles Times*, October 4, 1995, p. A-3; Richard C. Paddock and Jennifer Warren, " 'I Was Somebody Who Didn't Care About Anything,' " *Los Angeles Times*, June 18, 1994, p. A-8; Evelyn C. White, "Fallen Hero Stirs Complicated Feelings," *San Francisco Chronicle*, October 4, 1995, p. A-6; Craig Marine and Leslie Goldberg, "The Hill O.J. Left Behind," *San Francisco Chronicle*, June 26, 1994, pp. A-1, A-8; Simpson, *I Want to Tell You* (Boston: Little, Brown, 1995): pp. 87–89.

5.   Hoffer, "Fatal Attraction," p. 20. The 1996 HBO film of Arthur Ashe's *Hard Road to Glory: A History of the African-American Athlete Since 1946* (New York: Amistad Books, 1988) makes the point on Simpson's pioneering in crossover advertising most acutely, perhaps because Ashe knew the long odds against such crossover firsthand. On advertising, see Roland Marchand, *Advertising and the American Dream* (Berkeley: University of California Press: 1985), p. 193; Jackson Lears, *Fables of Abundance* (New

York: Basic Books, 1994), pp. 123–24; Stephen Fox, *The Mirror Makers: A History of American Advertising and Its Creators* (New York: Morrow, 1984), pp. 280–84; Harry Edwards, "The Black Professional Athlete," in John T. Talamini and Charles H. Page, eds., *Sport and Society: An Anthology* (Boston: Little, Brown, 1973), p. 260; McClintock, *Imperial Leather: Race, Gender and Sexuality in the Colonial Conquest* (New York and London: Routledge, 1995), pp. 31–35, 207–31.

6.   Louis J. Haugh, "O.J. Tops Year's Star Presenters," *Advertising Age*, June 20, 1977, p. 1; Deford, "Ready If You Are," p. 16; Cerasini, *O.J. Simpson*, pp. 84–85, 158–61, 192, 202–3; Edwin Shrake, "The Juice on a Juicy Road," *Sports Illustrated*, August 19, 1974, p. 36.

7.   Teresa Carpenter, "The Man Behind the Mask," *Esquire*, November 1994, p. 87; James Brady, "Sunlit Afternoons and O.J.," *Advertising Age*, June 20, 1994, p. 34.

8.   The best study of 1968 worldwide is George Katsiaficas, *The Imagination of the New Left: A Global Analysis of 1968* (Boston: South End Books, 1987); on the late 1960s in basketball and Chamberlain/Nixon, see Nelson George, *Elevating the Game; The History and Aesthetics of Black Men in Basketball* (New York: Fireside Books, 1992), pp. 152–78.

9.   Edwards, *The Revolt of the Black Athlete* (New York: Free Press, 1970); Talamini and Page, eds., *Sport and Society*, pp. 259–61; Othello Harris, "Muhammad Ali and the Revolt of the Black Athlete," in *Muhammad Ali: The People's Champ*, Elliott J. Gorn, ed. (Urbana and Chicago: University of Illinois Press, 1995), pp. 54–69.

10.   Edwards, *Revolt of the Black Athlete*; Jack Scott, *The Athletic Revolution* (New York: Free Press, 1971), pp. 86–88; Lee Ballinger, *In Your Face* (Chicago: Vanguard Books, 1981), pp. 34–38; George, *Elevating the Game*, pp. 147–48. See, however, Ashe, *Hard Road to Glory*, p. 192, for Simpson's brief support of the antiracist boycott of the New York Athletic Club, and Earl Hutchinson, *Beyond O.J.: Race, Sex and Class Lessons for America* (Los Angeles: Middle Passage Press, 1996), pp. 140, 149.

11.   George, *Elevating the Game*, p. 142; Cromwell quoted in Scott, *Athletic Revolution*, p. 81; "*Playboy* Interview: O. J. Simpson," p. 94; Dan Jenkins, "The Great One Confronts O.J.," *Sports Illustrated*, November 20, 1967, pp. 33, 38; Herman L. Masin, "All the Way with O.J.!" *Senior Scholastic*, October 18, 1968, p. 32; Carpenter, "The Man Behind the Mask," p. 87; A. S. Doc Young, "The Magnificent Six," Los Angeles *Sentinel*, January 17, 1980, p. A-7.

12.   Louie Robinson, "Two Superstars Vie for Heisman Trophy," *Ebony*, December 1968, p. 173.

13.   George, *Elevating the Game*, p. 164; *"Playboy* Interview: O.J. Simpson," pp. 78-B, 85–90, 98–99; Cerasini, *Simpson;* pp. 56, 145, 177–78; Carpenter, "The Man Behind the Mask," pp. 88–89; Frank Deford, "Ready If You Are, O.J.," *Sports Illustrated*, July 14, 1969, p. 19; Pete Axthelm, "The Juice Runs Wild," *Newsweek*, October 27, 1975, p. 10; Simpson with Axthelm, *O.J.: The Education of a Rich Rookie* (New York: Macmillan, 1970), pp. 12–17; Jenkins, "Great One Confronts O.J.," pp. 34–38; Krier, "What Makes O.J. Run?" p. 110; Peter Wood, "What Makes Simpson Run?" *New York Times Magazine*, December 14, 1975, pp. 6–38; Ballinger, *In Your Face*, pp. 47–51; Dave Meggyesy, *Out of Their League* (New York: Ramparts Press, 1971), p. 172.

14.   Michigan *Chronicle*, May 21, 1977; Jim Baker, *O.J. Simpson's Memorable Games* (New York: Putnam, 1978), p. 49.

15.   Deford, "Ready If You Are," pp. 16–19; Harry Edwards, *Sociology of Sport* (Homewood, IL: Dorsey, 1973), pp. 279–80; Simpson with Axthelm, *Rich Rookie*, pp. 9–17; Shrake, "First Taste of O.J.," pp. 20–22; *"Playboy* Interview: O.J. Simpson," pp. 78–85; Axthelm, "Juice Runs Wild," p. 72.

16.   Robert Weems, "The Revolution Will Be Marketed," *Radical History Review* 59 (Spring 1994): 94–107; Fox, *Mirror Makers*, pp. 281–84; on the "level playing field" image, see Mike Marquese, "Sport and Stereotype: From Role Model to Muhammad Ali," *Race and Class* 36 (April–June 1995): 4–5.

17.   Cerasini, *Simpson*, pp. 48–49; "Harsh Realities Haunt Simpson," p. 3-B; Robinson, "Two Superstars," p. 173; Simpson with Axthelm, *Rich Rookie*, p. 12; Edwin Shrake, "The First Taste of O.J. Is OK," *Sports Illustrated*, August 25, 1969, p. 20; Darden, "The Bloody Glove," *Newsweek*, March 25, 1968, p. 57.

18.   The most common misspelling, "Portero," recurs in Pulitzer Prize-winning journalist Teresa Carpenter's recent attempt to tie the murders to Simpson's putatively underclass youth in her "The Man Behind the Mask," pp. 84–100; Simpson's autobiographical (with Axthelm) *Rich Rookie*, p. 10, comes no closer than "Patero." See also *"Playboy* Interview: O.J. Simpson," p. 97; "Countdown to Pasadena," *Time*, October 11, 1968, p. 43; Paul Zimmerman, "All Dressed Up," *Sports Illustrated*, November 26, 1979, p. 40; "Meet O.J. Simpson: Home Is Always Where the Heart Is," *Parents' Magazine*, February 1977, pp. 42–43.

19. "*Playboy* Interview: O.J. Simpson," pp. 97–99; Carpenter, "The Man Behind the Mask," p. 86; Warren and Paddock, " 'I Was Somebody,' " p. A-8.

20. Robinson, "Two Superstars," p. 173; Brian Lowry, "Adams Turns Up the Juice with O.J. Simpson," *Advertising Age*, December 23, 1985, p. 6; Axthelm, "Juice Runs Wild," pp. 70–71; "The Juice Joins the Soda Wars," *Fortune*, September 30, 1985, pp. 9–10; Zimmerman, "All Dressed Up," p. 40; Paddocks and Warren, " 'I Was Somebody,' " p. A-9.

21. Chuck Wingis, "O.J. Tells How Ads Led to His Tinseltown Success," *Advertising Age*, June 20, 1977, p. 82.

22. Edwards, "Black Professional Athlete," pp. 263–64; Shrake, "First Taste of O.J.," p. 20.

23. "*Playboy* Interview: O.J. Simpson," pp. 78-A, 78-B; Shrake, "First Taste of O.J.," p. 20; "Simpson Settles In," *Time*, October 8, 1973, p. 68; "O.J. to Go," *Newsweek*, January 13, 1969, p. 76; Jack Slater, "O.J. Simpson: The Problems of a Super Superstar," *Ebony*, November 1976, p. 164.

24. The Carson joke is in Robert F. Jones, "The $2.5 Million Dollar Man," *Sports Illustrated*, September 27, 1976, pp. 20–21; see n. 23 above, especially for the quote, "Simpson Settles In," p. 68.

25. "Meet O.J. Simpson," pp. 42, 43; Axthelm, "Juice Is Loose," p. 66; Joe Marshall, "What's Making O.J. Go?" *Sports Illustrated*, July 25, 1976, p. 20; Carpenter, "Behind the Mask," p. 87. On debates over race, family, and pathology in this period, see Lee Rainwater and William Yancey, eds., *The Moynihan Report and the Politics of Controversy* (Cambridge: MIT Press, 1967).

26. On Ali and style, see Jose Torres and Bert Sugar, *Sting Like a Bee* (New York: Abelard-Schuman, 1971); Jeffrey T. Sammons, "Rebel With a Cause," in Gorn, ed., *Ali*, pp. 162–64; see also George, *Elevating the Game*, pp. 132–68.

27. "Year of the Okey-Doke," *Time*, December 24, 1973, p. 57; Marshall, "Now You See Him . . . ," p. 37; Axthelm, "Juice Really Flows," pp. 69–70; Bob Oates, "O.J.'s Way," Los Angeles *Times*, October 12, 1975, Section 3:1; "Simpson Settles In," p. 68; Robinson, "Two Supporters," p. 174; "*Playboy* Interview: O.J. Simpson," p. 102; Bob Oates, "There's a 'Coward' Loose in the NFL," Los Angeles *Times*, October 3, 1973; on *juke* (*jook*), see Clarence Major, *Dictionary of Afro-American Slang* (New York: International Publishers, 1970), p. 72; Robert L. Chapman, *New Dictionary of American Slang* (New York: Harper and Row, 1986), pp. 239–40.

28.   "Year of the Okey-Doke," p. 57; Herman L. Masin, "All the Way with
       O.J.," *Senior Scholastic*, October 18, 1968, p. 32; "2003: O.J.'s Odyssey,"
       Newsweek, December 31, 1977; on Ali, Simpson, and style, see also Cuda
       Brown, "O.J. Who?" *Vibe Meanderings* 205 (1995): World Wide Web.

29.   See n. 27 above and, on *okey-doke*, Major, *Dictionary of Afro-American Slang*,
       p. 87; Clarence Major, *Juba to Jive: A Dictionary of African-American Slang*
       (New York: Penguin, 1994), p. 329.

30.   Dyson, "Be Like Mike? Michael Jordan and the Pedagogy of Desire,"
       in *Reflecting Black: African-American Cultural Criticisms* (Minneapolis: Uni-
       versity of Minnesota Press, 1993), pp. 64–75, esp. 70.

31.   Jenkins, "Great One Confronts O.J.," p. 38; Cerasini, *Simpson*, p. 61ff;
       Wingis, "Tinseltown Success," p. 30; Dan Jenkins, "The Juice is
       Turned On Again," *Sports Illustrated*, October 13, 1975, p. 30; "O.J. Snags
       Real Juicy Contract with Tree Sweet," Los Angeles *Times*, July 14, 1976,
       Section 3, p. 15; Chapman, *New Dictionary*, p. 303; Stuart Berg Flexner,
       Listening to America (New York: Simon & Schuster, 1982), p. 474. See also
       n. 4 and 5 above.

32.   Robinson, "Two Superstars," p. 173.

33.   Gavin Power, "What the Marketing Experts See for O.J.," *San Francisco
       Chronicle*, June 16, 1994; *Time*, June 27, 1994, front cover.

34.   Cited by Michael Oriard, "Order and Chaos, Work and Play," chapter
       5 in *Reading Football: How the Popular Press Created an American Spectacle*
       (Chapel Hill: University of North Carolina Press, 1993), p. 185. See
       also Ballinger, *In Your Face*, pp. 33–35.

35.   From the beginning of his college career until the time of his trial, O.J.
       was constantly referred to by reporters as an affable, smiling Negro.
       For example, "The Great One Confronts O.J.," a 1967 *Sports Illustrated*
       story about a game between USC and UCLA, described O.J. as "a
       mild, warm, talkative transfer from City College of San Francisco,"
       November 20, 1967, p. 37.

36.   Shrake, "First Taste of O.J.," p. 20; Carpenter, "Behind the Mask,"
       pp. 84, 88; Deford, "Ready If You Are," pp. 16, 19; Michigan *Chroni-
       cle*, March 25, 1978, p. B-2; Zimmerman, "All Dressed Up," p. 38. See
       also Cerasini, *Simpson*, p. 196; Jenkins, "Great One Confronts O.J.,"
       p. 38.

37.   Perceptions of O.J.'s affability can be compared to the demonization of
       Kareem Abdul-Jabbar, who was deeply involved in black protests. See
       also Kareem Abdul-Jabbar, *Giant Steps* (New York: Bantam Books,

1983), p. 200: "My adversary relationship with the press started during my second week in the league."

38.   Among the many accounts of Arledge's years as head of ABC sports are: Ron Powers, *Supertube* (New York: Coward-McCann, 1984); Marc Gunther, *The House That Roone Built: The Inside Story of ABC News* (Boston: Little, Brown, 1994); Phil Patton, *Razzle Dazzle* (Garden City: Dial Press, 1984); Terry O'Neil, *The Game Behind the Game: High Pressure, High Stakes in Television Sports* (New York: Harper and Row, 1989); Bert Randolph Sugar, *"The Thrill of Victory": The Inside Story of ABC Sports* (New York: Hawthorn, 1978); and Jim Spence, *Up Close and Personal: The Inside Story of Network Television Sports* (New York: Atheneum, 1988).

39.   In *Supertube*, Ron Powers reproduces a memo in which Arledge maps out his philosophy of televised sports as spectacle designed to make specific gender appeals, and talks about the role of slow motion in this effort; see pp. 145–46. Patton elaborates on the history of slow motion in television, noting that NBC experimented with the technique before Arledge and CBS perfected the technique of instant replay in the late 1950s. But Arledge perfected its use on live broadcasts, largely because he had access to video technology and especially to the mini-cam. See *Razzle Dazzle*, pp. 63–75. Shortly after the first use of instant replay technology in a college football broadcast in 1963, the technique got its first mass exposure when it was used to replay Jack Ruby's shooting of Lee Harvey Oswald. See Erik Barnouw, *Tube of Plenty: The Evolution of American Television* (New York: Oxford University Press, 1975), p. 334, for an early example of the use of slow motion in sports; also see Dan Streible, "A History of the Boxing Film, 1894–1915," *Film History* 3, no. 3 (1989): 235–57.

40.   Powers, *Supertube*, pp. 160–70; Spence, "The Thrill of Victory . . . The Agony of Defeat: The Incredible Story of ABC's *Wide World of Sports*," in *Up Close and Personal*, pp. 66–79. The concept for *Wide World of Sports* was developed by Ed Sherick, Arledge's first boss at ABC Sports. But while Sherick developed the idea of covering offbeat sporting events, Arledge executed that idea, figuring out how to make the coverage "up close and personal."

41.   Lisa Fluor, "God of the Stadium: National Socialist Aesthetics and the Body in Leni Riefenstahl's *Olympia*" (Ph.D. diss., Univ. of California at San Diego, 1992). Streible, "Boxing Film," pp. 235–57 and n. 39 above.

42.   Ashe, *Hard Road to Glory*, pp. 138–39, adds, "In the early 1970s, tickets for
       NFL games became more sought after than those for any other type of
       athletic contest. Corporations bought up sections of season tickets,
       and sell-out crowds were the norm rather than the exception. There
       was a constant demand to make the game more exciting, and fans, espe-
       cially those watching on television, wanted more scoring; rules were
       changed to accommodate them, and in nearly every instance black
       players benefited because, aside from the white quarterbacks, they were
       the most gifted performers on the field." On "supernatural," see
       Robinson, "Two Superstars," p. 171.

43.   Gunther, *House That Roone Built*, describes some of the panic that struck
       the ABC news division after Arledge's appointment as its head, noting
       that one journalist joked that Roone would soon be hiring the likes of
       Geraldo Rivera. Geraldo, in fact, was one of Arledge's first hires in the
       news division; see pp. 32, 147. See also Howard Cosell, *I Never Played the
       Game* (New York: Avon, 1985), pp. 154, 177; and note Axthelm's contin-
       uing praises of Simpson in *Newsweek* after the two collaborated on *Rich
       Rookie*.

44.   Powers, *Supertube*, p. 146.

45.   *Ibid.*, pp. 137–41; Spence, "Forever a Man's World? Why Women Sports-
       casters Are Still So Far from Winning Equal Air Time," in *Up Close and
       Personal*, pp. 175–88.

46.   O'Neill, *The Game Behind the Game*, pp. 262–63.

47.   Spence, *Up Close and Personal*, pp. 147–48; Bill Russell, *Second Wind: The
       Memoirs of an Opinionated Man* (New York: Random House, 1979);
       Cosell, *I Never Played*, p. 334.

48.   Spence, *Up Close and Personal*, pp. 149–50; Cosell, *I Never Played*, pp.
       177–78.

49.   Cosell, *I Never Played*, pp. 155, 158.

50.   See, for example, Carpenter, "The Man Behind the Mask," pp. 87–101;
       Hoffer, "Fatal Attraction;" and "Harsh Realities Haunt Simpson," pp.
       1-B, 3-B.

51.   Interview with former *Newsday* writer Bob Drury, KFAN Radio in
       Minneapolis, May 8, 1996.

52.   James McBride, *War, Battering and Other Sports* (Atlantic Highlands, NJ:
       Humanities Press, 1995).

53.   Powers, *Supertube*, pp. 138–41. See also Hoffer, "Fatal Attraction," pp.
       30–32.

54. Spence, *Up Close and Personal*, p. 6. Also see Marlene Saunders, "Women in Management," in *Waiting for Prime Time* (Champaign-Urbana: University of Illinois Press, 1988), pp. 158–90, for a discussion of the climate for women at ABC and their struggles to break through the glass ceiling in sports as well as news.

55. Kate Bertrand, "O.J. Simpson Juices Hertz's Image," *Business Marketing*, August 1992, p. 28.

56. Cerasini, *Simpson*, pp. 180–82; Simpson with Axthelm, *Rich Rookie*, pp. 16–17; "Chalk Up One More Score for 'The Juice,'" Michigan *Chronicle*, April 16, 1977, p. B-1; Krier, "What Makes O.J. Run?" pp. 106, 110; Gertrude Gipson, "O.J. Signs Exclusive Contract with NBC-TV," Los Angeles *Sentinel*, May 5, 1977, p. Entertainment-1; Stu Black, "They Call Me Mister Juice," *Los Angeles Magazine*, April 1980, p. 174.

57. Buchanan, "18 Holes," p. 100; Lowry, "Adams Turns Up Juice," p. 6.

58. Deford, "Ready If You Are," p. 16; Bertrand, "Juices Hertz's Image," p. 28; Michigan *Chronicle*, July 16, 1977, p. B-1; Cerasini, *Simpson*, p. 204; Spangler, "Golf Legends," p. 26; Wood, "What Makes Simpson Run?" p. 38; "No Touchdowns," *Inc.*, October 1985, p. 18.

59. Lisa Disch and Mary Jo Kane, "When a Looker Is Really a Bitch: Lisa Olson, Sport and the Heterosexual Matrix," *Signs* 21 (Winter 1996): 284, 283–87.

60. Messner, as quoted in Disch and Kane, "Looker," p. 285.

61. Gates and West, "Affirmative Reaction," pp. 181–83; "Harsh Realities Haunt Simpson," p. 3-B.

62. Messner, "Masculinities and Athletic Careers: Bonding and Status Differences," in Messner and Don Sabo, eds., *Sport, Men and the Gender Order* (Champaign, IL: Human Kinetics Books, 1990), p. 103; Zimmerman, "All Dressed Up," p. 39; Shrake, "Juice on Juicy Road," p. 37; Gates and West, "Affirmative Reaction," p. 181; Hoffer, "Fatal Attraction," pp. 18, 20.

If the Genes Fit,
How Do You Acquit?

O.J. and Science

Andrew Ross

Loose Talk

I was only in Los Angeles once during the whole O.J. circus, but the memory of a brief encounter in the cocktail lounge of a Santa Monica hotel in August 1994 has stayed with me. A bar bore was getting cranked up, and soon he was broadcasting loud and clear on the topic du jour. He was a white businessman, whom the bartender seemed to know all too well and wished she didn't. He was claiming a special knowledge about football players on the basis of having once served on the board of trustees of an East Coast university. Without much egging on from his audience of two, one bluster led to another until he unveiled his theory that, of all football players, the success of running backs on the field depended less on brainpower than on their killer instinct, and that this disposition was probably genetic. In fact, he was sure this was the key to the O.J. Simpson case. When pressed to elaborate, he ventured that the scientists could prove this kind of genetic theory in the courts, but they would not be allowed to do so in the upcoming trial. At this point, because I had to leave to meet a friend, I discreetly expressed my sympathies to the bartender who would now bear the brunt of these pronouncements alone. What I thought I had encountered in the bar was a new kind of concoction—of half-truths about the links between genetics, law, and crime—that may be more potent and widely consumed than anyone would like to believe.

Back home in New York two weeks later, another friend—an O.J. trial junkie—who shares some of my interest in genetics sent me a clipping of a *New York Post* headline that read "Murder in O.J.'s Blood." The clipping confirmed my impressions in that throat-grabbing way tabloid headlines have when they tell us "this is where you live, here and now." The headline, no surprise, bore only an oblique relation to the newspaper story, which soberly recounted that preliminary results of two different DNA tests had matched O.J.'s blood with blood found leading from the crime scene. But the headline's telegraphic announcement suggested something else, much closer to my bar bore's woozy story about the genetic basis of criminality.

What was happening in August 1994 to explain this kind of nonsense? In "the Simpson matter" (as Judge Lance Ito would famously come to refer to the trial, day after day), the prosecution and the defense teams were both being assembled, shaped by the case that each was going to present. It looked as though the prosecution's case would rely heavily on DNA profiles of blood left at the crime scene and on various objects—the bloody glove, the Bronco—to identify Simpson as the murderer, and, to a much lesser extent, on the demonstration of motive provided in his history of domestic violence. It had just been announced that the defense would bring on board Barry Scheck and Peter Neufeld, directors of the Innocence Project, well known for using DNA testing to exonerate over a dozen clients who had previously been convicted and imprisoned. These attorneys would play a crucial, and perhaps decisive, role in casting reasonable doubt on the DNA evidence in the course of the trial. The prosecution, in turn, would call on the expert testimony of Rockne Harmon, George "Woody" Clarke, and other strong advocates of DNA forensic technology. In August, then, both sides were preparing for what the press was referring to as "the DNA Wars," scheduled to begin, and potentially end, in the pretrial hearings that would determine the admissibility of DNA evidence. There was reason to believe that some, if not all, of the forensic techniques would be considered inadmissible in the California courts.[1] This is what I think my bar bore might have had in mind when he speculated that the scientists would not be allowed to prove his theory in court.

To get to the pulpy core of his theory, however, we need to step outside of the Simpson matter and look briefly at the profound impact that modern genetics has had on public consciousness in the last fifteen years or so, to the degree that it has become routine fare in barroom conversations. In that period of time, it has become common to refer to genetic causation for virtually every aspect of human behavior—from medical disorders to ethnic traits and personal conduct. Science reporting has encouraged the view that such genetic links are simple and direct, and in popular culture it is currently acceptable to say there is a gene for almost everything, including the urge to make generalizations of this sort. Much of this attribution is droll, and therefore it mocks even as it reflects the exalted status of the Holy Gene.

Even so, the popular allure of biological explanations for
social behavior is encouraged not only by biotech companies but
also by scientists and policymakers who have helped, directly or
otherwise, to shape the attack on collective social responsibility
in general and the welfare state in particular. Absolving society
of all blame or responsibility for problems that can be seen
as genetically determined has been a significant element of the
conservative crusade to redefine social problems as a matter of
individual predisposition.[2] In this view, gene therapy is more
cost-efficient than social programs.

Of all the qualities that have been "linked" to specific
genes—selfishness, shyness, adventurousness—the association
with criminality is the most notorious. Talk about "natural-born
killers" with "bad seed" or "tainted blood" is almost universal
folklore, but its scientific basis has been consistently explored for
over a century, from Dr. Professor Cesare Lombroso's attempted
criminal typology on the basis of physical characteristics in the
late nineteenth century to theories of the criminal chromosome
(the extra Y chromosome in males that accounts for their aggres-
sivity) that surfaced in the 1970s. Ever since then, ideas about the
genetic basis of criminality have been riding the long wave of
resurgent biologism into the institutions of social and legal
policy-making. The currency of these ideas has been tied to the
fortunes of the eugenics movement over that same period of
time, rising with Galton in the late nineteenth century, collapsing in the aftermath of Nazism, and surfacing again in new
forms primarily in the U.K. and the U.S. through the developing
paradigms of sociobiology and evolutionary psychology in the
last two decades of the twentieth century.

The concept of genetic criminality has contributed specifically to the social psychology of racialization. Most studies of
genetic criminality survey incarcerated populations, and since

African Americans are incarcerated at a rate ten times that of Caucasians, it is hardly surprising that U.S. studies draw bogus conclusions about links between race and criminality.[3] Given the high public tolerance of the U.S.'s racially skewed incarceration rates, it is easy to imagine the appeal to racists of such conclusions, casually linked, in turn, to other spurious ideas about genetic causality and race, such as the link between race and intelligence.

By the end of the summer of 1994, there were very few public scandals that could have dislodged O.J. from the forefront of North American public conversation. In some circles, the publication of *The Bell Curve*, by Charles Murray and Richard Herrnstein, came very close. The cant about genetic links between race and IQ dredged up by Murray and Herrnstein was designed to feed intravenously the antiwelfare policies of the moment. Their ideas about the decline of the gene pool and the racialization of intelligence in the new cognitive hierarchies of information society seemed to be borne along by some autonomous principle of social motion, at a time when popular opinion is increasingly receptive to arguments that appeal to genetic authority.

The public debate about *The Bell Curve* lasted for several months, and, while it did not make much news in the tabloid press, it occupied many of the same media pages as the O.J. trial. However, my extensive data-base search for stories that mentioned both O.J. and *The Bell Curve* during the relevant period and shortly thereafter came up with very few matches and none at all that touch on genetics. This discovery surprised me. Both *The Bell Curve* and the DNA typing in the O.J. trial employed a controversial process of testing, appealed to racial or ethnic categories as classified by genetic scientists, and rested to some degree on assumptions about how genetics can be used to elucidate legal or social quandaries. Why then was discussion of one field of genetics so segregated from the other in the public media? Surely there was some reason other than that *The Bell Curve* appealed to a behavioral, and the O.J. trial to a forensic, field of genetics.

Was it because one had been marked as "contaminated" by its racist associations, while the other was seen as clean, at least where race is concerned? Given that DNA forensics have evolved in response to the needs of a law enforcement system with a systematically racist record, only those immune to skepticism would view this as a credible explanation. Indeed, it was partly on the basis of that racist record that members of the O.J. defense team argued their case for the incompetence of the LAPD criminologists and the racial biases of one or more of its detectives.

Or was it because *The Bell Curve* was perceived as a soft application of molecular biology, and DNA typing as harder, and more incontrovertible? Perhaps, but then one of the big media stories about the DNA wars was that the forensic methods were highly contestable. Ever since the 1989 case of *People v. Castro*,[4] which successfully challenged DNA typing as an infallible source of legal evidence, this complex technology has been fiercely disputed in courts and in scientific and law journals, and it was the object of bitter contention in the O.J. trial.

The reasons for the separation of interest in O.J. and *The Bell Curve* do not lie within molecular biology itself. Instead, they arise from the needs of those institutions—in education, law, medicine, commerce, the military, and government—that serve as clients for customized kinds of scientific knowledge. Specialized scientific fields are habitually made to order by powerful institutions or wealthy contractors or because they respond to prevailing ideological needs. In almost every field, the division of labor within the scientific community is shaped by the managerial needs of social and economic elites. Subfields of scientific knowledge are social arrangements of labor (many in the late twentieth century are spin-offs from the military-industrial system). The division between different fields of genetics corresponds in part to the select interests of clients. Invariably, demand from one field shapes developments in another; DNA forensics, for example, relies upon population genetics for its identification of suspects. Division of fields, moreover, does not preclude their independent reinforcement of the powerful philosophy of genetic determinism.

When it is not directly converted into capital, specialized scientific knowledge is habitually sought out to intensify respect for institutions and their policies. Consider some of the respective outcomes of the O.J. trial and *The Bell Curve*. While very few scholars leapt forward to defend the scientific premises of *The Bell Curve*, few would doubt that its poisonous theses about alleged links between race and intelligence have had considerable impact on framing the public reception of major changes in social legislation, especially those relating to affirmative action policies. Indeed, it could be said that conservative policymakers are proceeding toward the conclusions favored by the book without relying overtly on the junk science offered by Murray and Herrnstein. By contrast, mainstream media wisdom held that the DNA evidence against O.J., while scientifically sound, was somehow disregarded by the jurors. This perception helped to fuel widespread disrespect for the jury system in the months after the trial, and may even have contributed to the zeal with which powerful politicians from the White House down took up the old game of judge-bashing. In the case of *The Bell Curve*, the science, even though it was discredited, still helped in some way to "explain" the policy-making directed against social programs.

In the Simpson matter, more accredited science was called for to better calibrate the institutional fit between the forensics field and its legal interpretation.

Accordingly, the science establishment played its role in helping to restore post-O.J. public confidence in DNA forensics. In July 1996, the NRC (National Research Council, the operating arm of the National Academy of Sciences) published an updated report on DNA evidence that issued a clean bill of health for the forensic process: "The technology for DNA profiling and the methods for estimating frequencies and related statistics have progressed to the point where the reliability and validity of properly collected and analyzed DNA data should not be in doubt."[5] Among its recommendations, the report urged the professionalization and accreditation of all crime labs in accord with upgraded standards of performance and accountability. This resolve is consistent with the history of the development of criminological technologies, from fingerprinting to polygraph testing, voice printing, blood grouping, enzyme typing, and DNA profiling. Each has required its own credentialed field of experts, with a professionalized jargon, a supporting record of approval in peer-reviewed journals, and a bureaucratic system of accreditation with institutional authorities. When doubts are cast on the legal interpretation of such technologies, the response of the scientific community has been to increase funding in pursuit of more accurate data and to beef up the supporting legitimating network of professionalization.

From the time it was first challenged in U.S. courts in 1989, evidence for the fallibility of DNA profiling had been supported by indications that biotechnology companies had pushed hard for the legal admissibility of the tests, the FBI had intimidated scientists who were critical in print,[6] and the "community of experts" responsible for validating the techniques involved many scientists who had themselves established a good deal of their reputation through lengthy and lucrative courtroom testimony about the value of the field to criminal jurisprudence. Aside from these more obvious conflicts of interest, the debate about the increasing use of DNA sampling and profiling involves a host of ethical concerns about the threats to genetic privacy posed by the expansion of the state's DNA identification banks, compiled from compulsory testing of prisoners, soldiers, and patients by the Departments of Defense and Justice and other state agencies; the normalization of genetically defined population differences; the further sanctification of biological explanations of the truth; and the applicability of quantitative reasoning to courtroom procedures designed to respect principles and values other than those acknowledged by science. Despite its public visibility, and the unusually generous resources available to both the prosecution and defense, the O.J. trial highlighted very few of these concerns.

The trial involved an enormous amount of scientific testimony (10,000 references to DNA in the 50,000-page transcript), inordinately more than, say, the 1953 Rosenberg case, another great "trial of the century," in which the prosecutors had to argue that the lay defendants understood enough physics to pass on the secret of the atom bomb to the Soviet Union. Predictably, the press found much of this testimony regarding DNA "boring," and an obstacle to the unfolding drama of the trial. Some commentators, like William F. Buckley, found the trial itself to be an obstacle to those goals of justice that were clearly aligned, in his view, with the evidence presented by the science. Writing in the *National Review*, Buckley lamented that "justice is dying ... from the creeping immobilizations brought on in the name of civil liberties. ... The only obstacle to the establishment of the guilt of O.J. Simpson is legal. The whole of the epistemological apparatus of the modern world—psychology, science, logic, reason—establishes that he is guilty. Only the law stands in the way of the application, paradoxically, of justice."[7]

Voicing a standard conservative view, Buckley manifests his impatience with the legal system's overzealous protection of the civil rights and dignity of defendants. He sees the cart going before the horse: the law should be driven by science—not vice versa. In framing the debate over scientific evidence in this way, Buckley was rearticulating an age-old concern that the jury system poses a substantial threat to the rule of law (especially manifest in the principle of jury nullification). He was also anticipating the torrent of public impatience with the jurors' verdict in the O.J. case. At issue is the Federal Rules' entrustment in the judgment of jurors, over and above those of experts and professionals in science and the law. DNA evidence has presented the most acute challenge to that principle in recent years because it has stretched the capacity of experts to believe that lay people can understand advanced science. If complex scientific testimony increasingly becomes a customary presence in the courts, what are the prospects for continuing respect for lay judgment?

The Jury on Trial

The fierce public backlash against the O.J. jurors was immediate, palpable, and sustained long enough for it to have congealed into a media "fact." The main tenor of the hostility stemmed from the belief that a predominantly black jury had exonerated a wealthy black celebrity with a history of spousal abuse in defiance of Marcia Clark's "mountain of evidence," and had done so in retaliation not just for the racist record of the LAPD but also for centuries of "white justice." The reactionary version of this belief was downright ugly, but the more liberal interpretation of the verdict as a healthy exercise in jury nullification may have been no less insulting to many of the jurors. When such allegations were not being made directly, related charges were often insinuated by questioning the jurors' lack of education in the face of the cold, hard facts of the DNA evidence. On many a talk show, we heard again and again the claim that since smart people can increasingly find ways of evading jury duty, juries are inevitably made up of the dumbest folks in the community. This claim has clearly racist overtones if one considers that the substantial increase in minority voter registration (along with the dismantling of all-white juries who, unlike black juries, are statistically inclined to exonerate defendants of their own race) has brought more and more citizens of color into the jury pool in recent years. For example, a March 31, 1996, segment of *60 Minutes* suggested that Francine Florio-Bunten—a white juror removed from the trial after Judge Ito received a letter alleging she was working on a book with a literary agency—had been set up by the defense team. The segment implied that Florio-Bunten was the most educated of the jurors and was therefore capable of understanding the DNA evidence—and of swinging the jury against O.J. Similar insinuations and suspicions abound in the massive media archive. The famous Internet list, *alt.fan.oj-simpson,* featured a wave of repulsive postings after the verdict; typical sentiments included a posting that read "Hate to say it, but I think *The Bell Curve* hit the nail on the head," or another which confessed, "I don't know if I can look upon blacks as anything other than a subhuman mob with an average IQ of around 80."[8]

How did this backlash affect the jurors themselves? At least three—Armanda Cooley, Carrie Bess, and Marsha Rubin-Jackson, who published their accounts in *Madam Foreman: A Rush to Judg-*

ment?—have described their persistent discomfort at being under suspicion themselves. Such was their impression that, in addition to their resentment at the cameras monitoring the hotel hallways, these jurors imagined that the smoke detectors and fire alarm units in their bedrooms were audio and video monitors (Rubin-Jackson took appropriate measures: "One day I got up in front of it buck naked . . . and shook my bootie.").[9] This paranoia was heightened by the intimidating scene outside the courtroom on the day the verdict was announced. Confronting the jurors as they arrived were hundreds of police officers on horseback and in riot gear, while helicopters seemed to fill the sky above. In downtown Los Angeles, this display of a massed LAPD force is by no means a neutral sight, especially for its citizens of color. With the crowd outside considerably swelled and agitated by the announcement of the verdict, these three jurors had some reason to feel they were not only besieged in the courtroom but also in some physical danger: "Every time I looked there were more and more people and I just kept saying, 'Oh my God, are they going to riot, are they going to get us?' " (*MF,* 176).

In order to throw off the reporters and cameras, the jurors were ushered out of the courtroom through the route reserved for the transport of prisoners ("It was like running a gauntlet. I felt like I'd committed a crime and I was on my way to being locked up" (*MF,* 7). This route involved the use of the elevator ordinarily reserved for convicted felons, surrounded by walls of graffiti both poignant and defiant, scrawled by men and women en route to detention cells. Once outside, they were transported to a secret drop-off point in a "full-size black-and-white-bus with barred windows." Ordered to keep their heads down, some of the jurors were fearful at the sight of the full extent of the massed police force: "Why do they need so many policemen? Do they really think we're going to be assassinated?" (*MF,* 9). No wonder these jurors felt as if they were at the wrong end of the justice system, not only then but in the months to come.

These stories and impressions are important to recount because they are a record of how and why jurors feel that their involvement with the justice system can bring a share of its (and the media's) punitive power down upon them. Something is clearly wrong if the fulfillment of their civic duties renders them vulnerable in this way. Public bigotry will only intensify if the two chief allegations of the O.J. juror backlash—that they practiced reverse racism and that they were undereducated—are allowed to subsist. For the record, again, let us note what jurors had to say about these allegations.

Having lived "underground" for the period of sequestration in circumstances more akin to detention (with five-hour conjugal visits and routine searches of their belongings), these jurors seemed genuinely surprised to learn that the verdict was being interpreted as a racial message, especially since Simpson was perceived as living "in a white world" of privilege quite remote from their own black one: "You could say we were shocked . . . or outraged, that people would even think of us sitting there making decisions based on race. And it proved to me that they felt we had no intelligence whatsoever" (*MF,* 82–83). The lengthy DNA testimony elicited a similar impression: "When I got out [*sic*], I kept hearing more and more people saying there was only one graduate on the jury and so forth, so that indicates to me that they felt everyone else was illiterate. . . . I realize that if you have a Ph.D. and you're talking to someone who does not have training in the field of serology or forensic science, you might assume that they're not going to understand some of the basics. Of course, you're not going to understand the total details of that field, but you don't have to. Unfortunately, there's no way to let people know you got it. You can't just raise your hand and say, 'Dr. Cotton, I understand what you're talking about. Move on.' " (*MF,* 114).

As it happens, jurors rated Dr. Robin Cotton, from Cellmark Diagnostics, the Germantown testing laboratory, lowest among the scientists judged on their ability to communicate technical arguments: "She talked down to us like we were illiterates. . . . She talked down and when you talk down to people you tend to lose them" (*MF,* 114). On the prosecution side, Renee Montgomery and Gary Sims, from the California Department of Justice, and Dr. Lackshamanan Sathyavagiswaran from the LAPD, rated highly, as did Henry Lee from the Connecticut State Forensic Science Laboratory, and Barry Scheck, on the defense side. Collin Yamauchi, from the LAPD, who had cast doubt on Lee's handling of the evidence, was perceived as covering up for the egregious errors in gathering and handling of evidence by LAPD criminalist Dennis Fung and his assistant Andrea Mazzola.

In the final analysis, these jurors reported that they *had* in fact understood the testimony relating to the DNA matches. With the exception of one particularly degraded sample (from the rear gate at the Bundy condo) that had been collected weeks after the crime and found to contain high levels of EDTA, a blood preservative used in labs, the jury, in its deliberations, had not questioned any of the matches of the blood samples with Simpson's DNA type. Instead, it was the evidence of the LAPD mishandling and cross-contamination of the blood evidence that was relevant to establishing reasonable doubt.

Of course, no one is obliged to take the jurors' comments out of court at face value, but to ignore them is to add insult to their perceived injury. As it happens, these comments reveal a good deal about the balance between expert and lay opinion that has been affected by the legal admission of complex scientific evidence.

DNA on Trial

One public perception that emerged from the O.J. trial was that the science was only as good as the police lab that processed the blood evidence—a "cesspool of contamination" in the view of defense witnesses. Barry Scheck argued, in a 1994 article about the *Daubert* decision [see note 1], and unceasingly throughout the trial, that laboratory error is the primary flaw in the DNA-typing process, and that a lab's error rate should be considered a matter of admissibility, and not weight, as judges have been inclined to rule.[10] In the O.J. case, Scheck could hardly have hoped for a more vivid illustration of his contention that laboratory error rates are substantially higher than the DNA profiling estimates that labs draw from trace sample evidence. As if in response to the unspoken injunction of the O.J. verdict to put the house of DNA forensics in order, the 1996 NRC report issued strict recommendations about forensic protocols and lab proficiency testing. Convened to resolve the legacy of uncertainties bequeathed by the controversial report of the 1992 NRC commission, this second NRC committee was not charged with the task of assessing the impact of DNA sampling upon the criminal trial process, nor with its much wider role in the state's databanking of genetic information from a wide variety of convenience samples: criminal records, law enforcement officers, soldiers, paternity-testing centers, blood banks, hospitals. With respect to the former, the NRC committee confined itself to recommending "behavioral" (i.e., scientific) "research on juror comprehension" of evidence from DNA profiles. As is customary, then, the scientific focus on value-neutral fact was isolated from the legal and social concerns; "that's not our department." But in neither department is it possible, or socially prudent, to isolate facts from values in this way.

In recent years, genetic information has become a tool for decision-making in a variety of legal fields—torts, criminal, trust, and estate law—and is increasingly used as a defense on grounds of genetic predisposition. Despite its promise of absolute precision and irrefutable truth—its "aura of infallibility," as a Massachusetts Supreme Court decision put it—DNA evidence is commonly introduced in the form of quantified probability. For example, in the Simpson matter, the odds of some of the blood samples matching any African American or Caucasian other than O.J. were estimated as high as one in 170 million, and one in 6.8 billion Caucasians in the case of the genetic markers matching Nicole and Ron. These astronomical odds, however much they varied from estimate to estimate (another put the Nicole odds, in the case of a particular blood sample, at one in twenty-one billion) conveyed the message that you "can't argue" with such numbers. How could O.J. possibly be innocent, given these odds? Such statistics carry the patina of irrefutable truth in a manner that tends to outweigh other kinds of evidence, like those supporting the motive in the murder charge by reference to the history of spousal abuse. Indeed, these odds were frequently cited in the courtroom of public opinion as overwhelming confirmation that science had proved O.J.'s guilt, and that the jury had disregarded science and, in Buckley's words, the whole of modern epistemology. These are false and perilous assumptions.

In a classic 1971 article, "Trial by Mathematics" (long before DNA evidence became a controversial factor in legal adjudication), Lawrence Tribe summarized the problems raised by the practice of using statistical methods to resolve conflicting claims in lawsuits. Even if it were desirable for the legal system to defer to quantitative reasoning, Tribe asserts that statistical proofs "decrease the likelihood of accurate outcomes" in a trial.[11] The impact of introducing statistical evidence to a jury's prior probability assessment of a defendant's guilt has a distorting effect, rendering an inference of guilt that is much greater than the evidence warrants. The hard, quantitative evidence will dwarf other "soft variables" like impressionistic evidence, according to Tribe, and will indubitably warp the jurors' obligation to weigh all the evidence evenly. If the statistical assessment is introduced early, it is difficult for jurors not to focus on these overimpressive numbers, and hence the presumption of innocence is often thrown out before defendants have had their full say. So, too, the probability values attached to variables, such as estimating the risk of a frame-up, or an error in testimony, are something that only individual jurors can assign, and so, to give mathematical proofs full credence, each juror would have to be able to compute their own complex equations, involving hard and soft variables, to guarantee the accuracy of outcomes. In addition, the authoritative weight of statistics harm the chances of a peer community's accepting a defendant's acquittal (in O.J.'s case, this community would presumably be his white neighbors in Brentwood and not downtown African Americans). Finally, Tribe argues that the use of statistics threatens to alter the entire character of the trial process itself, imposing standards unconvincing to the "untutored contemporary intuition," making the legal system appear "even more alien and inhuman than it already does," and undermining its responsibility to protecting the defendant's rights as a person.

Given its "aura of infallibility," many believe that the subsequent introduction of DNA evidence in the courts has only exacerbated these problems and has further eroded defendants' rights, especially when the defendant's resources are too meager to muster counterevidence. O.J.'s privilege in this regard is truly exceptional, but it proved, nonetheless, *contra* Tribe, that a suc-

cessful defense can technically be mounted against an overwhelming array of quantitative evidence. The larger flaw with
Tribe's argument, however, is its assumption that quantitative
evidence and reasoning arise at the outset from value-free
knowledge. It is easy to conclude then that methodologies of
scientific reasoning and the adversarial procedures of the legal
system are difficult to reconcile. The one aims at isolating
absolute truths that are irrefutable in any time or place, the
other expresses the relationship between the individual and the
state as defined by civil principles and rights that pledge respect
for defendants as persons. As Marjorie Maguire Schultz puts it,
"science deals in particulars in order to determine generalizations, law deals in generalizations in order to determine partic-
ularities."[12] The legal process is supposed to resolve conflicts,
often involving the full coercive power of the state, in ways that
protect individual rights and in accord with normative community values. The quantitative reasoning of science is not well
suited to taking these values or rights into account. In times like
the present, when civil rights and community values are under
siege from social conservatives, scientific diagnoses in the service of law enforcement and legal adjudication have a particularly strong appeal to those swayed by right-wing ideas. Under
these coercive circumstances, the trust in lay judgment, under-
pinned in part by a particularly American skepticism regarding
the authority of experts, comes under fire.

But this acknowledged conflict between science's truth and
the law's social wisdom assumes that the domain of science is
indeed value-free, and sequestered from the social interests of
those institutions in government and law and commerce that
exercise their authority through the use of scientific knowledge
or expertise. A large body of scholarly literature in science studies has challenged this view and has demonstrated that science is

no less shaped by social interest than any other field of knowledge. The story about DNA profiling is no exception. It shows how the law enforcement system defines goals for researchers to deliver very particular kinds of knowledge. In a field largely created by the FBI, the direction of DNA forensic research has been wholly governed by the cliental needs of the Justice Department, while the vulnerability of its commercial and police laboratory environments has been fully exposed, and the infallibility of its scientific claims has been hotly contested. Indeed, the meaning of these claims is sufficiently contingent that the probative value of DNA evidence invariably has to be established in the courtroom through lengthy reviews of, or appeals to, the whole peer-review apparatus of scientific and legal literature, as was the case in the O.J. trial. Scientific knowledge, as Sheila Jasanoff concludes in *Science at the Bar,* is not a simple ancillary to the legal process, waiting to be employed in the pursuit of truth. In many instances, it is highly provisional knowledge, while its authority emerges out of the courtroom battle to prove that the claims of one side's experts are more contingent than the claims of the other side's experts.[13] *People v. Simpson* was a dramatic demonstration of this process.

When the probative value of genetic evidence becomes a norm in courtrooms, defendants are more and more likely to be reduced, as sociologists Rochelle Cooper Dreyfuss and Dorothy Nelkin have suggested, to genetic conceptions of "personhood." Instead of the fully entitled person the legal system is ideally supposed to respect, the defendant is seen as a construct of his or her DNA.[14] One of the grave dangers of this tendency is that people brought before the law are once again defined in part by their biological constitution. For centuries, minorities and women have been defined in precisely this way, and more often than not, by loose categories upheld by the law.

In his book *White by Law*, Ian Haney Lopez has shown that
courts historically relied on science and "common knowledge"
to determine racial categories, and in particular to determine
who counted as white and who did not. These categories used to
be governed by the five antique anthropological classifications of
Caucasian, Negro, Mongoloid, American (Indian), and Malay.
Even so, ethnic and national groups have always been subject to
reassignment from one race to another, often in response to
changes in immigration laws. By the 1920s, the U.S. Supreme
Court's reliance upon scientific definitions of race had become
untenable, and it decided to abandon the use of scientific evidence to adjudicate racial prerequisite cases, and to rely instead
upon common sense or popular knowledge. This resulted in the
1922 decision of *United States v. Thind*, where Bhagat Singh Thind,
an Asian Indian, had argued for naturalization on the basis of
the Court's own scientifically refereed equation of "Caucasian"
and "white." Lopez suggests that the Court was increasingly
frustrated with science's inability to accurately identify and
quantify racial differences, and that, beginning with *Thind*, it
accepted common knowledge as a more reliable way of policing
the boundaries of whiteness, most immediately for the purposes
of legislating the 1924 immigration bill.[15]

The judiciary has continued to play a major role in determining entitlements and benefits along racial lines, and it has
actively shaped social beliefs about race in doing so. Overtly
biological notions of race were put on the back burner for
at least fifty years. In the last two decades, however, these
biological definitions have hitched a return ride on the coat-
tails of the new molecular genetics. While genetic variation is
very slight among humans (and much greater between persons
than between population groups), those tiny differences have
attained immense cultural significance in a period when biolog-

ical explanations for social problems are increasingly sought out. The rise of the new genetics has been accompanied by, and, to some extent, utilized in, a brutal rollback of the U.S. state's affirmative, post–civil rights commitment to closing the racialized gap between the formal equality of its citizens and the material inequalities faced daily by them. Some social science scholarship has made a direct link between the two, none more explicitly than *The Bell Curve*, whose authors fleshed out their reactionary fantasy of an underclass that was both genetic and cognitive, resistant to all social and educational assistance, and marked by a specific racial profile. More generally, civil libertarians are concerned that the explosion in genetic testing and screening will usher in a social order governed in part by the rule of predictive information about the genetic predisposition of individuals. In this new eugenic dispensation, discrimination is institutionally directed against those genetically designated as risks to society, and thus beyond assistance, along with those profiled as menaces to society, and thus subject to preemptive discipline. This tendency has already been borne out, in the former case, in the realm of medical insurance denied to the "healthy ill," and in the latter case, in programs like the Violence Prevention Initiative—tried out by the Bush administration—which called for the screening of 100,000 inner-city children to identify potential criminals.

American courts have an appalling record when it comes to safeguarding the rights of minorities. In light of the history, noted above, of the law's use of science to categorize race, and with an eye to the scary neo-eugenic future of genetically screened population controls, is there any reason for citizens of color to regard the legal application of genetic evidence with anything approaching equanimity? And what bearing, if any, did these concerns have on the O.J. trial?

Race and Genetics

Despite his initial fame as a "black athlete," it was widely perceived that O.J. Simpson was less socially black than almost any other black man in America. As comfortable in Brentwood as he was schmoozing with his white friends at the Riviera Country Club in Pacific Palisades or at LAPD Christmas parties, he held down his job as a Hertz spokesperson for an astonishing seventeen years, shilling, in the famous ads, for predominantly white businessmen on tight airport schedules. In an angle already covered in the O.J. joke repertoire (What did Rodney King say to O.J.? "Good thing you didn't get out of the car, Juice."), Sistah Souljah declared that the blackest thing O.J. ever did was get chased by the police, even though it was a stretch to call it a chase. Just about the only place where O.J. could not be colorless was in a U.S. court of justice, where no black man has ever felt that the color of his skin has no relevance. More to the point, O.J. was in a court in Los Angeles in the 1990s, facing a charge investigated by law enforcement officers who had established the most racist reputation of any police force since the heyday of white justice in the South. By the end of the trial, many concluded that Simpson had purchased a role for himself in the game of identity politics he had assiduously avoided for so long, and may have done so in order to beat the rap for a gender crime.

From the moment L.A. district attorney Gil Garcetti decided to locate the trial downtown, where the jury pool would be more diverse and where the likelihood of a repeat scenario of the Rodney King uprisings was diminished, the trial had a racialized dimension. With the Fuhrman exposé and the defense case built around his racism by Johnnie Cochran (the legal profession's crown prince of identity politics), the trial's focus on race deepened and was amplified a thousandfold in the echo chamber of media reportage. The prevailing media account of public responses to the verdict fiercely reaffirmed all of the divisive fictions about the bichromatic Black and White nation. The most corrosive version suggested that this single, racially weighted, verdict had compensated for centuries of white justice, and that the judicial playing field would be newly leveled as a result. In retrospect, the whole trial became a racial Rosetta stone, endlessly scanned for clues to understanding a society on the brink of abandoning affirmative solutions to its most intractable race problems, while turning a blind eye yet again to the glyphs that spelled out its gender problems.

In all of this drama, little public attention was paid to the single feature of the trial—the data from population genetics used in DNA typing—that formally focused the legal process on O.J.'s racial identity. When the DNA profile obtained from a trace evidence is matched with that of a suspect, statistics derived from population data are applied to estimate the likelihood of a random match. The accuracy of the probability estimate depends on the criteria used for determining the relevant population from which data on allele frequencies can be drawn. In the early years of DNA typing evidence, the reference population was based on the FBI categories of Caucasian, African Americans, and Hispanics, which are far from genetically homogeneous. Dissenting biologists took issue with the treatment of these categories as random mating populations. In 1991, R.C. Lewontin and D.C. Hartl argued that genetic differentiation among ancestral populations in Europe is very complex, and immigrant history is too recent and endogamous mating within ethnic groups too high for Caucasian categories to be internally homogeneous. For African Americans, there exists very little reliable data about African slave populations, notwithstanding the extensive mixing with European and Indian ancestry, and the complex genealogical differences between recent Caribbean immigrants and northern urban and southern agrarian blacks. Hispanic is the most vague category, ranging from Guatemalan ancestry that is pure Indian to Argentinian that is pure Caucasian.[16] Lewontin, Hartl, and other critics of these categories insisted that significant differences among genetic markers in ethnic subgroups had to be empirically accounted for. Defenders of the process maintained that the degree of variance in population substructures would not substantially differ from profile frequencies calculated from population averages, and that the latter were good enough for estimating random-match probabilities with accuracy.[17]

The doubts about the subpopulation problem prompted the 1992 NRC commission to recommend a ceiling principle (or more accurately, an interim ceiling principle, in the absence of significant data on ethnic subgroups) based on conservative assessments of data within the major racial groups.[18] Since the principle appeared to favor the defendant, there were strong criticisms of this report from scientists and lawyers, and, as is common, questions were raised about conflict of interest: several members of the NRC panel were found to have financial links with companies involved in DNA testing.[19] In addition, it was apparent that science in the field was being driven by the urgent needs of the court system and, in particular, by the FBI, which tried to pressure the commission to tone down its reservations on the subpopulation issue. Not surprisingly, the technology's proponents also tried to clear the field's name in eminent journals. Lamenting that adversarial lawyers would soon be spreading confusion about science in the upcoming O.J. trial, Eric Lander and the FBI's Bruce Budowle published their exoneration, "DNA Fingerprinting Dispute Laid to Rest," in *Nature* in 1994, only to be further challenged in the journal by Lewontin

(who described their article as a "piece of propaganda") and
Hartl, who drew attention to the absurdity of FBI scientists
being in a position to determine what constitutes the exact
"forensic significance" of statistical differences between racial
and ethnic populations.[20] Not for the first time in the history of
the field, the cops were seen to be guarding the henhouse.

Many of these doubts and controversies were cited by
Neufeld and Scheck in *People v. Simpson*, both in their motion to
exclude DNA evidence and in their relentless attempts to cast
doubt on the expertise of prosecution witnesses, from lab assis-
tants to leading experts in population genetics. In the meantime,
the new NRC commission had been appointed at the request of
the FBI director William Sessions in 1993 to stave off a general
moratorium, and to settle the disputes about population subdi-
vision and its role in calculating random-match probabilities.
The 1996 report declared that the interim ceiling principle was
no longer necessary, given the advances in knowledge about the
frequency of genetic workers in ethnic subgroups and the overall statistical improvements in genetic profiling of populations.
There now existed an "appropriate data base" to support calculations about population substructures, and the data had shown
that differences between broad racial groups were more significant than within them.[21]

The publication of the 1996 report may put to rest some
public and institutional doubts about the scientific evidence presented in the O.J. trial, but it resolves none of the issues regarding
how complex scientific evidence should be handled in the courtroom nor what uses will be made of the state's data-banking of
DNA samples. For over a century, the state's criminal agencies
have petitioned science with demands for an identifiable self-
signature that would serve as a reliable medium of surveillance,
classification, and law enforcement. Such signatures, from finger-

prints to DNA profiles, have invariably raised, and dashed, the hopes of those looking for biological clues to social behavior. Paul Rabinow points out that the eugenicist Francis Galton was enthused about the first use of fingerprinting in India, motivated by the need of the colonial authorities to counteract the " 'proverbial unveracity' of the Oriental races," but was disappointed to find that fingerprints contained no information about race or temperament, no clues about natural or sexual selection.[22]

The last quarter-century's research in molecular biology has again attracted the interest of those who believe that people carry within their biological makeup the causes of their own crime, poverty, and poor health. The institutional contexts for DNA forensics in particular have been the laboratories of commercial biotechnology companies, local law enforcement, and the FBI itself, which has its own professionalized research team at Quantico, Virginia, responsible for training forensic specialists in the principles of molecular genetics. These techniques are linked to the FBI's National DNA Identification Index, developed in coordination with forensic data banks in at least thirty-two states, and based on extensive sampling studies of convicted felons and over two million armed personnel. A number of soldiers, in Hawaii notably, have already refused to be tested, citing the protection of their civil liberties. The DOD, which court-martialed the soldiers, refuses to guarantee that their data banks will not be used for purposes other than identification of the war dead.[23] Nonconsensual testing is nonetheless becoming a norm, as Phillip Bereano notes, "at a time of an unprecedented testing hysteria," where everyone from corporate employees to sex offenders is being subjected to scientific testing.[24]

The controversy over the courtroom use of DNA typing created a demand for population geneticists to research the differences in DNA marker frequencies among racial and ethnic groups. The FBI alone undertook extensive population surveys resulting in the DNA data-basing of racial and ethnic differences.[25] Thus the earlier doubts about population substructure, which were dismissed at the time by the FBI, turned out to be a convenient justification for extending the range of the FBI's DNA identification banks. The concerns about threats to genetic privacy from this data-banking are considerable. For example, who gets to use the results once the original demand for this kind of research has been satisfied and forgotten? However, there are also larger cultural and social ramifications. The potential outcome of such research will be to reinforce assumptions about the biological classification of ethnicity and race in a social and political climate where such classifications invariably have destructive consequences. Inevitably, it seems, people will once again link cultural and social traits to these biological classifications. Efforts at population control will be able to draw upon biological taxonomies that had proven elusive for centuries. More specifically, genetic testing may be used to affirm the ethnic authenticity of affirmative-action candidates.[26] In the world of identity politics, testing may also be used by spokespersons to buttress their claims to be "more black" or "more gay" than others. Anything is possible on this burned-over terrain, which is being cultivated yet again after centuries of overpopulation by destructive scientific and social fictions about race and sexuality.

In the case of DNA typing, there has been no easy separation of the scientific agenda from the social agenda. They have been beset by the same contradiction: Should our identities be analyzed on an individual basis or according to group type? Nothing could be more pivotal to liberalism's current agony over racial politics. Genetic research has the choice of focusing its resources on the emphasis of individual variation or on group variation. (The former happens to be by far the greater of the two, racial difference accounting for only a small percentage of human genetic diversity.)[27] The legal system is obliged to assess subjects as individuals, but it does so within a social climate and within the framework of community and group values where race and ethnicity often have a more powerful significance.

In the O.J. case, this contradiction played an important role. There was arguably less reason to racialize O.J. than with almost any other black American male. While still a black male before the U.S. legal system, he was as "individual" as it was possible to be. And yet, just as the genetic evidence in the trial was based, in part, on references to his racial identity, the social and cultural meaning of his trial was pushed and pulled into the arena of public opinion where race matters—big time. These contradictions between individual and group are nothing new; they lie at the heart of the liberal political system and are increasingly central to public and policy debates about the shape of a multiracial, multiethnic society. But there are many good reasons why appeals to biological authority should be kept to a minimum in such debates. If the criterion of judgment in matters legal, social, and political is whether the genes fit or not, then we are going to be in serious trouble. Consider the outcome in the O.J. trial: the virtual silencing of the prosecution's establishment of motive in the murder charge, along with much of the supporting evidence of domestic violence. The obsessive focus on DNA identification, which monopolized so much courtroom time, helped to overshadow the systematic evidence of spousal abuse on O.J.'s part. Along with its group-oriented counterpart—the morality play of race politics that Johnnie Cochran's summation evoked in religion-soaked terms—this drama about identification may well have buried the evidence for the gender crime that many believe lay at the heart of the O.J. case. If so, then the individual/group dualism of the liberal imagination proved yet again that it is not up to the feat of dealing more than two cards at a time.

Notes

Thanks are due to Christine Harrington and Dorothy Nelkin for comments and advice on this essay.

1. The California Appellate Court had issued conflicting rulings about the admissibility of the techniques, but was still adhering to the vague criteria of the *Frye* test for its rulings. The 1923 Washington, D.C., case of *Frye v. United States* (293 F.2d 1013 D.C. Cir.) had established a precedent for adjudicating the line between "the experimental and the demonstrable stages" of a science, whereby a conservative duration must have lapsed between discovery of a scientific procedure and its forensic application. While the newer techniques of the PCR (polymerase chain reaction) amplification method were at issue, concerns related to the older techniques of RFLP (restriction fragment length polymorphism) analysis were also presented by the O.J. defense team. Evidence based on both techniques was eventually admitted in the trial.

    By the time of the O.J. trial, some states, but not California, had adopted the approach favored by the decision in *Daubert v. Merrell Dow Pharmaceuticals, Inc.* (113 S. Ct. 2786, 1993), which called for a more sophisticated and informed analysis of scientific evidence than *Frye* had done. The *Daubert* decision was against *Frye*'s traditional bias towards peer review and general scientific acceptance, and it reaffirmed the discretionary power of judges to assess the relevance of the scientific evidence to the case in reviewing its admissibility.

2. See Dorothy Nelkin and Susan Lindee, *The DNA Mystique: The Gene as a Cultural Icon* (New York: Freeman and Co., 1996).

3. Troy Duster, *Backdoor to Eugenics* (New York: Routledge, 1990), pp. 99–100.

4. 545 N.Y.S. 2d 985 (Sup. Ct. 1989).

5.   National Research Council, *The Evaluation of DNA Forensic Evidence* (Washington, D.C.: National Academy Press, 1996), pp. 1–28.

6.   R.C. Lewontin, *Biology as Ideology: The Doctrine of DNA* (New York: HarperCollins, 1992), pp. 79–82.

7.   William F. Buckley, "O.J. on Our Mind," *National Review*, vol. 47, no. 12, June 26, 1995, p. 71.

8.   Cited in an editorial, *Atlanta Journal and Constitution*, October 4, 1995, p. 13A.

9.   *Madam Foreman: A Rush to Judgement?* featuring Armanda Cooley, Carrie Bess, and Marsha Rubin-Jackson (Los Angeles: Dove Books, 1995), p. 75. (Cited hereafter in the text as *MF.*)

10.   Barry Scheck, "DNA and *Daubert*," *Cardozo Law Review* 15 (1994): 1959–97.

11.   Lawrence Tribe, "Trial by Mathematics: Precision and Ritual in the Legal Process," *Harvard Law Review* 84 (1971): 1329.

12.   Marjorie Maguire Schultz, "Reasons for Doubt: Legal Issues in the Use of DNA Identification," in Paul R. Billings, ed., *DNA on Trial: Genetic Identification and Criminal Justice* (Plainview, NY: Cold Spring Harbor Laboratory Press, 1992), p. 20.

13.   Sheila Jasanoff, *Science at the Bar: Law, Science, and Technology in America* (Cambridge: Harvard University Press, 1995).

14.   Rochelle Cooper Dreyfuss and Dorothy Nelkin, "The Jurisprudence of Genetics," *Vanderbilt Law Review* 45, no. 2 (March 1992): 313–48.

15.   Ian Haney Lopez, *White by Law* (New York: NYU Press, 1996), pp. 79–110.

16.   R.C. Lewontin and Daniel Hartl, "Population Genetics Problems in the Forensic Use of DNA Profiles," *Science* 254, no. 1745 (1991).

17.   See Ranajit Chakraborty and Kenneth Kidd, "The Utility of DNA Typing in Forensic Work," *Science* 254, no. 1735 (1991); Bruce Weir, "Population Genetics in the Forensic DNA Debate," *Proceedings of the National Academy of Sciences* 89, no. 11, 654 (1992); William Thompson, "Evaluating the Admissibility of New Genetic Identification Tests: Lessons from the DNA Wars," *Journal of Criminal Law and Criminology* 84, no. 22 (1993): 42–61.

18.   National Research Council, *DNA Technology in Forensic Science* (Washington, D.C.: National Academy Press, 1992). Scheck points out that "since the NRC report was published, the overwhelming number of appellate decisions in Frye jurisdictions have rejected methods used by

the major forensic laboratories for making statistical estimates, and along with it, the DNA evidence." Scheck, note 20, p. 1965.

19. Ruth Hubbard and Elijah Wald, *Exploding the Gene Myth* (Boston: Beacon Press, 1993), p. 151.

20. Eric Lander and Bruce Budowle, "DNA Fingerprinting Dispute Laid to Rest," *Nature* 371 (1994): 735; and letters from R.C. Lewontin and Daniel Hartl, *Nature* 372 (1994): 398–99.

21. In fact, the 1996 report concludes that while "virtually all populations will show some statistically significant departures from random mating proportions ... many of the differences will be small enough to be practically unimportant." NRC (1996), pp. 1–11. The U.S. group that showed the most marked internal variation—a "statistically significant departure"—is American Indian; there do not yet exist adequate databases for many Native peoples' tribes.

22. Paul Rabinow, "Galton's Regret: Of Types and Individuals," in Billings, ed., *DNA on Trial*, p. 6. See also *Making PCR: A Story of Biotechnology* (Chicago: University of Chicago Press, 1996), in which Rabinow analyzes the commercial development of the polymerase chain reaction process.

23. The Council for Responsible Genetics and the ACLU have filed an amicus brief in the lawsuit challenging the building of DOD data banks.

24. Philip Bereano, "The Impact of DNA-Based Identification Systems on Civil Liberties," in Billings, ed., *DNA on Trial*, p. 121.

25. Federal Bureau of Investigation, *VNTR Population Data: A Worldwide Survey* (1993), and numerous studies, published by Bruce Budowle et al., in the *American Journal of Human Genetics* and the *Journal of Forensic Science* from 1992 to 1995. Even more extensive efforts to classify the genetic range of race have been initiated in the Human Genome Diversity Project, under the auspices of Stanford University.

26. Rabinow, "Galton's Regret," p. 17.

27. For all of the advances in DNA data-basing, the degree of human genetic diversity assignable to racial difference has not changed much since Lewontin provided the estimate of 6.3% in 1972. He ended his study with the following proposal: "Human racial classification is of no social value and is positively destructive of social and human relations. Since such racial classification is now seen to be of virtually no genetic or taxonomic significance either, no justification can be offered

for its continuance." "The Approportionment of Human Diversity," *Evolutionary Biology* 6 (1972): 397. In the letter in *Nature* (supra 19), he points out that the FBI's research efforts in the field of DNA typing would be better devoted to producing "idiotypes," or unique genetic identifications, rather than the system it has developed, which requires reference to racial groupings.

American Kabuki

Patricia J. Williams

It wasn't the riot so many soothsayers had almost longingly predicted but instead a soft rain of radioactive poison that began to fall, right on schedule, immediately after The Bomb of the Verdict.

In one of the more symptomatic confrontations, Tammy Bruce, a white radio talk-show host and head of the Los Angeles chapter of the National Organization for Women, declared on *Nightline* that the Simpson trial was "not about racism" but rather about "violence against women," and that focusing on domestic violence would provide "a needed break from all that talk of racism."[1] When Denny Bakewell, the head of a local black community group protested that "The statements she has made, somehow giving domestic violence a priority over racism, are unacceptable.... you should not attack one at the expense of the other,"[2] Bruce shot back, "I'm an advocate for women; what I work on is to try to improve the quality of women's lives. I'm not going to take seriously a man who, I think I can safely say, does not have his finger on the pulse of my community."

With the lines of "community" thus drawn, black feminists started feeling a too-familiar squeeze: Were we against domestic violence or were we against racism? Were we in favor of black men or on the side of white women? Were we going with the New Nationalist Race Woman Stance, standing by her rooting, tooting, raping, and a-looting Man (who, she hastens to explain, wasn't *really* raping but only hurrying because he could hear the hooded horsemen galloping round the house waiting to unsex him). Or would we follow in the grand tradition of those she-martyrs and great betrayers of the race, those intellectual bounty hunters who, following the lead of Anita Hill, sacrifice their "true" black selves for feminism—always beating the hooded horsemen to the job, always willing to sell black men down the river of Hollywood as long as We are played by Whitney Houston. . . .

Only in America.

I guess it's not surprising that in the months following the verdict, close to a million black men marched on Washington to protest, among other unfortunately less well-defined things, their image as criminals and "buffoons." During the same period of time, the membership of the Los Angeles chapter of the National Organization for Women swelled by ten percent. And, reflecting the complicated coalition politics within feminism itself, the national board of directors of NOW, one-third of whom are women of color, issued a resolution censuring Tammy Bruce and asserting "that women of color are often put in the unfair position of being told to choose between their allegiance to their communities of color or to the feminist community when responding to complex issues which encompass race, class, and/or gender." Bruce responded by threatening to sue the national board, saying, "I would think we would have a hard time finding anyone who would disagree that batterers or men who beat up women are not welcome in our culture."

It is easy to forget that O.J. Simpson began this particular chapter of the culture wars as the heroic "white black man." So revered was he that even as a fugitive murder suspect he could drive around the city of Los Angeles with a gun to his head being applauded by crowds of predominantly young white men—"Go O.J., Go!" they chanted—in as callously macabre and Halloween-ish a parade as anything seen in modern times. Yet the modern memory span is about as capacious as a flea's, and scarcely a year later Simpson was magically transformed back into that familiar pumpkin of a "black man's man," his verdict of legal-if-not-socially-accepted innocence greeted with those unforgettable frozen front-page images of exuberant young black men *and* some apparently lindy-hopping young black women. One was left to assume that "they were just so *happy* that 'the bitch' got what she deserved"—as I heard some white teenage girls on the uptown subway describe what they thought some black classmates were thinking. Later, on the downtown subway, I heard two young black boys describing what they thought their white classmates were thinking: "They'd like to see all black men with their balls cut off."

The media reiterated relentlessly the extremes of this divide. On the one hand, there were the images of young white women in West Los Angeles always, seemingly, interviewed at their health clubs while pedaling furiously on stationary bikes, with their lips pressed together in repressed anguish, tears coursing silently down their waxen cheeks. With a little urging, they might eke out a few choked words such as "This is the worst thing that has ever happened to me." Cut to the body of black opinion always, seemingly, located at some noisily devil-worshipping barbecue-rib joint in South Central, where undulating crowds of dark youth, barely distinguishable through the smoky din of misogynist rap lyrics, could be heard shouting things like "He was framed!"

And so the tension was posed in these extraordinary stereotypes—mythological terms that transport the real characters in this very real-life drama far into history and beyond themselves: White women, black men—each contesting their figurative disfigurement, the matter of their symbolic debasement. And as black men continue to be Willie Horton-ized to death, no less do white women continue to be Nicole Brown Simpson-ized into the beautiful shape of the sheet-covered dead. Yes, Willie Horton was a real rapist and Nicole Brown Simpson was a real victim of domestic violence, but as the public discussion turns him into all black men and her into all white women, real black men spend their lives trying to overcome an impossible burden of other people's run-amok fear, while real white women find themselves rendered archetypally fragile and pornographically prone to slasher plots, dismembered in the media with such relentless reiteration that it only goes to *prove* their endless miraculous powers of figurative resurrection.

In any event, the one constant seems to be that all the women are white, all the blacks are men (as Sojourner Truth, Ida B. Wells, Lorraine Hansberry, Pauli Murray, Audre Lorde, Angela Davis, Patricia Hill Collins, Barbara Christian, Deborah MacDowell, Michele Wallace, bell hooks, Hortense Spillers, and not-a-few others have so persistently observed). Any black woman left standing, better pick a side, quick. In the musical chairs that followed the Simpson verdict, black feminists were depicted either as those who had suddenly fallen silent for fear of dishonoring their always already dishonorable men, or as those who found their voices only long enough to agree to mud-wrestle white feminists on prime-time TV.

This much is not a new problem, of course. As literary theorist Ann duCille observes, "the longevity of the insider/outsider debate is reflected in [Anna Julia] Cooper's one-hundred-year-old pronouncement: 'Only the BLACK WOMAN can say when and where I enter, . . . then and there the whole *Negro race enters with me.*'"[3] And as legal theorist Kimberlé Crenshaw has noted, "the specific forms of domination to which black females are subject sometimes fall between the existing legal categories for recognizing injury. Underlying the legal parameters of racial discrimination are numerous narratives reflecting discrimination as it is experienced by black men, while the underlying imagery of gender discrimination incorporates the experiences of white women."[4]

Yet while even that skirmish rages, there have been some very odd silences and telling gaps in the media coverage of the post-O.J. moment. There has been, to return to my earlier example, no serious concern about what *on earth* was going on in the heads of those young white men who held up signs urging O.J. to "Go!" as though for gold while the fallen outlaw-hero played the doomed bull circling the city (in his white Bronco no less), followed closely by flashing cordons of L.A.'s finest *banderilleros.* What, if anything at all, did *they* think of Nicole Brown Simpson and Ronald Goldman? Whatever did *they* think of the verdict?

If there was very little inquiry into the possibility of "white male" misogyny as implicated in the O.J. drama, that silence seems particularly suspect against the backdrop of a bitter national debate about budget cuts that would defund precisely so many of the services upon which battered women must depend. Even as there has been lots of hindsighted handwringing of the "if only we had known" variety, there has been very little application of foresight in that will to know. One heard little in the national media about Nicole Brown Simpson in relation to efforts to cut off legal services for civil suits, including divorce proceedings and restraining orders; or to provide affordable child-care; or to restrict access to public services for undocumented battered women; or to slash welfare benefits and AFDC to levels far below subsistence; or to kill any whisper of a notion of guaranteed health care. If the Simpson verdict could be blamed for a rise in the number of men who battered their wives in his name, then perhaps there are some politicians and religious fundamentalists of various stripes who should be held further accountable for the lot of battered women who see no way out of their present lot except homelessness.

So, how to begin a recuperation of the emotions whose caricature made the case of *People v. Orenthal James Simpson* one of the most poisonously divisive political circuses in our history, such that the very sanctity of the jury system itself seemed to hang in the breach?

First, it is probably worth sifting out the real trial from the media sensation that surrounded it; it is probably worth acknowledging explicitly that there were actually two trials taking place: one in the courtroom, the other in the court of public opinion. Some barrier between the two worlds was supposedly ensured by the process of juror sequestration.

For those of us not living in that courtroom, it's hard to remember that this was a trial where jurors were locked away for the better part of a year precisely so that they would *not* see the instant and endless replays in slow motion of Geraldo Rivera's favorite 911 moment—which so convinced some that this case was about domestic violence alone. For those convinced the verdict was only about race, it's worth remembering that the jurors did not hear all Mark Furhman's racist rantings, and that they knew little more than what it took to show that he had perjured himself badly. They did not read, presumably, Faye Resnick's lurid tattling and prattling about wild cocaine parties where Brown and Simpson were seen doing the bump. They missed out, poor things, on Johnnie Cochran's first wife's promise to write a book about *her* trials and endless tribulations.

The purpose of sequestering the jurors is, after all, to protect them precisely from such tantalizing passions and scandal-soaked rumor. And in fact it is testament to how much the process worked in the Simpson case that the little knot of black, white, and Hispanic jurors came out at the end of that sequestration blinking like moles from a burrow, no doubt initially buoyed by naive faith in civic reward and their piece of the royalty pie, then stuttering and stunned by the blazing suns of bursting flashbulbs and accumulated public fury.

What the jurors (remembered now only as "predominantly black") had failed to take into account in their verdict, of course, was how dangerous it is to cross the largest viewing audience in television history—those whose Monday-morning quarterback status had been upgraded to the pseudointellectual rank of Armchair Jurist. "Johnnie Cochran deserves the *electric* chair!" snorted an impatient voice on the other side of the dressing room wall at my health club. Things had become pretty meanly inflamed in the world beyond the butterfly jar of that jury box.

It is, therefore, important, I think, to deal with what happened in the court of public opinion as its own kind of reality, if one related more to the kind of brawls one sees after a particularly close sports play-off.

Tammy Bruce, for one, "was so certain that he would be convicted of murder that she popped a bottle of champagne on air to celebrate his impending doom."[5] Assuming that there had been a conviction, this was hardly the response one would expect of anyone intimately involved with such a trial. While the Browns or the Goldmans might have felt something more like relief mingled with their grief had Simpson been convicted, the flowing-bubbly gesture of outright celebration probably signals a more distant and cynical emotional response, one more complicated by unrelated, if no less bitter, social projections—a bit like the crowds who gathered in picnicking clusters outside the prison walls to cheer the execution of serial killer Ted Bundy.

At this level, "O.J." (the trademark) was pure Hollywood spectacle, a bread-and-circus superbowl where "the blacks" and "the whites" cheered their sides, had orgiastic cathartic experiences, and if anyone gets hurt, well, it's kind of like a fraternity hazing; everyone knows it's a game and, after all, sports injuries are something one can take an odd but manly pride in. But spectator sport though it might have been, O.J.-mania was still a dangerous game, indeed a deadly political exercise. It *was* that great conversation about race Lani Guinier implored us Americans to have, albeit a conversation waged in a fan-danced pantomime of naked revelations followed by quick flutters of denial.

I fear bread-and-circus events, particularly when they remain as unmoored as they do in our culture, so unreclaimed as ritual. The investment of a normatively distant event with the dynamics of the obsessively experiential—this is the worst (or the best) thing that has ever happened to me—is one way of creating a symbolic vocabulary for public and private crises that remain otherwise unexpressed. In other cultures it can be an effective way of resolving such crises; and perhaps it would do us a world of good to just own up to the fact that racial passion plays, from the Scottsboro Boys to the Clarence Thomas hearings, have emerged as a uniquely American art form, like jazz—our own stylized form of Kabuki theater. However, reading those passion plays as sym-

bols of a legacy of trauma is a task that few in the popular media
have deemed worthy of sustained attention.

Let me first say that I do think that most (black and white)
feminist responses (including Tammy Bruce's) have been motivated by genuine concern about the extraordinary statistics documenting violence against women in America, regardless of race,
ethnicity, or class.

By the same token, I think that most (male and female)
black responses were genuinely and heavily influenced by the
tapes of Mark Fuhrman, combined with the tremendous toll
that overreactive and excessively violent police tactics have had
upon black Americans' willingness to allow for the possibility of
"framing," where whites might not.

It is deep concern about violence, then, that both unites
and divides those who turn to the police fearing predation from
loved ones, and those who fear the predation of corrupt police
upon loved ones—to say nothing of those who fear both.
Reconfiguring the problem in this fashion, however, underscores
the extent to which the basic problem of violence is one not easily divisible between those not-so-discrete boxes of "black versus
white" and "male versus female." It opens the inquiry to whether
extended family, unorthodox family configurations, gay couples,
and sexually harrassed employees may also expect protection in
either their public or private social relations. And it implicates
the degree to which police (who are not only "state actors" but
mortal men and women who have grown up watching *Terminator*
movies like the rest) bear a crucial burden in brokering the fragile line between protecting against, participating in, and just
plain collapsing beneath the complicated weight of our culture's
violence and general gun-craziness.

Yet to stop with even these observations conceals other
currents that, while having no place in the official courtroom

trial, probably played some role in the whirlpool of resentments that swept the nation in the wake of the verdict. Beauty, for example, was surely one of the more unspoken yet powerful sources of the obsessive nature of the public gaze.

While several of my white friends were quite ambivalent about whether Nicole Brown Simpson's extraordinary good looks had anything to do with the amount of attention (his celebrity-blackness and her whiteness were more easily acknowledged as factors), not one of my black friends doubted it for a moment. "Beauty is at the heart of race," says a friend. "That's why those 'black is beautiful' stickers in the sixties were all about politics."

"Yup," says another black friend. "An ugly woman, a black woman, wouldn't have cut the mustard for that poster-girl standard of public sympathy." She does not speak self-effacingly but unhappily, nonetheless, in a tone that underscores the way "ugly" is so often used as a synonym for "black."

While there are few such time-stopping bonfires of public relations with which to compare, I do suspect that this case would never have attracted the attention it did—even given O.J.'s celebrity—if Nicole Brown Simpson had been overweight or dark-skinned or somehow more flawed, more *ordinary.* Moreover, it does seem that if the attention had truly been about the milk of human compassion, the murder of Ronald Goldman would not have been so completely overshadowed. Indeed, there are thousands of cases that rival this for sheer savagery—cases, moreover, in which there are completely credible witnesses, full confessions, and smoking guns—yet where the perpetrator spends virtually no jail time, or where the "heat of male passion" is still an unspoken defense. If one knows anything at all about the general ho hum with which "ordinary" cases of battery and spousal killings are tolerated in the courts and in communities across

America, it is hard not to wonder if the reductively iconographic nature of a generally unattainable blond-beauty standard had something to do with the fascination—and the resentment.

But whether the death of a woman in a plain brown wrapper would have changed the outcome or not, the subterranean resentments of many black women toward the tyranny of white aesthetic ideals are too prevalent to ignore, and probably deserve attention if for no other reason than that they might otherwise be mistaken for resentment of Nicole Brown Simpson herself.

I can't help noticing, for example, how conspiratorial I felt among my black women friends who went on to whisper their significant animosity toward, of all things, Barbie dolls; there was a lot to fear, we agreed, in the kind of doll who would wear high heels while walking on the moon. We shared our shame with unbecoming glee.

Ann duCille, in a study of the history of Barbie dolls, writes of an encounter she had with a young black teenager in Toys 'R' Us who was laying in a stock of Barbie dolls for the sheer sadistic pleasure of snapping their heads off. "It's the hair," she confessed miserably. If, as white feminists Kim Chernin and Naomi Wolf imply, Barbie acts as a kind of codependent to white women afflicted with anorexia, one brave enough might also ask whether her idealized plastic puppetry serves as the tinder for—just possibly—a black woman's Farrah Fawcett fixation, the flintstone for a form of burning hair anxiety that is our own little waiting-to-be-discovered-by-medical-science form of racial bulemia.

In fact, of course, I would hate to see this catalogued in the annals of women's stress as just another neurotic female "thing." Black women's hair anxiety has a lot of history, even a legal history. Legal theorist Paulette Caldwell has written about how black women have actually had to sue for the right to wear their hair naturally—i.e., unstraightened, kinky, liberated from chemical "enhancement"—without being fired from their employment. (My favorite case in that litany involved a women who sued to be able to wear her hair in "cornrows," cornrowing being nothing less than an ancient African style of braiding hair. Not only was she required to conform to her employer's demands, she was then chided for "imitating Bo Derek.")

Nicole Brown Simpson never seemed to have had a bad hair day.

I remember an afternoon halfway through the trial when I was in the A&P with my neighbor D. We stood in line, leaning on carts full of staples, surveying the checkout racks of magazines. *Family Circle* was dusted for the one thousandth week in a row by the *National Enquirer*, which featured a racy front-page photo of Nicole Brown Simpson, her face purple with bruises from the blows O.J. had purportedly delivered. "Her hair," said D., arrested. "He roughed her up, and there's still not a hair out of place." It was spoken with both sympathy and wonder. It was only later we discovered that the picture had been a computer enhancement of a file photo, a high-tech artist's depiction based on reports of what she suffered.

The blasphemous repose of that image has lingered with me ever since. The "twist her arms! bend her legs! color in the bruises!" of that pornographic moment has left me with many questions.

Is not the idolatrous pornography of women like Nicole Brown Simpson, for example, related to the bestialization of Shannon Faulkner by her classmates who, during her embattled bid to study at the Citadel, called her an "ugly whale"? With what anxiety must the girlfriends and wives of such cruelly "disciplined" young men monitor the limits of their own bodies, in this world where solidity and strength in a woman are deemed so hyperbolically engulfing? And what of the complicated public condemnation of Faulkner's decision to quit: the jumbled sense that she wasn't "man" enough to "tough" it out and instead had proved to be a "real girl" prone to nervous breakdowns, a crybaby ingrate who never expressed a flicker of gratitude for all those thousands of dollars they spent building her that special high-security cage of a dorm room with the twenty-four-hour spotlight trained right on the door?

Similarly, is not the reservation of "feminism" to a certain perceptual "slip" of a "thing" of a white woman related to the de-aesthetizing masculinization of black women? That is, the sense that black women are figured more as "stand-ins" for men, sort of reverse drag queens, women pretending to be women but more male than men: bare-breasted, sweat-glistened, plough-pulling, sole supporters of their families. Arnold Schwarzenegger and Sylvester Stallone, meet Sojourner Truth—the *Real* Real Thing, the Ace-of-Spades Gender Card Herself, Thelma-and-Louise-knocked-up-by-Wesley Snipes, Battle Axis of all Battle Axes, the ultimate hard-drinking, tobacco-growing-and-a-spitting, nut-crushing ball-buster of all time. As historian Debra Gray White and psychologist Jessica Daniels have suggested in their studies of stereotypes of black women, how can such a one be raped?

Literary theorist Wahneema Lubiano observes that even successful black women find that their "disproportionate over-achievement stands for black cultural strangeness and . . . ensures the underachievement of 'the black male' in the lower classes."[6] Indeed, if black women are such thorough pretenders to the thrones of both femininity *and* masculinity, it is hardly surprising to see the figures of both the Black Mother and her unfathered, unmanly Wild Child so endlessly mocked with the ambiguously gendered, homophobically charged, crown-ofthorns imagery of "queen"—Madame Queen, snap queen, welfare queen, quota queen, Queenie Queen, Queen Queen Queen.

One of the most complicated and delicate issues that presents itself in all this is the degree to which Nicole Brown Simpson was elevated to tragic movie-star status à la Marilyn Monroe only posthumously. I want not just to suggest that there was something necessarily necrophiliac about the enslaving, consuming gaze to which her penultimately obedient photographic stillness was subjected. (Or perhaps I do. The slack, skeletal, empty-faced image of Kate Moss is no less waxen in those Calvin Klein ads.) But the more interesting question for me is whether Nicole Brown Simpson would have been able to retain the sympathetic power of her perfectly coiffed beauty if she had lived and left, *entirely*, the propertied protection of O.J. Simpson's control. Not just separated, mind you, but fled with her children the first time he hit her, giving up completely "his" house, "his" car, and "his" support payments.

Where, in other words, would Nicole Brown Simpson have realistically found herself if she'd decided to walk out years ago? Indeed, with a high school education and little employment experience, she stood a good chance of ending up in the same situation that her sister had only a few years before; yet Denise Brown's one-time status as a single mother, whose personal crises and bad fortune prompted her to take advantage of the safety net of welfare, has almost never been mentioned as a lesson in how welfare in fact might or might not have worked.

The degree to which battered women of all classes fall into poverty at greater rates and seek welfare in disproportionately large numbers is too often seen as their own irrationality—the choice of a bad man, the choice to be poor—rather than as part of a quite predictable chain of cause and effect. Battering inflicts trauma. Trauma paralyzes. It is the very logic of battery to exact debilitating social and economic cost; it is the rationality of the batterer to control his victim by making her as socially isolated and economically dependent as possible. Less apparent is that control sometimes involves seducing the vulnerabilities of the families of victims, no less than the battered themselves.

This brings me to the most difficult question of all. These days, the Brown family is properly and publicly exercised about the domestic abuse Nicole suffered over the years; but I do wonder some about news reports, around the time of the famous 911 call, that her family had urged her to try to preserve her marriage. Let me underscore the degree to which I have come to distrust all media reports in the wake of this trial—hence I suppose I risk hypothesizing about the Brown family dynamic in a way that is surely unfair and possibly dangerous—but hopefully to make a point that is illuminated even by the very glancing shape of such hypothesis. I keep wondering if the Browns' protective instincts at earlier times had at all been compromised, perhaps by Simpson's economic support of the entire Brown family, including providing Nicole's father with a profitable Hertz franchise.

This last is not as simple as wondering if the Brown family were uncaring or greedy. Concern about bottom-line economic survival is not as unrelated to issues of physical health and emotional well-being as the romantic lore of the solidly middle class might make it out to be. In an era when health benefits are so outrageously expensive even for the healthy well-to-do, when shelters are so limited, and when psychological services of all sorts are being wiped out, including counseling for batterers as well as for the battered, the fear of being out in the cold and literally homeless cannot be deemed a casual one.

There is a way in which this fear has sometimes worked itself out in the unspoken demand for what legal anthropologist

Deborah Post calls a "modern brideprice": in which beautiful women who become "trophy wives" not uncommonly purchase a degree of economic insurance for their extended families. That this aspect of such marriages can have many of the characteristics of an outright sale is not to disparage the possibility, even the heightening, of romantic love. For a long time in Western history the essence of femininity has meant beauty and grace; the essence of masculinity, power and wealth. Put the two together and, well, whether you call it commercial intercourse or romantic exchange, it almost doesn't matter in the high-powered world of contract law that is the well-made fairy-tale marriage.

Along class lines, however, less-well-made unions are the subject of considerably less pretty characterization. Women who use their bodies or their looks to get ahead in life will be classed as prostitutes, or not, depending on how discreetly the currency terms are negotiated and whether the price is high enough to purchase respectability as part of the bargain. If these precise terms make it sound crude and cynical, this discussion has nevertheless been one that has rent feminism since the earliest days of the women's movement. Historian Christine Stansell writes of debates in the mid- to late-nineteenth century that "while bourgeois men and women viewed ruin as the consequence of prostitution, working-class people reversed the terms. It was ruin, occasioned by a familial or economic calamity (for women the two were synonymous), that precipitated the 'fall' into prostitution."[7] Indeed, she maintains that for many poor women, "Prostitution was neither a tragic fate, as moralists viewed it (and continue to view it), nor an act of defiance, but a way of getting by, of making the best of bad luck."[8]

In a fascinating review of Carolyn Heilbrun's biography of Gloria Steinem, *The Education of a Woman,* Vivian Gornick, writing in *The Nation,* reports that "Steinem was born sixty-one years ago in the Midwest into a family whose drift toward the margin was steady. She was smart, and she was pretty. Like millions before and after, she thought pretty would be the passport to another life, but as it turned out it only meant 'coming in second in beauty contests in Toledo, Ohio.' . . . Then came a scholarship to Smith College. After Smith she knew how to do the world."[9]

The significance of being pretty from Toledo as opposed to being pretty from Smith reflects a class split whose rancor is reflected in the very Question: When women "use" their looks for their own ends, is it making the most of one's "assets" or is it some coy form of parlor prostitution?

And what of women who diminish the power of their wealthy husbands by breaching the contract, taking back their trophy selves, and suing for divorce? To return to the question of what might have happened if Nicole Brown Simpson had run for her life at the very first hint of violence: Would she have had savvy and capital enough to have ended up "liberated"? Or would she have fallen upon anonymous hard times, supporting children by herself, dodging the sanctimonious vilification of the Guardians of the Moral Order, the waist grown thick, the hair grown lank and ever lanker?

"As Steinem talks," writes Gornick, "one hears repeatedly the inevitable murmur of 'She's so beautiful,' but in the crowd stand countless women who also came in second in a beauty contest in Toledo, Ohio, and also needed to command the attention of the local Man of Power. The women who might have become Steinem, but instead became Thelma and Louise."[10]

If this much is complicated by class, how much more so it becomes when one throws race into the brew. The figure of "the" poor single mother in today's policy debates is always a black teenager, a younger yet tougher version of the picture Clarence Thomas painted of his sister: addicted to those HUGE welfare checks; given over to the life of lust and laziness to which her "pathological" dependence has presumably so accustomed her; bearing profligate (rather than prodigal) children, an over-ripe fruit of a Tattooed Harlot, spilling a profusion of Bad Seeds into an overtaxed world, a model of hard-hearted female calculation rather than maternal deference, a creature in whom willfulness and agency are subcategories of the irrational.

In this definitional collapse, race consumes class, to the degree that commentators like Dan Quayle and Charles Murray blame the loose morals of unmarried white women—even fictional upper-class white women like Murphy Brown—upon their purported imitation of "underclass" black mores. Racism thus becomes the ultimate weapon against the legacy of the women's liberation movement: white women who transgress will be tossed into the same demonized space as black women. This symbolic cohabitation has led to the inevitable error of some white women believing with all their hearts that their struggle comes from exactly the same "place" as that of black women: it's a simplistic reversal in which gender consumes race. Just as inevitably, this has left a lot of poor black women believing that "feminism" has nothing at all to do with them.

How much is lost by such oversimplifying is demonstrated by historian Nell Painter's recuperation of Emma Mae Martin, Clarence Thomas's much-maligned "welfare queen" of a sister—who in fact had gone on welfare only temporarily while nursing a sick aunt who had baby-sat her children while she worked two minimum-wage jobs: "She had followed a trajectory common in the experience of poor women, regardless of race.... He seemed not to have appreciated that he was the favored boy-child who was protected and sent to private schools and that she was the girl who stayed behind, married early, and cared for a relative who had fallen ill. If he realized how common his family's decision had been, he gave no indication of seeing those choices as gendered. His equation balanced one thing only, and that was individual enterprise."[11]

If we have difficulty imagining the beautiful Nicole Brown Simpson as a putative welfare mother, then surely this is as much a problem of race as it is of feminism. By the same token, if we have difficulty imagining Emma Mae Martin as the beautiful icon-of-the-checkout-line to whom our hearts rush out in all her ravishing fragility, then we must understand this as a problem of sexism as much as it is of race. The failure to see one in the embodied distress of the other is a cultural blindness that afflicts every segment of our culture. And the temptations to disembody ourselves in service to the ideal are everywhere: in the hair-straighteners and the curly perms, the surgery to make eyes bigger but noses smaller, the skin-lighteners and the tanning salon, the crash diets, the hidden currency of inflated bosoms. The life-or-death stakes to hold Ken's eye—for better or much worse—for in his gaze lies the Dream House of our existence . . .

The sadomasochistic dangers of self-elimination that accompany the beatification of Nicole Brown Simpson but not her living, struggling, browner, "less attractive" counterparts is peculiarly but succinctly summarized by the comment of a woman standing in front of me in line at the Food Emporium. Gazing at a photo of Princess Diana looking radiantly, elegantly melancholic on the cover of some women's magazine, she snapped: "God! Bulimia must work."

Notes

1.   Kenneth B. Noble, "Outspokenness on Simpson Case Has California Talk Show Host in a Cauldron" *New York Times,* December 17, 1995.

2.   *Ibid.*

3.   Ann duCille, "The Occult of True Black Womanhood: Critical Demeanor and Black Feminist Studies," *Signs* (Spring 1994): 599.

4.   Kimberlé Crenshaw, "Whose Story Is It, Anyway?" in Toni Morrison, ed., *Race-ing Justice, En-gendering Power* (New York: Pantheon, 1992), p. 404.

5.   Noble, "Outspokenness on Simpson Case."

6.   Wahneema Lubiano, "Black Ladies, Welfare Queens, and State Minstrels: Ideological War by Narrative Means," in Toni Morrison, ed., *Race-ing Justice, En-gendering Power* (New York: Pantheon, 1992), p. 335.

7.   Christine Stansell, *City of Women* (New York: Knopf, 1986), 19, p. 175.

8.   *Ibid.,* p. 176.

9.   Vivian Gornick, "What Feminism Looks Like," *The Nation,* November 6, 1995, p. 544.

10. *Ibid.,* p. 545.

11. Nell Irvin Painter, "Hill, Thomas, and The Use of Racial Stereotype," in Toni Morrison, ed., *Race-ing Justice, En-gendering Power* (New York: Pantheon, 1992), p. 210.

The Unbearable Darkness of Being: "Fresh" Thoughts on Race, Sex, and the Simpsons

Ann duCille

To understand why O.J. was so compulsively attracted to Nicole, you'd have to understand his mind-set. O.J. seemed to hate being black and, although he tried to conceal it, avoided any real connection with the black community. His marriage to Marguerite was in the days before he knew he could actually cross over the line and, except for the color of his skin, seemingly become white. Marguerite was probably the last black women [sic] O.J. would ever be with. Nicole was, in O.J.'s words, "angel white."

—Faye Resnick, *Nicole Brown Simpson*

I don't mean to diminish the horror of the crime . . . Everyone wants the murderer punished. But Nicole. Nicole. She embodies a little discussed wound in the heart of many African-Americans: the white wife.

—Jacqueline Adams, "The White Wife," *New York Times Magazine*

I marry white culture, white beauty, white whiteness. When my restless hands caress those white breasts, they grasp white civilization and dignity and make them mine.

—Frantz Fanon, *Black Skin, White Masks*

They stalk. They publicly humiliate. They murder. And afterward, they don't feel very bad. Welcome to the Othello Syndrome.

—*LosAngeles,* July 1995

Ancient civilizations often entertained themselves at the expense of the weakest among them: slaves, male prisoners of war, and female captives cum concubines forced to

dance, do battle, and die for the titillating pleasure of the populace. The Romans diverted themselves by throwing Christians to
the lions and by watching gladiators, usually male slaves, fight to
the death right before their eyes in the Coliseum. Today, we consider such human sacrifice barbaric. One could argue, however,
that in airing dirty laundry and personal tragedy as public spectacle, the mass media—tabloids, TV talk shows, and even the
more respectable press—play to the same coliseum mentality
that thrilled at the sight of human slaughter. We have become a
nation of voyeurs, who despite (or maybe because of) our
advancement as a civilization, retain what the black psychiatrist
Frantz Fanon described as "an irrational longing for unusual
eras of sexual license, of orgiastic scenes, of unpunished rapes,
of unrepressed incest."[1] And perhaps because the black male, as
Fanon also explained, is instantly reducible to his genitalia and
imagined transgressions, the black man for all seasons—*homo
erectus*—has superseded baseball's boys of summer as the one to
be watched.

For some time now, our national avocation of scopophilia
has been particularly well plied by supermarket tabloids (*Star,
Globe,* and the *National Enquirer*) and by TV talk shows (*Jenny Jones,
Jerry Springer, Richard Bey, Ricki Lake, Maury Povich, Montel Williams,* and
especially *Geraldo*). Black men who do all manner of socially
unacceptable things are the most frequent subjects of these
shows. But never in the history of mass communication has
there been a more voluptuously viewable male specimen than the
black body of O.J. Simpson or a more highly specularized
tragedy than what has come to be known as "the Simpson case":
the June 1994 murders of Nicole Brown Simpson and Ronald
Goldman and the subsequent arrest, trial, and acquittal of O.J.
Simpson. Simpson may have stalked his ex-wife and admittedly
peered through the window as she entertained other lovers, but,

with the help of the media, millions of us have had the opportunity to stalk him and to peek both at him and with him.

Part of what has made the man, the woman, and the case so delectable, so conspicuously consumable is the extent to which its details immediately draw our gaze below the belt. The December 1995 cover of *Spy* makes the focus of our collective attention graphically clear. Riffing the cover of the inaugural issue of *George*, John F. Kennedy, Jr.'s, glossy new political magazine, the *Spy* cover morphs O.J. Simpson's likeness into the same colonial garb and General Washington stance that Cindy Crawford sports in *George*. The bare midriff and spread legs of Cindy Crawford are replaced with those of O.J. Simpson, simultaneously positioning the former All-American as an object of desire and a false patriot. The caption spread across his crotch declares "By George, He's Guilty!" while a sidebar script promises "1,001 Reasons Why the O.J. Trial Is the Most Absurd Event in the History of America." Inside, a second photo depicts the putative O.J.—still in colonial costume but with added black leather gloves—grinning broadly, grabbing his crotch à la Michael Jackson, and giving the country a gloved finger. Themselves a clever hoax, the photographs speak volumes about race, sex, desire, and transgression. O.J. Simpson, the greatest trickster of all times, stands founding-father erect among his multiple transgressions, thumbing his dick at the nation, if not the world—the black man who broke all the taboos and literally got away with murder.

The not-guilty verdict has long since come down in *The People of the State California v. Orenthal James Simpson*, but the jury remains out on the issue of Simpson's innocence. Or it might be more accurate to say that, despite the not-guilty judgment, nearly all of the mainstream media and—if we believe the polls, reports, and postmortems—most people remain convinced of Simpson's guilt. This national presumption of guilt is nothing

new, of course. There was never a moment in the public production and consumption of the Simpson case when "O.J.," as the
media insist upon calling him familiarly, was innocent. From the
first repeatedly displayed image of the not-yet-accused Simpson
in handcuffs on June 13, 1994, to parting shots of the just-
acquitted Simpson in mid-smile (or was it a smirk?) on October
3, 1995, the graphics and the grammar of trial coverage both
assumed guilt and helped to produce it.

Elsewhere I have argued that not only was the presumption
of guilt overdetermined by the news *and* entertainment media, it
was also racially coded in predictable, deeply historical ways, as
the press at once subtly and overtly linked Simpson's assumed
crime to his color, to his gang past, to what black men to the
ghetto born are destined to do *by nature*.[2] In this essay, I want to
focus not on the blackening of O.J. Simpson—of which *Time*'s
darkened mug-shot cover photo is probably the most infamous
example—but on the browning of his white ex-wife, Nicole.

Like many who followed and commented on the trial, I
have been known to speculate that had the murder victim been
the black ex-wife instead of the white one, there would have been
far less media attention and public fascination. Here, I want to
advance a rather different theory. I want to argue the relative
irrelevance of Nicole Simpson *as a white woman*. I want to suggest
that although her marriage to a black man in possession of a
great fortune elevated her social and economic standing, it also
blackened her and robbed her of any claim to the cult of true
white womanhood or to favorite-daughter status. The narrative
that held its audience captive for more than two years is the fall
of a black man who would be white—not the death of a white
woman who did sleep black.

I came to this understanding of Nicole Simpson's relative
irrelevance when I began to wonder why O.J. Simpson is still

alive. If he is as guilty as we continue to assume he is, why isn't he dead? I understand why he isn't in prison: in a tragic but wholly predictable show of racial solidarity, twelve ignorant, mostly colored jurors let the brother go. But why isn't he dead? The blood of a white woman was spilled by a black man. Where are the avenging angels? Where are the angry white men of conscience? Why are Nicole's only male champions the Puerto Rican talk-show host Geraldo Rivera, who continues nightly to make Simpson's guilt his show's lead "news" story, and the black deputy district attorney, Christopher Darden, the self-proclaimed "lightning rod for the bigotry, insecurity, and misunderstanding of an entire nation," who has cast himself in the role of avenging lone ranger?[3] Where is the Klan? the lynch mob? Historically, black men have been strung up, castrated, and burned alive because someone said they looked at, spoke to, or thought about a white women. Yet here, there, and everywhere golfs the black man who bedded, beat up, and nearly beheaded a white woman and lived to deny it—at Oxford University, no less. Where is the irate father? Where is the hit man? I mean, as retribution goes, a civil suit is so *civil*.

I was genuinely baffled by this civility in the face of a white woman's murder until it came to me as I was preparing a lecture on captivity narratives that, like the captive colonial daughters I was reading about, Nicole Brown Simpson had ceased to be a white woman once she married a black man. Henry Louis Gates, Jr., was right, I thought: race is a trope. Her dead body may be worth millions in civil court, but Nicole Simpson had little surplus value in "real life," except perhaps her decorative female sexuality itself and the financial benefit her marriage to a black man of means and property brought—indeed, continues to bring— her white family. Her awful murder can be appropriated for a national campaign against domestic abuse that figures a bestial black man as the signifier for all male violence, but she herself is a lost cause, a disappeared daughter, curiously written out of anything other than a metaphorical role in a national narrative that might well be called "The Rebirth of a Nation," in dubious tribute to D.W. Griffith's hugely successful 1915 film. In the film, as in *The Clansman*, the novel on which it is based, the need to protect white women from the sexual threat posed by lusty black bucks serves as the rationale for the rise of the Ku Klux Klan.

But *Birth of a Nation* isn't the only drama that the Simpson saga has evoked; nor are its innocent southern belles the only specimens of sexually threatened white womanhood Nicole Brown recalls. As a white woman who married a black man, the second Mrs. Simpson serves a symbolic function in the white imagination roughly akin to that of Shakespeare's Desdemona. It should come as no surprise, then, that some experts have labeled the psychodrama in which her dead body plays a starring role the "Othello Syndrome."

A form of paranoid psychosis first identified and named by British psychiatrists in 1955, the Othello Syndrome is characterized by "intense jealousy of a spouse and delusions of infidelity, often leading to violence." According to Dr. Louis J. West, race is a key component of the disorder. Six months into the trial, a cover story in *LosAngeles* magazine summarized West's theory and applied it to O.J. Simpson: "Race discrimination leads to self-loathing in certain black men, causing them to believe that any white woman who accepts them is worthless. They project that autohatred onto their wives, experience irrational suspicion and lash out."[4] The article claimed, in fact, that Simpson fit the syndrome so perfectly that, "according to a well-placed source in the defense camp"—F. Lee Bailey, a longtime acquaintance of Dr. West—asked the psychiatrist to be an expert witness for the defense. Although he denied that he and Bailey ever discussed the case, West did offer a diagnosis: "If [Simpson's] guilty, it's quite likely this is a case of the Othello Syndrome," he's quoted as saying. "It's hard to find a more accurate model ... O.J., like Othello, was seen to be a heroic figure, larger than life, rich and famous. He was older and more experienced than his wife. He was black; she was white."[5]

Without an M.D. behind my name, I guess I can't just dismiss this kind of theorizing as armchair psychobabble, especially given the credentials of those making the Othello diagnosis: Dr. West is the former head of UCLA's Neuropsychiatric Institute, and the novelist Jonathan Kellerman, who authored the *LosAngeles* magazine article about the syndrome, is himself a trained psychologist. But what is it about this case—except the respective races of the subjects, black man/white woman—that makes it acceptable for professionals and clinicians to publicly comment on the mental state of a "patient" they haven't examined, interviewed, or studied? What is it about this case that lures men and women of conscience, decency, and intelligence into offering analyses and making judgments that their scholarly practice, if not their professional ethics, would otherwise forbid?

Although he acknowledged that his commentary was pure conjecture, Dr. Alvin Poussaint, a highly respected black professor of clinical psychiatry at Harvard Medical School, couldn't resist the opportunity to offer his own long-distance diagnosis in the pages of *Ebony*. After speculating that, if Simpson committed the murders, he might have been mentally ill or temporarily insane, the doctor went on to suggest that, if not crazy in the legal sense, a jealous, spurned O.J. may simply have snapped, allegedly murdering the woman he could no longer possess out of an "if I can't have her, nobody will" attitude. In a move that seems both to name the villain and blame the victim, Poussaint suggested that the abusive husband's "final heinous act may have been provoked by Nicole's rejection of him as a Black man. Perhaps she, as a so-called ideal California blonde, symbolized the American dream for O.J. and losing her revealed that he could never be totally accepted into the White world he coveted."[6]

Published four months before the case even went to trial—before the jury was empaneled, in fact—these if/perhaps/maybe speculations seem particularly irresponsible, coming as they do from a respected black psychiatrist with a public presence (he was a consultant to the *Cosby Show*) and a loyal following in *Ebony*, for which he frequently writes. Even with the caveat that he doesn't know what motivated O.J., Dr. Poussaint's conjectures are as dangerous as Dr. West's. In fact, woven throughout Poussaint's commentary are threads of the Othello Syndrome. From news reports, the doctor determined that Simpson "felt he owned Nicole like a piece of chattel" and, "in a bizarre twist," may have seen his white wife "as a rebellious slave who needed to be executed."

Worse still than this explanation that presumes guilt is the fact that Poussaint's psychoanalysis moves from the specific case of O.J. Simpson to the general psychic condition of all black men. "The Simpson case should be a reminder of the complexity of Black males' relationships with the White world and the emotional toll it takes," he opined, adding that the prevalence of crime and violence among black men is evidence of "their psychological vulnerability."

It is amazing to me—and may be a sign of the dementia that attacks all of us who touch this case—that so many attempts to explain Simpson's assumed crime, even those by well-intentioned, concerned citizens and expert witnesses, such as Alvin Poussaint, manage to simultaneously racialize the crime and criminalize and animalize all black men. Surely as a psychiatrist and as an educator Poussaint knows that the dominant/

submissive, master/slave domestic pattern remains the primary model of heterosexual (and perhaps even homosexual) coupling in the United States. Yet, if we follow the logic of his analysis, we must conclude that black men possess, dominate, beat, brutalize, and even murder their wives—especially their white wives—not because they are men functioning in a patriarchal society that condones and even suborns such behavior, but because they are black.

I'm one of those people who believes that race is always an issue in the United States, but I think that here a Marxist analysis of domestic economy under patriarchy might be more useful than a racial analysis of what has been figured as specifically or uniquely black male behavior. Historically, a major measure of a society's advancement as a civilization has been the status and treatment of "its" women. This appraisal not only has defined social advancement in terms of the female body, it has also made the woman's exemption from material production—that is, her leisure rather than her labor—the signifier of civic success and viable nationhood. Where men are civilized, women as wives, mothers, and daughters are the promoters, protectors, and preservers of high culture rather than the producers of material culture.

Within this patriarchal, capitalist framework, heterosexual coupling functions as a domain of male power in which labor or material culture (figured as male) has ultimate dominion over leisure or high culture (figured as female). The legitimate compensation for man's labor is the conspicuous consumption of the surplus value of women's leisure: her female sexuality. In other words, women's indebtedness to the men who "own" them through wedlock isn't limited to the concrete patriarchal possession of the female body but extends to the abstract ownership of what women produce in such relationships: desire.

The basic proprietary quality of marriage—what some have called its domestic slavery—is a deep structure that women have been challenging for centuries. It has found one of its most finely honed challenges in women's literature, including the work of black women writers. Zora Neale Hurston's fiction, for instance, can be read collectively as an extended critique of male dominance—a critique that I would argue comes to its fullest fruition not in *Their Eyes Were Watching God* (1937), for which she is best known, but in her last and perhaps least read novel, *Seraph on the Suwanee* (1948), where Jim Meserve, the white male protagonist says to Arvay Henson, his "useless . . . play-pretty" fiancée: "Women folks don't have no mind to make up nohow. They wasn't made for that. Lady folks were just made to laugh and act loving and kind and have a good man to do for them all he's able, and have him as many boy-children as he figgers he'd like to have, and make him so happy that he's willing to work and fetch in every dad-blamed thing his wife thinks she would like to have."[7]

For Jim Meserve, as for his real-life counterparts, the woman's physical beauty is of fundamental, commercial importance—the commodity she brings to the marriage like a dowry. Within the confines of middle- and upper-class marriages in particular, the husband's masculinity, economic status, and sexual prowess are confirmed by the ornamental display of his wife's beauty and by his perhaps less conspicuous but no less potent consumption of her sexual goods, her "labors of love," as it were—the outward and visible sign of which is the production of offspring, whom he also owns. Abstract ownership of female desire and real economic power over the nonlaboring wife entitle the husband to unlimited access to his mate, whose beautiful body excites or produces desire.

Although courts now acknowledge the possibility of marital rape, historically the wife's resistance or lack of desire has not been viewed as an impediment to her husband's "rightful" claims to the fruit not only of his labor but of hers as well. This has been the white man's way. But as black women have long noted, it's a model of patriarchal performance from which black men are by no means exempt. Sojourner Truth initially opposed the ratification of the fourteenth and fifteenth amendments precisely because they made no mention of the rights of black women. "If colored men get their rights, and not colored women theirs," she argued, "the colored men will be masters over women, and it will be just as bad as it was before."[8]

In *Their Eyes Were Watching God*, Janie Crawford, Hurston's most famous character, is initially attracted to Joe Starks, the man who would be mayor, because of his "like a white man" ways—his business sense and his willingness to work for her comfort in contrast to her first husband's plans to put her to work behind a plow. But as Janie is silenced and put on display merely as another of her husband's material possessions, she learns what the critic Sally Ferguson says white women have known for some time: "men who make women objects of their labor tend to treat them as things bought and owned."[9]

If O.J. Simpson treated his wife like property, it might be read as another way in which he functioned *like a white man*. It has been easier, however, to claim his behavior as part of a black syndrome rather than a patriarchal one—as a "black thing," rather than a "man thing." Whatever else black men may be guilty of, such interpretations make their original sin blackness itself.

The Mandingo Syndrome

This last observation leads me back to what I want to say about the browning of Nicole Simpson. The blackness of black men is evidently so potent that one drop of black semen can turn a white woman brown and a white man green with envy. This is the real meaning behind the "one-drop" rule: the law of "hypodescent," which historically has defined anyone with a percentage of "African blood" as black. It's not so-called black blood that is the issue, however; it's black semen. And the operative "psychosis" isn't the Othello Syndrome but what I am calling here the "Mandingo Syndrome": white women's penchant for and willing submission to black men and the national anxiety that even the possibility of such consensual coupling has traditionally evoked. As the media theorist John Fiske writes:

> America has a long tradition of using the beauty and vulnerability of the white woman as a metaphor for its social order. The nonwhite male out of sexual and social control, then, individualizes and sexualizes the threat of the other race, now primarily the Black race, though in the nineteenth century the figure of the male American Indian threatening the white female captive functioned identically. Sergeant Stacey Koon offered as justification for beating Rodney King the fear that King posed a "Mandingo" threat to a white policewoman.[10]

I doubt that Stacey Koon knew what he was actually implying when he invoked the Mandingo image, for if we trace his allusion to its literary and cinematic roots, it would be the white policewoman who posed a sexual threat to Rodney King, not the other way around. In *Mandingo*, both the trashy 1975 film and the steamy Kyle Onstott novel on which it is based, it's not the loyal African slave (played badly by boxer Ken Norton) who poses a sexual threat to the young white mistress (Susan George); it's the already ruined white plantation lady whose reckless sexual desire threatens the life of her husband's favorite slave, Mede—a tall, dark, handsome Mandingo she forces to "pleasure" her, both to satisfy her own lust and to punish her husband for preferring his black concubine to his white wife. Her threat to cry rape if Mede refuses to have *her* way with her places the moronically loyal slave in a dilemma of biblical proportions: he must serve two masters, one of whom is determined to make him her mistress.

Ultimately Mede pays a high price for his loyalty. (So does she, for that matter.) When the white wife gives birth to a baby too dark to be her husband's, the infant is made to bleed to death, and the African is shot, pushed into a vat of boiling water, and then run through with a pitchfork. The nigger-loving wife is merely given the same toxic toddy that's used to kill slaves too old or infirm to work, but the Mandingo's crimes—sleeping with a white woman and knocking her up—are so horrible that the cuckolded husband has to kill him three times over.

It's important to understand that in *Mandingo*, much as in the syndrome I've given its name, it's the white woman who aggressively pursues (or willingly submits to) the reluctant black man. Too terrible to contemplate, the Mandingo Syndrome has never been clinically diagnosed—except by me. (I'm not a doctor, but I play one in this essay.) Its dread and unspeakability lie precisely in its consensual nature: the fact that Mandingo-Syndrome sex isn't a matter of the black male's uncontrollable lust for and rape of white women, but of the white female's sexual desire for the black man.

But there's another aspect to the syndrome that is, if anything, even more unspeakable: white male desire for the black male body, or what I have decided to call "Mapplethorpism," in honor of the white gay photographer Robert Mapplethorpe, whose studies of nude black men are legendary for their homoerotic fetishizing of the black male body, especially the penis.[11] I mean by Mapplethorpism something more than mere homoeroticism, however.[12] I mean the term to identify an appetite that doesn't start or stop with simply gazing, but that acts out its desire in passionate, even violent deferral. White men's sexual desire for and exploitation of black women is historically manifest; their erotic desire for black men, however, is equally well covered up—so much so, in fact, that it most often masquerades as both hyperheterosexuality and rabid racism. What I am suggesting, then, is that not only does homophobia mask homophilia, as many have long maintained, but Negrophobia masks Negrophilia in much the same way. It is its implied literalness that has made the term "nigger-lover" such fighting words among white men.

The multiple repressions and displacements involved in both Mandingoism and Mapplethorpism are, of course, of Freudian proportions, but they also point out just how self-absorbed Freud really was. His phallocentric theory of female penis envy rises from a displacement only a man could make. Only a man could look at his own penis and assume that a woman would want to own it, wear it, have it. Only a white man could look at a black man's penis and assume that his white woman would want to have it. "Projecting his own desires onto the Negro," Fanon wrote, "the white man behaves 'as if' the Negro really had them."[13] This displacement represents the ultimate intentional "phallusy": white men project their own latent desire for the black male penis onto white women and punish black men for a desire that is finely their own: to fuck a black man, to fuck like a black man, to fuck white women with a black penis. The necessarily absolute repression of such desires may explain why the racism of someone like Mark Fuhrman particularizes itself in an acute animus against interracial—that is, black male–white female—coupling. (White male–black female couplings are either unremarked upon or sanctioned. Part of Fuhrman's defense against charges of racism was that he once dated a black woman.) Such racial hatred veils a triply transgressive desire that crosses the boundaries of gender, race, and sexuality. In a Lacanian analysis, the tyranny born of the white man's unrequitable desire for the black phallus might be known as the Out-Law of the Father.

I don't know for certain whether Mapplethorpism has its roots in slavery or the other way around. But it's no accident that both male and female slaves were often exhibited and sold in the nude, their naked bodies fondled, groped, and gazed upon by white men in the marketplace and on the plantation. Anyone who thinks that all of this nudity, gaping, and groping was just a matter of the master's dispassionately assessing the reproductive organs of his property may be interested in a certain bridge for sale in Connecticut. White homophilia can only countenance itself by feminizing the black male it desires. Thus the dominant/submissive, master/slave power relation of the peculiar institution was the perfect locus for playing out forbidden racial and sexual fantasies.

The sports arena, often dominated by beautifully athletic black male bodies, remains another. The 1996 Summer Olympics were blacker than ever; they were also nuder than ever in modern times, with athletes posing naked for a photo essay in the July issue of *Life* entitled "Naked Power, Amazing Grace." Most of the athletes displayed in the article, like the majority of the athletes in the Games, were black, giving an interesting import to the journalist's observation that "the Olympic body is another country, its beauty as exotic and varied as that of any distant terrain."[14] The athletic black body is an alien land, an exotic continent to be claimed and tamed by the camera in endless low-angle shots that chart the subject's nether regions.

It's also interesting to note how professional sports repeats the language, though not the economic relations, of slavery: owners, players—sometimes called properties—buying, selling, trading. The playing field is one place—perhaps the only place—where men of different races can openly grab and fondle each other, while hundreds, thousands, even millions watch. Law enforcement represents a possible third site for the exorcising of latent desires for the other: the black male body under arrest, frisked, patted down, probed, cuffed, spread, and ordered to "assume the position," which, after all, is the stance of anal intercourse. Placed under a certain kind of scrutiny, then, the most manly arts, acts, and attitudes may well be exposed as something else entirely. The king is dead; long live the queen.

The Brentwoodian Captivity of Nicole Brown

In order to situate the Mandingo Syndrome and my larger claims about the blackness of blackness within the metanarratives of domesticity, race, sex, and nation of which they are a part, I want to turn for a moment to one of the earliest articulations of American identity: the captivity narrative. Classic Anglo-American captivity narratives, such as Mary Rowlandson's 1682 autobiographical tale, tell the story of the white woman's abduction by and confinement among Indians and document what Nancy Armstrong and Leonard Tennenhouse describe as the lost daughter's "single-minded desire to return home," unsullied by native hands (or other parts of the male anatomy). According to Armstrong and Tennenhouse, the captivity narrative "described an experience that people of 'the middling sort' in England could not have imagined were it not for the colonial venture; it asked its readers to imagine being English in America."[15] I would add that in addition to advancing Englishness, such narratives also constructed whiteness: that is, they figured national identity as white, where what the Anglo- or Euro-American woman does is not just stand by her man in building the new nation but lie under him, bear his children, carry on his culture, and otherwise do her domestic duty. And the white woman's proper domestic duty is to preserve and reproduce the white household, or die trying.

This historical civilizing mission is well documented in fiction and film—westerns, for example—where just as the restless natives are about to attack, the frontiersman and his woman exchange a meaningful look as he hands her a gun. The audience understands what she is supposed to do: if all is lost, she is to shoot herself rather than "allow" herself to be captured and raped by Indians, even though we know that rape was not a part of native cultures. What the true woman/white daughter does under siege, then, as Nancy Armstrong has suggested, is die. It's the Anglo-American way: the custom of "a culture that abhors a mixture" and "prefers a dead daughter to an ethnically impure one."[16]

The "native" daughter—that is, the red daughter or the black daughter—by contrast, lives, survives her sexual assault, and in so surviving loses any possibility of achieving the national, domestic identity that her colored skin has already removed her from anyway. This is the theme that numerous black women writers take up in the nineteenth century and in the twentieth as well. Not only do these writers appropriate and combine the forms of the sentimental novel and the slave narrative, as many critics have argued, they also take back and *blacken* the white captivity narrative, though in their texts "captivity" refers to a variety of social and psychic forms of confinement as well as to the physical bondage of chattel slavery. How, for example, is Harriet Jacobs's (Linda Brent's) story like Mary Rowlandson's? What is the nature of Janie's confinement in Hurston's *Their Eyes Were Watching God* or Pecola's captivity in Toni Morrison's *The Bluest Eye*? Is Alice Walker's Celie in *The Color Purple* a modern version of Samuel Richardson's title character in *Pamela*?

If we ask these kinds of questions, we might begin to see a novel like Harriet Wilson's *Our Nig; or, Sketches from the Life of a Free Black* (1859) as both a captivity narrative and a quintessentially American text. *Our Nig* tells the autobiographical tale of Alfrado (Frado), a mulatto girl who is abandoned by her white mother and left to live and labor as a virtual slave in the New England household of a white mistress with an unlimited capacity for cruelty. But to tap into the Mandingo Syndrome and the meta-narrative of domesticity, race, sex, and nation that underpin the text, we have to look not only at the captivity of Frado, "Our Nig," the thrown-away mulatto daughter, but also at the blackening of her white mother, Mag Smith, whose poverty and general lack of *white* male protection already placed her in a vexed relation to the national romance, but whose marriage to a black man of better means than she pulled her "another step down the ladder of infamy."[17]

For Jim, the African Mag married in desperation, the white woman is a prize—the original trophy bride, what the novel describes as "his treasure—a white wife." In the national narrative—and *Our Nig* is a national allegory—Mag, the white wife, is completely lost once she marries and has children by a black man. She ceases to be a white daughter of potential service to the nation and becomes instead black like the man she sleeps with. In Wilson's words: "She was now expelled from companionship with white people; this last step—her union with a black man—was the climax of repulsion."

What a courageous move for Harriet Wilson: to write the unutterable but no less present American narrative of interracial coupling between black man and white woman, to speak the white daughter's black desire. I want to be careful not to overstate the case, however. Mag doesn't so much desire the African Jim sexually as need him economically. But in presenting the union of a black man and a white woman as chiefly an economic arrangement, Wilson joins white women writers such as Jane Austen in exposing holy matrimony as an affair of the pocketbook as well as the heart, at the same time that she also complicates and blackens the category of desire. Under the cover of convenience, she implicitly makes explicit the interracial sex act whose white female desire the national narrative (not to mention the nineteenth-century woman's narrative) must cover over.[18]

To see the power and perseverance of this covert narrative —the modern "climax of repulsion"—we have only to return to the psychosexual drama of the Simpsons that absorbed the nation for two years: to what the feminist theorist Wendy Kozol has described as a racially charged "story of domesticity gone awry."[19] I want to suggest that like Harriet Wilson's Mag Smith, Nicole Brown is both the white trophy wife and the disgraced lost daughter blackened by her marriage to and having brown babies with a black man. Rather than doing what the true white woman does in the face of the sexually threatening man of color—die—she willingly submitted to copulation and miscegenation. She slept with the enemy and populated the nation with his mulatto babies. Her murder has indeed been taken up by some feminists as a cause célèbre. (If you called the L.A. chapter of NOW during the first half of 1996, a recording informed you about the chapter's "No O.J. Project," including detailed information about the June 12 candlelight vigil, the chapter's "No O.J." Mother's Day project, and its campaign against the domestic violence for which Simpson is the symbol.) Yet Nicole Simpson herself is lost, disappeared, often absent in her own story.

She is absent, for example, from the magazine cover that O.J. Simpson's darkened mug shot made infamous: the June 27, 1994, issue of *Time*, whose caption announced "An American Tragedy." Simpson's altered image dominates the page, suggesting that "the bloody odyssey of O.J. Simpson," rather than the murders of Nicole Brown and Ronald Goldman, is the real American tragedy. Noting the victims' absence on *Time*'s "American Tragedy" cover, Wendy Kozol insists that we must ask not only for whom is this a tragedy but also "why is this specifically an 'American' tragedy? What is the linkage between the personal and national in this murder? And why is race an integral factor in this story of domesticity gone awry?"[20] She answers her own questions by suggesting that the murders of Nicole Brown Simpson and Ronald Goldman upset the very domestic ideals central to the American family romance.

I want to push Kozol's reading a little harder. The fact that images of Nicole Simpson and Ronald Goldman are missing from the cover, and the coverage more generally suggests just how much the racial drama of a black man of white means is the actual American tragedy, the real drama. Nicole Brown's function, however essential to the steamy, seamy plot, is, I will say again, primarily symbolic. *Time* followed up its "American Tragedy" issue with an eight-page cover story on domestic abuse, published the next week. Nicole Brown Simpson was neither on the cover nor much in the story. Not to be outdone, *Newsweek* also had a cover story on domestic violence in its July 4 issue.

Nicole Simpson was pictured on the cover, but, again, the story inside was not about her; she in fact merited only a paragraph in an eight-page article. Her absence, if not erasure, may be explained by the extent to which her "naughty Nicole" image upsets the "Birth of a Nation" narrative in which *innocent* white women throw themselves off cliffs to spare themselves and the nation the stain of African blood.

Far from jumping off cliffs to escape black men, Nicole Brown Simpson reportedly jumped into bed with several of them, and that was her undoing as a white daughter. If we didn't know it from her sexual liaisons with black men (O.J., Marcus Allen), the endless tabloid photos of her in bikinis, short, tight, black dresses, halter tops, and skimpy cutoffs tell the tale: they incite us to conclude that the lady was a tramp. What other kind of white woman would so willingly receive the polluting semen of black men? A cover photo in the *Enquirer* of Nicole in a close encounter with two white men, one of whom has his hands on her breasts, even managed in some circles to divert sympathy from her as the murdered wife to O.J. as the cuckolded husband.[21] Such trashy photos and the news that Simpson caught her fellating one of her lovers on the living room couch, while the children slept upstairs, were enough to win O.J. sympathetic nods from the likes of Rush Limbaugh.

Family members like Denise Brown and friends like Candace Garvey were anxious to tell the world that Nicole was a devoted mother who cared for her children herself rather than employing a nanny. But other, mostly anonymous friends and associates, were equally eager to tell the tabloids and the talk shows and the TV cameras that the second Mrs. Simpson was a party girl, who drank too much, danced too late, and dated too often. Nicole "was no young innocent"; she "knew what buttons to push"; "she wasn't little Miss Suzy Homemaker," members of the Simpson circle have been quoted as saying. "She had an alcohol problem. She'd get drunk and say and do things you normally wouldn't do."[22] Even the vanity plate on her white Ferrari—L84AD8 (late for a date)—was evidence against her.

But of course the most damning "truths" about Nicole are those told by her best friend, Faye Resnick, in her bestselling instabook *Nicole Brown Simpson: The Private Diary of a Life Interrupted* (1994). In what I think is supposed to be an authenticating commentary, novelist Dominick Dunne, who covered the Simpson trial for *Vanity Fair*, says of Resnick's first book:

> Sure it was dirty. Sure I could have done without the blow-job episode, where the guy wakes up from his sleep and says "Thanks" to Nicole. But the book had a sense of truth to it, even honor, in a Brentwoodian sort of way. She portrayed expertly the telling moments of control, belittlement, and cruelty in the post-marital relationship of Nicole and O.J. Simpson.[23]

What qualifies Dunne to judge the "truth" of Resnick's storytelling I'm not sure, but he's hardly alone in treating the author like the oracle of Brentwood and her potboiler like the gospel. Confirming every stereotype about black male brutality, sexual prowess, penis size, and animal appetites, Resnick's book blackened O.J., to be sure, but it also darkened Nicole along with him. Purporting to speak for Nicole through her private thoughts and confidences, the book told white fathers what they most fear and least want to hear about their daughters:

> Nicole was ruined by O.J. because she would never be able to be with a white man, ever . . . The truth was that the two men who had truly satisfied her in bed were O.J.

Simpson and Marcus Allen. Because of them, Nicole was becoming convinced that only a black man could really satisfy her.

It was an inside joke that O.J. would never lose Nicole because she would never find another man who could give her the quantity and quality she was used to.[24]

In case we missed the size of the point, Resnick went on to share Nicole's confidence that "almost every white man she'd been with didn't satisfy her, didn't measure up." Hence her irresistible attraction to and insatiable appetite for the black football star Marcus Allen, whose penis Resnick claims Nicole once likened to a large piece of driftwood.

Like Mapplethorpe's photographs, Faye Resnick's exposé, which might well have been titled *She Had to Have It*, focused on the black male penis (O.J. was "one of the fastest cocksmen in town") and Nicole's fondness for it. Explicit details about her bedroom raiding and barhopping painted a portrait of a party girl you wouldn't necessarily want next door—unless perhaps you were the black male neighbor awakened in the middle of the night by her, shall we say, lip service. The defense implied it, but Resnick's portrait proved it: no innocent damsel to be championed, Nicole Brown Simpson was a "player" (Resnick's word) whose lifestyle invited her murder. If you lie down with dogs, you might not wake up.

Brown Like Me

But of all the images of the Sensuous Simpsons, the most haunting may be a certain family portrait, versions of which have made several appearances, including on the covers of *People* (June

27, 1994) and *Star* (July 12, 1994) magazines. Taken in 1986, the photograph to which I refer depicts a seemingly naked (at least from the waist up) O.J. and Nicole embracing each other and cradling their infant daughter Sydney between them. At any other moment, this portrait of nude black and white parents and brown child would invite a biological or sociological reading; its wide circulation after the murder of the white wife/mother, however, invites an hysterical one—all the more so because of the way the magazines presented the pictures. *Star* included an inflammatory caption: "How this dream family portrait turned into a murderous nightmare." Using large, blood-red type, *People* titled its cover "LOVE AND DEATH," adding in only slightly smaller black letters, "The Nicole Simpson Murders: The shocking story of the volatile relationship between O.J. and his beautiful ex-wife." For the brain-dead who might have missed the point, *People* inserted alongside the family portrait a snapshot of Nicole's body being removed from the scene "where she and Ronald Goldman were slain."

In its naked, sensual display of interracial sex and the bira-cial family, the Simpson family portrait is an *un*American Gothic, whose black presence and white absence simultaneously speak the nation's secret sins, great hopes, and worst fears. I must admit, however, that my reading of this photograph is impacted by my inability to separate it entirely from another image that seems to me to repeat it: a two-paged Benetton ad of a white child and a black child embracing each other in almost exactly the same way as the Simpsons.

The white child is blond, blue-eyed, and rosy-cheeked, with Shirley Temple curls and a cherubic glow that is in part the effect of lighting. The black child, presumably a boy, is dark-skinned and dark-eyed, with kinky short black hair combed to resemble two horns. Like the Simpsons, the boy and girl in this photograph are—at least as far as we see—naked, but because they are children, their bare shoulders don't bespeak sexual intercourse and miscegenation as the Simpson family photo does. Yet, it is exactly their youthful innocence that presents itself as a false clue. As the Simpson photo becomes more than ever a cautionary tale in light of the white wife's murder and the black husband's presumed guilt, so too does the overdetermined angelic white innocence and demonic black guilt of the embracing children. The spectator reads the danger of their profound *unlikeness* in ways that their youthful innocence belies.

American consumers have bought (although not entirely without complaint) another widely published two-page Benetton ad—this one depicting a white baby nursing at black breasts. We see only the black breasts and the white baby, not the black woman, and, because the racial signifiers are, as Henry Giroux says, "so overdetermined,"[25] we know that the unseen woman behind the breasts is irrelevant beyond her wet-nurse function. If we follow what I think is the logic of Benetton's United Colors advertising campaign, an image like this one is supposed to disrupt precisely because it doesn't disrupt, because it is taken for natural. The truly disruptive or shocking image would be that of a black child suckling the breast of a white woman. As the legal theorist Patricia Williams has asked:

> Is there not something unseemly, in our society, about the spectacle of a white woman mothering a black child? A white woman giving totally to a black child; a black child totally and demandingly dependent for everything, sustenance itself, from a white woman. The image of a white woman suckling a black child; the image of a black child sucking for its life from the bosom of a white woman.[26]

Although such questions might be asked of the Simpson family portrait, Williams actually raised these issues in the context of reading the case of surrogate mother Mary Beth Whitehead, whom the court decided was contractually obligated to surrender her daughter Sara, the so-called Baby M., to William Stern, the man whose child Whitehead had contracted to bear. The judge's decision in the custody suit turned in part on "the supposition that it is natural for people to want children 'like' themselves." But exactly what constitutes likeness, Williams asks. What if instead of producing a visibly white child, Whitehead had given birth to a "recessively and visibly black" one? "Would the sperm of Stern have been so powerful as to make this child 'his,' " Williams asks, and, moreover, what constitutes "the collective understanding of 'unlikeness'?"

Historically, in the United States, race has been an important constitutive factor, both in the reproduction of family likeness and in the construction of national identity. The outward and visible *unlikeness* of blacks and Asians in particular was used to deny citizenship and the rights and privileges thereof. Nancy Armstrong argues that, although the dominant model of Anglo-American nationalism depends on white colonists and their descendants marrying their own kind, another permits the white daughter to "go native"—to mate with the Indian—and reproduce the English household with other than entirely white players.[27] "No matter who makes up this household or where it comes from, it can incorporate, imitate, reenact, parody, or otherwise replicate whatever appears to be most English [read white] about the English family. Such a household," Armstrong concludes, "produces a family peculiar to the settler colonies."[28]

It seems to me, however, that such families have been most readily tolerated where the ethnic and racial mixing has occurred between whites and those who look least different, that is, those who come closest to looking *like* the white founding fathers and mothers. I'm not convinced that such acceptance has ever been grandly or largely offered the Anglo-African family. There has been little or no room in the national romance for white women who "go African," who marry black like Nicole Brown, and reproduce a mulatto household.

So unspeakable is such coupling in the Anglo-American scenario that the English language has no name of its own for it and its offspring. The terms that have historically been used to describe the products of black-white miscegenation—mulatto, quadroon, octoroon—are borrowed from Spanish and French. The *Oxford English Dictionary* defines the word *mulatto*, for instance, as "a person having one White and one Black parent; a person of mixed White and Black parentage"; it traces the term's origins to the Spanish and Portuguese word *mulato*, meaning "young mule."

Now, I wouldn't presume to challenge the *OED*, but having been well trained by my *profesora de español*, Señorita Lenore Padula, I know that young mule in Spanish is *muleto*, not *mulato*. *Cassell's Spanish Dictionary* confirms my understanding, defining *muleto* as "young he-mule" and *mulato* as "tawny colored"; however, *el diccionario de la lengua española* traces the etymology of *mulato* to the Arabic *muwallad*, meaning "someone of mixed ancestry." The Arabic influence makes sense, given that the Moors were in Spain from 711 to 1492. The Arabic root for *muwallad* appears to be *walada*, "to be born," or *tawallad*, "to give birth." Other related forms of the word, according to the *Arab-English Dictionary of the Literary Language*, include *mawled*, "a time of birth"; *milad*, "day of birth, pertaining to the birth of Christ"; and, especially, *mawaled*, "special birth."

It's interesting that in all of the Spanish dictionaries I consulted, the origins of the word *mulato* relate to color and to mixed or otherwise "special" or unusual birth, while all of the English lexicons trace the word's origin to the Latin *mulus* or *mula*, meaning "mule," or to the Spanish for mule, an animal whose birth is of course also unusual. Whatever its actual derivation, the word *mulatto* clearly has a far more complicated and culturally impacted etymology than any given dictionary definition suggests. What's at stake in these various myths of word origin? Is there some cultural rationale behind the mule train of thought that is so clearly evident in English lexicons? English derivations yoke together as "unnatural" the offspring of ass and horse, on the one hand, and white and black, on the other, imputing to the progeny of humans of different races the same strangeness and sterility of the mixed-specied animal. *Muwallad, mulus, mula, muleto, mulato, mulatto,* mule. Would it even be possible to accurately trace the derivation of such a culturally loaded word? I think not, because, much as with the "mountain of evidence" in the Simpson case, it is impossible to separate provable fact from racially tainted fiction.

The Returns of the Native

There are circumstances under which the lost daughter, the daughter gone native, and even the dead daughter can be returned to the home and the law of the father. Sometimes ruined daughters are returned to the community through the redemption of great suffering, sacrifice, and good works. (Hawthorne's Hester Prynne comes to mind.) Other times they are returned through death, as in the case of Richardson's Clarissa, or reborn through their own daughters, as with Charlotte Temple in Susanna Rowson's novel of the same name.[29]

As a lost daughter come back to and embraced anew by her white family—both through her death and through the life of her own daughter, Sydney, so like her—Nicole Brown Simpson fits into each of the last two categories of return. But some have suggested another classification for her entirely, one not of return but of *returns;* for, as a daughter whose marriage not only elevated her own social and economic standing but that of her family as well, Nicole Brown Simpson and the seventeen years of abuse she endured have already brought the Browns considerable dividends. The hard, mean fact is that, given the pending multi-million-dollar wrongful death suit her family has filed against O.J. Simpson, she may be worth even more in death than she was in life.

Occasionally, where class, success, and social position seem almost to trump race, the white daughter who marries the black other can be returned to her family by virtue of the marriage itself—by having married up, if not entirely well. This phenomenon might be called the *Guess Who's Coming to Dinner* Syndrome, after the 1967 Stanley Kramer film, starring Sidney Poitier as a thirty-seven-year-old black research physician taken home to meet the parents (Katharine Hepburn and Spencer Tracy) of his twenty-three-year-old white fiancée (Katharine Houghton). The parents, a well-to-do liberal couple, both of whom work, are not thrilled at the prospect of a black son-in-law. (Nor are his parents happy with their son's choice of a white wife.) But Poitier as the dashing, distinguished doctor is so perfect—so well-mannered, well-educated, and well-professioned—that he transcends both his black skin and his black working-class background (his father's a mailman). Awestruck by the doctor's professional credentials and personal charm, Tracy's character asks his wife: "How do you suppose a colored mailman produced a son with all the qualities he has?" In other words: how did a black man produce a "white" son? After considerable hand-wringing and soul-searching, mother and father of the bride decide to tolerate their daughter's choice. The daughter, by the way, appears to have nothing much to recommend her as a suitable mate for this extraordinary man other than what O.J. Simpson might have called her "angel whiteness."

Like the film's fictional daughter, Nicole Brown made an uplifting marriage to a black man of means, although her parents, too, it seems, were not initially thrilled with their daughter's choice. In his deposition for the civil suit, Lou Brown reportedly testified that he initially opposed the marriage because O.J. had beaten Nicole even before the couple tied the knot. We don't know exactly what it was that made the concerned father change his mind, but with his fame, fortune, generosity, and even-better-than-Sidney Poitier good looks, Simpson no doubt seemed a better catch than a high-school-educated teenaged waitress from a working- or middle-class family might otherwise have hooked, even with her much-remarked classic white American beauty. Moreover, in terms of color and class, Simpson, even more so than Poitier's character, had been whitened by wealth and fame. *Sports Illustrated*, in fact, described him as a man "who not only seemed just like us [read "white"] but also seemed better—richer, more handsome, more popular, an overwhelming success."[30] Perhaps the Browns, like the Tracy and Hepburn characters in *Guess Who's Coming to Dinner*, were overwhelmed by their son-in-law's "credentials."

From a Hertz dealership and college tuitions to shopping sprees and Club Med vacations, the Browns, according to the defense attorney Johnnie Cochran, were part of a "circle of benevolence" for which O.J. Simpson footed the bill. Many speculate that it was the glitter of Simpson's gold that blinded the Browns to the high price their daughter was paying for the good life. Unfortunately, the family's otherwise inexplicable behavior leaves room for such nasty speculation. Lou Brown acknowledged in one of the family's numerous TV appearances that Nicole once tried to show him pictures of her bruised body, but he brushed them aside. In the more recent court depositions, both Mr. and Mrs. Brown testified that Nicole told them that O.J. was going to kill her; "we passed it off," Juditha Brown said. Amazingly, Mrs. Brown also admitted that when Nicole expressed such fears just weeks before her murder she assured her that "he's not going to kill you; he's not going to leave his money to everybody else."[31]

An apparent non sequitur, the allusion to O.J.'s money seems an odd response to a daughter's expressed fear for her life. But then this is the same mother who kissed the lips of the man she says treated her daughter like a common prostitute, offering her $5,000 for a one-night stand just weeks before he made good on his repeated threats to kill her. Ironically, by virtue of the very details that they now want the world to accept as evidence of a pattern of abuse, the Browns evidently had good reason to believe that their daughter wasn't just crying big bad wolf. However, far from challenging the man who they believe abused their daughter—even on the day she died, a day they say Simpson glowered at Nicole menacingly throughout their granddaughter's dance recital—the Browns were caught on video warmly embracing, laughing with, and kissing their former in-law.[32]

According to Faye Resnick, Nicole herself had made the connection between Simpson's generosity to her family and their deference to him at her expense. Nicole supposedly complained that her parents and sisters "weren't at all supportive" when she left her husband. "They absolutely wanted me to stay with O.J.," Resnick writes, quoting a conversation she allegedly had with Nicole in Cabo San Lucas. "O.J.'s done a lot for my family. They love him. I'm not saying they don't love me. They do. They're wonderful. They just love him more." Other perhaps more reliable evidence—including the Browns' own inadvertently self-incriminating testimony—suggests that her family was hardly a port in the stormy marriage.

In any case, fair or not, the sense that Nicole Simpson's life was sacrificed on the altar of a bad marriage from which her family did nothing to save her has led some of the most cynical among us to put the Browns on trial for crimes ranging from negligence to pandering. It's cruel, however, to lay such an indictment at the feet of a family suffering the loss of a loved one. But the mainstream media's failure to question the Browns' motives, while at the same time giving them a forum to solicit not only sympathy but money, may be tantamount to aiding and abetting the pursuit of something other than truth and justice. Now that millions of dollars are at stake instead of a mere conviction, the Browns are bearing witness to Simpson's abusive behavior and death threats in a way often quite different from the heard-no-evil-saw-no-evil ignorance they claimed earlier. And, perhaps out of respect for their grief, few if any in the media have called them on their contradictions or on the complicity that their testimony suggests. If what they say about Simpson's treatment of Nicole is true—if she told them that he beat her, stalked her, threatened to kill her, and nearly raped her in a "sexual rage," as they now claim, what does this same testimony say about *them* and their continued affectionate relationship with Simpson?

But while vilifying the Browns for the past is a fruitless exercise, watching them in the future may be a justifiable scrutiny, given their guardianship of the Simpson children. The attorneys representing O.J. Simpson in the civil suit have implied that the Browns are profiting financially from Nicole's death, raising questions about her personal effects, the possible exploitation of the children, and the fiscal management of the Nicole Brown Simpson Charitable Foundation for Battered Women, of which Denise Brown is chair and Lou Brown president.

In addition to donations to the charitable foundation, the Browns (and the Goldmans) have also solicited and received monetary contributions to help defray the costs of their civil suits.[33] Simpson and his counsel aren't the only ones wondering about the foundation's finances and Simpson's hefty child support payments, but the charge that the Browns have benefited financially from the tragedy is more than a little hypocritical coming from the Simpson camp, since O.J., who clearly spent a fortune defending himself, has also made millions on the murders and, having copyrighted himself, stands to make considerably more.[34]

However hypocritical, such loaded questions from the defense forced Dominique Brown to admit during her July 25, 1996, deposition that she was paid $25,000 by the *National Enquirer* for four photos of her dead sister—including at least one of Nicole sunbathing topless in Mexico—and another $7,500 for three snapshots of her niece and nephew, Sydney and Justin Simpson. One of these photos is of Justin visiting his mother's grave; the other two show the children at the beach and at Sea World. Having earlier refused to answer questions about the photographs, Dominique Brown was ordered to testify by a judge who ruled that her testimony could reveal a financial interest in the outcome of the civil suit, thus raising questions about her credibility as a witness.[35]

Other members of the Brown family either refused to comment on or denied any knowledge of Dominique's public sale of such private moments. But while mother, father, and sisters may claim a blissful ignorance of Dominique's action, there have been other occasions when the entire family has sanctioned the intrusion of journalists and the public viewing of the children. The *New York Post* columnist and tabloid TV personality Steve Dunleavy claims to have spent a day in the life of the Browns, observing the Simpson children at play in their grandparents' home, which he characterized as a sanctuary, despite his own apparently easy, welcomed penetration of the so-called safe house.

Geraldo Rivera has similarly described himself as a good friend of the Browns and a frequent guest at the Dana Point home, where the children live. A picture is worth a thousand words, they say, and although Geraldo has frequently had his picture taken with the Browns, *Life* magazine has a cover and eight pages of hearthside and graveside photographs of the Simpson children to back up its claims of intimate knowledge of their home life. An "exclusive" photo essay on the family appeared as the cover story in the June 1995 issue.

Photographed and published apparently with the Browns' full cooperation and participation, the *Life* cover story, "The Simpson Children One Year Later," displays Sydney and Justin, then nine and six, at their mother's grave and at their grandparents' home. "Here's who Sydney and Justin live with now," the article explains, listing Nicole's parents; two of her three sisters, Denise and Dominique; and their sons. Although the article goes on to describe how friendly neighbors in this gated Orange County community, three blocks from the beach, "thoughtfully turn over the tabloids in local stores when family members come in,"[36] it doesn't explain how or why a *Life* photographer and his assistant were offered such intimate access to the Brown household and the Simpson children. On the contrary, *Life*, like Dunleavy and Rivera, lauds the Brown home as "a place to heal," where the children are "protected from the frenzy surrounding their father's trial by the nurturing love of their extended family."

It is particularly ironic that this gushy tribute to the Browns as long-suffering guardian angels opens with a page-and-one-half color shot of Sydney wrapped in what are supposed to be the protective arms of her godmother, Dominique, "the aunt who most reminds her of mom." This of course is the same aunt who sold pictures of her beloved niece and her slain sister to the *National Enquirer.*

Life's day-in-the-life photo essay may represent an unread chapter in the Simpson saga from yet another angle. The Browns are everywhere in the photos and in the children's lives; the Simpsons are nowhere. A caption reports, without critical comment, that at school Sydney and Justin use the last name "Brown." It is an extraordinary thing that these children, who historically would be considered black, have been returned to the home of the white father, entrusted into the care of their white grandparents, aunts, and cousins, while their black relatives, including a half-sister and a half-brother, have been virtually disappeared by the media as part of their extended family.

It seems we have come full circle: from the lost daughter, blackened by her marriage to a black man, to the reclaimed children, whitened by their return to the household of the white maternal grandfather. Despite the historical potency of the one-drop rule, the Simpson children are never spoken of as black or even mulatto. I might think this a good thing, if I didn't know that race unremarked really means "white," even as it is their unspoken blackness—the skin and sin of their black father—that makes them, like him, curiosities, fitting subjects for commerce and cover stories, despite their youth and absolute innocence.

In an interview with Geraldo Rivera the day of the verdict, Lou Brown—whom *People* aptly described as "remarkably conciliatory toward his former son-in-law"—said that he feels "a friendly approach to custodianship is better for the children." In a cynical reading, "friendly" (as opposed to, say, "cooperative") represents a telling word choice: Brown doesn't want to bite the hand that feeds his grandchildren. From the children's perspective, he is no doubt right about the importance of cordiality: the kids love their grandparents and their father and would surely be further traumatized by open hostility between the two camps. But even if they are not actually beaten themselves, children are never completely outside the physical and emotional abuse inflicted on their mothers. It's difficult, therefore, to reconcile Lou Brown's conciliatory attitude toward his former son-in-law with his conviction that Simpson habitually battered and then brutally murdered Nicole.

Taking up for the Browns on the talk shows on which she has become a frequent guest, attorney Gloria Allred, who at one time represented the family, has condemned as "outrageous" the suggestion that the grandparents' desire to retain custody of Sydney and Justin has anything to do with the substantial child support payments they receive from Simpson (a figure considerably less than the $10,000 a month he reportedly paid to his ex-wife for the children's support). Allred accused Simpson and his lawyers of further victimizing the Browns by trying to turn public sentiment against them just as the civil suit is about to begin. She and others implied, in fact, that Simpson's attempt to regain custody, initiated on the eve of the wrongful death hearings, was strategically timed to win him sympathy as a loving father kept from his children by greedy, vengeful grandparents. The tabloids clearly agreed, with the *Globe*, declaring that the "evil," "heartless," "devious O.J. Simpson" was "using every trick in the book" in a desperate attempt "to wrench his kids away from his murdered wife's parents"—"even leveling charges of racism at them" (Sept. 17, 1996).

For the most part, the battle over the children took place (as well it should) outside the glare of television cameras. Neither side was silent, however, about the other's alleged dirty tricks and ulterior motives or the righteousness of its own claim to custody. In the same Geraldo interview mentioned earlier, Lou Brown indicated that where the children are concerned he intends to utilize "all the advantages of a bicultural upbringing so we can get away from this racial crap that came out at the trial."[37] It's not clear what "advantages" Brown has in mind, but I would take this tacit acknowledgment of the children's biraciality as a sign of good intentions if I weren't left wondering how this "bicultural upbringing" will happen under the guardianship of a white man who dismisses as "crap" the profoundly historical racial issues surrounding the case and the culture of which his grandchildren are a part.

Only those wrapped in the skin privileged by the dominant culture have the luxury of taking race lightly or cavalierly dismissing its social, economic, and *legal* consequences. Well-intentioned, loving, white liberal efforts to erase race—to transcend color—can leave mixed-race children unprepared to survive in a hostile world that will ultimately identify and treat them not as white or raceless or even biracial, but as black. At least that's the argument Simpson made the cornerstone of his campaign to regain custody of his children. Claiming that the white Browns aren't culturally equipped to raise black children, the "nouveau-black" Simpson and his attorneys reportedly argued in effect that Sydney and Justin were being whitened by their environment.

Truth is stranger than fiction, and such an argument worked for Halle Berry's character in the popular 1995 film

Losing Isaiah. Berry plays a recovered dope addict who regains custody of the son she abandoned as a baby, not simply because
she's the birth mother but because her militant black lawyer
(Samuel L. Jackson), who believes that "black babies belong
with black mothers," shows that the white adoptive parents (Jessica Lange and David Strathairn) are raising the black child in a
completely white environment "where he never sees anyone like
himself," not even in children's books. Interestingly enough,
some of Simpson's public statements about his concern that his
children be immersed in their African-American heritage sound
remarkably like dialogue from the movie.

What troubles me about the custody question, however, is
less the whitening of these historically black children than their
possible exploitation within an "extended family," which, if its
principals were black, would likely be labeled dysfunctional,
given what the media would certainly identify as the "unwed
mother" status of the resident daughters, the history of alco-
holism and unemployment, and the absence of fathers or male
role models other than the aged grandfather who's already
demonstrated that he can't control or protect his daughters.

But if the thought of the Browns raising Sydney and Justin
is disquieting for a few, the likelihood of their being returned to
the man presumed to have murdered their mother is horrifying
for the many—perhaps the most tragic turn of all in a saga suffused with outrages, insults, and abominations. Those who
shudder at the thought of what these children have already lived
through, including the murder of their mother, can't bear the
idea of their living with their father or with what much of the
world believes about their father. For some, then, the most
disturbing questions of the Simpson case are not about O.J.'s
unpunished guilt, but about his children's much-punished innocence.

In considering the custody question, it may be important to note that O.J., too, sold family photographs to the tabloids—not of Sydney and Justin, as far as I know, but of his post-trial reunion with his older children, Arnelle and Jason, and other family members and friends. Shot on location at the Brentwood estate, two *Star* "world exclusive" special issues featured cover stories and "dozens of fabulous intimate photos" of Simpson welcomed home by his "nearest and dearest," including his older children, his sisters, and his aged, infirmed mother (Oct. 17 and 24, 1995). Both *Star* exclusives were sanctioned by Simpson and stamped with his corporate seal of approval—"Copyright © 1995 Orenthal Productions and Polaris Communications." Both carried the warning "Publication without written permission is prohibited."

Directly rebutting reports that "Simpson intended to exploit the youngsters he fathered with Nicole," *Star* took pains to point out that the reunion with Sydney and Justin occurred in private. "Even though STAR was with O.J. during the days after his release from jail, we left him and his children alone to cherish their first hours," the magazine hastened to explain. Yet in a case where nothing is sacred, where everything and everyone is up for sale, including family, one has to wonder if there is any house that can be a home for the Simpson children. Is there any place where they can indeed be safe, protected as children instead of pandered as commodities, as Orenthal's most marketable productions?

Life magazine concluded its day-in-the-life photo essay on the Simpson children with the claim that there are two families residing within the larger Brown household:

> There is a family that longs to be understood, to share the burden of its grief with the wider world, to make a con-

nection that might bring meaning to the violence that has
visited them; and there is a family that shies from the public, that doesn't care for the media, that wants to be by
itself.

The children may prefer to mourn in private. (Sydney has been
photographed sticking out her tongue defiantly at paparazzi,
and the *Life* article noted unselfconsciously that "Justin doesn't
want to have his picture taken. He's had so many hard things in
his life.") The adult Browns, however, have always been very public in their grief, regularly allowing journalists such as Diane
Sawyer or Geraldo Rivera to pick their festering wounds on
national television. Since his acquittal, O.J. Simpson has been
similarly public in his efforts to reinvent himself as victim
instead of villain and to market himself as a godfearing, Bible-
quoting crusader for racial justice who will go wherever there's a
paying audience. I've grown used to the adults' ringside grieving
and multimedia street hawking, but the pictures of Nicole and
the children sold to the tabloids and the graveside and hearthside photo shoots in Dana Point and Brentwood continue to
haunt me because I can't figure out why "victims" would subject
themselves and their families, especially innocent children, to the
kind of public exhibition that the *National Enquirer, Star,* and *Life*
magazines represent. I can't fathom it—not for love nor
money—but I suspect it's one or the other.

Dark Men Walking

Often great tragedy offers up some degree of redemption, some
lesson, some element of hope. I have followed the Simpson case
closely for more than two years, but even in my most optimistic

and generous moments I have been unable to discern either hopeful light or redeeming end to the tunnel into which this particular tragedy has plunged the media and the masses. We are in no way that I can see the better for our obsessive immersion in the life and death details of the Simpsons, the Browns, and the Goldmans—for the endless trial coverage, the legal, social, and psychological analyses, the inspections, dissections, cross sections, postmortems, and projections. And, if we are not actually the worse for it all—for "feasting on the buffet of O.J. Simpson," as one network executive put it—we have most certainly been shown at our worst by it.

We kid ourselves and swallow whole the junk food we've been fed for over two years if we believe that any of this—the endless mediation of the Simpson saga—is really about a man and a woman who were murdered, about two young children robbed of their mother, a family robbed of a daughter, another bereft of a son. It's about race; it's about sex; it's about money. It has long ceased to be about truth and justice, but it is very much about the American way: our desire as a nation of voyeurs to return to the Colosseum, to be titillated by the sexual transgressions and personal tragedies of others.

Although we have all danced to the undulating tom-tom rhythms of the Simpson samba, some of us will pay more dearly to the piper than others. For some the consequences of the Simpson case, like the story itself, may well be endless. Here I'm thinking not only about the children and the families of the victims, but also about the black masses smeared by the backsplash from the same grime and guilty pleasures that made Simpson a national obsession.

Shortly after the verdict, a writer in L.A. e-mailed a friend at the *New York Times* the "intentionally provocative" message that once Simpson walks, "whites will riot the way we whites do:

leave the city, go to Idaho, Oregon, or Arizona, vote for Ging-rich . . . and punish blacks by closing their day-care programs and cutting off their Medicaid."[38] Simpson's acquittal con-firmed the widely held, though intensely erroneous, belief that blacks are getting away with murder in this country: that they are doing as well or better than whites. Punitive measures aimed pri-marily at African Americans—the perceived source of all the nation's ills and the assumed beneficiaries of its *noblesse oblige*— have extended way beyond white flight and Medicaid cutbacks. While we were preoccupied with the trials of the century (crim-inal, civil, and custodial)—while we were sleeping with O.J. and Nicole and Ron and Kato and Chris and Marcia, Marcia, Mar-cia—reactionary legislation at the federal, state, and local levels ended "welfare as we know it," rolled back public assistance, Head Start, and affirmative action programs; limited immigra-tion from the third world; and initiated the three strikes law designed to put even more black men permanently behind bars.

O.J. Simpson is by no means the cause of the white rage that blames and punishes the black other for the nation's woes, but in his always-already-sexual black male guilt, he is its vindi-cation, its "I-told-you-so." The perception that "the black com-munity," constructed in the press as a mindless monolith, is solidly behind Simpson has made black people all the more complicit with his crimes, all the more guilty of malfeasances ranging from unAmericanness to literally and figuratively getting away with murder.

Newsweek columnist Jonathan Alter voiced the thoughts of millions, I'm sure, when he wrote after Simpson's acquittal: "We expected more blacks to look beyond race to facts, as many whites had during the Rodney King trial. When so many blacks didn't, it shocked us—and hardened us in ways that shocked us even more."[39] Pharaoh's heart has been hardened, and he's not about to let my people go. Because of the way racial mythology operates in America, Simpson's fall from grace could never be just one horrendous step for *a* man; it has to be a giant leap backward for his kind. O.J. may have walked, but millions of dark people have already begun to pay for his sins.

Notes

1. Frantz Fanon, *Black Skin, White Masks* (New York: Grove Press, 1967), p. 165.

2. See Ann duCille, "The Blacker the Juice: O.J. Simpson and the Squeeze Play of Race," in *Skin Trade* (Cambridge: Harvard University Press, 1996), pp. 136–69.

3. Christopher Darden, *In Contempt* (New York: Regan Books/Harper-Collins, 1996), p. 12.

4. Jonathan Kellerman, "The Othello Syndrome," *LosAngeles* 40 (July 1995): 53–58; quotations from pages 55 and 57.

5. Terry Mulgannon, "Not Wisely but Too Well . . . ," *LosAngeles* 40 (July 1995): 54.

6. "The O.J. Simpson Case: Prominent Blacks Discuss Race, Sex, Crime and 'the Case of the Century,'" *Ebony* XLIX (September 1994): 29, 34.

7. Zora Neale Hurston, *Seraph on the Suwanee* (New York: Scribner's, 1948); reprinted with an introduction by Hazel Carby (New York: Harper-Collins, 1991), p. 25.

8. Elizabeth Cady Stanton, Susan B. Anthony, and M.J. Gage, eds., *History of Woman Suffrage*, vol. 1 (Rochester, NY: Fowler & Wells, 1881), pp. 567–68. See also Gerda Lerner, *Black Women in White America: A Documentary History* (New York: Pantheon), p. 569.

9. Sally Ann Ferguson, "Folkloric Men and Female Growth in *Their Eyes Were Watching God*," *Black American Literature Forum* 21 (Spring-Summer 1987): 185–97; quotation from page 189.

10. John Fiske, *Media Matters: Everyday Culture and Political Change* (Minneapolis: University of Minnesota Press, 1994), p. xvii.

11. I mean to evoke here the photographer Robert Mapplethorpe's controversial studies of black male nudes rather than his entire oeuvre.

12.   See, for example, Leslie Fiedler's reading of homoeroticism in "Come Back to the Raft Ag'in, Huck Honey," *Partisan Review* 15 (June 1948): 664–71; reprinted in Thomas Inge, ed., *Huck Finn Among the Critics* (Frederick, MD: University Publications of America, 1985), pp. 93–101.

13.   Fanon, *Black Skin, White Masks,* p. 165.

14.   Lisa Grunwald, "The Soul of These Beautiful Machines," *Life,* July 1996, p. 65.

15.   Nancy Armstrong and Leonard Tennenhouse, *The Imaginary Puritan: Literature, Intellectual Labor, and the Origins of Personal Life* (Berkeley: University of California Press, 1992), p. 205.

16.   Nancy Armstrong, "Why Daughters Die: The Racial Logic of American Sentimentalism," *Yale Journal of Criticism* 7 (Winter 1994): 1–24; quotation from page 12.

17.   Harriet Wilson, *Our Nig; or, Sketches from the Life of a Free Black, in a Two-Story White House, North* (1859); reprinted with an introduction and notes by Henry Louis Gates, Jr. (New York: Vintage, 1983), p. 13.

18.   On this point, see Hortense Spillers, "Changing the Letter: The Yokes, the Jokes of Discourse, or, Mrs. Stowe, Mr. Reed," Deborah E. McDowell and Arnold Rampersad, eds., *Slavery and the Literary Imagination* (Baltimore: Johns Hopkins University Press, 1989), pp. 25–61. In a brilliant reading of desire in *Uncle Tom's Cabin,* Spillers argues that Stowe "dispatches the child [Little Eva] to do a woman's job; that is, the white woman's desire for the black man is displaced onto Little Eva ("I want him.") and thus made prepubescent pure. As Spillers writes, "the female child figure—in her daring and impermissible *desire*— stands in here for the symptoms of a disturbed female sexuality that American women of Stowe's era could neither articulate nor cancel, only loudly proclaim in the ornamental language, which counterfeits the 'sacrificial,' of disguise and substitution" (p. 44).

19.   Wendy Kozol, "Fracturing Domesticity: Media, Nationalism, and the Question of Feminist Influence," *Signs* 20 (Spring 1995): 646–67; quotation from page 659.

20.   *Ibid.,* pp. 658–59.

21.   See the *National Enquirer,* July 19, 1994, cover and pp. 36–37.

22.   Richard Hoffer, "Fatal Attraction," *Sports Illustrated,* June 27, 1994, pp. 16–31; quotation from page 22.

23.   Dominick Dunne, Foreword to *Shattered: In the Eye of the Storm,* by Faye D. Resnick (Los Angeles: Dove Books, 1996), pp. vii-viii. Dunne is refer-

ring here to an incident, recounted in *Nicole Brown Simpson: The Private Diary of a Life Interrupted,* in which Nicole allegedly slipped into the bedroom of a sleeping neighbor—whom Resnick describes as "black, great-looking, and seemingly totally absorbed in his fiancée and his studies at an Ivy League college"—and woke him up with "a lovely surprise—the blow-job of his life" (p. 45).

24. Faye D. Resnick, *Nicole Brown Simpson: The Private Diary of a Life Interrupted* (Los Angeles: Dove Books, 1994), pp. 100–1. Resnick penned a second book in 1996, *Shattered: In the Eye of the Storm,* also published by Dove. This book includes a foreword—an authenticating stamp of approval—from the novelist Dominick Dunne, who covered the trial for *Vanity Fair.*

25. Henry A. Giroux, *Disturbing Pleasures: Learning Popular Culture* (New York: Routledge, 1994), p. 20.

26. Patricia J. Williams, *The Alchemy of Race and Right: Diary of a Law Professor* (Cambridge: Harvard University Press, 1991), p. 226.

27. Richard Slotkin calls these two models captivity and conversion. See Richard Slotkin, *Regeneration Through Violence: The Mythology of the American Frontier* (Middletown, CT: Wesleyan University Press, 1973). See also Gary L. Ebersole, *Captured by the Texts: Puritan to Postmodern Images of Indian Captivity* (Charlottesville: University of Virginia Press, 1995).

28. Armstrong, "Why Daughters Die," p. 12.

29. *Ibid.,* pp. 10–11.

30. Hoffer, "Fatal Attraction," p. 31.

31. As quoted by Geraldo Rivera reading from the deposition transcripts.

32. Although Denise Brown and others testified that Simpson glowered menacingly at Nicole throughout Sydney Simpson's June 12 dance recital, a videotape shows an amiable Simpson laughing and schmoozing with the Browns after the event. Lou Brown shakes his hand and both Denise and Judith Brown kiss him on the lips. And although the Browns would later claim that they believed Simpson, who had long threatened to kill Nicole, was responsible the moment they heard she was dead, the family initially supported their former in-law in his claims of innocence. A full ten days after the murders, Denise Brown told the *New York Times* that her sister was not a battered wife and implied that the 1989 incident was the only instance of domestic discord of which she was aware. See Sara Rimer, "Nicole Simpson: Private Pain Amid Life in the Public Eye," *New York Times,* June 23, 1994, pp. A1, A20.

33.   *Parade* reports that the Ronald Goldman Justice Fund has raised several hundred thousand dollars, while the Nicole Brown Legal Fund has collected "only a minimal amount." A lawyer close to the civil suit attributes the difference to the fact that "Ron's father, Fred, and sister, Kim, have appeared on TV almost daily, attacking O.J." The Browns, according to *Parade's* analysis, "have been reluctant to attack O.J. publicly, because they don't want to jeopardize their right to the custody of his children." *Parade* concludes that the family's reticence has hampered its fund-raising ability. Possibly, but the Browns actually have been, if anything, more visible in their grief than the Goldmans. The difference in the success of their respective fund-raising may be that the Goldmans are perceived as the more innocent, and thus the more sympathetic victims.

33.   Some reports claim in fact that from his book, *I Want to Tell You*, and from autographing football cards and other memorabilia he earned more during his fifteen months in jail than he had during previous years.

34.   Matt Krasnowski, "Topless photos of Nicole at issue," *San Diego Union-Tribune*, July 26, 1996, p. A-5. As near as I can tell, Dominique Brown's revelation was dramatically underreported in the press. *Rivera Live*, whose notoriously pro-Brown coverage of the case led Simpson's lawyers to "theorize" an affair between Denise Brown and Geraldo Rivera, barely mentioned this rather startling revelation in the last five minutes of its July 26 show. Interviewed briefly by phone, a lawyer for the Browns claimed that Dominique left the photographs in question with a close friend, who sold them to the *Enquirer*. According to the attorney, Brown put the $32,500 *she* received for the photos in a separate account, which she has not touched. Although it defies common sense, the lawyer's attempt to portray Dominique Brown as the innocent victim of a friend's betrayal went unchallenged by the news reporter, John Gibson, who was sitting in for Geraldo Rivera as host. (The wire service reported that Brown sold seven photographs; *Newsweek* placed the number at five. See "Selling Her Sister's Memory," *Newsweek*, August 5, 1996, p. 68.)

35.   Roger E. Sandler and Marilyn Johnson, "The Way We Live: A Place to Heal," *Life*, June 1995, pp. 37–44; quotations from page 38. As the article explains, a *Life* photographer and his assistant spent the day before Easter 1995 with the Browns and Sidney and Justin—before, during, and after the family's visit to Nicole Simpson's grave.

36.   *Rivera Live*, October 4, 1995. See also *People*, October 16, 1995, p. 50.

Eye, the Jury

Armond White

If the word "nigger" could light up the sky, Los Angeles wouldn't need streetlights; that's how angry white people are.

—a Los Angeles disk jockey to *Emerge* magazine

Tenderly leaning his head on O.J. Simpson's shoulder, Johnnie Cochran displayed caring that went immediately beyond lawyer-client privilege. This image of bonding, coming at the end of the trial, when the country held its breath, was shocking—it vibrated relief, even a sense of love. For all the many Black male images the media flaunts—brothers slapping five on basketball courts, knocking heads in boxing rings, and break dancing in hip-hop videos—none has the intimacy expressed between Cochran and Simpson. It was all the more surprising for their silent communication, a confidence based in trust, a trust the jury might have refuted. Contrast to this was seen soon after in assistant prosecutor Christopher Darden's own emotional moment—his blockage—behind a podium at a postverdict press conference with Los Angeles district attorney Gil Garcetti. Pausing, searching, disconnecting his thoughts from his speech, Darden fell into the arms of the family of Ronald Goldman then, finding no comfort there, broke free and dashed offstage.

These scenes of trust and distrust, broadcast around the world as if they were formal government ceremonies, revealed nuances in black American male behavior that burst apart the almost obscenely presented public events that occasioned them. Disclosing fraternal alliances and secret fears through a subtle gesture and an impulsive bolting, each scene unsettled whatever disposition one had on the entire trial. The surface of Black men's public composure cracked open with unexpected behavioral truth.

Such winner-loser reflexes climaxed the hysteria most Americans felt at the O.J. trial. And yet the momentum of the larger event rolled on. Once again, the trial's revelations trailed in the debris of steamroller speculation and contention, all meaning lost—except in memory. Understanding the broadcast of the trial as an uncanny public concurrence of cultural suspicion and social apprehension requires that we recall it with focus on the three black men it showcased—representatives of what in mainstream America is still an alien existence. Black men of dissenting orientations reflect lives foreign to media conventions. It's in the mythology of pop culture that the image of Black Americans, particularly the male, is subject to distortion, followed by mistrust. Empirical psychology may help describe the poignancy of certain developments during the trial (and of its key players), but it will also uncover some motivations and meanings in the workings of the media (what pathologists call a videognosis), in the many shades of reporting and editorializing that comprise corrupt contemporary journalism and harden our view of one another.

Our news media, like our fiction films, seem committed to condemning—nullifying—the standing of Black men. It happens so consistently that our culture is at a new, cruel crisis point, relegating Black men to cannon fodder, boldly dreaming O.J.'s conviction unto death. You've noticed the media doesn't keep asserting that brutal cops exonerated from manslaughter trials or celebrity criminal Oliver North are guilty; the press is selective in its commitment to "truth." And the media may never rebound from this betrayal of ethics. Continuous denigration of Simpson becomes another political utility—not assertions of opinion but an insistence on vilification. Through "He's guilty!" moralizing, media elitism contrives to coverup daily, historical racial antagonism and injustice.

The last socialquake comparable to this trial (the concussive John F. Kennedy Malcolm X Martin Luther King Robert F. Kennedy assassinations) proved a similar, terrible truth: democracy does not protect against tragedy. And while decades of searching, sorrowful, and honorable American journalism happened in the wake of those calamities (exposing patriotic platitudes), today democracy itself is undermined by media's insidious allegiance to class and race division—the foundation of lucrative empire. In this onslaught Black American grievance and loving go unaccounted for; various oppressions and hurts of the unempowered go ignored.

As spectators it is crucial to defend what we actually saw of the trial against the avalanche of slanted interpretations. Simpson, Cochran, and Darden—media stars and media targets—challenged conventional pop images of Black men. Each of them refused stereotype in the sensitivity, the spontaneity, of plenary session actions, but especially through their individuality. Those three separate responses to the verdict demonstrated an American plurality (specifically, differences in political positions).

These Black men showed moral sensitivity generally thought impossible of their race due to degraded social expectations. It is the limits of the courtroom roles that media assigned to them—criminal, con man, statesman—tied to the proverbial diminutions of Black males that obscures what, in those touching, impromptu gestures, is authentic evidence of American experience, the complexes of masculine rectitude, and the much-needed proof that there's more to people than we easily presume.

Letting their guards down on Verdict Day, Simpson cringed, then smiled, Cochran closed his eyes in gratitude, and Darden collapsed. These exhibitions are part of what made the O.J. Simpson verdict an historically great moment. (I will always remember the afternoon of the verdict announcement for the tense, eerie calm in Manhattan streets broken only by a few young Black men striking the air and laughing in victory.) Seeing two Black men touch—Cochran's cheek leaning into Simpson, head to shoulder (repeatedly), mind to body (repeatedly), thought to feeling (repeatedly)—seemed natural enough to miss. But if noticed, without the structure of sports or entertainment to banalize their show of affection, it revealed a Black emotional richness swamped by trial turmoil with its varieties of stoicism and outrage. Simpson and Cochran were expected to gloat, or at least leer, according to monstrous legend. And precisely because of such ass-backward, programmed expectation, their subtle grace, like the laughter of the boys on the street, seems plangent. Their humanity was momentarily given back to us.

How was it ever denied? Through the strange license of popular mythology, Blacks usually enter the national pop dream/nightmare awkwardly. Rather than fulfilling imagination as human ideals, they appear in "news" form as social convicts—potentialities born of the happenstances of politics and history. Denied human richness, they're then "understood" only as social problems. A trial becomes an occasion for justifying this already warped convention: the malfeasance of murder asserts a problem to be solved, and a Black suspect easily fits a social dilemma. By running with this formula, the media gets to present a case of Black perfidy no different from its usual assumption of Black guilt, treachery, licentiousness, and anarchy. Instead of sensibly following and investigating events in and around the trial, ideological commotion takes over in the name-calling style of 1990s' tabloid culture. These stereotypes are familiar, but the *stereotyping* is less obvious because it carries so much unconscious ideology of white-owned and -operated institutions about race, sex, and rights to power. Prejudices then get abstracted into notions of reporting and "truth" speaking—privileges the empowered secure for themselves.

Both George Eliot and Ralph Ellison had words for this occurrence. (It's not new; it must be an intrinsic part of the post–Industrial Revolution tendency to control popular thought through carefully contrived communication industries.) Eliot answered nineteenth-century social despair with the cry: "While the creative brain can still throb with the sense of injustice, with the yearning for brotherly recognition—make haste—oppress it with your ill-considered judgements, your trivial comparisons, your careless misrepresentations."[1] She meant the social hostility toward nonconformity, while Ellison's twentieth-century vantage pinpointed the race problem: "[N]ot only have our popular culture, our newspapers, radio and cinema been devoted to justifying the Negro's condition and the conflict created thereby, but even our social sciences and serious literature have been conscripted—all in the effort to drown out the persistent voice of outraged conscience."[2]

Had Ellison lived to witness the Simpson trial, even he might have been shocked to see the absurd lengths to which "our" media goes in perpetuation of white supremacy—taking an individual matter to extremes of public castigation, fury, and, ultimately, widespread intellectual chaos. When surveillance camera footage is pilfered and fitted into TV broadcasts (as did the All-O.J.-All-the-Time CNBC) to show Simpson entering the courtroom of his *untelevised* civil trial deposition (implying further, on-the-prowl criminality to Simpson), we get media stalking, another form of vigilantism. Obviously some white people are pissed. And because some of the angriest control the media, their outrage, their hypocritical indignation, as they let go professional and ethical ideals, lights up the sky.

During the current civil trial phase of the O.J. pogrom (what the aftermath of the Nicole Brown Simpson-Ron Goldman murders have become), the media has dropped its pretense about victims' rights, victims' honor. Bloodthirst rules. There can be no question that the media's interest is race-denunciation. A mere murder case or civil rights investigation, government office bombing or airplane crash, *never* commands this much industry. Due to proliferating modern media, news stories often swell obscenely out of their proper social size, but O.J. busy-ness is actually designed to distract from our social, thereby racial, tensions. Throughout the fifteen months of the hearing and trial, media angled to construct public thinking. Sustaining an individual perception meant constantly firing up skepticism, a wearisome process but also an intrinsic, necessary—and liberating—Black American activity.

Not surprisingly, hip-hop music offers the most remarkable, rigorous example of how differently the Simpson trial has entered our culture's bloodstream. In the rap group A Tribe Called Quest's "Ince Again," Q-Tip chants, "I'm gettin' off like O.J." Then, in "Soul Food," Goodie Mob gripes, "Fuck Chris

Darden"—a reference to the deputy prosecutor evoking Willie D's classic 1992 recording "Rodney K (Fuck Rodney King!)." There are more illustrations, but these two represent an *ordinary* cultural process where news events are relayed to personal experience—evidence of a subjective Black interpretation that, in this case, has almost nothing to do with the official mainstream media's way of presenting and contextualizing the Simpson trial.

By "ordinary cultural process" I want to indicate a natural social reflex at work—especially as it differs from the dominant culture's view—since the process of understanding public events and evaluating them has been so oppressively governed by the uniformity of the mainstream's disdain of O.J.—what some are able to recognize as overweening arrogance. In those rappers' free expression, there's nothing so petty as the typical tendency to judge Simpson. A Tribe Called Quest understands his acquittal as part of an historical chain where a Black man's fate is once again in jeopardy, trapped in America's legal hell. The phrase "gettin' off" brashly combines sexual metaphor with an allusion to escape—from the clutches of the court system (these days the bane of one out of every four young Black men, *every* Black family). Symbolizing rare or ironic freedom, Simpson, in this cultural reading, proves "right or wrong don't matter" (as Billie Holiday sang in "Don't Explain") when the preservation of Black sanity, Black healing, is foremost in mind. You'd have to go to the Black press to find a good analysis of this, such as Sylvester Monroe's in *Emerge* (January 1996):

> When Simpson reverted to being "just another Black
> male under arrest," the African-American community, as
> usual, reclaimed its Black prodigal son. They demanded
> that he be given a fair trial and all the rights of an inno-

cent defendant until proven guilty beyond a reasonable doubt. And in the end, it was a reasonable doubt, according to the jurors, that allowed Simpson to go free.

In mainstream trial accounts and references, what passes for journalistic objectivity favors something other than Black sanity and racial healing. From ferocious public accusations by deliberately chosen interview subjects to TV newsreaders' tones of repugnance, a distinct antipathy came through—as an official viewpoint that is by and large undeniably white—and inexcusably biased. At least A Tribe Called Quest's use of "gettin' off" rather than "gettin' over" (or *New York* magazine's October 16, 1995, cover story "Getting Away With It") steers honorably clear of condemnation. By refusing rightness or wrongness, rappers preserve the greater principle of Simpson's right to a fair trial and abide by its acquit-and-release rules—a pledge many journalists have forgotten in their zeal to discard professional integrity and ethical precedent, perpetuating social division. This perversion of justice is what Goodie Mob nails in "Soul Food's" mention of Darden.

Although he could not win his case, Darden has nevertheless been vindicated to the point of heroism by many mainstream commentators, such as the *New York Times Book Review* or numerous TV talk-show hosts. Darden has entered the cultural bloodstream, too. Propped up as the System's preferred version of a Black public figure, he's a Black knight/almost-slayer of Simpson who can be idealized as a better Black man (a TV network plans to cast him as a gospel preacher). But this is not hip-hop's outsider, underground view in which Darden is seen as untrustworthy. Darden's trial behavior contrasts arduous, set-upon Black folkloric experience as an ignominious performance. For rappers concerned with the integrity of Black appearance, his petulance and diffidence amounts to "wackness," in the Uncle Tom sense. (The mainstream, meanwhile, pretends to be above racializing its standards of masculine nobility, *especially* when it is a Black person carrying out the white majority's will.) Goodie Mob's displeasure comes as part of a grass-roots ideational flow, colorfully enunciating modern Black American thoughts and experiences in casual hip-hop narrative. Darden gets ruefully taken back into the fold, taken in stride like mundane failure or a passing cab driven by a Third Worlder; his name affording wide recognition to what, here, is a minority definition of self-abnegation.

But it is genuine. As a cultural alternative to both the established media and its implicitly politicized distortions of the Simpson trial, hip-hop manages this feat of representation succinctly (as does social comic Paul Mooney who praised Johnnie Cochran as "My nigga! He's damned near a rapper!"). These practices recover the ordinary process of observation and interpretation, summarizing events in ways a subculture finds useful and authentic. Simply saying most Blacks view America's race situation differently from most whites shows lazy thinking. Responses to the verdict proved that many Blacks *and* whites actively, joyously, *reject* white media's leaning on their sense of reality. They *knew* the meaning of race was the trial's central subject because of the impact trial coverage has on our psychic well-being. Yet we have virtually relinquished our social intuition in this era of mass media ubiquity. Intricate ambivalence, an ability to observe a social calamity without coarsening our feelings, is endangered. Humanism, its depth and surprise, comes with maintaining a sense of historical proportion. We dare not lose it. Rap group De La Soul puts the trial and the media's dubious outrage in perspective when its album *Stakes Is High* ends with the cry, "Fuck O.J. Simpson, who killed Emmet Till?"

Less astute trial pundits seem intent on hanging O.J. as an effigy for Black America itself, but Ellison's decades-old media-assessment fits even tighter around the necks of these opinion makers:

> This unwillingness to resolve the conflict in keeping with ... democratic ideals has compelled the white American, figuratively, to force the Negro down into the deeper level of his consciousness, into the inner world, where reason and madness mingle with hope and memory and endlessly give birth to nightmare and to dream; down into the province of the psychiatrist and the artist, from whence spring the lunatic's fancy and the work of art.[3]

In reaction to a troubling verdict, a new, dark, antihuman mythology has been created in which mainstream media's judgment against O.J. is similar to its usual judgments against Blacks. This includes the trial's TV broadcast and recent movies such as *Before and After, Eye for an Eye,* and *A Time to Kill,*[4] that exploit Simpson trial controversy. They raise phantoms to prevent people from thinking clearly about the hatred of Blacks saturated in mainstream habit. We must become Doubting Thomases, pull the thorn of race out of the media's side, and, resisting our guilt-tainted taste for salaciousness, probe the national wound, grabbing evidence to show how racism is allowed to evade awareness. In recognizing that panic and repression must some way be let loose, we should still recognize openly sanctioned, self-righteous media racism as demagoguery.

If Ellison wasn't sharp on this, it's because even his litterateur's mind underestimated mass culture's cunning deceptions. Keep in mind how the initial outrage of homicide got reduced by partisan journalists' crimes. (Two examples out of many: *Ms.* magazine and *Esquire* magazine traducing feminism by praising "Woman of the Year" Marcia Clark's bungling of the prosecution.) Thus, the ethics of criminal justice, of journalistic responsibility, are steadily diminished. These days (prior to a late-summer '96 gag order), TV news reports on the civil trial phase go straight to the Goldman family only for a daily perspective, ignoring balance or even a show of fairness. It is blatant to us because movies exploiting social fear through mixed-up liberal concern are a relatively recent development—post–World War II, even post-1960s, when the barrier sank on B-movie topics and acceptable tactics of public discourse. For instance, the viciously manipulative mother-daughter rape and murder in *Death Wish* (1975) is echoed in the rape-murder scene in *Eye for an Eye* (1996), in which a mother overhears on the phone her daughter's violation and killing. Such ugliness, on screen or off, is by now familiar, generic—part of the sensations audiences settle for when insight ain't comin'. Opening in the Nixon law-and-order era, *Death Wish,* a popular genre prototype, used 1970s' paranoia (which was really just an aftershock of sixties' urban uprisings) as its exploitation subject. Today, the arrow of fear hits the heart of darkness. It's the racial threat plain and Simpson. (His trial is one of the first images in *Eye for an Eye.*) Refusing to admit contemporary race fears is what sets the nineties apart from the seventies as an era of denial. Calling the Simpson trial "the Trial of the Century" is part of it—a grotesque, ignorant tabloid conceit. Yet in its unwieldy way it is our great racial drama, our fin-de-siècle *Birth of a Nation* or Death of a Republic. This new culture industry habit of fomenting consensus by turning movie houses or TV rooms into courts of public opinion (horrendous concept) only means one thing: keeping people in the dark.

To redefine Ellison: Popular media is the method society uses to reify its fantasies—and biases. Black Americans, being

the object of much media fascination, harassment, and scorn
know this well. You grow up witnessing how the political contempt for nonwhite, nonaffluent people is directly reflected in
how those people are portrayed in movies, newspapers, fiction,
and nonfiction TV shows, fantasies from the pious middle class.
The fact of demonization backs up the constant illusion of
those people's worthlessness, dangerousness, and burdensome
existence. It's a short jump from the pattern of disparagement in
American films and television to its seeming hard proof in news
reporting and essayistic journalism. Just a hop, in fact, from
Stepin' Fetchit to Willie Horton; from the white racist specter of
Black villainy to the media's castigation of O.J. Simpson.

Racist illusions suffuse trial coverage so that consideration
of trial facts and court protocol is second to society's traditional,
ingrained practice of making a monster. In England such trials
are closed to the media to prevent incitement; to insure it, the
O.J. Simpson trial was conducted on two fronts: in the courtroom and the exterior social sphere that received, televised, or
mediated reportage of the trial. In both instances, racist illusion
came back to the center of the event. Media workers, under the
delusion of "fairness," object to discussing America's racist history—the legacy of biased indoctrination—as irrelevant to the
Simpson trial. But if so, why did the issue of race constantly
come up? Because it cannot be suppressed, neither in the Black
reflex for self-defense nor in the white reflex to control (blame).
We can't get beyond it, and shouldn't want to, until we understand clearly where these ideas come from and exactly how they
affect our country's capacity for tolerance and judgment. What
has happened in our media and daily lives is a changed attitude
toward individual social relations in response to the changes in
political and economic power since the 1960s. Social fear and
depression control the terms in which whites and Blacks regard

each other plus the language and laws they use to express that pervasive suspicion. Movies are infected with this miasma as much as journalism—the former expounds the latter's anxiety and both are a perversion of good will. The trial has been over for months, but the witch-hunt continues in press reports and Simpson-bashing long after the legal resolution that is supposed to absolve the accused and quell accusations. That's because the mainstream's preoccupation with Simpson still perplexes as essentially a "problem" of the Black male.

With Simpson Black male denigration reaches an absurd peak, obliterating most attempts at dispassionate disinterest and legal integrity. It proves when white media goes after Black folks, civilians become stars, celebs become criminals—word becomes bondage.

This is what's behind the insistent proclamation: "I think he did it!" (Saying so falls in line only with the empowered's view of what is important or true.) It's become a new password of white solidarity, even for some Blacks who feel it necessary to separate themselves from O.J. by proclaiming their distaste, instead of insight or compassion. (Not since Desert Storm have so many people made themselves this unfeeling, this vengeful, this appalling.) They corroborate the Black male criminal myth without thinking about how it began, what it means, or who it benefits. Embroiled in mythmaking, O.J. coverage emphasizes dread instead of clarifying the social inequities, conditioning Black folks for more abuse, more disenfranchisement.

None of us feel adrift in the O.J. matter; forms of uneasy solidarity have come from it, but our wounded social conscious-ness hurts worse than our (un)certainty about the actual mur-ders. African Americans rightly discern this confusion as a psychic pressure. The feeling of hatred and domination that comes across must be urgently vanquished. And if it takes a jury to strike this blow, cheering will be then understandable. That's what determined reactions to the courtroom circus and the disputatious verdict. Cheers or jeers were political reflexes, not moral responses (which must be tempered by grief and solemnity). Yet American media's arrogant certitude regarding the evil of Black misconduct forsakes ambivalence to exploit bristling, long-standing cultural notions of Black insufficiency. Instead of complexity, the media creates huge, tragic misrepresentations, excoriations. Few political/cultural commentators, from Anna Quindlen on *The Charlie Rose Show* to *People* magazine, are able, or willing, to see through this white hegemony. Consciousness of social mythology could help here because when pundits argue that O.J. is not a worthy subject for Black America's symbology (as did the one Black political columnist for *The Village Voice*), they ignore how pop myths work; they forget that O.J. degraded is still the image of the white's Negro.

You can feel for the man's manipulation—even if you disapprove his doings—because his downfall, perhaps more than his past out-of-reach "success," resonates with the common Black plight (O.J.'s failure is bound to the prospect of Black achievement in this country, evoking the passions of those who have felt the oppressive stress of white society). O.J. affects any Black person's sense of self. That's why there's so much turmoil over whether O.J. deserted "the Black community"; he's tied to it no matter who doesn't like it. Plus, the media won't let O.J.'s downfall be his own—joining the panoply of Black belittling, he's become a lightning rod for the frustrations of this era's Angry White Men (and Women.)

These unconfronted issues fit what Wendell B. Harris, writer-director of *Chameleon Street*, the 1991 tragicomedy about Black identity, was moved to call "the kind of story God would invent William Shakespeare to write." Simpson's trial didn't transcend American racism, but it did something media workers who are not artists are conventionally loathe to do: give racism a mythic, plain-to-see dimension. This is as convenient as it is agonizing, a neat, chagrined way to grasp our society's racist inclinations. But it's difficult; one must be conscientious about not getting tangled in the arguments of guilt versus innocence or succumbing to biased journalism's tricky, insidious fiats. Morality requires that a delicate balance be maintained by viewers of the trial; that they be better than Court TV by placing observation before judgment. It's the appraisals and evaluations of devious media, such as Court TV's brutish game-show-style commentators who offered daily rundowns and critiques of the trial in progress, that intruded upon the trial's moral issues. Media became meddlesome, unholy participants—as much agents of venality, cruelty, dishonesty, conspiracy, hate, *soul murder*, as anyone whose name was actually stenotyped into the record.

Taboo explains it all. If not for the mixed-race element of the Simpson-Brown marriage, the murder case might have been investigated and news of it broadcast unexceptionally. What Shakespeare knew in the dramatizing of Othello was the perpetual frisson of sexual innuendo. Trial accounts that refuse to parse titillation also fail the necessary examination of our cultural biases—centering instead on the object of a sole malefactor. Dominant culture's sense of offense subordinated law. Simpson plainly was on trial for more than murder—for audacity, rebellion, the sexual rights he claimed as an American citizen and an American victor. His race, held against him in the mind-blowing way only the white establishment knows, overwhelmed the rationality of the law and most media officials. We now have to extract the trial from its media presentation, sifting out bigoted commentary and the commercializing of sex and violence, relying on our own intelligence and experience to get closer to the truth—not of what happened the night of the killings (that's not the nation's business), but to find out what did occur within Simpson's and Darden's beloved-now-bizarro worlds, their two paths to upward mobility.

The Simpson trial as pop myth *is* a Shakespearean drama with great characters confronting the moral limits of one world after having crossed the tribal bounds of another. All viewers of this intrigue, by the fact of cultural engagement, take part in the perpetuation of certain ideas of race and class transience. Thus implicated—and our fantasies of social progress detoured—we are compelled to reexamine the motile figure of the Black American male and every vicissitude affecting the way he is perceived. But the seriousness of the trial and its dread effect also forces us to split criminal social illusion from complicated fact of who Black men—the persons of O.J. Simpson himself, defense attorney Johnnie Cochran, and prosecutor Christopher Darden— really are. *They're all on Chameleon Street.* It's the tragicomedy of Black identity mired in media distortion and desperate for rational, humane rescue. Yes, Shakespeare (not Dominick Dunne) could do justice to Wendell B. Harris's assumption, but the dramatic personae are all America's own.

Unlike the bourgeois sideshow that came out for the Anita Hill–Clarence Thomas carnival, this was a more incendiary roster. These three represented the interchangeable potential open to Black men. It was a grim joke seeing them televised, on exhibit, in the trial's public space: their middle-class lifestyles (not evening news stereotypes) yet converged over an evening news issue—Black criminality. O.J. represented a fall from grace, Darden a trip-up into the white establishment's uneasy good graces. Cochran remains an intermediate figure because he occupies blameless adversarial space, although he did receive much censure, almost as a sign of the cultural opprobrium that always circumscribes Black performance. Whether it's questionable social assertion like O.J.'s glib climbing or Darden's similar desperation to succeed, Black American social activity cannot escape seeming aggressive, impolitic. Somehow it exposes the awkward trade-offs of racial pride (solidarity) and ambition (isolation). Public exposure demands wiliness of each man as the three of them try to lift themselves out of the directives, proscriptions, and constraints of a wretched, biased social ethos. Seeking various ways to escape cultural censure and disgust, they must make themselves up out of imagination and experience, against the world's vicissitudes, but also against its disinterest and cruelty. *Chameleon Street* perceived and prophesied this. So how did carpet-bombing press denunciations miss it? And fail to appreciate the crucial Simpson-Cochran interplay of stressed unity and Darden's desolate flight? In such moments these men exposed their own destinies, their personal allegiances: a striving lawyer and client bound by subconscious fraternal needs that Faulkner would call "not-terror"; a panicky prosecutor in free fall like a trapeze artist reaching in midair for a partner he cannot truly believe in. But it's something journalists would have to be already sensitive to. If Simpson-Cochran's bond suggested collusion to cynics, Darden's bust-out should also have rung alarms. (And probably did—a silent alarm that shames.) The Goldman family and district attorney office were there for Darden (as Cochran was for Simpson), but Darden couldn't *see* them because he didn't feel right there or fit with them.

These were not just matters of racial or cultural likeness; they go deeper, to a society's fundamental assumptions, its daily structure of support and practice of mores as three Black men lived them out. The trial did not create these race tensions, but every aspect of them—from the miscegenation issues of the Brown-Simpson marriage to the formal, political alliance of

Darden and lead prosecutor Marcia Clark—surely grew out of them. But Darden himself won't admit it (in his self-exculpatory book *In Contempt*). With all his prosecutorial history, and pride in it, Darden was certainly privy to the system's inequities and mendacities. But when his inner Faust awoke, he attempted, in one brief moment of public candor, to shake it off. Establishment media would have us deny or ignore such complex ambivalence; it so disturbs the outward appearance of justice and fairness that lay politicians don't want to touch it, even though it reveals alienation common to any mixed-group American workplace. Equally, noticing it would sensitize witnesses to the spontaneous compassion in Simpson's and Cochran's summary embrace.

When pundits further perverted the trial by assigning its strangeness to the cult of celebrity, this was merely more evasion. The media's excessive concentration on Simpson was based in a racist illusion that the crime was "important." The Bronco chase was a clear case of media exploitation. His celebrity didn't warrant live, preemptive TV coverage at all. Face it: it was the scandal one could attach to the circumstances of a killing, a fleeing, an impending arrest that made media moguls slather. We are used to having our worst instincts pandered to by the media, thus ungluing the fragile trust of community that we live by. Still, race exploitation was the convenient selling point, the goal. The Bronco chase—with its indecent hovering over the Simpson estate to peek in on catastrophe—was the first offense. (I refuse to borrow the trivializing metaphor "playing the race card" because it is itself loaded with the media elite's disrespect, and reluctance, for any discourse on race.) Next, *Time* magazine's darkened mug shot was proof again of how media wrought this issue along lines of stereotype and fear. Simpson would be made over in the Black monster mode by any graphic, sophistic means necessary. (The magazine itself explained: "To many whites, O.J. entered the trial as a fellow White man and grew darker as the proceedings went on. He was the perfectly assimilated minority hero until he was associated with terrible crimes. Then he became just another Black male under arrest, presumed to be guilty of everything.")

This betrayal of a former hero is actually a common turn-about, causing Black distrust of whites and their official institutions—from *Time* magazine to executive office cabinet firings such as Clinton's axing Jocelyn Elders. The *Time* magazine cover and the televised Bronco chase were ideological salvos that short-circuited empathy. Both linked with the justice system's media-friendly, cash-cooperative inclusion of courtroom cameras to announce and prepare the audience for a new level of public spectacle.

Media frequently bends itself into formats that promote its essential allegiance to white supremacy. Americans know that throughout history, rules customarily are broken to disfavor Blacks (the media has been no less willing to do this than police investigators). Before the trial Simpson was but one of many Black sports stars, now one whose field achievements are virtually forgotten after years of lame movies and TV commercials. Some think these promotions of capitalism proved his acceptance by an open America. But accepted how far? Within the admiration by which the mainstream makes racist exceptions of Black atheletes is a repressed contempt that here gets expressed in all-out vengeance. One of the most peculiar instances was the *Entertainment Tonight* show that, in treating Simpson's travail as entertainment news, overlooked Simpson and devoted an entire segment to idolizing "The Hunk of the Hearings," Lt. Mark

Fuhrman—as if what this soap opera needed was a white, square-jawed romantic figure. (Their folly eventually turned to horror.) Simpson himself was never hunkier. He looked different, a changed figure—the gravity of the situation knocked the banal pitchman's smile off his face. He appeared solemn, more handsome, an embodiment of the Black man in trouble (for some an evil, for others an image of fascination). If you could recognize the defamation Black people endure daily, you would sense what Black celebrities oppose by their efforts to withstand suffering and affirm (document) perseverance. They're *expressing themselves* and their people—a load Simpson would always carry whether on the field or in court. Although Simpson had never been a community hero like Cochran, whose legal career in civilian rights (as opposed to Darden) inspired trust by demonstrating consciousness about racial conditions in this country, he became a poetic figure anyway. History was turning on Simpson's shoulders, returning his relevance to Black America at last.

By now Simpson must feel himself transmogrified, taken out of his own life into a psychic desolation very much like slavery's abduction and dislocation. No matter what else Simpson may have done in his life—won football games, trophies, made movies, babies, driven cars, etc.—the fame, adulation, resentment, happiness, anger it produced could not prepare him for this current persecution. Such stress, coming in waves from the hostile atmosphere and not the result of one's own conscious, physical endeavor, must astonish a celebrity as well as a jaded public. It's wilder than mere fame because it's full of the judgmental society's menace. Whites may not understand this sense of paranoid disorder, although Black Americans have long endured it even in situations as mundane as being watched then followed by security guards: society's suspicion and disrespect crowds your sense of free movement, shadowing your anticipation. Even the innocent would feel resentful and the dispassionate, protective. In this climate, the dominant society has won: Simpson's already a prisoner—as are we all—social captives trapped in the media's purge, suffering the phenomenon of white supremacy in which a group, explaining itself to itself (and the world), does so at the expense of our health and social stability.

This media transference of dominant group hatred is the evidence of unjust power—the bequest of a guilt- and evil-gripped culture. Overtalking the Simpson case, white media reinforced racist ideology, erecting white sepulchres, white plantations, white abattoirs, white schools, all edifices of white dominance. When *The New Yorker*'s Jeffrey Toobin, the trial's most "respected" reporter, castigates Simpson as a "semiliterate," he means untutored, unprincipled, savage. The whole witch-hunt is plainly exposed as part of a class- and race-based need to pronounce guilt, thus to ostracize O.J.—the Other.

Cochran is the second most-vilified figure in this event, but it must be said that his infamy is largely a white projection. The distraught Fred Goldman, still mourning his son, took political objection to Cochran's comparing Fuhrman's racism to Adolf Hitler. Goldman railed incoherently against Cochran: "We have seen a man who perhaps is the worst kind of racist himself. This man is the worst kind of human being imaginable. He suggests that racism ought to be the most important thing that any one of us ought to listen to in this court, that any one of us in this nation ought to be listening to, and it's because of racism we should put aside all other thought, all other reason, and set his murdering client free. He's a sick man. He ought to be put away."[5] This is incoherent but it blares mainstream race fear, race hysteria.

Sure, Cochran's "slick"—that's just American culture's word for being successfully competitive. In his book Darden envies and despises the way Cochran dresses, but an honest view of Cochran saw no courtroom misconduct, no pouting (despite Judge Lance Ito's own biased contempt citations). He claimed the moral high ground in arguing against Darden's racial stigmatizing. (And in smoothly setting up the glove-fitting routine that Darden vainly fell for, Cochran trumped his opponent.) Cochran's professionalism perfectly analogizes the rigorously maintained perspective of those whites and Blacks who were unwilling to go with hunches and moralize about the case. The opposite to Cochran's intelligent approach showed in the brash conclusions of observers who refused to wait for the legal process to play out, especially the prosecution team.

Their remarkable sense of superiority (and embattlement) came out in Marcia Clark's flirty arrogance and Darden's testy fretting. Basically inept, they relied on an inordinate manipulation of a daily press-conference forum. An important instance of institutional conspiracy showed the media's willingness to perform public relations for the district attorney's office (typically part of hack journalists' dependence on "official source" press statements rather than hunting down a story). No actual trial participant misunderstood his or her role more than Darden, who gambled on the tactic of personalizing the deceased to win sympathy. Darden's unctuous plea (repeated in *In Contempt*) that "Ron and Nicole" were his clients immediately unbalanced the issues. A prosecutor serves a state's interests; currying favor from individuals with a private stake in a trial's outcome is not his job. Such specious empathy exposed Darden's allegiance to an unofficial prejudice disparaging Blackness (intimated in Darden's bitter phrases describing Simpson's behavior and history). The district attorney's office used Darden's own ethnicity to disguise its chosen low strategy of character assassination. But more than willing to deceive, Darden became the System's eager dupe.

If in Shakespearean terms Simpson was Othello, Darden Iago, it remains a toss-up who was the most interesting, most tragic, figure. Certainly Darden was the most duplicitous, since his ethical contradictions were not merely a matter of preserving a public front but serving two communities—Enterprising Black America versus Imperial White America—a poignant, enraging schizophrenia. What was ultimately a self-betrayal began in Darden's own career history that prepared for his courtroom mendacity.

A Black person's decision to become a public prosecutor requires holding an antipathetic regard for the ongoing facts of America's institutional abuse of Black people or perhaps an ignorance of the social history and political facts that contribute to Black troubles. It arbitrarily imputes lawlessness to people without power or opportunity. Darden never ponders his requisite callousness in *In Contempt*, which would get in the way of his convenient belief that Blacks are to blame for his losing the case, for Ron and Nicole being murdered, for every pathological effect of racism in the United States. Iago was jealous, but Darden was contemptuous of blacks who reject his middle-class, assimilationist notion of correct behavior. A little fascism poisons the law-and-order tendency that compels cops and prosecutors to do their job. It was strange to see Darden's boyish obstreperousness (so much like an insolent young rapper) taking the side of power—and still steaming, irate. His immature scowls betrayed a lack of moral courage, an insufficiency we know can never be satisfied. Matching tempers with Cochran, Darden frequently lost more than his cool: his head flew off in the way of delinquents caught in the wrong but too vain to admit it.

The entire prosecution team playacted denial on the issue of Mark Fuhrman—the suspicious, unfit, racist Los Angeles cop Darden was assigned to prepare as a state witness. For many viewers this is where the state lost its case: *knowing* Fuhrman's history, *knowing* he lied to F. Lee Bailey's questions, yet persisting in a Fuhrman cover-up until the defense team doggedly exposed him. This grievous offense, added to bumbled investigations, mishandled evidence, Judge Kennedy-Powell's prejudiced bench rulings that okayed warrantless search-and-seizure, shook the foundations of the criminal justice system. And—oops!—cameras stayed on, exposing the errors. Pundits, of course, looked the other way, blaming the derailment on the defense team and forestalling the fair-enough notions of a mistrial.

Here's how ego defeats the person: In his book, Darden excuses Fuhrman, proposing that his racist statements be forgiven, by outrageously linking Fuhrman to post–Mecca Malcolm X as a man with a change of heart. Darden is able to flip the script on Malcolm X—and on the problem of racism—because fundamentally he, like his white cohorts in the district attorney's office and the media, disdains untoward Black behavior. House-Negro fealty to his boss, camera hog Gil Garcetti, led Darden to disgrace a figure of Black empowerment by comparing him to a Black oppressor. If we mistake Darden's confusion for tragic heroism, we cheapen human aspiration as nothing more than a craving for authority's favor. Interestingly Darden never sympathetically compares himself to Cochran or Simpson; he personally circumscribes Black male potential, acquiescing to Black abasement.

Eventually, good sense got lost in Darden's contest over race with Cochran. No media person seemed able to see through this crucial moment of the trial. Black men pitted against each other had the nation's attention, but resolved nothing. Watching tempers volley could have enlightened the judge, jury, and world. Instead, their altercation was a plantation owner's divide-and-conquer dream. Their case positions prevented them from sharing truths about race culture and race mythology. They couldn't converge their different experiences as Black men in America because the separation probably started long before the trial in different, class-bound attitudes about what constitutes necessary or legitimate ethnic sensibility. (Cochran also began his legal career as a young prosecutor, apparently a *rite de passage* for many Black attorneys in Los Angeles. But he made his reputation defending Blacks—most significantly Black Panther Geronimo Pratt—in police abuse cases. Cochran termed this "the most remarkable civics lesson you could learn in that you don't accept the official version. But when I started trying cases as a young city attorney thirty-one years ago, you would be almost held in contempt of court if you said a police officer was lying.")[6]

Loyal Darden didn't efface himself for the good of the case. He went ego and started an ideological street fight. More than prosecuting, Darden became the spokesman for white insensitivity and impatience, going for conviction at the cost of moral restraint. It happened when he insisted a Black voice is in itself identifiable, invoking and attempting to legitimate racial stigma, dredging up American weakness and suspicion lurking in posthumous details of the Simpson-Brown marriage. Cochran's calling out Darden's racist ploy argued for equity and impartiality in the "evidence" presented. But in the now-exacerbated terms of the public spectacle, Cochran's fair-mindedness was discredited by mediacrats as militancy. It was, but only in the way that opposition to racist practice required a militant forthrightness. When Darden claimed that Blacks go blind and irrational upon hearing the word *nigger*, Cochran launched a passionate retort: "It's demeaning to our jurors to say that African-Americans, who have lived under oppression for 200-plus years in this country, cannot work within the mainstream, cannot hear these offensive words.

African-Americans live with offensive words, offensive looks, offensive treatment every day of their lives. But yet they still believe in this country . . ."[7]

The standoff between Cochran and Darden aired out suppositions about race that floated freely during the trial, sparking here and there with no place to be proven or debated as needed. This was the most important determinant of the trial's tone and its ramifications. If the prosecution was willing to argue a witness's not-hearing/hearing "a Black voice," then there was nowhere it would stop, no ideal it held important except winning its case at all costs—lynch-mob justice. It is within this racist rigidity—America's unacknowledged prevailing prejudices—that Simpson, Darden, and Cochran were seen, regardless of the content of their characters. We know such things as accident, hormones, health, environment determine the quality of a voice. Similar variables also influence how a voice is perceived, how people who turn up in a ring or courtroom together come to oppose each other's very sense of humanity. These highly Visible Men turned a courtroom into Ellison's hellacious boxing ring.

Observers who sided with Cochran or Darden or Simpson, stuck on deciding guilt or innocence, chose an irrelevant dilemma easier to deal with than this lonely, devastating awareness: that our forces of justice and communication are arrayed against the unempowered—especially converting Black males into grist for our contemporary prison/criminal justice industry. In spite of the jury's verdict, Simpson can't receive the rights due him by legal process because these are benefits reserved for (rich) whites who are able to "work within the system's" money-driven apparatus. Broadcast outlets who seek ad revenue by exploiting Simpson news hypocritically renege on his right to advertise a videotape.

Such malevolence is heinously defended by the ploy of guilt or innocence. But if that abreaction prevents us from practicing our supposed democratic principles, our society is despoiled.

Understanding the social and personal urges that made us eye-jurors of the trial, bringing all our fates together with Simpson's, Brown's, and Goldman's, is more important than merely adducing who murdered two people. George Orwell asked, "Who Cares Who Killed Roger Ackroyd?" Its 1990s' paraphrase would be a proper response to the relentless shit-stirring of media jackals like Geraldo Rivera, who turned this tragedy into a morbid, maniacal bid for ratings. It's when you consider the millions of lives (Black and white) to be corrupted this media catastrophe that the two murders come to seem relatively unimportant, and the media's disservice amounts to social devastation. The Simpson trial manifests more than a good read or "sexy" TV. It indicates to us what we are as a nation—social hypocrites and compromisers.

I avoided the word *brotherly* to describe Simpson and Cochran's postverdict gestures, even though that's exactly what distinguished them, because I want to impress a larger sense of human empathy, to suggest, by example, a more complicated writing of history than the mainstream has ordained. But brotherhood is, in the end, unavoidable. It endows some Black men with an understanding of each other that whites may only comprehend as aberrant, an exotic trait, and thus disrespect. But it's also deeply affectionate, deeply judicious, in the way Cochran intuited the need to press his body to Simpson's rather than any glib form of encouragement. Nothing could mean more than that sentient assurance. It's the essence of contact and a base of civilization. Many whites—and Blacks—may have had this connection worn out of them by the chaotic trial, yet it persists in the communal response to larger issues—the political scandal of law run amuck and broken by prosecutors, police, and media. Black people felt enthusiastic about beating a system of corrupt vengeance, a euphoria that surpasses feeling for O.J. himself (though it certainly embraces him). It's proof of a vibrant, long-offended moral intelligence that, by dint of will and passion, keeps going in spite of domineering media propaganda. Within that tight, tender exchange between Simpson and Cochran is the sustenance one need only observe to hold as a social faith. Darden's judgmental response to Black trouble is dehumanizing. It can only lead to distress.

Seeing or hearing these voluminous aspersions of O.J. will always, despite the remote abstractions of TV and press, put one back in the moment where every American's soul hung in anguished suspense. But that moment is also profoundly ordinary: it's when you decide to clasp humanity or to run away from its difficulty—feeling sorry and terrified.

Notes

1. George Eliot, *The Lifted Veil* (New York: Viking Penguin reprint, 1986).
2. Ralph Ellison, *Shadow and Act* (New York: Random House/Vintage reprint, 1972).
3. Ibid.
4. Each film was a box-office failure. Along with *Devil in a Blue Dress* and *Seven*, their refashioned social dread could not compete with the O.J. trial's suspense, drama, and scandal. I detail this phenomenon in "Simpson Sensibility: Black Male Shows in the Year Mythology Broke Down," *The City Sun*, December 20, 1995.
5. *Emerge*, January 1996.
6. Ibid.
7. Ibid.

The "Interest" of the Simpson Trial: Spectacle, National History, and the Notion of Disinterested Judgment
Claudia Brodsky Lacour

"The public use of one's reason must always be free, and it alone can bring about enlightenment among human beings."[1]

—Immanuel Kant

That there was altogether too much interest in the Simpson criminal trial was a view espoused only by a vocal minority and, even by that minority, more often espoused than acted upon. If the level and depth of interest in the trial took an even smaller minority by surprise,[2] crisscrossing nearly all the social divisions in America that we know of— including race, class, religion, gender, ethnicity, profession, and region—then still more surprising is that so much and such diverse interest was not enough to warrant serious reflection and analysis. The basis for this discrepancy now appears evident. While in other adversarial contexts that engage the "undivided" attention of the nation, ranging from political contests and sporting events to the staged slaughter of domestic bombings, we are eager to designate the divisions among us as national strengths to be both admired *and* overcome, those same differences or divisions were never intended to be transcended through the spectacle of the Simpson trial. For all their outspoken fervor, and self-proclaimed assumption of a higher moral ground, the various commentaries relating to the trial have remained bereft of the presupposition of a common ground that is the necessary prerequisite, neither of premature appeals to "healing," nor of instant caricatures of national schisms, but of any possible understanding of them achieved through analysis.

By analysis is not meant "analysis" of the trial itself, the ongoing volume and dubious value of which may soon outstrip those counterfeit hundreds that caused the U.S. Treasury to mint more complicated bills. What is here meant by and ascribed the role of serious public analysis is an investigation of the interest the trial aroused in its spectators—an interest surpassing even common, sensationalist curiosity about the brutal crime itself, indeed surpassing, most unusually and almost perversely, compassion felt for the victims themselves and for their families. Leaving aside for a moment the industry and individuals that stoked that interest for their own benefit, as well as the many ancillary, national, and local companies that profited from "expanded coverage" of the trial, from airlines and hotels to shops, bookstores, and restaurants (the spectacle of the trial doing for all commercial media and the tourist economy of L.A. what the '96 Olympics—despite many more black American athletes in the spotlight and the constant hum of editorial sentimentalization—have failed to do financially for NBC and a relatively racially harmonious, well-intentioned Atlanta), we would do well to analyze the nature of the attraction of the Simpson trial, the grounds and consequences of the intense personal involvement it stirred, and this for one obvious, oddly overlooked reason. The profiteering cultivation of a tautological, unreasoning interest in the spectacle of the trial notwithstanding, interest in any trial is itself an oxymoron, for such interest renders impossible the very activity upon which legal procedures and outcomes are predicated, the larger mental activity which, since the invention of the modern republic, we call judgment.

Judgment is, by definition, disinterested, or it is something else; no more fundamental concept comes to us from the Enlightenment, whose theorists and adherents both conceived the notion of the nation and actually wrote this nation into existence. In order to approach, with some degree of reason, the nature of our national interest in a trial that—even before the trial's beginning—was spoken and exhibited for us, through an incessant transmission of selected words and skewed images, it would first be helpful to consider closely the nature of the activity in which this or any trial should issue the act of judgment whose formulation and practice were central to the international pursuit of intellectual development then and now called enlightenment. For the so-called Age of Enlightenment, or much-maligned Age of Reason, might best be viewed as an age we must all want to attain, the age when, rather than spoken for by other authorities and interests, we can speak for ourselves—when, to use Kant's famous term, we become *mündig* (literally, capable of giving voice to oneself, from *Mund*, "mouth").[3] The pivotal thinker of his age, which he preferred to call "the Age of Criticism" [*Zeitalter der Kritik*],[4] Kant formulated a notion of disinterested judgment as powerful and as necessary in its scope as were ancient beliefs in fate or the will of the gods or God, the medieval doctrine of enduring, original sin and thus inherent human weakness, and the clashing, early modern philosophical premises of primal egotism, mechanical causality, idealist metaphysics, and rational skepticism—all rationalizations of the limits of human action which Kant's notion of judgment effectively replaced.

If, given our negligence of the term, it seems an exaggeration to attribute to judgment the effective origin of enlightenment and the theoretical and actual basis of the modern republic—that of a free *and* lawful, or self-legislating, nation— we should recall that it is also upon the notion of disinterested judgment that, at least since the Enlightenment, the possibility of distinctly moral action rests. For Kant, the only moral law was the law of universality; the simple principle of "conformity to universal law" was the entire contents of his so-called categorical imperative, the unfortunate phrase coined in his *Groundwork of the Metaphysic of Morals* to describe nothing more (nor less) than the moral intelligence evidenced every day by "ordinary" or "common human reason" [*gemein[e] Menschenvernunft*].[5] Discarded in *The Critique of Practical Reason*—Kant's later attempt to *deduce*, from within the limits set by his critical philosophy, the certainty of the moral law he then defined as "freedom"—Kant's "imperative" or "first principle" of "moral knowledge" was a single straightforward statement: "I ought never to act except in such a way *that I can also will that my maxim should become a universal law.*"[6] In other words, I should act with a view to, and a wish for, the universal translatability of my action, the realization that any particular act *can and must* be a possible sentence in the grammar of all actors. What *I* do must be rewriteable without contradiction in the second and third persons, making of every first person a potential first person plural.

It was *not* the case, Kant noted, that "ordinary human reason" conceives "this principle" "thus abstractly in its universal form."[7] Rather, in place of conceiving of such a statement, it *acts* upon it, "us[ing] it as a norm of judgment."[8] Judgment and, as we shall see, all the so-called mental faculties or capacities judgment entails, is the activity that links an abstract, universal law—the law of universal law or applicability itself—to the particular instances of action. Judgment is the bridge between what Kant in his critical writings called "understanding" and "reason:" theory and theoretical knowledge, limited to understanding given phenomena, on the one hand, and the "pure," noncontingent reason of moral action, or practice, on the other.[9] It is the only faculty, in a world ruled by no nonhuman power, that makes specifically *moral* action *within* contingent circumstances possible, which is to say with the Enlightenment, necessarily possible for all. It is judgment, and no particular moral precept, that undermines the wall posed—sometimes rigorously, more often cynically—between theory and praxis precisely by finding itself obligated to overcome the intellectual vacuity and moral sterility that such a barrier between thought and action facilitates. Judgment questions the conscious or effective compartmentalization of theory and practice that, erected and appealed to out of bad faith or stupidity, prepares the ground only for universally degrading gameplaying and self-inflating opportunism.

Yet, it is not that theory, relating to the understanding of the empirical world, and practice, taking place in and affecting the empirical world, are or can be equated, least of all according to Kant: the internal and external, mental and material, private and public realms only have reality insofar as they involve each other against the grain, the conceptual and physical delineations that compose them. If reflection were action with no difference or opposition between them, there would be no one and nothing we could either recognize or imagine, no form of representation, no language, not even speech acts, but a single conflation of will and matter surpassing even the power over things of all the gods we have said we cannot know. It is judgment that must move between these two realms, just as private reason must be externalized, made public, according to Kant, who defined the chief "promoter" of enlightenment as exactly this kind of translation.

Without the pressure applied to the division between theory and practice by judgment, Kant reasoned, "the concept of right" or *public* moral principles which should inform the politics and laws crafted by and between nations, and which "only the republican constitution" of a representative government "fits entirely," would be no more than a chimera of reason, a wholly impracticable "thought, empty of content" [*ein sachleerer Gedanke*].[10] If representative government, republican constitutions of laws, and their corresponding concept of "universal principles of right" are not yet realized, the "*sign[s] of history*," Kant suggested, show that they are nonetheless "the tendency of the human race viewed in *its entirety*."[11] Such signs are neither static images nor active "cause[s] of history" but rather indications of a certain movement, just as the most significant among these signs for Kant, the event of the French Revolution, would, according to him, prove mentally and empirically irreversible—a "phenomenon . . . *not to be forgotten* in human history"—regardless of its specific, concrete outcome ("[d]enn ein solches Phänomen in der Menschengeschichte *vergisst sich nicht mehr*").[12] Most important for the present analysis is Kant's thesis that such efficacy lay not in the Revolution itself but *in the "mode of thinking" it produced in its "spectators*," a *Denkungsart* which Kant defined as follows: "universal yet disinterested sympathy for the players on one side against those on the other, even at the risk that this partiality could become very disadvantageous for them if discovered."[13] The French Revolution, then, is not a sign; it is a concrete event, an occurrence. Yet it produces the additional, semiotic event of its reception, a mental response that constitutes a sign of something else by overriding the personal interests—indeed, the very persons—of its subjects, those who are literally subjected to the response they undergo.

This "mode of thought" which, not directly engaged in action, instead considers action from a "disinterested" viewpoint, nonetheless commits its thinker to an unequivocal position ("partiality" [*Teilnehmung*] or "sympathy" [*Parteilichkeit*]) that is the joint product of reason and practice: a conceptual and historical sense of "the right" ("der blosse Rechtsbegriff").[14] To conceive *and* recognize what is right (or wrong) within the context of actions committed in contingent, phenomenal circumstances makes not those actions but one's ability to view them disinterestedly and partially into a "sign of history." Advocacy which may pose a threat to an individual's own contingent interests, including, in the first place, the safety and fortune of that individual's material self, is the *disinterested partiality*, or heterogeneous "mode of thought," Kant otherwise called judgment, the faculty of moving between theoretical and practical reason whose historical and political manifestations, he reasoned, must always be a movement forward.

But judgment is also *aesthetic* judgment in Kant, and this is where the exercise of disinterestedness is both absolute and immediate, rather than "progressive," in effect, and thus also where the issue of the concrete, particular instance becomes more complicated.[15] That is, one may look forward to achieving the "ideal" "common being" that is "the eternal norm for all civil organization in general," "one namely in which the citizens obedient to the law, at the same united, ought also to be legislative [*gesetzgebend sein sollen*]"—

a nation, in short, in which disinterested judgment is actually mutual law.[16] One may also act in freedom from all individual objectives, as if in conformity to a moral law prescribing nothing but its own universality. But aesthetic experience is necessarily momentary and particular; and aesthetic *judgment*—the activity for which Kant reserved that term alone—must be disinterested about distinct, sensory objects perceived here and now. Distinct, sensory objects are not events whose spectatorship, interested only in the advent of what is right, can in turn be viewed as "signs" of the eventual and irrevocable "improvement" that is the "tendency" of "human nature," the historical and internal tendency toward the public "goal" of constituting a nation "in conformity with inner principles of right."[17] The sensory objects of aesthetic judgment affect their viewer without the intervention of a sense of (universal) lawfulness, (future) purpose, or (fundamental) right. Judgments that are aesthetic are not "signs of history," at least in the sense Kant presented, because, properly abstracted from action as from content, they preclude even the viewer's selfless interest, a personally overriding partiality for just moral outcomes.

Unlike judgment in the viewing of actions, specifically aesthetic judgments are disinterested with regard not to the self who judges but to the object judged. Kant defines this disinterest in the practical "existence" of such an object as follows:

> when the question is if a thing is beautiful, we do not want to know whether anything depends or can depend on the existence of the thing, either for myself or for anyone else, but how we judge it by mere observation (intuition and reflection). If anyone asks me if I find that palace beautiful which I see before me, I may answer: I do not like things of that kind which are made merely to be

stared at. Or I can answer like that Iroquois Sachem, who was pleased in Paris by nothing more than by the cook shops. Or again, after the manner of Rousseau, I may rebuke the vanity of the great who waste the sweat of the people on such superfluous things. In fine, I could easily convince myself that if I found myself on an uninhabited island without the hope of ever again coming among men, and could conjure up just such a splendid building by my mere wish, I should not even give myself the trouble if I had a sufficiently comfortable hut. This may all be admitted and approved, *but we are not now talking of this* [*nur davon ist es nicht die Rede*]. We wish only to know if this mere representation of the object is accompanied in me with satisfaction, however indifferent I may be as regards the existence of the object of this representation.... Everyone must admit, that a judgment about beauty, in which the least interest mingles, *is very partial* and is not a pure judgment of taste [*sehr parteilich und kein reines Geschmacksurteil sei*]. We must not be in the least prejudiced in favor of the existence of the things, but be quite indifferent in this respect, in order to play the judge in things of taste.[18]

As opposed to political and historical judgment, aesthetic judgment is that which pleases "without any interest" [*ohne alles Interesse*] in its object, and the way in which we experience such aesthetic pleasure is in contemplation not of that object itself but of its "form."[19] Form alone allows for "the free play of imagination and understanding" [*freies Spiel der Einbildungskraft und des Verstandes*] that defines aesthetic judgment,[20] and our experience of form is opposed to our necessarily "partial" view of content. Yet, unlike the equation of "formalism" with an empty and static intellectual method that, with time, succeeded Kant's introduction of the concept of formal considerations into aesthetic theory, Kant specifically equates form with the *dynamic* quality of an aesthetic object. Famously defined in the terms of his *Critique* as "purposiveness without purpose" [*Zweckmässigkeit ohne Zweck*], the dynamic aspect of form Kant has in mind may best be described as the appearance of indicating something more than a mere appearance: it is the *form* of an aesthetic object which signifies, in the most fundamental sense, that it is not only an object but a carrier of meaning.[21] Unlike the cognitive apprehension of objects which, in Kant, is always based on concepts and related to knowledge of other things, in judging the beautiful we experience a discrete object not as an object of conceptual knowledge but as "pleasing." At the same time, the beautiful appearance of "purposive" form "pleases" its perceiver without representing any specific, "subjective" *or* "objective" "purpose" or aim, the very purposes which appeal to "interest," including the moral interest in "the good." Neither a cause nor an effect of the immediate pleasure of aesthetic experience, moral interest instead takes the form of what is no longer or is not yet experience, and thus has to be read rather than felt: the legible, semiotic form of a "sign of history" [*Geschichtszeichen*].[22]

If dynamic, "purposive" form causes our pleasure in the aesthetic according to this first modern redefinition of the word, then specific content considered in isolation from form remains tied to its original, ancient meaning [αισθητικοσ], that of pertaining to any sensory experience at all. Rather than presenting an object for aesthetic judgment—"the play of imagination and understanding"—content or "matter" offers only the "empirical" occasion for "mere sensations," and the first of these unformed, "simply" or "merely" sensational experiences is the perception of color:

A mere color, e.g., the green of a grass plot, a mere tone
(as distinguished from sound and noise), like that of a
violin, are by most people described as beautiful in themselves, although both seem to have at their basis merely the
matter of representations, viz. simply sensation, and therefore only deserve to be called pleasant . . . ; for we cannot
assume that the quality of sensations is the same in all
subjects, and we can hardly say that the pleasantness of
one color or the tone of one musical instrument is judged
preferable to that of another in the same way by everyone. . . .

In painting, sculpture, and in all the formative
arts—in architecture and horticulture, so far as they are
beautiful arts—the *delineation* is the essential thing; and
here it is not what gratifies in sensation but what pleases
by means of its form that is fundamental for taste. The
colors which light up the sketch belong to the *charm;* they
may indeed enliven the object for sensation, but they cannot make it worthy of contemplation, and beautiful.[23]

In a closely related anthropological observation, Kant
remarks that any "average" or "normal idea of the beauty [of
the human figure]" [*Normalidee der Schönheit der Gestalt*]—like the
"pleasantness" of a specific color to an individual—must differ
according to the "country *where* the comparison is instituted"
[*dem Lande, w o diese Vergleichung angestellt wird*] and the specific, given
or "empirical conditions" from which such an idea is drawn,
declaring matter-of-factly: "[t]hus necessarily under these
empirical conditions a Negro must have a different normal idea
of the beauty [of the human figure] from a white man, a China-
man a different normal idea from a European, etc. And the same

is the case with the model of a beautiful horse or dog (of distinct breeds)."[24] The "presentation," or physical rendering of such "a normal idea," under which Kant goes so far as to include the "celebrated" "Canon" of Polycletus—the statue of Doryphorus traditionally considered not a particular cultural "idea," but the universal ideal of human beauty—would please "not by its beauty, but merely because it contradicts no condition:" based on an "average" "image" of the individuals a people are empirically, and thus contingently accustomed to seeing, and which, at the same time, "no one individual" among that people "fully reaches," it "is merely [institutionally or pedantically] correct" [*schulgerecht*].[25]

Like those who would raise a single, cultural idea of bodily beauty to an ideal, painters and historians of painting may take issue with Kant's subordination of coloration to line: the debate on the artistic significance of color is at least as old as the discovery of painted Roman imitations of Greek statuary. But in relegating specific colors, like specific musical tones, to the mere "charm" (*Reiz*) of an object we judge aesthetically, Kant makes all the "formative arts," in their differing cultural forms, available to judgment in the same, disinterested way: as objects whose status depends not on their most "sensational" or arbitrary[26] aspect— the reception of which would naturally differ from culture to culture, from person to person, and even from moment to moment within cultures and persons—but rather on their formally achieved, dynamic "purposiveness," their ability to please by engaging a corresponding purposiveness in their perceiver, the formally dynamic interplay of imagination and understanding that makes aesthetic *judgment* possible. Entertaining no prejudice with regard to possible aesthetic objects, Kant extended the notion of the beautiful from *les beaux arts* to seashells, from representations of the human body to the pleasing patterns of wallpaper, raising the latter of these—seashells and wallpaper—to the category of "free beauties," since, like "music without words," "they represent nothing" [*sie stellen nichts vor*], that is, no specific object which, like the human body, would be related to a concept of its purpose.[27]

The purposelessness of seashells and wallpaper may seem to lead one rather far from the spectators of the French Revolution—not to speak of our own spectatorship of televised courtroom "drama"—and make aesthetic judgment and moral and legal judgment appear disinterested not only in different but in entirely divergent ways. Yet another example of aesthetic judgment can serve to illustrate the way in which the two realms of judgment inevitably intersect.

The example—only as apparently trivial as Kant's—concerns a public judgment with potential legal consequences in an aesthetic matter that occupied, not very long ago, the gradual attention of the press.[28] This was not a judgment of whether something was or had the right to be considered art, by which the act of publicly and legally defining the proper sensory content of art objects is made into the medium for a sensationalist politics. Such "judgments" enact only the external pretense of judging, according to Kant; having no relation to disinterested experience, their correlates are calculable rather than aesthetic. These include not only the institution of artistic censorship and exclusion so invaluable to reducing to one single view all representations of the real under tyranny, but also, as recently enacted in our democratic nation, both the reduction or abolition of legally institutionalized public funding of the arts and their exhibition, and the enhancement of personal political (and financial) fortunes achieved on the back of these same arts at the ballot box.

Rather than a publicly enacted, political imposition of a single definition of the content and purpose of art, this relatively minor incident involved a private, profit-making body whose very existence as a public showcase depends on the celebrated universal appeal of the art it makes and exhibits. The art in question was dance, specifically, the single kind of dance that offers an obvious analogy to Kant's "free" or objectless beauty— line dancing—and the question raised was whether the aesthetic effect of one of the most viewed spectacles in the world would change if elements of its coloration changed. The decision was that it would, that the inclusion of another skin tone would destroy a famous model of dynamic form. Black dancers, it was argued aesthetically and, implicitly, legally, would mean the ruin of the Radio City Music Hall Rockettes.[29]

Now one might be tempted to say that the subject who made such a judgment had no understanding of aesthetic experience in the Kantian sense. But one could also say that he or she understood too well exactly that sense. What was being protected by an all-white dance company—so went the claim—was the much vaunted uniformity of the dancers, to which Kant's theory of aesthetic judgment responds unequivocally that uniformity, indeed, any foregrounding of formal delineation whatsoever, is the very basis of aesthetic experience to which color is fundamentally irrelevant. Precisely because line dancing, like "music without words," "represents nothing"—no object but its perceivable, formal self, or rather the dynamic impression it gives of form in motion—the color of the individual line segments that constitute it cannot matter in the least to its aesthetic effect. Just as those constitutive lines are drawn by scores of legs practiced to resemble the weightless limbs of marionettes—legs that please aesthetically precisely because, performing together, as part of a larger composition, they are no longer seen immediately as individual, objective legs—so the taint of the single line beneath leotard and stocking is no more significant, if indeed visible, than paint added, if ever it would be added, to an inanimate marionette. What matters alone is the "delineation" whose movement we follow with our eye, and, whatever we may think of them as a cultural institution, the uniform movements of nonpurposeful, uniform, and uniformed bodies may be as close to the "free," or objectively and conceptually undetermined "beauty" of wallpaper and seashells as conceptually weighted human bodies can get.

Yet what the artistic director(s) who made this decision historically ostensibly believed is that any visibility of another skin tone would destroy the aesthetic experience of uniformity itself: that there could be no objective "free beauty" of uniform patterns of movement and no subjective "free play of understanding and imagination" in their perception—in short, that there could be no possibility whatsoever of universal aesthetic judgment—when color instead came first, and color, they reasoned (from the "empirical conditions" of their "country"[30]), would always come first. In Kant, color—the most superficial of sensory qualities—does indeed come first, as pure surface without formal, i.e., effective or meaningful content, and for that very reason comes last aesthetically and matters least to judgment. But in a theater whose private productions of purposeless "free beauty" are at once based on the "presentation" and formation of a "normal idea of the beauty [of the human figure]" in an entire nation (and, by anthropologically ignorant extension, the world)—a venue of shows whose tourist spectators converge like TV viewers upon an "average" "image" they do not "fully reach" as individuals, nor see any individual attain in life,[31] but pay to see simulated by dint of the repetitive optical effect of staged " 'mirror images' "[32]—in such a theater, its artistic director might suppose, true aesthetic experience requires the artificial exclusion of color which the mind itself does not perform. Not only might color appear to blot out the delineation of pure movement being performed, making the dynamic, formal purposiveness of the dance appear instead invisible, but even worse: were a different color allowed to be visible and seen instead to make *no* visible difference in the compositional form, the result for the viewer might seem as disorderly as if the whole line of uniform movements had in fact fallen to pieces.

Thus it has proved harder to integrate the Christmas Show at Radio City than to sing "Ave Maria" at Carnegie Hall.[33] The comparison (while real) may, once again, appear trivial, but it is also no less apt. For, in direct contrast to the viewing of spectacles, in attending musical performances we both see and look past the performers before our eyes; were this not the case, we would not be attending the performance of *music*, and, along with the art of listening, the theatrical art of opera would not exist. It is vocal quality and not qualities of bodily image that make an operatic performer incorporate a specific dramatic part, and operatic staging, gesture, and costuming, while aiming at anything but uniformity, are all finally without effect upon the quality of tone one hears. In music, even or especially in its "highest" cultural forms, it is the invisible quality of sound that—true to Kant's description[34]—prevails. The aesthetic pleasure experienced in any musical tone cannot be confined to an "institutionally correct" skin "tone"; the "beauty" of musical "color" upstages all national "ideas"[35] concerning any other. For, were musicality linked directly and exclusively to spectatorship, the listening public, while still far from color-blind, would be obliged to be neither listening nor public: neither to hear music aesthetically, to experience pleasure in it, without consideration of visual, nonmusical information, nor to do so without the intervention of a country's privative "ideas" of beauty, merely "institutionally correct," contextually "average" images.

The culture of conventions and concepts that prescribes the norms of vision for spectatorship can rule music only when there is no music, no invisible art of movement to hear. Yet, in addition, it can or can be presumed to supplant pleasure in vision itself: its merely contingent interest in promoting a "normal idea" of beauty can be conceived as capable of overpowering the very act of disinterested judgment that occurs when we perceive dynamic form. We may never know, nor especially care to know, whether a commercial spectacle of line dancing would have indeed appeared any less pleasing were formal relations not preconceived in this culture as requiring, rather than precluding, the perception of (a single) color. We may never know in the case of the Radio City Music Hall what we may not know at higher institutions of cultural transmission for generations to come: in short, whether the *integrity* of aesthetic experience needs—nonsensically—to be protected from its own *integration*. Before raising the question of whether the culture of spectatorship, whose interest ruled in such a relatively innocuous (but, for that same reason, all the more memorable) matter, can also prevail in another, obviously more significant realm of judgment regarding uniform yet dynamic human form—that of the formal delineation of human life by universal law—it would be helpful to consider next a controversial legal proceeding of opposite stature that did in fact take place, a case involving documented crimes of inexaggerable dimension and gravity. In this criminal proceeding, purposefully staged in order to present the most arduous of international spectacles, the very different interests of another nation were at stake.

. . .

A "trial of the century" which had a real historical claim to that name, because it sought to try the crime of the century in both the objective and subjective senses—a crime without equal in kind whose commission also had the unique subjective requirement *that it be done disinterestedly, for its own sake,* while with a modern enthusiasm for inventing and implementing technology—the trial of Adolf Eichmann in Jerusalem in 1961 dealt with the mental abyss, the ultimate nonimagability to the mind's eye, of the most criminal performance of uniformity imaginable: no dance but the international synchronization of total extermination, the organized, repetitive production of determinedly uniform death. No trial since the Dreyfus Affair could have been of greater interest to an individual nation than the Eichmann trial, and none put the notion of disinterested judgment to a greater test, for the subject to be judged was the known and admitted director of the industrialized torture and murder of millions of civilians, including, and especially, children. The killing took place throughout, and across the boundaries of, the nations of Europe, usually with those nations' assistance; and the trial took place in the nation that succeeded Europe as the "home" of the victims, individuals sorted into infinitesimal fractions of mountains of shoes, teeth, and bone, unlocatable dead who had to find a metaphorical locus or dwelling—a place to be known as long as there was the will to know, and memory—as well as those few who, in surviving bodily, would never *themselves* survive, that is, mentally, and those others who would always know that their "escape" from universal annihilation had happened merely by historical and geographical accident. The trial of Adolf Eichmann was of supreme interest to the people of the nation in which it was held; it was that interest which, more than any religious laws, effectively made its disparate, immigrant population into a nation. Ignoring entirely the nature of the crime under consideration, one could call such a trial, staged to represent the national interest, a "show trial," but Ben-Gurion's government argued that the singular interest of its people in bringing Eichmann to justice was in fact what most qualified it to do so. Regarding the naive notion that such national interest was not and need not be at stake, or that the lack of its international equivalent lay in the previous unavailability of Eichmann alone—that "the Nuremberg Trials, where the defendants had been 'indicted for crimes against the members of various nations,' had left the Jewish tragedy out of account for the simple reason that Eichmann had not been there"—Hannah Arendt speculates in her landmark *Eichmann in Jerusalem*:

> Did Mr. Hausner [the prosecutor] really believe the Nuremberg Trials would have paid greater attention to the fate of the Jews if Eichmann had been in the dock? Hardly. Like almost everybody else in Israel, he believed that only a Jewish court could render justice to Jews, and that it was the business of Jews to sit in judgment on their enemies. Hence the almost universal hostility in Israel to the mere mention of an international court which would have indicted Eichmann, not for crimes "against the Jewish people," but for crimes against mankind committed on the body of the Jewish people. Hence the strange boast [of the prosecution]: "We make no ethnic distinctions" ["if we shall charge (Eichmann) also with crimes against non-Jews"].[36]

Thus, in the "trial of the century" in Jerusalem, interest and disinterest exchanged places. For if it was their own avowed interest that representatives of a specific nation argued qualified them alone to pass judgment on the architect of mass murder whose actions, give or take chance and circumstance, would have resulted in their death too, it was Eichmann, who, not only admitting but boasting of his actions,[37] pled his own *disinterestedness* in what he did as his defense. In what remains one of the most infamous, public references to moral philosophy, he claimed that the roots of that disinterest lay in his early reading of Kant. Arendt's comments on Eichmann's perversion of the notion of universal law are worth citing at length:

> The first indication of Eichmann's vague notion that there was more involved in this whole business than the question of the soldier's carrying out orders that are clearly criminal in nature and intent appeared during the police examination, when he suddenly declared with great emphasis that he had lived his whole life according to Kant's moral precepts, and especially according to a Kantian definition of duty. This was outrageous, on the face of it, and also incomprehensible, since Kant's moral philosophy is so closely bound up with man's faculty of judgment, which rules out blind obedience.... Judge Raveh, either out of curiosity or out of indignation at Eichmann's having dared to invoke Kant's name in connection with his crimes, decided to question the accused. And, to the surprise of everybody, Eichmann came up with an approximately correct definition of the categorical imperative: "I meant by my remark about Kant that the principle of my will must always be such that it can become the principle of general laws".... He then proceeded to explain that from the moment he was charged with carrying out the Final Solution he had ceased to live according to Kantian principles, that he had known it, and that he had consoled

himself with the thought that he no longer "was the master of his own deeds".... What he failed to point out in
court was that ... he had not simply dismissed the Kantian formula as no longer applicable, he had distorted it to
read: ... "Act in such a way that the Führer, if he knew
your action, would approve it".... Kant, to be sure, had
never intended to say anything of the sort; on the contrary, to him every man was a legislator the moment he
started to act: by using his "practical reason" man found
the principles that could and should be the principles of
law. But it is true that Eichmann's unconscious distortion
agrees with what he himself called the version of Kant
"for the household use of the little man." In this household use, all that is left of Kant's spirit is the demand that
a man do more than obey the law, that he go beyond the
mere call of obedience and identify his own will with the
principle behind the law.... In Kant's philosophy, that
source was practical reason; in Eichmann's household use
of him, it was the will of the Führer.[38]

If Eichmann was doing disinterestedly—or, as he repeatedly claimed, "idealistically"[39]—that which his nation, in the
person of the Führer, willed, thereby destroying utterly the
translatable content of the Kantian principle he continued to
follow only in its barest form, then in staging the kidnapping
and trial of Eichmann—a "spectacle" whose "sensational,"
"theatrical" quality Arendt critiques unsparingly from the outset
of her account[40]—Ben-Gurion's government was acting, as no
other government would for his, on the principle of a people's
and a nation's historical interest: "[f]or it was history that, as far
as the prosecution was concerned, stood in the center of the
trial."[41] Yet it was also history, in all its excruciating detail, that

ultimately undid the spectacle staged for its sake, the play in which, more than the individual under prosecution, it was made to occupy the central role and spotlight: "[i]t was precisely the play aspect of the trial that collapsed under the weight of the hair-raising atrocities" recounted by scores of survivors, Arendt states.[42]

While objecting to the trial as an ultimately unsustainable spectacle, Arendt argues against those critics of its staging, who, whatever their view of attempts to try history, "everywhere seem to be in . . . agreement that no one has the right to judge somebody else."[43] Judgment, she reminds us, has to be exercised upon an individual if a crime is to be tried at all: "insofar as [the Final Solution] remains a crime—and that, of course, is the premise for a trial—all the cogs in the machinery, no matter how insignificant, are in court forthwith transformed back into perpetrators, that is to say, into human beings [. . .] [a]nd the questions of individual guilt or innocence, the act of meting out justice to both the defendant and the victim, are the only things at stake in a criminal court."[44] While the theatrics of the trial, both desired and unavoidable, were undone by the unheard-of testimony of witnesses on the one hand, and, on the other, by Eichmann's exactly opposite inability to utter "a single sentence that was not a cliché" (including the most "thoughtless," "outrageous cliché" that, the war now being over, "he 'would like to find peace with [his] former enemies' "—"Eichmann's mind," Arendt notes, by way of a *sobering* resort to cliché, "was filled to the brim with such sentences"), the failure to have judged the accused at a particular moment in time as a particular individual, would have been the undoing of "the nature and function of human judgment."[45]

Arendt's defense of the Eichmann trial as a necessary proceeding, flawed in circumstance but not in substance, thus rests on the notion of defending the possibility of judgment itself. Reflecting back on the different conditions of judgment in Kant's related aesthetic and moral theory, we can say that practical legal judgment may be their nearest, while always imperfect synthesis, the necessary and necessarily incomplete union of objective and subjective disinterest. The failure to judge legally would thus constitute the failure of understanding and imagination to make moral principles apparent here and now: to themselves delineate the dynamic particulars of lived *and* perceived experience by the universal form of law.[46]

Rather than judge Eichmann, the individual, for his admitted crimes, even when those crimes presented the terrible precondition of destroying all known legal norms for judging, Ben-Gurion (unlike the three presiding judges) wished to present the trial itself as a "show" or spectacle of national and international interest, for, as Arendt observes, the Israeli government had " 'lessons' " to teach—"to Jews and Gentiles, to Israelis and Arabs, in short to the whole world."[47] And while those lessons, as "outlined" by Ben-Gurion himself, "before the trial started, in ... articles designed to explain why Israel had kidnapped the accused," "were meant to be different for the different recipients," it would not be unfair to summarize them now by a single hyperbole, a phrase of outrage and admonition, as warranted as it is wishful, which, despite its specificity, has become a stock phrase of political discourse, and even—when appropriated by those committing new criminal acts—a blinding, thoughtless cliché.

The lesson of the Eichmann criminal trial—as national (and international) spectacle—was the historical lesson and hyperbole: Never again. If it is worthwhile reviewing and analyzing the issues raised by the staging of that truly historic trial, in which the seats of interest and disinterest perversely, and perhaps uniquely, exchanged places, in the attempt to understand our own passionate conviction that in viewing the Simpson criminal trial, we were indeed watching, as advertised, "the trial of the century," it is because the national interest in trying history by trying Eichmann—rather than in trying and bringing to justice an individual[48]—reflects and reveals the nature and circumstances of the interest in the Simpson trial by inverting them. The specific empirical conditions that made the Eichmann trial, unlike the Nuremberg trials, a spectacle with a lesson to teach turn the conditions of interest in the Simpson trial upside down. They do this *instructively* because the Simpson trial, too, had a lesson to teach.

The lesson of the Simpson criminal trial—as national (and international) spectacle—was the historical lesson and hyperbole: Never again. Before examining the content of that formally identical lesson, we should note some of the major inversions of judicial circumstances between the two trials: a public crime of murder of unprecedented magnitude, dispassion, and technological sophistication on the one hand, and a brutal private crime, grouped under the far-too-familiar heading of "crime of passion," on the other; admitted, exhaustively and meticulously documented and witnessed criminal actions on the one hand, and an unwitnessed, inconclusively and sloppily documented and denied act on the other; volumes of open, if self-deceiving, evidence testified to by the only absolute expert in the matter, the avowedly unbiased, personally "disinterested" accused himself, on the one hand, and volumes of contradictory testimony by teams of experts assembled to investigate disputed evidence largely gathered by an official who formally deceived others regarding his own active bias against a group of people that includes the accused, on the other; the admission by the accused, not only of his systematic criminal actions, committed from an administrative remove, over several years, but of their "objective" motivation, his desire for professional advancement in a society in which (thanks to "disinterested," ambitious individuals like himself) mass murder was law, on the one hand, and the inability of the prosecution to construct a plausible motive or time frame for two murders committed manually, at closest range, on the part of someone who knew that his ambition for professional advancement in society would always depend on the safeguarding of his own unthreatening image, on the other.

Even such a perfunctory contrast of the concrete rudiments of these two "trial[s] of the century" can serve to demonstrate the enormous circumstantial gulf between them. But, in addition, it can help to give us some insight into the extraordinary interest in the Simpson trial by bringing the deepest inversion of circumstance between them into relief. That circumstance concerns elements not of the crimes themselves, nor of their trials, but, again, of those trials' receptions, indicating what "never again" in each of their national contexts means.

Never again, the lesson and interest of the trial of Eichmann in Jerusalem, would have meant: no more trust in others to protect us and render us justice, and no more trust in others not to persecute us "by law," not to murder us, or to shelter us from murderers and enslavers. Never again, the lesson and interest of the trial of Simpson in Los Angeles, would carry the same meaning, *just inverted:* no more trust in those we enacted laws against, persecuted, murdered, and had enslaved. "Never again," meaning *not:* no more suffering of injustice and deferral of justice for the crimes committed against us as a specific people, since we, as a people, can remember; but rather: *no more* justice or remedy sought for a people historically made the anonymous objects of crimes that continue to be committed precisely by changing with the times, thereby causing them to be defined (as crimes) only and always after the fact by individual judges deemed miraculously enlightened, since their own brethren had long defined them as innocent or beneficent practices in accordance with national norms. In short: no more rhetoric about colorblindness; absolutely no more non-color-blind affirmative action; and above, or underneath all, no more miscegenation.

For surely no one in this nation can reasonably doubt, that had Simpson, *the individual*, been tried for the murder of *individuals*, his trial would never have "made it to prime time"—or only occasionally, on slow news nights—and his acquittal, founded on the universal *legal* principle of reasonable doubt, would never have provoked calls for the abolition of the jury system (as the acquittal in Simi Valley of *all* the policemen *filmed* beating an unarmed black motorist nearly to death did not, and generations of hanging or—if the defendants were white—walking juries in the Jim Crow south also did not). What made it every night to prime time, and what made viewers contemptuous in their certainty of conviction of such legal "niceties" as perjury and noncredible testimony and preparation and presentation of evidence, was our particular national history, a history of which, suddenly, these viewers no longer saw themselves the victors. If through the spectacle of the Eichmann trial a nation of citizens directly affected by the defendant's undisputed crimes said to the world, we who try this defendant will never be anyone's victims again, the spectacle of the Simpson trial said to its (nonblack) viewers, not only two brutally murdered individuals but you, too, are Simpson's victims, and Simpson could be anyone who "passed" when you weren't looking—that is, exactly when you were looking—so that now you see the whole natural order of things come, as it always had to come, crashing down. Performing in such perfect and superficial synchrony with the norms of the spectacles that most please us as a nation—in collegiate and professional sports, in TV and film, even as a profitable image for corporations—Simpson momentarily became invisible to us for what he really is: someone whose skin tone we were fooled into not seeing by our pleasure in seeing his beauty, a pleasure—*undisturbed by any appeal to content on Simpson's part*—which began when, as if forgetting what comes first in our normal idea of the beauty of the human form, we watched his uniformed body move dynamically within the purposive play of a game.

That, of course, was before black "crossover" stars from sports and entertainment became a new American cultural norm, not to speak of the propagation in advertising of a painter's palette aesthetic of human form. It was before kids of all classes and colors, and scores of competing white designers, made the visual aesthetics of blackness into their stock costume and pose. And that, of course, is precisely the problem: we need only see where history has taken us. That was once, that was then; this is going on and on, ineluctably, now, and Benetton ads aim at the consumption of clothes in many colors, not the multicultures that can eventuate in interracial marriage. The altogether extraordinary sensory experience where color, mattering least, must be recalled to matter most; the pleasure other languages and cultures unsentimentally call love and we, as if to bring the body even more literally before our eyes, call sex—the possibility of a deep, personal interest whose *public* acknowledgement wreaks havoc on our national interest in maintaining normative ideas of beauty—this is what we have come to since Simpson crossed the color line decades ago. The Simpson trial showed its spectators that the direct result of such historical "progress" was bloody murder: they need not read the "signs of history"—and certainly not the countersign of their own passionately self-interested reception of the trial—for they need no longer wonder where history was tending; like Simpson's guilt and the "reason" for it, the course of history, past and future, was not even a subject of speculation. For they could see the spectacle of its final image and exchange places with its victims. Day after day, viewers could say, look: Never again.

If we have come to the point where a black and a white individual can find *each other* beautiful, in public view, we have come to the breaking point in the logic of the historical idea that remains the motor and springboard of our civilization. In the remarkable early article on totalitarianism, "Ideology and Terror: A Novel Form of Government," Arendt describes the contradiction between "totalitarian lawfulness" and "legality" in terms later echoed by her analysis of the Eichmann trial: the accused's perverse use of Kantian universal law as a basis for nullifying the need for judgment, and the Israeli government's understandable, if infeasible attempt to try the history of anti-Semitism in trying the individual criminal, Eichmann:

> Totalitarian lawfulness pretends to have found a way to establish the rule of justice on earth—something which the legality of positive law admittedly could never attain. The discrepancy between legality and justice could never be bridged because the standards of right and wrong into which positive law translates its own source of authority—"natural law" governing the whole universe, or divine law revealed in human history or customs and traditions expressing the law common to the sentiments of all men—are necessarily general and must be valid for a countless and unpredictable number of cases, so that each

concrete individual case with its unrepeatable set of circumstances somehow escapes it.

Totalitarian lawfulness, defying legality and pretending to establish the direct reign of justice on earth, executes the law of History or of Nature without translating it into standards of right and wrong for individual behavior. It applies the law directly to mankind without bothering with the behavior of men.[49]

The necessary "preparation" for embracing the rule of "Nature or History" on earth, and thereby obliterating all consideration of the individual case, is the explanation of the world in purely formal terms that for Arendt defines "ideology:" "[a]n ideology is quite literally what its name indicates: it is the *logic of an idea*."[50] That idea defines "the movement of history" the way one deducts a conclusion from a premise: "[]ideologies always assume that one idea is sufficient to explain everything in the development from the premise, and that no experience can teach anything because everything is comprehended in this consistent process of logical deduction."[51] Thus, "[r]acism is the belief that there is a motion inherent in the very 'idea' of race, just as deism is the belief that a motion is inherent in the very notion of God."[52]

According to this analysis, founded by Arendt in a biting critique of "the logical" or analytic "movement in philosophy," rather than of Marx or the Frankfurt School, as one might expect,[53] ideology—at least in totalitarian society—is not a sophisticated superstructure for mediating and disarming active forms of opposition but an atrociously simplistic, literalistic primer for action. Ideology says that we must indeed mean what we say; it creates and then takes literally its own clichés:

"[w]hoever agreed that there are such things as 'dying classes' and did not draw the consequence of killing their members, or that the right to live had something to do with race and did not draw the consequence of killing 'unfit races,' was plainly either stupid or a coward."[54]

It is not the idea of an ideology but its "stringent logicality" that brooks no exceptions, Arendt notes. Reminding us of the symbolic alphabet of mental progress that so menaced Mr. Ramsay, Virginia Woolf's stymied analytic philosopher ("Q he could demonstrate. If Q then is Q—R—. . . . What is R?"), she explains that such logicality admits to absolutely no mental impediments: "an argument of which Hitler like Stalin was very fond, is: You can't say A without saying B and C and so on, down to the end of the murderous alphabet."[55] "You" have to draw out the deduction from the premise to its ultimate conclusion (as if such endgames were ever possible), and the "you" indicated here is no mere rhetorical device or floating pronominal marker, for it puts the individual who defined his or her own life's actions in accordance with a specific premise directly on the spot. Critiquing, again, the intellectual abyss of a universally leveling logicality, rather than ruminating about modern mass psychology, with its imponderable calculations of group to individual will,[56] Arendt proceeds to make her most striking observation regarding the deeply personal motivation for maintaining the logic of ideology. "Here"—in the apparently "disinterested" adherence to an idea—"the coercive force of logicality seems to have its source; it springs from our fear of contradicting ourselves."[57]

If, contrary to the view of a war criminal whose effort to realize the enforcement of logicality on earth reached nearly to "z," "the murderous alphabet" of ideology is indeed always profoundly and unthinkingly *self-interested*, the self-contradiction that adherents of ideology fear is not the "disinterested" "partiality" of Kant's judgment: it is the destruction of the "premise" (literally, presetting) or stage upon which they view themselves as subjects acting in sync with History, and the fear of self-contradiction is not the fear of history but the feeling that one may have taken contingently fabricated clichés for eternal verities, "self"-evident tautologies for "signs of history," and so read the "tendency" of history, and thus of one's own life, wrong, if at all.

If there is an underlying idea whose logic levels the differences of individual existence in our democratic nation, it is the ideology of racial separation as the basis of civilization. Nothing that took place in the Simpson trial *could* contradict the idea of guilt beyond any reasonable doubt because, having broken the surface of this idea—having successfully and legally crossed the color line without indicating that, once on the "other" side, he would still know how to maintain that line (and, with it, civilized society)—Simpson, by the higher laws of History and Nature, would ultimately kill most savagely, and so was not entitled to the due process of law upon which the society to be protected was based. Arendt had importantly noted that one of the peculiarities of the logic of ideology was its inevitable tendency to "devour" its content, "the original substance upon which the ideologies based themselves as long as they had appeal to the masses."[58] Thus the ideology that appealed to "the national aspirations of Germany ... did not pay the slightest regard to the minimum requirements for survival of the German nation:" "it is the nature of ideological politics," she observes, "that the real content of the ideology ... which originally had brought about the 'idea' (the struggle of classes as the law of history or the struggle of races as the law of nature), is devoured by the logic with which the 'idea' is carried out."[59] The "inherent" logic of an idea, or, rather, its active production as ideology, eventually destroys the originally appealing basis for its formulation.

A civilized, democratically lawful society that ideologically equates the content of civilization with the idea of racial separation (and ours is not the only one) would devour that very content in the spectacle of laws being applied where, "logically," they would no longer apply. And the interest of such a society in such a spectacle would have to be absolutely compelling, for what could be more compelling—terrifying and spellbinding—than the sight of a civilization, by its own logic, devouring its own substance, the universal legal procedures, limits, and constraints devised to protect not only each individual defendant but the greater principle of disinterested judgment itself. The interest of the Simpson trial was in disrespecting disinterest, in watching guilt defined in advance by the logic of an idea concerning civilization, redefine the very principles of the society to be protected as outrageous formalities. While by no means the trial of the century, *as received by the public* the Simpson trial did have this particularity: never in America was a trial so desired and detested *as a trial*, never were legal procedures and *all* their agents—the presiding judge, lawyers from both sides of the aisle, and the entire jury—subjected to more detailed scrutiny *and* contempt. In a fundamental sense, the trial went on and on, consuming the gaze of the nation in prime time, because, from the point of view of the nation, it should never have gone on at all. According to its intensely interested viewers, the trial (as the verdict only proved) was a painstaking exercise in superfluity, yet it was an exercise which they—without fear of contradicting themselves—*wanted to see take place.* Their eyes remained trained on the central character of the spectacle, a defendant whose image, trespassing upon and partly altering national aesthetic norms, they had formerly viewed with pleasure. Now, thanks to the trial that should not have been, they could see him for "what" he was; day after day they could "see" his previously invisible culpability, his "true colors" (a "thoughtless" cliché whose content was also literalized and destroyed in the course of the trial, in the only "logical" way it could have been—through actual, visible *falsification*, the darkened photograph of the defendant disseminated nationally on the cover of *Time*). The eyes of the trial's viewers may have focused with undivided interest on Simpson, but the intensity of their gaze was that of a nation of laws hungrily consuming itself.

In effect, nothing in the Simpson trial could constitute the legal basis for reasonable doubt—no conflicting "expert" testimony, no evidence of a botched investigation, no lying under oath, nor voluntary, taped admission by an investigating officer of his hatred for interracial couples, of his having already actively harassed them, and framed black citizens; and certainly not the first available body of evidence, that of the defendant himself, which showed no indication of having engaged in the extremely violent struggle to commit especially gruesome and bloody murder upon two fully conscious victims fighting for their lives. Reasonable doubt could not be applied by anyone, black or white, to this particular trial because there could be no doubt how and why this crime occurred. The logic of racial separation already showed beyond a doubt that if A and B, then C..., the formula for understanding history which in this instance may be fairly parsed as follows: With every step taken in this nation since Lincoln, with every new piece of legislation bought with blood, sewn into the fabric of society as if to suture the wounds of flesh whipped by fellow citizens and bitten by police dogs, as if to mend forever bones cracked by clubs, to restore bodies seared by flames; with every provision focused on the future as if to continue in imagination the lives of murdered children, with every motion, word, thought, law and statute meant to make the absence of racism imaginable, to make the bridging of racial separation imaginable, and one day, which will not look or feel like history till that day, reality—with every movement away from the logic of racial separation we have moved closer and closer to the murder of Nicole Brown Simpson and Ronald Goldman. If A and B, then C: the consuming interest of the trial was to know not whether Simpson was guilty, but to know by seeing with one's own eyes that freeing the slaves, and all the fiercely embattled, legal increments of freedom that have followed the end of violently enforced racial separation in our nation's history, killed most savagely these most unfortunate, (racially) incautious, (white) people.

For the disproportionate public focus on the victimization of Nicole Brown Simpson, and marginalization of Ronald Goldman, underscored by a newfound, universal abhorrence of thoroughly condemnable—but in this case legally inconclusive—incidents of domestic violence (bolstered again in the public mind by doctored photography, this time on national television: a computer-generated image, rotated in three dimensions, of what the beaten Mrs. Simpson "really" looked like), indicate the strange mental hybrid that took the place of disinterested judgment in this trial. For like every ideology, the "pure" or inherent logic of racial separation has its own binding aesthetic and moral laws; indeed, like every ideology, it binds those laws into an aesthetic moralism, a single dogmatic norm. The Simpson trial has been readily identified with *Othello*, but its drama lay elsewhere, for no one can read or view *Othello* and believe the root of evil lay not with Iago, or that Othello and Desdemona did not love each other, or that their "mixed" marriage was blasphemy. Too many white husbands murder too many white wives, and cause the ruin of too many white lovers and daughters in Shakespeare (and in the everyday history of the world), and they do so for more ignominious reasons than carefully fomented jealousy, for the tragedy of Desdemona and Othello to offer anything but another thoughtless cliché in relation to our nation's consuming spectacle. But the clumsy application of Shakespeare does serve to illustrate the mental rules of thumb that united in the reception of the Simpson trial. While no writer or artist in the entire English-American tradition may be further removed from the limits prescribed by aesthetic moralisms than Shakespeare, viewers of the trial understood the death that most interested them according to a simple equation of morals with aesthetics: its primary victim was tragically blind to the fact that mixing skin tones is evil.

While to Americans, and not to the author of *Othello*, miscegenation remains the ultimate, logical catastrophe for an ideology of racial separation—so that some black American viewers, more divided over the probability of Simpson's guilt than the media were interested to present, could quip ironically that the nation had certainly come full circle from the time when the crime a black man was most terrified and likely to be accused of was that of seeming to think about a white woman; and so that some white viewers, more divided than the media were interested to present, could call the verdict, most bizarrely and tellingly, a thirty-year "setback to civil rights" (all those incremental gains of freedom which, ostensibly, they had *previously* supported)—the prospect of miscegenation also ensures that the logic of that ideology can be palpably demonstrated: that A and B can indeed *be seen* to result in C. The fact of this particular "C," of no accidental or arbitrary union but a mixing of colors based on free and mutual personal interest, similarly left none of these viewers in doubt that what they had seen was not the trying of an individual for the murder of individuals but the trying of national history.

In saying the Simpson trial was viewed as a trying of national history "now" concluded in the form of an admonishing lesson, we should, however, remember the dynamic that is fundamental to the history of this nation in particular, and virtually impossible to conclude, in any place or at any time, as a lesson. In America, perhaps more than any other nation, national history is, brutally and blissfully, the complex history of freedom. In America this has meant—from the beginning—the freedom both to be free *and* enslave another people; the freedom to live where you want *and* kill another people already living there; the freedom to live the way you want *and* to censure anyone who does not live as you do; the freedom to pursue your own happiness and prosperity *and* in so doing use your wealth to "protect your own interests" and destroy the happiness of others. Freedom, in America especially, has always been two-faced, for it has never followed a single chain of command. A nation that prizes its freedom of religious belief, has no history whatsoever of religious justification for authority, or of any order defined and administered from the top down, and yet always needs its leaders to remind it (when they themselves can recall) that they do not live in a pre-enlightenment theocracy; a nation that originated as a "universal" democracy *for some people*, and that, *composed exclusively of immigrants* (whether voluntary or enslaved), is or can be made hostile to immigrants in every succeeding generation—such a nation, as *all* its citizens do seem to notice, cannot afford to take freedom lightly. For they never know when "theirs" will become the victim of someone else's.

Freedom in this nation has the unfortunate tendency to act, not like Kant's universal law, but like a direct hit, a transitive verb. Rather than ensuring acts that must be viewed as translatable, without contradiction, into the second and third persons, the "enjoyment" of freedom in America often includes activities that make those persons their objects, taking from them their right as subjects to speak publicly for themselves. Yet for the same structural reason it has never managed to follow to its single "logical" conclusion the simple formulaic replacement for thinking that states, if A, then B and C. . . . Finally—and even if the defendant had not been acquitted—what the terribly interested viewers of the Simpson trial were watching in a very concrete way was the trying of that formula, *and of its opposite*, the nation's freedom. And what they wanted to know was certainly not whether this particular defendant "did it," but rather: how free can we, can "I," afford to be? Is freedom freedom, or does it require an ideology of cause and effect, of agent and object of action; is freedom the law or is it war? If the history of the freedom of action some of us are born with and some of us have to win daily has resulted in the Simpsons (and only in America could that name double simultaneously as the title of a comic cartoon show about the freedom of a white family to do, essentially, nothing), has history—have "we"—not gone "too far"? Must we not say *to freedom*, with all the dangers of its dynamic, formal delineations of every kind, from the apparently most trivial performances to the most substantive legal decisions; to freedom, with its interplay of understanding and imagination, the inability of its aesthetic content to remain normative, and of its judgments to be self-interested; must we not say to our history, the history not of oppression by another power but of freedom for some, a legal democracy of which we now see ourselves the victims: never again?

To which one can only respond, when? When *was* freedom ours alone and uncomplicated; when did it give anyone the right to speak for someone else and say, you shall never think, never judge for yourself, and when did it not include contradicting ourselves, lest we define our own selves as the merely interested agents of ideology. "Freedom as an inner capacity of man"—Arendt (echoing Kant) concludes in her analysis of ideology—"is identical with the capacity to begin, just as freedom as a political reality is identical with a space of movement between men.... Over the beginning, no logic, no cogent deduction can have any power," and just "[a]s terror is needed lest with the birth of each new human being a new beginning arise and raise its voice in the world, so the self-coercive force of logicality is mobilized lest anybody ever start thinking—which as the freest and purest of all human activities is the very opposite of the compulsory process of deduction."[60] Profit-minded television rather than state terror may be the user-friendly medium for reinforcing the iron chain of "logicality" in our democracy, the "compulsive process of deduction" of ideology that made the Simpson trial a spectacle of compelling national interest. But before deciding we have all had enough of freedom (for others), the viewers of the trial who concluded the necessary end of history from A and B might try instead to *begin* to be free; and that would have little to do with a private murder trial made public moral theater by a mixing of colors disallowed in the public aesthetics of private theaters, and everything to do instead with the private capacity for disinterested public judgment, with thinking. For we cannot know in advance—and so must judge here and now—whether our own personally disinterested partiality in any instance will spell a true "sign of history," but we can agree that only in the mix of such disinterestedness do we freely compose a "mode of thought," and perhaps progress.

Notes

1. Immanuel Kant, "Was ist Aufklärung?" in *Was ist Aufklarung?*, ed. Erhard
    Bahr (Stuttgart: Reclam, 1976), p. 11; "What is Enlightenment?" in *Kant
    on History*, ed. Lewis White Beck (Indianapolis: Bobbs-Merrill, 1963),
    p. 5 (translation modified to better reflect the German text).

2. On a single personal note, I should state that I myself was able to dis-
    regard that interest—as transparently voyeuristic, racially motivated,
    and embarrassingly self-interested—until a casual encounter instructed
    me how much was at stake for others in Simpson's fate. Upon congrat-
    ulating in passing a professedly apolitical acquaintance on the recogni-
    tion recently awarded what had been up to then *his life's work*, I was told
    with exasperation that the outcome of the Simpson trial had negated
    any pleasure he could have taken in his good fortune. By contrast, the
    same individual responded with a nonchalance bordering on heedless-
    ness to the assassination, roughly one month thereafter, of Yitzhak
    Rabin. Now, by any account—that is, including his assassin's—Rabin
    was a genuinely unique, historic figure, one whose compelling *symbolic*
    significance, based on *actual*, nationally and internationally significant
    deeds, was the bittersweet fruit of a lifetime of hard-fought accom-
    plishments. If not those real achievements, then surely Rabin's stature,
    character, and ethnicity should have made him of considerable, even
    vital interest to my acquaintance, or, at very least, made his murder—
    committed so as to alter the lives of millions, to alter history itself—
    give pause. It did not in the slightest. I mention and compare these
    incidents only to underscore the extraordinary nature of the interest
    (and, in this case, ire) that the Simpson trial, the trying of a particular
    private crime, aroused in the viewing public, an interest capable—as tra-
    ditionally befits a monumental public crime—even of eclipsing one's
    own personal happiness.

3. Kant, "Was ist Aufklärung?" para. 1–2, p. 9; "What is Enlighten-
    ment?" p. 3.

4. Kant, *Schriften zur Metaphysik und Logik 2, Werkausgabe* Bd. VI, ed. Wilhelm
    Weischedel (Frankfurt: Suhrkamp, 1981), p. 457; *Logic*, tr. Richard Hart-
    man and Wolfgang Schwartz (Indianapolis: Bobbs-Merrill, 1974), p. 37.

5. Kant, *Grundlegung zur Metaphysik der Sitten* (2d ed. 1789) (Stuttgart:
    Reclam, 1996), pp. 40–42; *Groundwork of the Metaphysic of Morals*, tr. H. J.
    Paxton (New York: Harper & Row, 1964), pp. 70–71. The very term

"categorical," signifying independent or unconditional, was primarily
used by Kant as a way to distinguish one single universal principle from
all "hypothetical imperatives," those "concerned [instead] with the
choice of means" to obtaining a certain end (see Ger. pp. 58–61; Eng.
pp. 82–84).

6.   *Ibid.*, pp. 40, 43 (Ger. [emphasis in text]); pp. 70–71 ([Eng.]). On Kant's
      own skepticism regarding the purely speculative notion of a categori-
      cal imperative, see my " 'Is that Helen?': Contemporary Pictorialism,
      Lessing, and Kant," *Comparative Literature* 45 (Summer 1993): 230–57
      (253–54).

7.   *Ibid.*, p. 43 (Ger.); p. 71 (Eng.).

8.   *Ibid.*

9.   See Kant's description of the place of judgment in his critical "sys-
      tem," or tripartite, systematic critique of reason, in the Introduction to
      his *Kritik der Urteilskraft, Werkausgabe* Bd. X, ed. Wilhelm Weischedel
      (Frankfurt: Suhrkamp, 1974), pp. 85–87; *Critique of Judgment,* tr. J. H.
      Bernard (New York: Macmillan, 1951), pp. 13–15: "in the family of the
      supreme cognitive faculties there is a middle term between the under-
      standing and the reason [*ein Mittelglied zwischen dem Verstande und der Ver-
      nunft*]. This is the *judgment.* . . . Although . . . philosophy can be divided
      only into two main parts, the theoretical and the practical, and
      although all that we may be able to say of the special principles of
      judgment must be counted as belonging in it to the theoretical
      part . . . , yet the critique of pure reason, which must decide all this, as
      regards the possibility of the system before undertaking it, consists of
      three parts: the critique of pure understanding, of pure judgment, and
      of pure reason. . . . Judgment in general is the faculty of thinking the
      particular as contained under the universal."

10.   See Kant, "Zum ewigen Frieden: ein philosophischer Entwurf," in
      *Schriften zur Anthropologie, Geschichtsphilosophie, Politik und Pädagogik 1, Werkaus-
      gabe* Bd. XI, ed. Wilhelm Weischedel (Frankfurt: Suhrkamp, 1993), pp.
      193–251 (208, 223, 232); "Perpetual Peace," in *Kant on History,* pp. 83–136
      (97, 111, 119 [translation modified]).

11.   Kant, *Der Streit der Fakultäten,* in *Schriften zur Anthropologie,* pp. 357, 361
      (emphasis in text); *The Contest of the Faculties,* Part II: "An Old Question
      Raised Again: Is the Human Race Constantly Progressing?" in *Kant on
      History,* pp. 137–54 (pp. 147, 143 [translation modified to better reflect
      the German text]).

12. *Ibid.* (emphasis in text).

13. *Ibid.*, p. 357 (Ger.); p. 143 (Eng.).

14. *Ibid.*, pp. 357–59 (Ger.); pp. 143–45 (Eng.).

15. The question, familiar by Kant's time, of whether humanity was steadily, intellectually, and morally "progressing," provides the title, noted in n11 above, of Part II of *The Contest of the Faculties* in which the spectatorship of the French Revolution is discussed: "An Old Question Raised Again: Is the Human Race Constantly Progressing?" ("Erneuerte Frage: ob das menschliche Geschlecht im Beständigen Fortschreiten zum Besseren sei?"). Kant's ultimate answer to this question—"a proposition valid for the most rigorous theory, in spite of all skeptics, and not just a well-meaning and practically commendable proposition: that the human race has always been in progress toward the better and will continue to so progress henceforth" (*Ibid.*, p. 362 [Ger.]; pp. 147–48 [Eng.; translation modified to better reflect the German text])—stands in direct opposition to the view argued earlier by Rousseau, in his prize-winning *Discours sur les arts et les sciences* (1751), although it was Rousseau whom Kant credited with his own awakening to the critically crucial concept of self-legislating, or moral, freedom.

16. *Ibid.*, p. 364 (Ger.); p. 150 (Eng. [translation modified to better reflect the German text]).

17. *Ibid.*, p. 361 (Ger.); p. 147 (Eng.).

18. Kant, *Kritik der Urteilskraft*, sec. 2, pp. 116–17; *Critique of Judgment*, pp. 38–39 (my emphasis [translation modified to better reflect the German text]).

19. *Ibid.*, sec. 5, p. 124 (Ger.); p. 45 (Eng.). On form, see Introduction, pp. 102ff (Ger.); pp. 28ff (Eng.); sec. 10, p. 135 (Ger.); p. 55 (Eng.) *et al.*

20. *Ibid.*, sec. 9, p. 132 (Ger.); p. 52 (Eng.).

21. *Ibid.*, sec. 10, p. 135 *et al.* (Ger.), ; p. 55 *et al.* (Eng.).

22. "Every purpose, if it be regarded as the ground of satisfaction, always carries with it—as the determining ground of the judgment—an interest about the object of pleasure. Therefore no subjective purpose can lie at the basis of the judgment of taste. But the judgment of taste can also not be determined by the representation of an objective purpose, i.e., of the possibility of the object itself in accordance with principles of purposive combination, and consequently by no concept of the good, because it is an aesthetical and not a cognitive judgment. . . . [T]hus it is the mere form of purposiveness in the represen-

tation by which an object is *given* to us, so far as we are conscious of it, which constitutes the satisfaction that we, without a concept, judge to be universally communicable and, with it, the determining ground of the judgment of taste" (*Ibid.*, sec. 11, p. 136 [Ger.; emphasis in text]; p. 56 [Eng.; translation modified to better reflect the German text]); *Der Streit der Fakultäten*, p. 357 (Ger.); p. 143 (Eng.).

23.   *Ibid.*, sec. 14, pp. 139–41 (Ger. [emphasis in text]); pp. 59–61 (Eng. [translation modified to better reflect the German text]).

24.   *Ibid.*, sec. 17, pp. 152–53 (Ger. [emphasis in text]); pp. 71–72 (Eng.).

25.   *Ibid.*

26.   "Arbitrary" here does not mean that any tone of music or color may simply be substituted for another, but rather that their composition, by *its* own formal nature, means that all constitutive tones can be—and regularly are—"transposed," shifted to fit different keys, scales, ranges, fields, and instruments. No musician and no painter, not even—as we say of both—a "colorist," could work in his or her art if this were not the case.

27.   *Ibid.*, sec. 16, p. 146 (Ger.); p. 66 (Eng.).

28.   See *The New York Times*, March 21, 1982, II, 1:5; May 31, 1985, I, 27:2; December 26, 1987, II, 25:5, 27:1; January 13, 1988, I, 22:2.

29.   When the issue was first raised in print, on the occasion of Radio City's fiftieth-anniversary celebration, the then director of the Rockettes stated that while, on the one hand, black auditioners in New York had not been qualified for the job, another consideration quite outweighed the question of qualifications: "the No. 1 reason is that the Rockettes are a precision line, and they are supposed to be mirror images on stage. One or two black girls in the line would definitely distract. You would lose *the look* of precision which is the hallmark of the Rockettes" (*NY Times*, March 21, 1982, II, 1:5 [my emphasis]). Recalling these comments in an Op-Ed piece that appeared in the *Times* a few years later, a lawyer, Gregory J. Peterson, made the direct connection between a racially based aesthetics and potential illegality, suggesting that while it may indeed be difficult to apply "the Civil Rights Act of 1964" to performing arts, racial "authenticity" must be viewed as having nothing to do with the nature and success of the Rockettes' performance; that no suit had been brought against the Rockettes was due to their own high profile and well-known discouragement of black applicants, he suggested (*NY Times*, May 31, 1985, I, 27:2). When the first

black dancer was chosen "to be on call for vacancies," some years after the publication of Peterson's Op-Ed article, a brief editorial comment in the *Times* again took up the issue of why "no one ever filed a complaint" against the Rockettes' management, stating that New York City's Human Rights Commission "gave priority to other discrimination less visible but more pervasive," but insisting: "[c]onsidering the Rockettes' dazzling visibility, it's disappointing that no one kicked loud enough to change the routine before now" (*NY Times*, January 13, 1988, I, 22:2).

30. On national, "normal idea[s]," see Kant, n24, this essay, and the representative comment by the founder of the Rockettes, quoted in the *Times*, that he had never allowed a Rockette to get a suntan, " 'because it would make her look like a colored girl' " (*NY Times*, December 26, 1987, II, 27:1).

31. See n25, this essay.

32. See n29, this essay.

33. While in response to a recent informal inquiry it was suggested that the Rockettes have now "long" been integrated, it was also stated, upon questioning, that such integration may not in fact be visible on the mainstage, at Radio City, but may take place instead in satellite shows and events around the country (just as the first black Rockette, chosen as a substitute nine years ago, was to perform at halftime at the Superbowl).

34. Cf. n27, this essay.

35. See n23, n24, n25, this essay.

36. Hannah Arendt, *Eichmann in Jerusalem: A Report on the Banality of Evil* (New York: Penguin Books, 1977 [1st ed. 1963]), pp. 6–7.

37. Arendt quotes Eichmann "bragging" to "his men during the last days of the war: 'I will jump into my grave laughing, because the fact that I have the death of five million Jews [or 'enemies of the Reich,' as he always claimed to have said] on my conscience gives me extraordinary satisfaction.' . . . [H]e had kept repeating the damning sentence *ad nauseam* to everyone who would listen, even twelve years later in Argentina, because it gave him 'an extraordinary sense of elation to think that [he] was exiting from the stage in this way" (*Ibid.*, pp. 46–47; see also p. 52). On the other hand, while admitting to the "facts, established 'beyond reasonable doubt' long before the trial started" (p. 56), Eichmann "steadfastly insisted that he was guilty only of 'aiding and abetting' in

the commission of the crimes with which he was charged, that he himself had never committed an overt act" (p. 246).

38. *Ibid.,* pp. 135–37.

39. See *ibid.,* pp. 41–42: "The perfect 'idealist,' like everybody else, had of course his personal feelings and emotions, but he would never permit them to interfere with his actions if they came into conflict with his 'idea' " (p. 42).

40. See *ibid.,* pp. 4–6, 8–9. Excepting from her critique the presiding judges alone—"[a]t no time is there anything theatrical in the conduct of the judges" (p. 4)—Arendt nonetheless observes: "[y]et no matter how consistently the judges shunned the limelight, there they were, seated at the top of the raised platform, facing the audience as from the stage in a play. The audience was supposed to represent the whole world, and in the first few weeks it indeed consisted chiefly of newspapermen and magazine writers who had flocked to Jerusalem from the four corners of the earth. They were to watch a spectacle as sensational as the Nuremberg Trials, only this time 'the tragedy of Jewry as a whole was to be the central concern' " (p. 6).

41. *Ibid.,* p. 19.

42. *Ibid.,* pp. 8–9.

43. *Ibid.,* p. 296.

44. *Ibid.,* pp. 289, 298.

45. *Ibid.,* pp. 48, 53, 294. It was the "sheer thoughtlessness" of Eichmann's overwhelming reliance upon cliché, the "inability to speak . . . connected with an inability to *think,* namely, to think from the stand point of somebody else," that Arendt controversially termed "the banality of evil," indicating thereby not the evil committed, but the profound stupidity or "lack of imagination" that eases, and even finds "the words" to justify its commission (pp. 287, 49).

46. While this particular connection between Kant's aesthetic and moral theory is not drawn out by Arendt, her writings, consistently concerned with the public and political act of judgment, paid increasing attention, after the Eichmann trial, to the ramifications she found implicit in the definition of judgment by Kant. In at least one instance identifying judgment with thinking itself, she sought to recast the power of imagination elaborated positively, for the first time in philosophy, in Kant's *Third Critique*—the same capacity so absolutely, murderously absent in the "sheer thoughtlessness" of Eichmann—as a

Socratic ability to conduct a dialogue with one's self by imagining events from the point of view of another within the self. See her important statement in Arendt, "Personal Responsibility under Dictatorship" (published in *The Listener*, Aug. 6, 1964, pp. 185–87, 205), that those who refused to participate in fascism "were unwilling to live together with a murderer—themselves. The presupposition for this kind of judging is not a highly developed intelligence or sophistication in moral matters, but merely the habit of living together explicitly with oneself, that is, of being engaged in that silent dialogue between me and myself which since Socrates and Plato we usually call thinking. . . . This kind of thought, though at the root of all philosophical thinking, is not technical and does not concern theoretical problems. The dividing line between those who judge and those who do not strikes across all social and cultural or education differences" (p. 205). See also Arendt, "Ideology and Terror: A Novel Form of Government," *The Review of Politics* 15 (July 1953): 303–27: "All thinking, strictly speaking, is done in solitude and is a dialogue between me and myself" (p. 324); and the slightly different, Heideggerian emphasis in Arendt, "Understanding and Politics," *Partisan Review* 20 (1953): 377–92: "Even though we have lost yardsticks by which to measure, and rules under which to subsume the particular, a being whose essence is beginning may have enough of origin within himself to understand without preconceived categories and to judge without the set of customary rules which is morality" (p. 391), and Arendt, "Thinking and Moral Considerations," *Social Research* 38 (1971): 417–46: "We call *consciousness* (literally 'to know with myself') the curious fact that in a sense I also am for myself . . . ; I am not only for others, but for myself, and in this latter case, I clearly am not just one. A difference is inserted in my Oneness. . . . I am inevitably *two-in-one*. . . . If thinking, the two-in-one of the soundless dialogue, actualizes the difference within our identity as given in consciousness and thereby results in conscience as its by-product, then judging, the by-product of the liberating effect of thinking, realizes thinking, makes it manifest in the world of appearances, where I am never alone and always much too busy to be able to think" (pp. 441–46). See also Arendt, "The Crisis in Culture," in *Between Past and Future: Eight Exercises in Political Thought* (New York: Penguin, 1993 [1st ed. 1968]), pp. 197–226: "Judging is one, if not the most important activity in which this sharing-the-world-with-others comes to pass. . . . By his manner of judging, the person discloses to an extent also himself, what kind of person he is, and this disclosure, which is involuntary, gains in validity to the degree that it has liberated itself from merely individual idiosyncrasies" (pp. 221, 223). On Kant's introduction of the key role of imagination within judgment, see "Understanding and Politics," p. 392: "Imagination alone enables us . . . to put that which is too close at a certain distance so that we can see and understand it without bias and prejudice" (see also p. 383); "A Reply to Eric Voegelin," *The Review of Politics* 15 (1953): 76–85: "I am convinced that understanding is closely related to that faculty of imagination which Kant called *Einbildungskraft* and which has nothing in common with fictional ability" (p. 79); "Freedom and Politics," in *Freedom and Serfdom: An Anthology of Western Thought,* ed. Albert Hunold (Dordrecht, Holland: Reidel, 1961), pp. 191–217: "In the 'Critique of Judgement' freedom is portrayed as a predicate of the power of imagination and not of the will, and the power of imagination is linked most closely with that wider manner of thinking which is political thinking par excellence, because it enables us to 'put ourselves in the minds of other men' " (p. 207); "The Crisis in Culture," esp. pp. 220–24; and Arendt's posthumously published *Lectures on Kant's Political Philosophy,* ed. Ronald Beiner (Chicago: University of Chicago Press, 1982), pp. 42–43, 73, 79–85 *et al.* (see also "Hannah Arendt on Judging," Beiner's closing "Interpretive Essay" in the same volume, pp. 89–156).

47. Arendt, *Eichmann in Jerusalem,* p. 9.

48. It should be noted that in its recent exculpation and freeing of John Demjanjuk, whose identity as Treblinka's "Ivan the Terrible" was disproved to the satisfaction of two separate Supreme Court panels, even as Demjanjuk was found to have been a guard at Sobibor, another death camp in Poland, the Israeli Court maintained, to the outrage of many Israeli citizens, its practice of trying the individual for individual crimes. While, according to *The New York Times* correspondent, Clyde Haberman, the Israeli government had recommended along pragmatic national lines that "the case here be closed because it was not in the public interest to have a new trial, given the assessment that a conviction was not guaranteed" (*NY Times,* August 18, 1993, I, 3), it was on overarching historical grounds that Israelis openly protested the Court's undisputedly lawful decision: "[a]nother survivor, Dov Shilansky, a senior Likud Part member of Parliament, said, 'The judges may

have acted according to the way of the law, but they have not done historical justice' " (*NY Times*, August 19, 1993, I, 8).

49. Arendt, "Ideology and Terror: A Novel Form of Government," *The Review of Politics* 15 (July 1953): 303–27 (307).

50. *Ibid.*, p. 316 (emphasis in text).

51. *Ibid.*, p. 317.

52. *Ibid.*

53. See Arendt, "Understanding and Politics," p. 387: "The new logical movement in philosophy, which grew out of pragmatism, has a frightening affinity with the totalitarian transformation of the pragmatic elements, inherent in all ideologies, into logicality, which severs its ties to reality and experience altogether.... Only under conditions where the common realm *between* men is destroyed and the only reliability left consists in the meaningless tautologies of the self-evident, can this capacity [for logical reasoning] become 'productive,' develop its own lines of thought whose chief political characteristic is that they always carry with them a compulsory power of persuasion. To equate thought and understanding with these logical operations means to level down the capacity for thought ... to its lowest common denominator where no differences in actual existence count any longer...." (emphasis in text).

54. *Ibid.*, p. 318.

55. *Ibid.*, pp. 318–19.

56. The earnest controversy that immediately enveloped Daniel Jonah Goldhagen's *Hitler's Willing Executioners: Ordinary Germans and the Holocaust* (New York: Knopf, 1996), which dares argue that individuals in Germany might have actually subscribed to, and been instrumental in carrying to its conclusion the racist premise of the Nazi ideology of anti-Semitism, only serves to demonstrate the questionableness, if not ultimate absurdity, of attempts to safeguard the sanctity of the individual or society by pretending to be able to separate the "free will" of the one from the coercive "evil" of the other (or vice versa).

57. Arendt, "Ideology and Terror," p. 319.

58. *Ibid.*

59. *Ibid.*

60. *Ibid.*, pp. 320–21.

About the Contributors

TONI MORRISON is the Robert F. Goheen Professor, Council of the Humanities, Princeton University, and winner of the 1993 Nobel Prize for Literature. Her most recent publications are *Jazz* and *Playing in the Dark.*

GEORGE LIPSITZ is a professor of ethnic studies at the University of California, San Diego. His book *A Life in the Struggle: Ivory Perry and the Culture of Opposition* won the Anisfield-Wolf Award and the Kayden Prize. His other publications include *Dangerous Crossroads, Rainbow at Midnight, Sidewalks of St. Louis,* and *Time Passages.*

A. LEON HIGGINBOTHAM, JR., is Chief Judge Emeritus of the United States Court of Appeals for the Third Circuit. Currently he is Public Service Professor of Jurisprudence at the John F. Kennedy School of Government at Harvard University and of counsel to Paul, Weiss, Rifkind, Wharton & Garrison. He also serves as a commissioner of the United States Commission on Civil Rights. Judge Higginbotham was awarded the Presidential Medal of Freedom in 1995, the highest civilian honor in the nation.

ADERSON BELLEGARDE FRANÇOIS is an attorney and a freelance writer.

LINDA Y. YUEH is Research Associate to Judge A. Leon Higginbotham, Jr.

NIKOL G. ALEXANDER is a graduate of Southern University and A&M College and the University of Texas School of Law. She is a Ph.D. student in political science at Rutgers University, where she studies women and politics, public law, and Africana. Her current research focuses on sexism in the nation of Islam and black-Jewish relations.

DRUCILLA CORNELL is a professor of law, women's studies, and political science at Rutgers University School of Law. She played a key role in organizing the conferences on Deconstruction and Justice with Jacques Derrida, held at the Benjamin N. Cardozo School of Law in 1989, 1990, and 1993. She has worked to coordinate the Law and Humanitarian Speakers Series with the Jacob Burns Institute for Advanced Legal Studies and the Committee on Liberal Studies at the New School for Social Research. Professor Cornell taught at the Benjamin N. Cardozo School of Law from 1989–94 and spent the 1991–92 academic year at the Institute for Advanced Study at Princeton. She has authored numerous articles on critical theory, feminism, and "Postmodern" theories of ethics. She is the co-editor, with Seyla Benhabib, of *Feminism as Critique: On the Politics of Gender;* with Michel Rosenfeld and David Gray Carlson, of *Deconstruction and the Possibility of Justice;* and author of four books: *The Imaginary Domain: Abortion, Pornography and Sexual Harassment; Beyond Accommodation: Ethical Feminism, Deconstruction and the Law; Philosophy of the Limit;* and *Transformations: Recollective Imagination and Sexual Difference.* Productions of her plays *The Dream Cure* and *Background Interference* have been performed in New York and Los Angeles.

KIMBERLÉ WILLIAMS CRENSHAW is a professor of law at Columbia University Law School and the UCLA Law School. She is a founding member of the Critical Race Theory Workshop. Her articles on race and gender have appeared in the *Harvard Law Review,* the *Stanford Law Review,* and the *University of Chicago Law Review.* She assisted the legal team representing Anita Hill and is co-editor of the recently published *Critical Race Theory: Key Documents That Formed the Movement.*

ISHMAEL REED is the author of nine novels, including *Japanese by Spring,* recently issued in paperback.

LEOLA A. JOHNSON is an assistant professor in the program in American Studies at the University of Minnesota, where she teaches a course on black popular culture in the period after World War II. She is currently at work on a manuscript about the gangsta image in black popular culture (*Un(w)rapping Gangstas*), which focuses on the influence of a character from black pulp fiction by the name of Iceberg Slim.

DAVID ROEDIGER teaches working-class history and chairs the American Studies Program at the University of Minnesota. His recent books include *The Wages of Whiteness* and *Towards the Abolition of Whiteness,* both from Verso. He is currently editing a collection of African-American writings on whites and whiteness, forthcoming from Schocken, and completing *Shades of Pale,* forthcoming from Free Press.

ANDREW ROSS is a professor and the director of the American Studies Program at New York University. His books include *The Chicago Gangster Theory of Life: Nature's Debt to Society* (1994), *Strange Weather: Culture, Science, and Technology in the Age of Limits* (1991), and *No Respect: Intellectuals and Popular Culture* (1989). A columnist for *Artforum*, he is also the editor of *Universal Abandon?* (1988) and the co-editor of *Microphone Fiends* (1994) and *Technoculture* (1990). His edited collection, *Fashion Victims: Sweatshops, Free Trade and the Rights of Garment Workers*, will appear in the spring of 1997.

PATRICIA J. WILLIAMS is the author of *The Alchemy of Race and Rights* and *The Rooster's Egg*. A professor of law at Columbia Law School, she is a contributing editor of *The Nation* and serves on the boards of the Center for Constitutional Rights and NOW-LDEF. Her essays and reviews have appeared in *Contemporary Sociology, Harvard Law Review, The New Yorker, The New York Times Book Review, USA Today, The Village Voice,* and *The Women's Review of Books.*

ANN DUCILLE is a professor of American and African-American literature at the University of California, San Diego. She is the author of *The Coupling Convention: Sex Text and Tradition in Black Women's Fiction* (Oxford University Press, 1993) and *Skin Trade* (Harvard University Press, 1996).

ARMOND WHITE is the author of *The Resistance: Ten Years of Pop Culture that Shook the World* published by The Overlook Press. He is the arts editor and film critic for *The City Sun,* and won the ASCAP-Deems Taylor Film Festival award for music criticism in 1992 and served on the jury for the Sundance Film Festival. His music video presentations *Change the Style, West of MTV, Romanek Fiction,* and *Cross Culture Dreams* have been presented by the Film Society of Lincoln Center.

CLAUDIA BRODSKY LACOUR is a professor of comparative literature at Princeton University and Directeur de Programme at the Collège International de Philosophie, Paris. She is the author of *The Imposition of Form: Studies in Narrative Representation and Knowledge* and *Lines of Thought: Discourse, Architectonics, and the Origin of Modern Philosophy,* and a contributor to *Race-ing Justice, En-gendering Power: Essays on Anita Hill, Clarence Thomas, and the Construction of Social Reality,* edited by Toni Morrison.

Grateful acknowledgment is made to the following for permission to reprint previously published material:

Dove Books: Excerpts from *Madam Foreman: A Rush to Judgement?* by Armanda Cooley, Carrie Bess, and Marsha Rubin-Jackson. Copyright © 1995 by Dove Books. Reprinted by permission of Dove Books. • *The Free Press:* Excerpts from *Critique of Judgement* by Immanuel Kant, translated by J.H. Bernard. Copyright © 1951 by Hafner Press. Reprinted by permission of The Free Press, an imprint of Simon & Schuster. • *Harcourt Brace & Co.:* Excerpts from "Understanding and Politics" by Hannah Arendt. Reprinted by permission of Harcourt Brace & Co. • *HarperCollins Publishers, Inc.:* Excerpts from *In Contempt* by Christopher Darden. Copyright © 1996 by Christopher Darden. Reprinted by permission of HarperCollins Publishers, Inc. • *The New Republic:* Excerpts from "My Race, My Gender" by Jonetta Rose Barras. Copyright © 1995 by The New Republic, Inc. Reprinted by permission of *The New Republic.* • *Prentice Hall:* Excerpts from *Kant on History,* edited by Lewis White Beck (Bobbs-Merrill, 1963). Reprinted by permission of Prentice Hall, Upper Saddle River, New Jersey. • *The Review of Politics:* Excerpts from "Ideology and Terror: A Novel Form of Government" by Hannah Arendt (*The Review of Politics,* No. 15, July 1953). Reprinted by permission of *The Review of Politics.* • *Social Research:* Excerpts from "Thinking and Moral Considerations" by Hannah Arendt (Social Research, No. 38, 1971). Reprinted by permission of *Social Research.* • *Viking Penguin:* Excerpts from *Eichmann in Jerusalem* by Hannah Arendt. Copyright © 1963, 1964 by Hannah Arendt. Reprinted by permission of Viking Penguin, a division of Penguin Books USA Inc. • *The Washington Post:* Excerpts from "Circus of the Ce_____" by _____ Will (*Th_ W_____ P_st O_____* 1995). Copyright © 199_ _____ by permission of *The W_*